Congressional Parties,
Institutional Ambition, and the
Financing of Majority Control

Congressional Parties, Institutional Ambition, and the Financing of Majority Control

Eric S. Heberlig and Bruce A. Larson

THE UNIVERSITY OF MICHIGAN PRESS

Ann Arbor

Published in the United States of America by
The University of Michigan Press
Manufactured in the United States of America
♾ Printed on acid-free paper

2015   2014   2013   2012   4   3   2   1

A CIP catalog record for this book is available from the British Library.

Library of Congress Cataloging-in-Publication Data

Heberlig, Eric S., 1970–
   Congressional parties, institutional ambition, and the financing
of majority control / Eric S. Heberlig and Bruce A. Larson.
      p. cm.
   Includes bibliographical references and index.
   ISBN 978-0-472-11813-7 (cloth : alk. paper) —
   ISBN 978-0-472-02823-8 (e-book)
   1. Campaign funds—United States.   I. Larson, Bruce
A., 1960–
II. Title.
JK1991.H42   2012
324.7'80973—dc23   2011043627

For Tracy, Colin, Mena, and Ellie
    —E. S. H.
For Bill and Elsie Carter
    —B. A. L.

Contents

Preface

We started our research on member campaign contributions and advancement independently. Fascinated by the so-called Waxman-Berman machine and curious about whether other U.S. House members were engaging in similar campaign contribution practices, Larson wrote about member contribution activity in the U.S. House for his PhD dissertation. He found that U.S. House members were in fact increasingly redistributing campaign funds to other candidates and to the congressional campaign committees, and he characterized this activity as an extension of the party campaign finance system. Heberlig came to the topic thanks to the American Political Science Association's Congressional Fellowship Program. Working for a member of the Democratic Party's Steering and Policy Committee, Heberlig was given the task of making a list of which members were requesting which committees, how many seats were available on that committee, and so on. In reading the "Dear Colleague" letters in which members justified their committee requests, he noticed that few members mentioned party loyalty on the floor—either generally or even when casting a particularly tough vote. Instead, many members used the contributions they had made to party candidates in competitive races as evidence of party loyalty. Knowing the literature on committee assignments (and the strong theories but weak evidence on the relationship between voting loyalty and assignments), he thought, "Aha! A testable hypothesis," and he filed it away for after the fellowship.

Several years later, after presenting a conference paper on the subject, Heberlig received an e-mail from Larson saying, "Hey, I'm working on this, too. Why don't we pool our data and work together?" Never having met in person, we coauthored a paper (the forerunner of our 2005 *Legislative Studies Quarterly* piece) for the 2002 meeting of the Midwest Political Science Association (MPSA). Larson showed up at the panel and asked Paul Herrnson, the panel chair, if Eric Heberlig had arrived yet. Paul looked at him incredulously and said, "You don't know your own coauthor? . . . He's over there." After nine years of working together on this research, we now easily recognize each other at conferences.

Over the years of our research, we have had the critical support of a vast number of people (far too many to thank individually) who have read and commented on all or various parts of our research. These individuals include numerous conference panelists and discussants as well as many anonymous reviewers of journal articles we have published. We would especially like to thank the three anonymous reviewers who read and commented on the manuscript for the University of Michigan Press. All three provided excellent and detailed feedback, and their comments and suggestions have substantially improved the manuscript. Marc Hetherington, with whom we coauthored a 2006 *Journal of Politics* piece on member contributions and leadership polarization, deserves special thanks for helping us to shape our thoughts on this topic (and for his good humor and friendship). We are also thankful for grants from the University of North Carolina at Charlotte (UNCC) and the Dirksen Congressional Center, which supported the gathering and coding of data, and for a UNCC research leave for Heberlig, which afforded him additional time to work on the manuscript. We would also like to thank Gettysburg College's Political Science department for a grant that supported the preparation of the book's index.

At the University of Michigan Press, we would especially like to thank Melody Herr. Our relationship with the Press began when we were milling about its book display booth at the 2009 MPSA meeting, talking about how much we liked Ray La Raja's book *Small Change* (2008). Overhearing our conversation, Melody graciously introduced herself and inquired about our own work. The rest, as they say, is history. We thank Melody for her unabashed and ongoing enthusiasm for the project and for her patience, support, and encouragement as we developed the manuscript. We would also like to thank Susan Cronin and Kevin Rennells at the Press, who expertly worked with us to ready the manuscript for publication.

Heberlig would like to thank his family for their support and tolerance. All of them (Tracy, Colin, Mena, and Ellie) joined the team as the project developed. Heberlig chooses to defy the conventions of academic diplomacy and admits that his family did not develop hypotheses, run tobit equations, edit the manuscript, or urge him to spend more time working on the book. They do make life infinitely more enjoyable in every way. Heberlig may not have ever figured out how to make FEC data usable at the origins of the project without Peter Radcliffe, whose friendship (and availability for consultation) over the years has been valued. Heberlig also thanks his colleagues at UNCC for their support and feedback: Ted Arrington, Ken Godwin, Bob Kravchuk, and everyone else who attended brown-bag presentations. Gathering the data for this project was a huge task. UNCC students Ivan Blackwell, Chris Gonyar, Hannah Sawyer, Michael Staley, Jerry Wilson, and Chase Woodall provided conscientious research assistance at UNCC.

Larson would like to thank his colleagues and students at Gettysburg College for providing an intellectually stimulating environment in which to teach and do research. Rob Bohrer and Char Weise of Gettysburg College deserve special thanks for tolerating Larson's incessant fascination with campaign finance. It would be impossible to list all of the people who have helped shape Larson's thinking over the years on political parties and Congress, but those deserving special recognition include Steve Finkel, Paul Herrnson, Marc Hetherington, Bruce Peabody, and Larry Sabato.

Finally, Larson would like to thank his wonderful spouse, Alice Carter, and their lovely daughter, Lily, for their boundless love, support, and encouragement throughout this project. They bring tremendous joy to each day. Over the years, Alice has endured far more discussion of congressional party campaign finance than any nonspecialist should be expected to endure, and it is a safe bet that Lily knows more about the U.S. House than nearly any other 10-year-old. A person could not ask for a more loving and supportive family. Larson also thanks Alice for her invaluable editorial assistance over the years. Despite a hectic schedule of her own, she has always found time to read and comment thoughtfully on his work, and her insightful comments and suggestions have always substantially improved the final product—including this book.

Portions of chapters 4 and 5 are elaborations of work previously published in *Legislative Studies Quarterly* and *Party Politics*, respectively. We gratefully acknowledge these journals for allowing us to use materials from these works here.

1 | Introduction

The [Congress] is a dues-paying organization now. Junior members
have to raise this much, committee chairs have to raise that much.
Find that in a civics book.
—Senator Evan Bayh (D-IN) in an interview with *Newsweek* (2010)

The 2004 elections were over, and Republicans retained majority control
of the House by a slim margin. As is customary following the November
congressional elections, both House parties caucused in Washington,
D.C., to select their party and committee leaders for the following Congress (in this case, the 109th). For Democrats, one of the many tasks was to
fill a vacancy for the top minority party position (called the ranking member) on the Agriculture Committee, which was left open by the defeat of
Texas Democrat Charles Stenholm.

In the "committee government" era of Congress (1910–74)—when
committee slots were largely determined by seniority—the most senior
Democrat on the committee, Representative Collin Peterson, would have
automatically gotten the post. But much has changed in Congress, and Peterson, who had represented a largely rural district in Minnesota since
1990, had several problems. For one, with a moderate swing district, Peterson often opposed the Democratic Party, particularly on key votes such
as the Medicare prescription drug bill pushed through by the GOP in
2003. But an arguably bigger problem for Peterson was his uninspiring
record of financial loyalty to the House Democratic Party. Of the $70,000
he owed in party "dues" to the Democratic Congressional Campaign
Committee (DCCC) for the 2004 election cycle, for example, Peterson had
paid only $25,000—and he did even that reluctantly, only a few days prior
to the 2004 election (Eilperin 2006).

Peterson's anemic party fundraising record did not sit well with House
Democrats. The House Democratic Steering Committee, which makes

recommendations on committee assignments to the full House Democratic caucus, criticized Peterson for paying party dues only two times during his entire House career (Billings 2005).[1] Even fellow moderates in the House Democratic Party, who understood that Peterson's district forces him to take moderate legislative positions, criticized the Minnesota lawmaker for insufficiently helping the party and its candidates during election time (Billings 2004). "Democrats were in the fight of our lives to regain the House this cycle," added a Democratic staffer. "We truly need team players to take back the House. He's not been a member of the Democratic team" (Billings 2004). Democratic leader Nancy Pelosi made it clear that if Peterson did not cough up his party dues—and pledge to donate more to the DCCC in the future—he would be passed over for the top slot on the Agriculture Committee, in favor of a less senior member with more enthusiasm for party fundraising (Billings 2004).

Recognizing that his promotion was in jeopardy, Peterson paid the balance of his dues for 2004 and assured Pelosi that he would donate more in the years to come. For some in the House Democratic Party, Peterson's efforts were too little, too late. "It's awfully ironic that after having done nothing to help the Democrats retake the House since we went into the minority, all of a sudden when he stands to benefit . . . he wants to help the Democrats," complained one House Democratic aide (Billings 2004). But Pelosi, apparently satisfied with Peterson's assurances, backed him for the post.

Peterson made good on his promise to support the House Democratic Party and its candidates. In the 2006 election cycle, he contributed $200,000 to the DCCC and $44,000 to House Democratic candidates from his principal campaign committee. After Democrats won control of the House in 2006, Peterson became chair of the Agriculture Committee and gave even more money from his campaign committee: $310,200 to the DCCC and $87,406 to Democratic candidates in the 2007–8 election cycle. In 2008, Peterson also created his own political action committee—the Valley PAC—from which he contributed an additional $55,234 to House Democratic incumbents in competitive districts.

The money to pay for Peterson's growing contributions did not materialize out of thin air. In 2006, he financed his contributions to the DCCC and House Democratic candidates in part by cutting off his donations to the Minnesota Democratic-Farmer-Labor Party (the DFL). But this apparent strategy was short lived. In 2008, he resumed giving to the DFL, funneling $74,150 to its coffers. Instead, Peterson offset his growing contributions to the DCCC and House candidates mostly by raising more money. While Peterson raised $422,906 for his principal campaign committee in 2004, he took in more than twice that sum in 2006 ($938,128) and increased his overall receipts again in 2008 to $1,218,264. In 2008, moreover, he raised $297,004 for his new political action committee. Most of the growth in Peterson's campaign receipts can be accounted for by the increasing sums he raised from business PACs and from large individual donors.

Peterson's story is not exceptional. Instead, it is now an expectation that incumbents who desire any influence in the House regularly make substantial campaign contributions to the party's congressional campaign committee and to fellow party candidates. Parties have increasingly used their control over the institutional structures of Congress, particularly prestigious party and committee positions, to motivate members to support the parties' fundraising efforts.

This brings us to the central points of our book. In the U.S. House of Representatives, the congressional parties now wield unprecedented influence over how incumbents spend their campaign money. The influence is wielded largely through the party congressional campaign committees, which—having moved beyond the service model of the late twentieth century—now serve as key organizers and directors of the financial resources amassed by party incumbents from their donor networks. Party leaders enforce compliance with party fundraising quotas by using powers originally granted by the party caucus for legislative purposes. The congressional party, analyzed by most congressional scholars as a legislative organization, has become a formidable fundraising network. We follow Cox and McCubbins (2005) by treating the congressional party as a cartel-like entity. As they note, legislative party cartels "seek to establish a collective monopoly on a particular resource (in this case, agenda-setting power), seek to restrict supply of products made with this resource (in this case, bills that are placed on the floor agenda), and face problems of free-riding (in this case, members reluctant to vote for a party measure when such a vote will not sell well back home, or members eager to use their delegated agenda powers for personal gain)" (2005, 24). But in our perspective, the cartel is designed not only to monopolize power for setting the legislative agenda but also to corner the market on campaign cash. When majority party control is up for grabs, the congressional parties attempt to accomplish this by harnessing incumbent power. Monopolizing campaign funds is especially important for parties that veer from the ideological center, as Democrats and Republicans have done in the past three decades. The more a majority party veers off center, the more

campaign funds it will need to retain the swing districts on which majority control hinges.

The New Party Orientation of Incumbent
Campaign Spending

Although his conversion was more dramatic than that of others, Congressman Peterson is not the only member to increase contributions to
the party's campaign committee and to other candidates. As demonstrated by figure 1.1, U.S. House members as a group have sharply increased the sums of campaign money they donate to their party and to fellow party candidates.[2]

House members have several ways of contributing to other candidates
and to the congressional campaign committees (also known as the Hill
committees). First, members can make contributions through their principal campaign committees (PCCs), the committees they organize to
finance their own reelections. Second, members may contribute through a
leadership political action committee (LPAC), committees sponsored by
incumbents to finance political activities outside of their own reelection
campaigns. Both types of committees are themselves financed by contributions from individual donors, political action committees (PACs), and
political parties. Thus, when members of Congress contribute money
from their principal campaign committees and LPACs to parties and candidates, they are redistributing funds they raised from other political

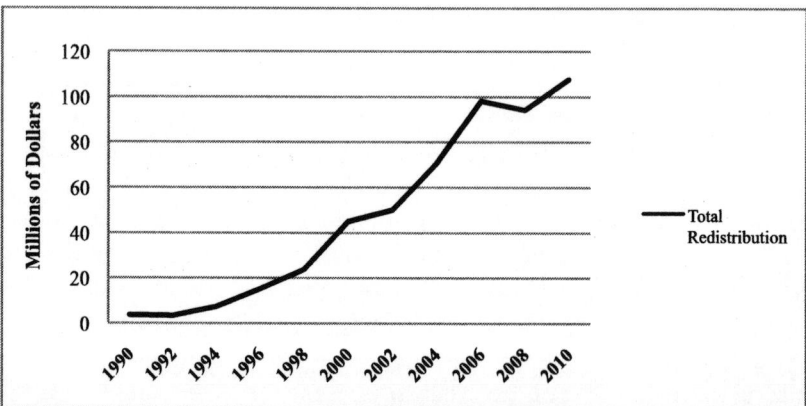

Fig. 1.1.   Increases in House incumbent campaign contributions, 1990–2010

donors. We therefore regularly refer to the campaign donations by incumbent members of Congress as their "redistribution" activity.

As donors, members of Congress are governed by federal campaign finance law. From their LPACs, incumbents may contribute $5,000 per candidate per election and $15,000 per year to national political parties—the same limits governing all PACs that engage in federal electioneering. From their principal campaign committees, members are limited to giving $2,000 per candidate per election.[3] However, federal law permits a federal candidate's principal campaign committee to transfer unlimited sums of unobligated hard money to any national party committee (11 CFR 113.2). In the most recent election cycles, numerous House and Senate incumbents have taken advantage of this rule and transferred six- and even seven-figure sums to the party congressional campaign committees (table 1.1).

Figure 1.1 shows that incumbent contributions to the party congressional campaign committees grew especially sharply in the 2004 election—the first election in which the 2002 Bipartisan Campaign Reform Act (BCRA) was in effect. The reason for this sharp growth is straightforward. BCRA prohibited the national parties, including the DCCC and its Republican counterpart—the National Republican Congressional Committee (NRCC)—from raising soft money. To offset loss of this lucrative source of funds, the parties pressed incumbents for even more campaign contributions (Carney 2004). The result is that a growing portion of the congressional campaign committees' campaign receipts now come from House incumbents. In fact, in 2008, Democratic House incumbents transferred $38.9 million to the DCCC—22 percent of the DCCC's total receipts in 2008. GOP incumbents, facing a more difficult electoral environ-

TABLE 1.1. Federal Regulations Governing Incumbent Hard Money Contributions to Candidates and the Congressional Campaign Committees

	Contributions to House Candidates	Contributions to the Congressional Campaign Committees
Leadership PACs	$5,000 per candidate, per election	$15,000 per calendar year
Incumbents' principal campaign committees	$2,000 per candidate, per election[a]	Unlimited[b]

Source: Data from the Federal Election Commission.
[a]Congress raised the limit from $1,000 to $2,000 in the 2005 Appropriations Act [2 U.S.C. 432(e)(3)(B)]. But the new limit was not indexed for inflation.
[b]The only condition is that the money must be unobligated (11 CFR 113.2).

ment in 2008, still managed to give $22.8 million (19 percent of NRCC receipts) to the NRCC.

House incumbents have also become an increasingly important source of campaign money to other candidates in the congressional campaign finance regime. Figure 1.2 compares incumbent contributions to House candidates with contributions from other high-profile industries: gun rights groups, lobbyists, banks, and the entertainment industry. (Other politically potent industries, such as oil and pharmaceuticals, show similar patterns.) The incumbent contribution data include only hard money contributions from House incumbents to other House candidates. By contrast, the industry data, which come from the Center for Responsive Politics, combine hard and soft money contributions, individual and PAC contributions associated with an industry, and contributions to House and Senate candidates.[4] Even so, by 2006, incumbent contributions from House members to other candidates surpassed the contributions of each of these politically potent industries.[5]

Contributions from House incumbents are now also the most important source of direct contributions to candidates in the party network. This is demonstrated by figure 1.3, which compares incumbent contributions to House candidates with DCCC and NRCC direct contributions to and coordinated expenditures on behalf of House candidates. Direct party contributions are simply dollar contributions made by the parties to candidates; party coordinated expenditures are expenditures coordinated by the party with candidates. The congressional campaign committees do-

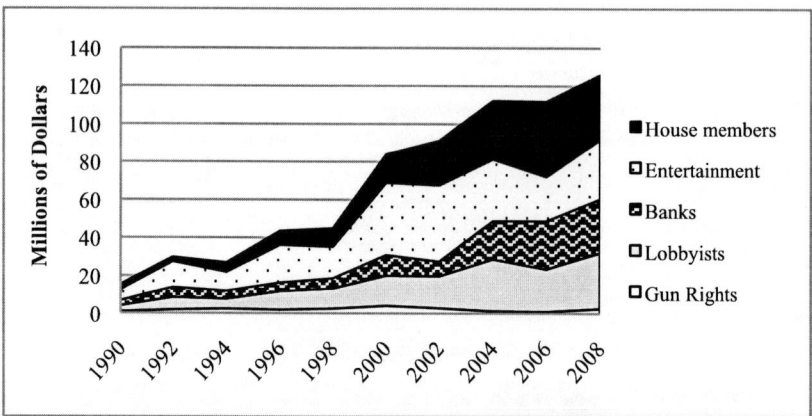

Fig. 1.2. Donations to House candidates by House incumbents compared to select industry contributions, 1990–2008

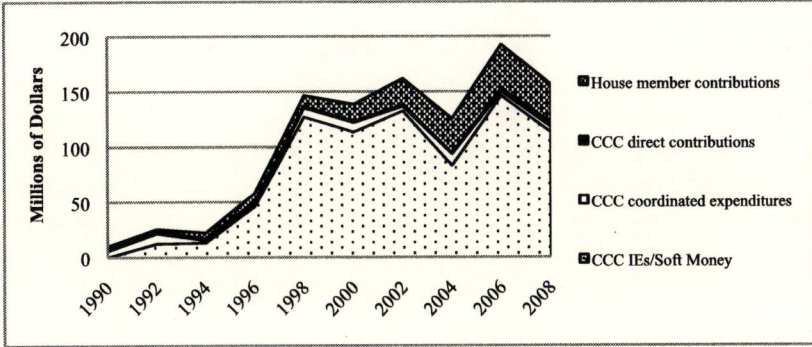

Fig. 1.3. House incumbents' redistribution of campaign funds compared to spending by party congressional campaign committees in House campaigns

nate relatively little directly to their candidates, and the levels of these contributions have remained largely stable over the decade. In federal campaign finance law, there is a key distinction between contributions and expenditures, and it is important to recognize that independent expenditures/soft money and coordinated expenditures are expenditures, not contributions. So while figure 1.2 shows that the CCCs make considerable independent expenditures, the sums of contributions (and coordinated expenditures) they make are far surpassed by contributions from House members.

Furthermore, the congressional campaign committees themselves are now increasingly financed by incumbent contributions, and this financial support has been vital in allowing the parties to make increasingly large independent expenditures in House contests. Banned by BCRA from raising and spending soft money to influence federal election outcomes, the congressional campaign committees have spent increasing sums of hard money in support of party candidates and, more often, against opposition party candidates. The parties may legally make such expenditures without limit, as long as they are financed with hard money and made independently of the benefited candidate.[6] In the 2007–8 election cycle, the DCCC spent $81.6 million on independent expenditures, while the NRCC spent $31 million.[7] Deployed strategically, independent expenditures made by the Hill committees can surely influence the outcome of close races. Indeed, in 2008 the DCCC pumped $2.4 million in independent expenditures into the House contest in New Hampshire's first congressional district. This was $800,000 more than the $1.6 million spent by the Democratic incumbent Carol Shea-Porter.[8] Party independent expenditures have transformed the electoral landscape in the past few election cycles by giving parties a greater capacity to communicate with voters in high-priority campaigns.[9] The funding for such expenditures has been increasingly supplied by the party's incumbents themselves. In 2008, contributions from House Democratic incumbents accounted for 22 percent of the DCCC's overall receipts, whereas contributions from House Republican incumbents accounted for 19 percent of the NRCC's total receipts. In contrast, prior to 1996, incumbent contributions comprised less than 5 percent of CCC receipts in both parties.

The Institutionalization of Incumbent Financial Support for the Parties

Contributing money to achieve political goals is not an entirely new strategy for House incumbents, as we will detail in chapter 2. But organized efforts by the congressional party to co-opt incumbent campaign funds are in fact very new. Indeed, as recently as the 1982 elections, Jacobson (1985–86) observed that Democratic incumbents hoarded their excess campaign funds and ignored the DCCC's appeals to assist the party's strapped challengers—preventing the party from capitalizing on favorable national partisan trends. The individual reelection interests of House incumbents, Jacobson noted, clashed with the collective electoral interests of the congressional parties, and the party had insufficient power to induce incumbents to share their campaign funds.

With the Democratic Party safely ensconced as the majority party, Democrats merely had to reelect their incumbents to maintain their power. Financially, Democratic incumbents managed this mostly on their own, by raising money from access-seeking PACs and local donors. The DCCC tended to employ an "incumbent protection" strategy in distributing its campaign resources, sometimes even giving to safe incumbents to help them scare off potential challengers. Seeing little opportunity to win majority control of the House, Republicans likewise had little reason to share funds that could more fruitfully be used to advance their own individual reelections. When incumbents did give away campaign funds, it was typically to candidates who were personal friends or key strategic allies (R. Baker 1989; Wilcox 1989). Contributions to party organizations, which would remove the link between incumbent donors and party-funded candidates who were the ultimate beneficiaries of the funds, were especially uncommon.

Wilcox (1989) and Bedlington and Malbin (2003) document the low level of member contribution activity in the 1970s and 1980s. As these researchers show, the sums of money redistributed by members of Congress during this period remained small and quite constant—typically under $5 million per election cycle. While members raised substantial funds during the seventies and eighties, there was simply no expectation that they would redistribute this money to the party or to other candidates. Instead, incumbents actively resisted even suggestions from party leaders that they might share their wealth for the benefit of the team (Jacobson 1985–86; Kolodny and Dwyre 1998).

Much has changed. In the 1990s, both party committees in the House developed programs to encourage hard money financial support from incumbents (Larson 2004). The DCCC formally initiated the practice of soliciting contributions from incumbents during the 1991–92 electoral cycle, when campaign committee chair Vic Fazio (D-CA) requested that all Democratic incumbents chip in $5,000 (Larson 2004; Sabato and Larson 2002). The NRCC launched its own program to induce incumbent financial support during the 1993–94 election cycle, and GOP whip Newt Gingrich personally solicited contributions from senior Republicans who were positioned to become committee chairs should the Republicans win majority status (Gimpel 1996, 10–11; Herrnson 1997, 108–9).

By the mid-1990s, the parties went beyond raising money for the Hill committees and began coordinating and targeting member contributions to other candidates. Party leaders increasingly made appeals for campaign funds to the membership as a whole, and congressional campaign committee members would even inform nonincumbents which incumbents were most likely to contribute to them (Larson 1998). One House Democrat at the time observed, "The DCCC is very helpful. They publish their lists and we have briefings by the DCCC chair, who says, 'these guys are on the watch list, these guys are in trouble'" (Sabato and Larson 2002, 86–87). Another House Democrat reported that "sometimes the DCCC will come to us directly, and ask if you could give to, say, any of these eight seats. . . . That's usually on behalf of incumbents" (Sabato and Larson 2002, 86–87).

After winning the House majority in 1994, the NRCC developed programs to harness incumbent power in the service of party fundraising. In 1996, the NRCC created "victory accounts" to encourage members to raise campaign money in their home states for the NRCC (Kolodny and Dwyre 1998, 289). In 1999, then GOP majority whip Tom DeLay (R-TX) developed ROMP—the Retain Our Majority Program—which organized members of the GOP whip structure to raise $30,000 each for the Republicans' ten most vulnerable incumbents (Corrado 2000, 100). The goal was to provide money to potentially endangered incumbents early in the election cycle in order to help them scare off the most threatening challengers. GOP leaders became increasingly willing to take action against insufficiently generous incumbents. "There will be some serious fallout if members don't reach the targets assigned to them," announced former NRCC chair Tom Davis in 2000 (Bresnahan 2000).

The DCCC followed suit in developing increasingly imaginative ways to tap into incumbent fundraising bases. For example, House Democrats established a "buddy system" in which safe incumbents are matched to a nonincumbent candidate in a similar district. The program calls on the incumbent to visit the candidate's district, offer campaign advice, and—most important for our purposes—provide the candidate with assistance raising PAC money (Firestone 2002; Herrnson 2008, 115)

In some cases, the parties' efforts to extract contributions from their members have become quite elaborate, using the time-tested techniques of charitable fundraising. In the GOP's "Battleground 2000" campaign, for example, the leadership gave each member a "non-voluntary" yellow pledge card with the pledge amount already filled in. The amount listed was determined by a sliding scale based on a member's position in the party leadership, committee, and seniority hierarchy. A United Way–style contribution thermometer, delineating each member's individual contribution, was posted outside of the NRCC suites from which members made fundraising calls. A special seventeen-member whip organization monitored progress and exerted peer pressure (M. Allen 2000). Former NRCC chair Tom Cole (R-OK) described the whipping process to get members to meet their party fundraising goals: "It's a brutal exercise in peer pressure" (quoted in Kucinich 2010b). When whipping is unsuccessful, other party leaders follow up personally. GOP whip Eric Cantor (R-VA) extended the work of the legislative whips to party fundraising. He and Kevin McCarthy (R-CA) raised over $1 million for the campaigns of whip team members so that the team could focus on raising money for the party rather than their own campaigns (Kucinich 2010a). By 2005, the GOP gave crystal elephants to members who had met fundraising targets set by the party (Kanthak 2007).

Party leaders use sticks as well as carrots to gain the fundraising compliance of their members. Sometimes the sticks are in the form of social incentives. For example, GOP leaders disseminate update tallies of incumbent contributions in order to embarrass lackadaisical members into increasing their efforts (M. Allen 2005). Similarly, at House Democratic caucus meetings, former Democratic House leader Richard Gephardt would announce member contributions to the DCCC, hoping to apply peer pressure on remiss incumbents (Kolodny and Dwyre 1998, 289–90). These practices continued under the next House Democratic leader, Nancy Pelosi: "Laggards in supporting the campaign effort are singled out to the rest of the caucus with a gentle but pointed message so as to 'encourage them to be part of the team'" (Peters and Rosenthal 2010, 115). Other inducements were more hard core. In June 2005, Pelosi sent a memo to her Democratic colleagues in the House informing them that members who failed to pay their DCCC dues would be unable to use the DCCC phones or other services or amenities (Eilperin 2006, 24). The episode in which Peterson was promoted to ranking member of the Agriculture Committee only after he pledged to be a more energetic party fundraiser further underscores the seriousness with which party leaders now view incumbent financial support for the party.

By 2008, both congressional campaign committees had institutionalized programs to facilitate the collection of incumbent campaign donations. The primary Democratic program is called "Frontline"; its GOP counterpart is called "Battleground." In both parties, leaders now set party contribution "quotas" for incumbents. Although the details differ for each party's program in a given year, the quotas for contributions to the Hill committees typically range from $75,000 for rank-and-file members to $200,000 for committee chairs and ranking members (more for exclusive committees) to $600,000 for top party leaders (Bolton 2006; Zeleny 2006). Many members now routinely give in excess of the quotas, including seven-figure contributions in several instances. Parties' assertive efforts to mobilize financial support from incumbents and incumbents' widespread compliance with party demands represent striking changes in party and incumbent behavior. A critical contribution of this book is explaining why these changes occurred, why they occurred so quickly, and why they occurred in both parties.

Several factors spurred the institutionalization of member contributions. The GOP's surprising takeover of the House in 1994 launched an intense battle for majority control of the House. Incumbents would enter each election year uncertain about which party would control the House majority in the next Congress. Paradoxically, however, nearly all House incumbents had a lock on their own House seats, with partisan control hinging on only thirty or so swing districts. Secure in their reelections, most incumbents increased their fundraising advantage over their challengers and retained significant sums of campaign cash from one election cycle to the next. Using powers originally granted by the party caucus for legislative purposes, party leaders increasingly developed and enforced compliance with programs designed to induce incumbents to redistribute those dollars to the party's campaign committee and needy candidates. Party leaders could reward members who actively shared their campaign resources with the party and its candidates, with valuable institutional positions (Cann 2008; Heberlig 2003) and with consideration of their legislation under favorable conditions (Hasecke and Mycoff 2007).

Broadly speaking, members also understood that achieving their individual goals in Congress required their party to hold the majority. In the House, the majority party is like a cartel (Cox and McCubbins 1993), holding almost all of the institutional power. The majority party, through its domination of the Rules Committee, determines what legislation comes to the floor for debate, how much time is allowed for debate, and what proposed amendments are allowed for debate. This certainly gives an advantage to legislative priorities of the majority party. At the very least, this gives the majority party the ability to block consideration of ideas that major factions of the party intensely dislike (Cox and McCubbins 1993, 2005). The majority party has similar power over the committee system, as members of the majority party hold the full and subcommittee chairmanships and thus set the committee agendas. Without agenda-setting authority, members of the minority party face the choice of either collaborating with members of the majority and getting whatever compromises they can or protesting and taking their case to the public in hopes that voters will reject the majority party's actions and give minority party candidates wins in sufficient numbers of districts to promote them to majority status.

For members seeking institutional influence, leadership positions in the majority are far more powerful than leadership positions in the minority party. For members with policy goals, the majority party's control of the legislative process is a crucial resource, and control has become even more important as the parties have polarized ideologically (Fiorina 2006; Sinclair 2006). A Congress controlled by a member's party will produce legislation reasonably consistent with the member's policy preferences; a Congress controlled by the opposition party will produce legislation that diverges substantially from the member's policy goals. Membership in the majority party even advances members' reelection goal, because majority party members can extract significantly more campaign dollars from corporate and trade PACs than can minority party members (Cox and Magar 1999; Rudolph 1999).

Once majority control was on the line and incumbent contributions could make a difference in whether their party captured it, members of each party were more receptive to leaders' appeals for financial assistance. As Kolodny and Dwyre (1998, 289) put it, "the collective goal of majority status was more valuable to these incumbents than the extra few thousand dollars would be." Texas Democrat Charlie Gonzalez similarly argued, "I have no problem understanding that several of my colleagues can't be with me on certain issues. . . . I want them to come back because they will be voting for the same person for Speaker, we have a majority in the committees and such. They empower me. So I have a vested interest in their success" (quoted in Hunter 2010). But since no single member's contributions would be sufficient to fund the party's campaign for majority control, each member would want to contribute to the party effort only if a sufficient number of his or her colleagues did. To encourage widespread participation, party leaders, acting as agents of the party, would not shy from denying insufficiently generous members, such as Peterson, the full benefits of majority control. With majority control up for grabs and more crucial to members than ever and with powerful party leaders able to prevent members from free riding on the efforts of their colleagues, member contributions became a substantial source of funding for the congressional parties.

Redistribution and Representative Democracy

There are several practical and scholarly reasons why we should care that the congressional parties now wield considerable influence over incumbent campaign money. On a practical level, party influence over incumbent campaign funds has significant implications for congressional parties, political representation, and the congressional campaign system. Most political scientists agree that political parties serve several valuable goals in democratic societies. While some researchers argue that the party congressional campaign committees do not provide the same laudable benefits to the political system as do traditional party organizations (La Raja 2008b; Shea 1995), American representative democracy is surely better off with robust congressional campaign committees than with weak ones. Motivated by winning party majorities, the congressional parties, led by the congressional campaign committees, are some of the most important supporters of nonincumbents in congressional elections. Parties donate to promising challengers; most interest groups, concerned with gaining access to incumbents, do not. Without well-funded congressional campaign committees boosted by incumbent contributions, congressional elections might be even less competitive than they currently are. Indeed, by helping to offset the loss of soft money, incumbent money has ensured that BCRA's soft money ban did not inflict a fatal blow to the congressional campaign committees.

Incumbent funding of congressional campaign committees (CCCs) may also have positive benefits for political representation. Money redistributed by incumbents originates from an array of donor networks. Incumbents, for example, have access to many local donors who would not contribute to the national parties. Incumbent donor networks thus expand and broaden the party's fundraising base (Heberlig et al. 2008). To be sure, donors to congressional incumbents are hardly representative of the overall population (Francia et al. 2003). But the money raised by hundreds of incumbents from thousands of donors and then redistributed to the party CCCs surely represents a far broader spectrum of motivations and political interests than did the large soft money contributions given by a relatively small number of well-heeled megadonors.

Oddly enough, party reliance on member money may also keep parties more broadly representative of factions within the party. A strong record of financial support for the party may help a member compensate for policy preferences that depart from the party mainstream (Heberlig, Hetherington, and Larson 2006). Indeed, Democrats would have almost surely had less of a problem with Peterson's relatively conservative voting record had he compiled a generous record of supporting the party and its candidates financially. Financial generosity as a standard for advancement may help ensure that even members who occasionally defect from the party can still win committee and party leadership positions.

Of course, the CCCs' growing reliance on incumbents to finance party operations has troubling implications as well. First, the need to support the party CCC at greater and greater levels has likely intensified the money chase among incumbents (Carney 2004). It is a safe bet that nobody would think this is a healthy development. In turn, the increasingly intense scramble for hard dollars may well make incumbents more reliant on lobbyists who can use their wide connections to amass and bundle large numbers of individual contributions for members of Congress (La Raja 2008b). Such a development would serve to strengthen incumbent ties with well-entrenched political interests that have so consistently vexed advocates of campaign finance reform (Sorauf 1992).

Second, with incumbent contributions increasingly tied to winning powerful party and committee posts (Cann 2008; Heberlig 2003), party reliance on incumbent contributions could well shape the kinds of members who advance within the institution. In particular, rewarding members for their fundraising may advantage leadership aspirants who have built "dense donor networks" over members who are less enthusiastic about nonstop fundraising (La Raja 2008b, 217). Fundraising as a standard for promotion would likewise disadvantage or at least compete with traditional promotion criteria, such as seniority, legislative prowess, and party loyalty voting. Advocates of good government would be rightly concerned if the nation's premiere lawmaking body is led predominantly by members who are skilled at fundraising and electioneering rather than legislative craftsmanship and coalition building (Wawro 2000)—though members may of course be skilled at both activities. Alternatively, it may be that ambitious members will simply adapt to whatever advancement norms are in place, so that the new party fundraising requirements will not change the type of members who gain positions of influence. This is in fact what Peterson did.

Finally, some critics see an accountability problem with incumbents redistributing money donated to their principal reelection committees. When individuals or interest groups' PACs contribute to a member's reelection account, these critics argue, they do so with the expectation that the funds will go toward the member's own reelection campaign. Consequently, when a member turns around and gives that money to another candidate, the member violates the expectations of his or her own benefactors (Novak 1988, 39; Alston 1991). Of course, this claim depends on the premise that outside contributors have specific expectations about how their donations will be used. Indeed, just as the trusteeship form of representation conceives of voters as electing members of Congress to use their own judgment on policy matters (Pitkin 1967), contributors to a member's campaign may be fine with letting the member decide how best to spend the money. It may also be that this problem applies less to members' leadership PACs than to their principal reelection committees, since donors to LPACs are more likely to be strategic insiders who understand that the main purpose of the LPAC is to redistribute funds.

There are also purely scholarly reasons to study member contributions. Party influence over incumbent campaign money is vital to an understanding of how the contemporary congressional parties now operate. Much of the scholarly understanding of Congress is based on the view of members as independent entrepreneurs who maximize their individual goals with little help from and few constraints imposed by political parties (Mayhew 1974; Fiorina 1989). This perspective sees congressional parties as the creation of their incumbents (Aldrich 1995), who have traditionally granted their parties only minimal powers. The parties, in turn, provided only nominal electoral assistance and exerted only minimal leverage over members to produce coherent policy outcomes. The congressional parties documented in our book differ drastically from this traditional image.

Recent theories of congressional parties have done much to illuminate the trends toward much more powerful parties and party leaders (Cox and McCubbins 1993, 2005; Rohde 1991). Yet these theories, even those that characterize congressional party goals as primarily electoral (Cox and Mc-Cubbins 1993, 2005), have focused exclusively on party influence on incumbent behavior in the legislative process (S. Smith 2007). They do not consider party influence over incumbent fundraising. While spelling out the logic of the congressional parties' increasingly coordinated legislative activities, scholars have all but missed their increasingly coordinated electoral activities—activities designed to win or retain majority control in an era of thin party margins. Along these lines, Rohde rightly exhorts scholars studying congressional parties to give more sustained attention to the continuous battle for majority control of the House, ushered in by the 1994 election.

> [T]heories of congressional parties need to more fully assess the impact of the 1994 GOP landslide. This event separates two vastly different congressional worlds. For a long time preceding the 1994 election, congressional politics were shaped by a high degree of certainty about which party would be in the majority in the next election. Since 1994, majority control has been constantly at issue, and leaders of both parties have conditioned virtually every strategic decision on its possible effect on the parties' collective electoral fortunes. The full effects of this shift on all aspects of congressional politics are still not entirely clear, and analysts would profit by giving it diligent consideration. (Rohde 2010, 338)

We argue that the parties' battle for majority control has led them to extend their cartel powers over legislation to fundraising. To amass the funds necessary to conduct a "permanent campaign," parties have used their control over congressional institutions to induce their members to leverage money from their own networks of donors on behalf of the party's collective electoral fortunes.

To the extent that the electoral efforts of the congressional parties have been studied, it has been by scholars studying campaign finance and political parties (Herrnson 1988; Kolodny 1998). These scholars have focused mostly on the congressional campaign committees themselves. Only recently has research on party fundraising begun to explore the connection between the Hill committees and incumbent campaign money (Dwyre et al. 2006). Perhaps even more important, the rich empirical work of scholars studying party campaign finance has not been informed by the theoretical work on congressional parties. Yet in our view, the literature on congressional parties is vital for understanding how and why congressional parties have wielded increasing influence over incumbent campaign money. Absent work integrating party campaign finance and congressional parties, we are left with various incomplete pictures of congressional party politics—and with no understanding of why Collin Peterson nearly failed to secure an important committee post.

By incorporating new developments in party fundraising into current theoretical perspectives on congressional parties, we build a long-overdue bridge between the literature on party campaigning and the literature on congressional party organization. We also present evidence that campaign contributions affect advancement in the House of Representatives. Our evidence shows that ambitious members do not simply buy off their colleagues with campaign contributions, as the simple analogy "pay to play" implies. Instead, when the party's predominant goal is attaining majority status, members who allocate their contributions in ways that help the party achieve majority status are advantaged in advancement. In particular, we show that the parties play an important role in compelling members to allocate their funds in ways that promote the party's collective electoral goals, not just their own individual ambitions. The party's control over powerful institutional positions supplies the party with leverage over its incumbents, and such leverage affects incumbent contribution strategies, how much incumbents allocate to party organizations, and even how incumbents raise campaign money. Thus, we argue that members who redistribute are signaling their fitness for party offices: they can supply the party and its candidates with the resources that are needed for the party to succeed electorally, and they can put the party's collective interests ahead of (or at least on par with) their own. Incumbents who reject the new party norms risk undermining their ability to achieve their individual goals.

More broadly, however, current research leaves largely unaddressed the larger implications of congressional political parties strong enough essentially to co-opt incumbent fundraising. We seek to use increasing contributions made by incumbents—and the increasing party control of these contributions—to offer a fresh understanding of congressional parties. Such an understanding revises the textbook view of American political parties, which conceives of parties as tripartite entities: parties in the electorate, party organizations, and parties in the government (Hershey 2008). In this conception, the strength of party organizations has typically been evaluated by the extent to which they exert control over electoral resources (money, workers, patronage, etc.). By contrast, as the central institutions in the "party-in-the-government," congressional parties have been (and continue to be) evaluated largely by their ability to produce party loyalty in the legislative process.

These conceptual divisions no longer clearly hold. The congressional parties are far more than legislative parties attempting to move legislation. They now house the main party networks serving the fundraising needs of congressional candidates. Indeed, some time ago, Salmore and Salmore (1989) urged scholars studying the party-in-the-government to pay greater attention to its electioneering functions rather than focusing only on its legislative functions. Similarly, Wright (2000) argued that the best way to understand congressional organization is not from a policy perspective but, rather, from a party fundraising perspective. More generally, Lee (2009, 190–91) argues that to understand congressional parties, scholars must look beyond ideology and toward members' "shared interest in winning office and in wielding power." We take these recommendations seriously.

In our conception, congressional party strength is indicated not only by a party's ability to enforce legislative party loyalty but also by its ability to control fundraising resources. By this measure, the contemporary congressional parties are stronger now than at any point in the past 30 years—perhaps in history—because they now exert substantial influence over a vital electoral resource: incumbent campaign money. Our book demonstrates how and why this has happened and explores whether it is good or bad for American politics.

Chapter Overview

Chapter 2 reviews the history of congressional parties' intermittent and largely unsuccessful efforts to solicit financial support from their incumbents. Campaign finance law has played an important role in shaping the relationship between party and candidate fundraising activities. Moreover, changes in campaigning and campaign finance have created incentives for parties to mobilize House incumbents to act as brokers for the party by tapping their personal fundraising networks on the parties' behalf.

Chapter 3 lays the theoretical groundwork for understanding House incumbents as key donors in the party network. We extend Cox and Mc-Cubbins's cartel theory of legislative parties to argue that parties use their monopoly over access to powerful institutional positions to create selective incentives for ambitious members to provide financial support to the party. When party control of the House is up from grabs, party campaign money is just as important to the congressional parties as legislation burnishing the party's reputation. After all, without sufficient campaign money, the party cannot communicate its legislative record to voters. Consequently, when party margins are thin, party leaders use their powers to enforce not only legislative loyalty but financial loyalty as well. Meanwhile, ambitious members who seek promotion within the institution will signal their financial loyalty by donating to the party and its candidates. Essentially, our theory generalizes the Peterson vignette that opened this chapter.

Chapter 4 details the changes in electoral and fundraising behavior by members of Congress. We show how the battle for majority control of the House and the parties' responses to campaign finance reform laws have created a fundamental change in members' use of campaign funds to assist the party and its candidates, including how the new expectations of redistribution on Capitol Hill have created a spillover effect of giving to state and local party organizations.

By examining the contribution strategies employed by members who contribute to other candidates, chapter 5 further explores the tension confronting House incumbents between redistributing campaign money to advance one's individual goals and doing so to advance the party's collective goals. Consistent with our partisan theory, we find that the extent to which a member employs a party-oriented contribution strategy is a function of his or her formal position in (and thus responsibility to) the party. We also demonstrate that the contribution strategies of all members, leaders and nonleaders alike, have become more party oriented over time, as the battle for majority control intensified and party leaders acted more aggressively to solicit member contributions and channel them to the most competitive contests on which majority status would hinge.

In chapter 6, we argue that advancement within the institution is dependent on three criteria: a member's commitment of time to the party, a member's legislative loyalty to the party, and a member's fundraising loyalty to the party. We also expect, however, that the relative weight parties place on each of these factors will be sensitive to the political setting—in particular to whether majority party control is up for grabs. Ambitious members signal their qualifications for positions by helping the party achieve its most important collective goal (passing the party's legislative agenda or providing campaign funds to achieve majority status) in a particular political context. We argue that money is not simply exchanged for institutional positions in a crude "pay-to-play" scheme. Rather, the party promotes members whose donations most effectively advance the goal of majority status: contributions to the party campaign committee and to party candidates in competitive contests on which majority control hinges. Promotion within the institution, we conclude, is a function of the institutional arrangements developed by the congressional party, which themselves depend on the political context. When party margins are thin, money looms large in determining who moves up.

Chapter 7 explores how incumbents have financed the growing campaign contributions they have been making to the party and its candidates. We demonstrate that members are paying for the new party fundraising demands in part by increasing the campaign cash they raise from donors least able to decline incumbent solicitations: access-motivated business PACs and large individual contributors. Members also form leadership PACs when their redistribution activities begin to put pressure on their reelection spending. By prohibiting the national parties from raising soft money—which made the congressional parties more reliant on member contributions—BCRA unwittingly increased the extent to which incumbents raised money from large individual donors to finance their growing contributions to the party and its candidates.

Chapter 8 examines the extent to which the strains associated with the new party fundraising requirements increase the likelihood of retirement for incumbents. We find that the new fundraising pressures have no impact on the decision to retire, even for members most likely to be disaffected by the new party fundraising regime. Our findings imply that senior members have adapted to the new party fundraising expectations and that new members enter the institution knowing what to expect. Chapter 8 also demonstrates that members seeking statewide office predictably redistribute fewer campaign dollars to the congressional party and its candidates, save more of their campaign funds for the statewide run, and contribute more to state (but not to local) party organizations.

We interpret these findings as further evidence that how members allocate their campaign funds is a signal of the direction of their political ambitions.

In the concluding chapter, we elaborate on the normative implications of our findings. In particular, we discuss how the battle for majority status has changed congressional party behavior, thereby changing the institutional operation of Congress. Where electoral competition has traditionally been assumed to be entirely positive, we discuss why the battle for majority status has not made Congress any more sensitive to public sentiment in its policy making. The fact that members of Congress—particularly those with the greatest power and legislative responsibilities—are more dependent than ever on access-oriented donors is a reason to be concerned with Congress's ability to represent unorganized and financially unendowed constituencies.

2 | Parties, Incumbents, and Campaign Finance in American Politics

Recent publications on Congress have used some unusual language:

> Confessore (2003): "Welcome to the Machine."
> Continetti (2006): "The Rise and Fall of the Republican Machine."
> Dionne (2005): "Republicans' congressional machine."
> Eilperin (2006, 24): "Party bosses."
> Edsall (2006, 138): "A Republican fundraising and patronage machine."

While journalists and activists might be forgiven for hyperbole, even usually cautious academics have used similar language:

> Hacker and Pierson (2005, 135): "The Republican Machine."
> Mann and Ornstein (2006, 179): "The Dominance of Machine Politics."
> Parker (2008, 8): "Parties' golden age."
> Norm Ornstein (quoted in Dubose and Reid 2004, 258): "It's Tammany Hall all over again."

While the U.S. Congress has never enjoyed a particularly positive reputation, the "machine politics" frame supplied by recent critics implies substantial changes in congressional party politics over the past two decades.

Tammany Hall is the model of the urban party machine style of government in the nineteenth and early twentieth centuries. In classic party machines, the mayor controlled the jobs and contracts, the private sector participants were developers or city service providers, and the patronage appointees were the local precinct captains. Power in machines is top down: party leaders give instructions to other city politicians and provide the rewards and sanctions to induce them to implement the edicts of party officials. Machines are extremely hierarchical organizations. City councilmen vote the way party leaders want them to vote, because they cannot win renomination without party leaders' support, nor can they win an election without their party's resources and workers. Government officials offer contracts and access to corporations in exchange for contributions. Politicians use their control of government jobs to reward their campaign workers. With resources from private interests, its ability to provide services to voters, and the electoral shoe leather of their campaign (i.e., government) workers, the party is able to help its candidates win election, thereby perpetuating the cycle. The mutual exchange of favors between a political party controlling government, its officeholders and activists, and private interests is one of the hallmarks of political machines.

Congress, in contrast, has typically been understood as the antithesis of machine government. Representatives and senators were loyal to the constituents in their states or districts who elected them. Representatives and senators mostly built their own personal electoral constituencies of voters and donors. Interest groups seeking access to government built relationships with individual members of Congress, particularly those serving on committees with jurisdiction over their organizations' interests. Committees, not party leaders, wrote the bills. Party leaders, cognizant of their need to be reelected by the members of their caucus, prioritized helping to reelect their members and asked for little party loyalty in return.[1] The national parties provided a brand name, a record of accomplishment on national issues, and basic electioneering support to assist their candidates. But the party organizations had access to relatively few resources. Candidates, interest groups, and parties worked together on an ad hoc basis to achieve mutual goals. The party rarely provided the coordination that brought the players together or held them together after a short-term objective had been reached.

While we can forgive the hyperbole that congressional parties now operate like classic party machines, there is little doubt that the comparison is closer than it has been at any time historically. The strengthening of congressional parties' capacities to enact the party agenda legislatively has been well documented (e.g., Rohde 1991; Sinclair 1995; Lee 2009), and the dramatic increase in the redistribution of campaign funds to party candidates and committees (as illustrated in figure 1.1 in the previous chapter) suggests that parties are successfully coordinating the efforts of their incumbents in the electoral arena, too. Incumbent contributions did not amount to much until recently, yet they are not unprecedented. Indeed, incumbents supported their parties financially during the machine era of the late nineteenth and early twentieth centuries. Such financial support has varied considerably over time as the parties' ability to help members achieve their individual goals has waxed and waned.

Although the purpose of the party organization is to serve the party's collective electoral interests, such interests do not always easily coexist with members' individual reelection concerns (Jacobson 1985–86; Sorauf 1992). Tensions between the individual reelection interests of members and the collective electoral interests of the parties can be particularly acute in a party system such as that in the United States, without dues-paying party identifiers or public financing for parties or congressional candidates. Such a system inevitably prompts the question of "who should pay to produce the collective good of the party organization" (Hopkin 2004, 632).

In the United States, the short answer to that question has always been the same: well-heeled private interests (e.g., Ferguson 1995). From local machines, to candidate-centered campaigns, to the strong national party organizations of the early twenty-first century, private interests have been the primary financial supporters of the parties' collective electoral efforts. Yet how parties have raised funds from private interests and the role of the party's officeholders in the process has changed significantly over time. The purpose of this chapter, which pays special attention to the relationship between congressional incumbents and their parties, is to situate historically the present regime of congressional party campaign finance. Exploring the interplay between incumbent fundraising, congressional organization, federal campaign finance laws, and partisan competition, we describe how incumbents have emerged as central financiers of the congressional parties' collective campaign efforts. We conclude by noting that well-financed party organizations in the United States now necessarily depend on the presence and cooperation of powerful incumbents, who can use their leverage over well-heeled interests to finance not only their own reelections but the party's collective electoral efforts as well.

Parties, Incumbents, and Campaign Finance prior to FECA

Over the past century, political parties have always sought financial contributions from members of Congress. More often than not, they have been unsuccessful in getting their incumbents to contribute much to the team efforts. During the strong party era of the late nineteenth and early twentieth centuries, parties requested and received regular contributions from members of Congress. But the party organizations that received those funds were usually the local parties—the machines. The congressional campaign committees were much less successful, despite the fact that their activities were most directly relevant to helping to reelect the incumbent members of Congress. The parties' efforts to mobilize contributions were halfhearted, and therefore members' compliance was inconsistent at best.

In the nineteenth century, traditional local party machines mobilized money and time from activists in exchange for jobs, contracts, or social benefits. Individuals desiring a government job or contract paid the party for it with kickbacks. In contrast to parties today, there was little or no policy content to the party agenda. Indeed, the first mass party—that created by Jackson and Van Buren—was designed precisely to de-emphasize policy (Aldrich 1995; Frymer 1999). Parties wanted power, and they doled out taxpayer-funded largesse to their supporters in order to get it (Banfield and Wilson 1963).

Parties were also the dominant players in elections. They determined which candidates ran for office, they ran their campaigns, and they controlled volunteer and financial resources. Although many campaign activities were conducted by volunteers—many of whom had their eyes on patronage jobs after the election—funds were used to pay for the partisan "spectacles": the parades, fireworks, and celebrations that attracted ordinary citizens to hear the candidates and their surrogates (McGerr 1986).

To finance these spectacles, party leaders used their control over officeholders and access to official government resources to extract the (usually small) sums of money needed to underwrite congressional campaigns from incumbents themselves, assessed patronage employees, and—when necessary—solicited "fat cats" to whom leaders could provide government favors (Salmore and Salmore 1989, 27; Sorauf 1992, 3; Summers 2002) The parties' first systematic attempt to raise money from individuals came from "taxing" their own members through placing partisan assessments on their positions, in essence requiring "dues" not only from patronage employees but from officeholders as well (Mutch 2002; Summers 2002). These payments went, for the most part, to state and local parties that conducted the campaigns, rather than to national party organizations. Officeholders were often assessed a percentage of their salaries. Nonincumbent candidates were also expected to help pay for the party's campaign activities. The exact amount the parties would seek from candidates would depend on the importance of the office, the candidate's own financial resources, whether the candidate had sought nomination or was persuaded reluctantly to run, and whether the candidate was in a competitive contest or merely a sacrificial lamb. Other party organizations would leave the size of the contribution to the party to the candidate's "conscience," but the party would negotiate a "schedule of payments" (Overacker 1932, 100).

During the strong party era, state and local party organizations were more powerful than the national party organizations, since they controlled the nomination of candidates and the means of mobilizing voters and resources. National parties were a "loose coalition of sectional, ethnic, and class factions." They did not have a mass membership base or a stable national constituency of donors (La Raja 2008b, 119). In fact, national party organizations were dependent on state and local organizations for funds: each state was given a funding quota by the national party, which the states often did not meet (Heard 1960, 287). Although there were strong legislative parties in Congress during the late nineteenth and early twentieth centuries, congressional parties did not operate as electoral machines. House and Senate incumbents may have been part of state or local machines (Peters 1997, 88; Strahan 1998, 57), but the party caucuses in Congress at best supplemented local party electoral activity (Herrnson 1994, 46; Kolodny 1998, 66). The primary focus of local party organizations was candidates for local offices; the primary focus of state party organizations was state candidates; the primary focus of the Republican and Democratic national committees was the presidential candidates. Parties typically organized around state and local political units, not congressional districts. As a consequence, party assessments of congressional incumbents and candidates, as well as additional requests to help pay for specific campaign activities on behalf of the candidate, often came from each of the county, ward, and precinct party organizations within the congressional district (Summers 2002, 60–61).

Since congressional districts often did not fit well within existing party organizational structures—which were typically organized around cities and counties—members established party congressional campaign committees in the late 1860s. The CCCs were funded primarily by members of Congress and congressional staffers (Kolodny 1998, 31), since, as new and emerging party organizations, they did not have an outside constituency of party activists to solicit. The CCCs were created to provide congressional candidates with resources that could more easily be obtained in Washington, D.C., than in individual congressional districts, thereby reducing the transaction costs of coordinating, producing, and distributing such resources (Kolodny 1998, 9). The primary services they provided to congressional candidates included model speeches, traveling speakers, and books containing information on issues. The CCCs gave only limited financial assistance to candidates in this era. As characterized by historian Mark Wahlgren Summers (2002, 53), the early CCCs "doled out dribs and drabs, and then only to the worthiest applicants." Party leaders generally did not supplement the CCCs financially, nor was their power based on their fundraising capacity. Despite his reputation as a powerful House leader, for example, Speaker Thomas B. Reed raised minimal funds even for his own campaign, accepting money only from personal friends (Overacker 1932, 176). Examples of redistribution in this era, such as Senator Nelson Aldrich (R-RI) steering corporate contributions and giving campaign funds to needy Senate and House candidates (Schickler 2001, 57, 65), appear to be the exception. In terms of overall campaign involvement during this era, the efforts of the congressional parties were clearly secondary to those of the local parties (Kolodny 1998, 66).

Soon, progressive reforms of the early twentieth century eviscerated powerful state and local party leaders. The reforms did not simultaneously strengthen national party organizations. Primary elections eliminated external party leaders' nomination power, while civil service reform and court decisions largely did away with patronage to reward party foot soldiers. Reform legislation limited the ability of parties to raise funds from government workers and contractors. Most far-reaching was the Pendleton Civil Service Act of 1883, which reduced the number of federal patronage positions and banned the assessment of appointed federal employees. During this same period, big businesses—particularly railroads, banks, and steel and oil companies—began to dominate the national economy. These corporations became important sources of funding for parties, filling the void created by civil service reform (Corrado 2005, 9–10). When federal law prohibited corporate contributions in 1907, parties relied mainly on their traditional source of funding from wealthy individuals (P. Baker 2002). As La Raja (2008b, 39) notes, the antiparty roots of campaign finance laws are one reason why national parties have been slow to develop as stable campaign organizations. Regulations restricted parties just as money became an increasingly important campaign resource and as national politics was becoming more relevant in the lives of ordinary Americans.

A few local machines survived the reforms and remained strong until the mid-twentieth century, but they were more concerned with gubernatorial and mayoral elections than with congressional campaigns (Sabato and Larson 2002). The result was that congressional incumbents were left largely to fend for themselves. Forced by necessity to construct their own personal political organizations, incumbents funded their campaigns, which were still relatively inexpensive grassroots affairs (at least until the 1960s), with funds raised largely from groups within their constituencies (Salmore and Salmore 1989, 47).

Meanwhile, the demise of the partisan press and the rising education levels of the American electorate forced members of Congress to develop more sophisticated and expensive methods of campaigning. The CCCs increased their level of activity in response and added opposition research to the menu of services they already offered. To finance their increased activity, the CCCs, like their party counterparts at the local, state, and presidential levels, were forced to engage in fundraising efforts beyond member subscriptions (Kolodny 1998, 65). When funding from wealthy contributors was insufficient and party leaders needed to expand their funding sources to individual contributors of more modest incomes, they "borrowed techniques from World War I bond sales and charity organizations such as the Community Chest to orchestrate their own fund drives" (P. Baker 2002, 19). Local party committees were assigned fundraising quotas from donors in their area. The large-scale industrial unions that emerged in the 1930s became an important source of funding to the Democratic Party, and business and trade groups followed suit, emerging as especially powerful in the 1950s and 1960s and bestowing their gifts primarily on Republicans (Corrado 2005, 15–18).

Rank-and-file incumbent involvement in party campaign efforts was uneven in the period of party campaign finance prior to the 1974 Federal Election Campaign Act (FECA). The Democratic Congressional Campaign Committee levied an assessment on its members for decades, but it failed to enforce it consistently (Caro 1983, 608; Overacker 1932, 101–2; Thayer 1973, 38). On the GOP side, the National Republican Congressional Committee raised $100,000 at one point by asking all federal officeholders making more than $1,000 to contribute 1 percent of their incomes (Keller 1977, 243). But such efforts were not systematic. In contrast to rank-and-file members, leaders of the congressional party began to play a more active role in the party's collective efforts over the course of the twentieth century, and they saw it as their responsibility to raise money to elect party candidates (R. Baker 1989; Salmore and Salmore 1989; Wilcox 1989, 1990). Moreover, a few enterprising leadership aspirants began to understand the utility of party fundraising as a means to advancing their political goals. Probably no story of twentieth-century fundraising is recounted as much as that involving then House member Lyndon Johnson. With House Democrats in need of campaign money for the 1940 election, Johnson established a personal organization parallel to the DCCC to raise funds from Texas oilmen and routed them to Democratic candidates in competitive races who often had trouble getting money from the DCCC. Johnson ensured that the recipients knew he was responsible for getting them the money, and he used candidates' gratitude to help build a national political base (Caro 1983, 606–64).

Toward the end of the pre-FECA period (the 1960s and 1970s), entrepreneurial state-level leaders such as California Assembly Speakers Jesse Unruh and Willie Brown increasingly understood the utility of redistributing campaign funds as a means to achieving and solidifying political power (Clucas 1992, 1994; Jacobs 1995). Ambitious Californian Phillip Burton, who cut his political teeth in California's state legislature, brought fundraising lessons learned from Unruh and Brown to the U.S. House (R. Baker 1989; Jacobs 1995). But stories about these ambitious political entrepreneurs are recounted so often, it seems, precisely because they were such exceptional efforts at the time, not part of a systematic pattern of activity by members to achieve collective goals (R. Baker 1989; Kolodny 1998). Indeed, Johnson's efforts were entirely personal (they did not continue as part of the House Democrats' election efforts once he moved on to the Senate),[2] and it would be years before the kinds of fundraising practices initiated by politicians such as Unruh, Brown, and Burton would become widespread in Congress.

Parties, Incumbents, and Campaign Finance after FECA

The 1974 FECA Amendments

A pivotal event affecting the relationship between House candidates and national party organizations was the passage of the 1974 amendments to the 1971 Federal Election Campaign Act.[3] The amendments imposed contribution limits on various types of contributors to congressional candidates: $1,000 per candidate per election on individuals, $5,000 per candidate per election on political action committees, and $5,000 per candidate per election on party organizations. The 1974 FECA amendments also limited to $10,000, adjusted for inflation, the sum that national party organizations could spend in coordination with House candidates.[4] (The limits on party coordinated expenditures for Senate candidates depended on the size of a state's voting-age population.)[5] Additionally, the new law imposed a $25,000 aggregate contribution limit on individuals (though no aggregate limit on interest groups or parties), and it created a system for the public reporting of all contributions and expenditures by candidates. Finally, the 1974 amendments placed limits on campaign expenditures by federal candidates, as well as on independent expenditures by groups and individuals, though all of these limits were overturned by the Supreme Court in its landmark ruling *Buckley v. Valeo* in 1976.

By limiting the sums of direct contributions that national party organizations could make to congressional candidates, FECA further advanced the trend of candidate-centered congressional campaigns and reduced the importance of parties in congressional elections. With party expenditures on behalf of candidates capped but overall candidate spending unlimited (due to *Buckley*), party money would make for only a small slice of total incumbent campaign receipts. The implication for candidates' fundraising strategies was clear. If a candidate needed hundreds of thousands of dollars to run a competitive campaign, creating contacts with many individual donors and many PACs—not relying on the parties—was the way to do it. Indeed, such arrangements were seen as key to advancing FECA's goal of curbing corruption: a member of Congress would solicit and receive contributions from many different sources, and no contribution would be inordinately larger than the others, so that the member would not be beholden to any one set of contributors, thus lowering the probability of corruption. But cumulatively, contributions from PACs and individual donors would dwarf the financial assistance provided by the national party organizations.

The advent of electronic mass media, developments in campaign technology, the growing suburbanization of the electorate, and the emergence of high-priced political consultants made congressional campaigns increasingly expensive. As a result, raising sufficient funds to wage an effective campaign would soon turn into "a campaign in and of itself" (Herrnson 2004, 159). The 1974 FECA served to cement an already strong incumbency advantage in fundraising that was increasingly necessary to bankroll a professional congressional election campaign, further stacking the deck against challengers. With contributions capped at $1,000 for individuals and $5,000 for PACs, having a large number of donors became essential to ensure the necessary stable flow of campaign funds.

In theory, incumbents, open-seat candidates, challengers, and parties all have the same basic types of donors to whom they can appeal for funds. But in practice, incumbent members of Congress enjoy major advantages over challengers and parties in developing broad networks of small donors. Incumbents are better positioned than challengers or national party organizations to develop extensive fundraising networks of individual donors at the local level, particularly among less politically active or attentive individuals. Parties can appeal to individual donors, but they are usually ideological donors with an orientation toward national policy concerns (La Raja 2008a). Incumbents also are able to take advantage of their power within Congress to raise funds from interest groups who desire access and policy benefits and who contribute to get the attention of the legislators who preside over their interests. Challengers obviously have no access, votes, or legislative favors to provide; parties may have majority status as a selling point but it is the party's incumbents who have influence over the details of policy of most concern to interest groups.

Individual Donor Networks

The structure of Congress facilitates member fundraising through broad networks of donors. Members represent geographic districts and spend considerable time in their districts getting to know constituents personally and providing them with services (Fenno 1978; Fiorina 1989). They promote local businesses, government agencies, and nonprofit organizations, protect their specific needs in the details of legislation, help them cut through the red tape of federal executive agencies, and help them obtain government grants and contracts. They vote their districts, often taking pains to distinguish their own position from that of their national party. Their presence in the district allows members to build networks not only of voters but of donors as well. A local picnic or barbecue, for example, could serve both as a small donation fundraiser (e.g., dinner tickets for less than $50) and a chance for the member of Congress and local constituents to meet in a relaxed setting. Candidates commonly draw most of their money from face-to-face solicitations and efficiently raise funds by drawing geographically concentrated donors together at a single event (Cho and Gimpel 2007).

Building donor networks through their local representational activities allows members of Congress to appeal to many of the common types of individual donors. Francia and others (2003) classify individual congressional donors into four types. "Ideologues" contribute based on their issue agreement with the candidate. Many ideologues are partisan supporters of the candidate. These contributors often have intense policy demands and seek out candidates who will reliably promote their policy interests (Cohen et al. 2008). In fact, interest groups of policy demanders can, officially or informally, form the backbone of the party at the local level (Masket 2009). They may recruit candidates directly, and even if they do not, their support is often necessary to win party nominations. Members of Congress are obviously likely to seek support from their ideological base. But developing relationships in the district allows a member of Congress to attract donors from beyond the usual suspects of partisan and issue activists in the district. "Investors" are those who give to gain access to the political process, often to protect their professional or business interests, and they often will donate regardless of the candidate's party affiliation. Members of Congress can gain donations from members of the local business community to whom they have provided access and assistance. They are also often successful in forging ties with nearby donors "outside of their home districts but within their economic region" (Bednar and Gerber 2011). "Intimates" contribute based on personal relationships, perhaps with the member of Congress him- or herself, perhaps with the friend or coworker who makes a solicitation on behalf of the candidate. Expanding their network of personal connections within the district allows members of Congress to expand their network of donors who contribute for social reasons. Finally, "incidental" contributors give as the spirit moves them to give. Providing more opportunities for more people to be in contact with the member of Congress and his or her activities is likely to increase the number of incidental contributions. As a consequence, the vast proportion of incumbents' individual contributions traditionally comes from in-district or in-state contributors (Grenzke 1988).

Local connections also facilitate PAC fundraising. Although large, national PACs provide most of the total PAC contributions, small "mom-and-pop" PACs make up the largest number of PACs (Biersack, Herrnson, and Wilcox 1994). These PACs, especially in the corporate sector, are often locally oriented in their contribution strategies (giving about half their contributions to home-state candidates) and, like national corporate PACs, are willing to fund local representatives regardless of ideology (Eismeier and Pollack 1986; Radcliffe 1998).

Relationships with constituents affect national PAC fundraising as well. Wright (1985) noted that PAC money often went to members of Congress who were not ideological allies of the group. The contribution was directed to the incumbent by a local member of the PAC who had helped to raise the money; the local fundraiser was given influence over the allocation of PAC money in exchange for his or her efforts soliciting on behalf of the PAC. The local PAC fundraiser liked his or her representative and wanted the PAC to fund the incumbent regardless of the incumbent's relationships with the organization's Washington lobbyists. In short, voters and donors would support the incumbent if they felt a personal connection with him or her and out of respect for the incumbent's experience and ability to deliver, even if they ordinarily would support candidates from the other party. Just as incumbents have an incentive to work their district to maintain or expand their reelection margins, they have the same incentive for fundraising purposes.

Institutional Positions and Leverage

Members of Congress also take advantage of their institutional positions in Congress to attract contributions from interest groups. Throughout much of the twentieth century, power in Congress was fragmented. The power and responsibility for writing legislation was held by committees, each of which was comprised of members with intense personal or constituency interests in the policies over which the committee had jurisdiction (Adler and Lapinski 1997; Shepsle and Weingast 1987). There was often a very close relationship between the committees, the executive branch agencies they oversaw, and the interest groups affected by their policy decisions (Lowi 1964; Ripley and Franklin 1991). Committee members used their gatekeeping powers to block policies they disliked, wrote the details of the legislation—including targeting the costs and benefits—to protect favored groups and constituencies, used their status as "experts" on the legislation to provide voting cues to other members on the floor, engaged in logrolls to pass legislation without substantial changes on the floor, and used their influence in conference committees to delete changes made on the floor that they disliked (Shepsle and Weingast 1987). Committee outsiders, including party leaders, rarely interfered in committees' monopoly over policy making.

In such a system, constituents and organizations affected by federal policies had to turn to the committee of jurisdiction to make their views known and to make policy changes that reflected their views. Legislation could cost a company millions of dollars (or produce like benefits), thus giving organizations substantial incentive to monitor the committee's actions and to attempt to communicate the real-life effects of legislation to committee members. Incumbents' policy-making leverage gave them substantial ability to attract campaign contributions from individuals and organizations who would be affected by their decisions.

Organizations can attempt to influence committee-based policy making by helping to ensure that like-minded legislators populate Congress. Some PACs thus follow an "electoral" strategy, contributing to candidates who share their ideological or issue positions. Motivated by changing the composition of Congress, such PACs typically contribute to candidates in close races, where their money will have the largest electoral impact. By electing allies to Congress, donors need not put much effort into persuading members to take the "correct" actions. (As allies, recipients will naturally do so.) Although individual contributors frequently give to support ideologically allied candidates (Francia et al. 2003), only a minority of PACs do so (Wright 1985; Herrnson 2008). These donors are primarily the ideological groups that constitute the core constituencies of the party coalition (Cohen et al. 2008).

Instead, most PACs follow an access or "investor" strategy (e.g., Snyder 1990). Recognizing that FECA contribution limits prevent them from providing enough money in particular contests to change the overall election outcome and that incumbents are almost always reelected, they contribute not to alter the composition of Congress but, rather, to build good relationships with incumbents already in Congress. As such, they give overwhelmingly to incumbents—not so much to help them win but because they will win—and with little regard for the recipient's ideology or party label. What motivates investor PACs is the return on their investment.

Exactly what form such a return takes has fueled fierce and long-standing debate in the scholarly literature. Many scholars have argued that contributors attempt to "buy" the votes of members of Congress, though evidence to support this is decidedly weak (for reviews, see Baumgartner and Leech 1998; Leech 2010; R. Smith 1995). The safest conclusion to draw from studies that show some influence of campaign contributions (Esterling 2007; Fellows and Wolf 2004; Godwin and Seldon 2002; Gordon and Hafer 2005; Gordon, Hafer, and Landa 2007; Hall and Wayman 1990; Keim and Zardkoohi 1988; McChesney 1997; Miler 2007) is that there are a wide variety of ways that donors could seek to influence Congress—including obtaining a legislator's assistance in shaping legislation or dealing with the executive branch—and a variety of legislators in positions to provide assistance. Regardless of the specific motivations of the "investor" donors, they contribute to members of Congress because of the leverage incumbents have over policies affecting the organization's interests.

The bottom line is that PACs give disproportionately to members of committees with jurisdictions over their issues and particularly to the committee and party leaders who have the greatest agenda-setting powers (Grier and Munger 1991, 1993; Grenzke 1989; Romer and Snyder 1994; Kroszner and Stratmann 1998). Even junior committee members can attract substantial contributions from PACs and lobbyists by sponsoring receptions at which the committee chair/ranking member or party leaders serve as the main draw. PACs also contribute more generously to members of the majority party, who dominate all stages of the legislative process (Cox and Magar 1999; Rudolph 1999).

That congressional organization facilitates incumbent fundraising is not a coincidence. Indeed, Wright (2000) argues that House Democrats were particularly attentive to fundraising needs in crafting the institutional decentralization of the 1970s. As the cost of campaigns began to skyrocket and Republicans began making gains in the House during the late 1960s, rapidly forming business PACs increasingly allocated their funds to Republican incumbents on the basis of committee assignments. Decentralizing power to subcommittees thus gave more House members—especially majority party Democrats—leverage over policy, providing investor PACs with an incentive to contribute to them. Similarly, weakening the power of committee chairs and empowering junior members gave PACs an incentive to contribute to the most vulnerable members, helping Democrats retain majority status.

In sum, members of Congress could take advantage of their relationships with many individual donors in their districts, as well as with organizations in Washington that had business before their committees, to develop wide networks of small donors, consistent with the demands of the legal fundraising regime. The implication of this fundraising system from the party's perspective is that each member of Congress has developed an independent, somewhat different fundraising network, based on the nature of a member's local constituency and committee assignments.[6] Many of these investor or personal donors would not contribute to the party but will indirectly help the party win majority control by helping to reelect its incumbents.

National Fundraising by Incumbents

To be sure, not all congressional fundraising is based on distinct local networks for each member. Some members, particularly prominent spokespersons for party factions, successfully tap networks of ideological donors through direct mail lists and the Internet. Both parties heavily tap wealthy regions for donations, especially New York City, Los Angeles, Chicago, and so on, regardless of the region's voting behavior (Gimpel, Lee, and Kaminski 2006). Because many districts are safe, wealthy donors often must contribute to nonlocal candidates or to the parties to make a difference. Some candidates tap national networks of contributors sharing their ethnicity, and organizations such as Emily's List have formed to assist candidates with desired demographic and political traits.

Consistent with these trends, out-of-district individual contributions to House incumbents have grown during the last 25 years. Gimpel, Lee, and Pearson-Merkowitz (2008) demonstrate that the typical House incumbent received individual contributions from 70 different congressional districts in 2004. Moreover, a significant percentage of individual contributions flow from the wealthiest districts, and many of these contributions are likely brokered through party networks. Successful national fundraising, however, is facilitated by celebrity, a position of power, or some other means of national political visibility. Thus, while national fundraising provides at least some campaign funds for the typical member of Congress, it is not an equally feasible fundraising strategy for all incumbents. It is surely a less feasible strategy for the typical nonincumbent candidate.

By forcing candidates to finance their campaigns by raising small contributions, FECA gave a decided advantage to those with the contacts and ability to build a network of reliable donors. In other words, it gave a clear advantage to congressional incumbents. Incumbents have the personal connection to donors, the leverage over public policy, and the likelihood of victory that nonincumbents do not have. They have a distinct fundraising advantage over parties for the same reasons. The major exception to donors' preferences for candidates over parties may be the activist who lives in a one-party region. The activists' contribution is unlikely to affect any local congressional contests but may help the party win majority status by allowing the party to spend the money in competitive contests nationwide.

The fact that incumbents have considerably more fundraising capacity than the CCCs suggests that if the parties could enlist incumbents as their fundraising agents, the parties could vastly improve their financial positions. Traditionally, incumbents' fundraising capacity allowed incumbents to amass large war chests, spend lavishly for election activities and services to constituents and donors (Fritz and Morris 1990; Morris and Gamache 1994), and dole out small sums to their friends in Congress (R. Baker 1989). But with the rise of party power and the competition for majority status, incumbents would become a tempting target for parties to expand their fundraising efforts with minimal cost or effort.

The Parties and FECA

FECA set higher contribution limits for contributions to parties than to candidates. Individuals were permitted to give $20,000 to the national party committees, and PACs were permitted to contribute $15,000.[7] The higher limits on individual contributions to parties presumably gave the parties incentive to target wealthy individuals for large contributions. But despite the higher contribution limits, the initial result of the 1974 FECA amendments was to weaken the parties' ability to fund congressional campaigns.

The national parties had to create their own infrastructure for raising money, as FECA's contribution limitations prohibited their past reliance on large donors. The GOP took the lead in developing a direct mail operation in the late 1970s (Herrnson 1988; Sabato and Larson 2002). As the minority party in Congress, the GOP could not rely on funding from access-oriented interest groups and had to seek funds countrywide from activists on conservative issues. The Republican National Committee's donor list increased from 24,000 names in 1975 to more than a million in 1980 (Klinkner 1994). The Democrats followed the Republicans' lead, with their national committees becoming more aggressive fundraisers after the party lost control of the presidency and the Senate in 1980. But Democrats consistently trailed Republicans in the sums of money they raised from direct mail and small contributors.

Both parties developed lists of small contributors who would send checks in response to regular requests sent by the party and usually signed by party leaders. They had particular success appealing to ideological donors with emotionally charged direct mail, which typically outlined the alleged dire threats to the nation posed by the opposition party (Godwin 1988). Party funds were also obtained from more traditional methods such as party dinners. These events often featured a "celebrity" draw, such as a national party leader, in order to maximize turnout among party regulars. Even so, the national parties could not offer the benefits of social camaraderie among activists that local party organizations or candidates' campaign operations can generate with regular grassroots activities. PACs contributed to parties, too, but were generally a limited source of party funding (Rozell and Wilcox 1999, 107).

The parties' reliance on direct mail solicitation for fundraising resulted in donor profiles markedly different from those developed by candidates. Grant and Rudolph (2002) and Lowry (2005) find that party donors are more likely than candidate donors to be strong party identifiers, highly politically interested, and wealthy. In other words, parties came to rely on a narrower network of individual donors than did candidates. Moreover, parties had to compete for the contributions of these donors with interest groups. As Cohen and others (2008) observe, ideologically motivated activists are first and foremost concerned with promoting their policy demands. They may contribute to political parties in addition to candidates and interest groups but primarily see parties as a means to an end. To the extent that interest groups allow policy demanders to register their ideal preferences without the compromises entailed by party politics, interest groups are likely to have a competitive advantage in attracting their financial support.

Thanks to the rebuilding of the 1970s and early 1980s, the finances of the CCCs remained largely stable through the 1980s. After the initial scare of the Reagan landslide in 1980, the Democrats remained firmly in control of the House throughout the decade. In the mid-1980s, DCCC chair Tony Coehlo responded to business PACs' affinity for GOP candidates by reminding PAC directors that Democrats would likely remain in the majority for the foreseeable future—and that it would be Democrats, therefore, writing the legislation that affected business interests (Jackson 1988). Corporate PACs responded by distributing their contributions relatively evenly between Democratic and Republican candidates, rather than disproportionately to Republicans, as they had in the past. Corporate PAC money thus helped House Democrats cement their majority by adding to Democratic incumbents' campaign resources. With the percentage for incumbent reelection rates in both parties hovering in the low to middle 90s in the latter half of the decade, members of Congress did not press the CCCs to innovate in fundraising.

CCC contribution patterns reinforced the stalemate in the 1970s and 1980s. In theory, each party formed a CCC to maximize the number of chamber seats it holds—with gaining or maintaining majority control of the institution the ultimate goal. An efficient distribution of party campaign money would benefit all party members by maximizing a party's chances of winning a House majority. Yet as the creatures of congressional incumbents, the CCCs contributed disproportionately to incumbents of their parties rather than to challengers who could change the balance of power in Congress (Jacobson 1985–86; Kolodny 1998). The CCCs had a history of giving relatively equal—and small—amounts to each incumbent (Salmore and Salmore 1989, 266). Incumbents felt "unsafe at any margin" (Mann 1978), and despite their substantial fundraising advantage over potential challengers, they demanded increasingly more money from the party CCCs. For their part, CCC chairs served short terms and consequently had little incentive to upset their colleagues by making investments in the long-term electoral health of the party. The remoteness of the chance that Republicans could actually win control of the House reduced the incentives for each party to allocate resources in a manner that would benefit its collective electoral fortunes. As a result, the CCCs would devote more resources than warranted to assuage the fears of nervous incumbents rather than spending it on open-seat and quality challengers.

Finding New Party Money, Part I: Adaptation to Modern Candidate-Centered Campaigns

Over the course of the 1980s, parties were increasingly caught in a financial bind: campaign costs increased more rapidly than the parties' ability to raise funds. Campaign expenses continued to swell, as the cost of television advertising and the professionalization of campaigns soared. Meanwhile, the number of individual contributors and the number of PACs stagnated (Sorauf 1988). With the dollar limits on contributions capped, the value of contributions declined due to the effects of inflation. To keep up with the rising costs of campaigning, the donor pool would have to expand substantially, yet the opposite was happening.

The declining efficiency of traditional funding sources gave the parties incentives to find new sources of money. One of these new sources became known as soft money. Whereas the FECA tightly regulated contributions to candidates and spending to endorse candidates, soft money went to the parties, flowing outside of the FECA's regulatory structures, and could be raised in unlimited amounts. But soft money could only be spent on "party-building" activities—activities benefiting the entire party rather than particular federal candidates—such as get-out-the-vote drives, generic party advertising, and overhead and building expenses. Since soft money could not legally be spent to elect federal candidates, it played only a relatively small role in the 1980s. It was used mostly for overhead expenses, such as the new DCCC headquarters, thus freeing hard money to be used for candidates. Parties did gain some advantage from the substitution effect, but soft money did not (yet) have a substantial impact on party involvement in congressional campaigns.

The national parties also innovated programmatically during the 1980s. They expanded their offering of services (Herrnson 1988), financing polls, ad buys, voter research, opposition research, and candidate training and recruitment. They also offered links to consultants and PACs. Providing a kind of one-stop shopping for campaign services, the national parties developed a niche in the market of campaign services that depended on expertise. Candidates were encouraged to conduct professionally run campaigns, but the CCCs would serve as the central repository of specialized services that would be too expensive and inefficient to be purchased by individual campaigns. Interest groups and PACs were better sources than parties of hard money (money that could legally be used to help federal candidates), and local parties were better sources than national parties of volunteers. But the national parties had a competitive advantage over interest groups and local parties in providing expertise-related campaign services.

A key to the national parties' growth in power was their increased use of "agency agreements" with state parties. FECA gave state party committees the same coordinated expenditure limits it gave the national party committees. States often did not spend their entire allotment, either because they did not have sufficient funds or because their spending priorities were on other campaigns. Agency agreements allowed the national parties to assume a state party's coordinated expenditure allotment. Such agreements sometimes involved "money swaps," whereby a state party would spend hard money in specific congressional races and the national party would compensate it by providing equal or somewhat larger amounts of soft money (which a state party could often legally use to finance state candidates). Swaps with state parties also allowed national parties to concentrate larger amounts of money in a few races, since the agreements would be reached in states that had competitive congressional campaigns (Dwyre 1996). The cumulative effect of these spending innovations was that they increased national committee activity while still complying with FECA spending limits and made state parties increasingly financially dependent on national parties. Sorauf (2002, 88) concluded that, for the first time, national parties were now the "dominant" party organizations in the federal system.

At the same time, the CCCs slowly began to focus more money on competitive nonincumbents (Buchler 2004). With sizable war chests enjoyed by both the CCCs and members of Congress (Sorauf 1992, 114), incumbents finally became comfortable with having CCC funds diverted to nonincumbents. Parties were becoming more internally ideologically homogenous during this time, which no doubt facilitated members' willingness to see party money going to other members. With fewer conservatives in the House Democratic Party, for example, liberal House

Democrats could worry less that DCCC money was going to ideological opponents within the party.

While incumbents increasingly supported CCC expenditures on non-incumbents, they remained reluctant to share their own campaign resources with the party and its candidates. Analyzing the 1982 elections, Jacobson (1985–86) observed that Democratic incumbents hoarded their excess campaign funds and ignored the DCCC's appeals to assist the party's strapped challengers—preventing the party from capitalizing on favorable national partisan trends. Similarly, Kolodny and Dwyre (1998, 289) recount unsuccessful efforts by former NRCC chairman Guy Vander Jagt to persuade House GOP incumbents to contribute to the NRCC during his tenure in the 1980s and early 1990s.

Anecdotal evidence suggests that party leaders, outside of the CCC chairs, were not heavily involved in soliciting member donations to the CCCs or other party candidates. One House Democrat who actively redistributed funds—and who routinely asked colleagues to give to candidates in competitive races—noted, "I can't ever remember having a call from a party leader. I've gotten calls from the DCCC, or I've talked to Vic Fazio [the DCCC chair] and, before him, the other chairs of the DCCC, because that's their function. But that's once we're in the campaign season, and they're saying, 'This is the turn these races have taken.' I can't ever remember receiving a call from one of the leadership people about it."[8] Party mobilization was limited and late in the game, not a coordinated effort to amass resources early in the campaign for candidates in potentially competitive contests.

Yet member fundraising on behalf of the party and its candidates gradually increased, almost entirely among party leaders and legislative entrepreneurs (R. Baker 1989; Salmore and Salmore 1989; Wilcox 1989, 1990). A new breed of entrepreneurial member—skilled at raising funds and operating in an increasingly open and decentralized Congress—understood the utility of sharing campaign resources as a means of accumulating political influence (Loomis 1988). The "major departure from past fundraising practice," according to Ross Baker (1989, 26–27), occurred in 1976, when Californian Phillip Burton provided colleagues with funds from his campaign account with the open expectation that the recipients would support his campaign for majority leader. Two of the three other competitors for the majority leader's post, Gillis Long (D-LA) and Jim Wright (D-TX), responded with contributions of their own, creating "the first documented example" (R. Baker 1989, 28) of campaign funds being a core strategy of winning a House leadership election. Burton lost the campaign to Jim Wright but set the precedent for redistributing campaign funds to advance within the institution.

In 1978, Representative Henry Waxman (D-CA), a liberal ally of Phillip Burton, distributed campaign contributions from his principal campaign committee and formed the first leadership PAC to secure an influential subcommittee chairmanship over a more senior member, on the Energy and Commerce Committee (R. Baker 1989; Sabato 1984). Waxman's actions received much notice because contributions to colleagues were unusual for junior members and because senior members were threatened by junior members willing to use campaign money to leapfrog over them instead of following the norms of seniority. Moreover, in a modern take on the old-style political machine, Waxman and fellow California House members Howard Berman and Mel Levine coordinated and targeted their campaign donations to like-minded House candidates (Fritz and Morris 1990; Sabato 1988).

Another Californian, Tony Coehlo, parlayed his fundraising successes as DCCC chair to selection as Democratic majority whip (Jackson 1988; Loomis 1988). Coehlo had a number of disadvantages in the whip contest. Should he win, all members of the Democratic leadership would be from the West. Perhaps a more important liability was that he faced formidable opposition. His key opponent, Charles Rangel of New York, was popular in the caucus, had the support of the Speaker, and had a base of support in the Congressional Black Caucus (R. Baker 1989, 37). Coehlo's prolific contributions from his leadership PAC overcame these hurdles and allowed him to win by a large margin, thus making the creation of an LPAC a near requirement for serious leadership aspirants (R. Baker 1989; Salmore and Salmore 1989; Wilcox 1989, 1990). Even Rangel, who had been a vocal critic of LPACs, formed one to contest the whip's race (Benenson 1986).

The dynamics of the intersection of position and redistribution largesse, which would become commonplace in later years, can be seen in the leadership career of Bill Gray (D-PA) (R. Baker 1989, 37–40). Gray first sought the chairmanship of the House Budget Committee and contributed generously from his principal campaign committee to non-incumbent Democratic candidates in the 1984 election. Candidates who won were then members of the Democratic caucus and, as such, eligible to vote for him to be chair. Chairing a committee allowed Gray to increase his fundraising activities substantially and to turn his sights on an elective party leadership post. Gray campaigned for the open chairmanship of the

Democratic caucus by inviting colleagues to an extravagant dinner at which he handed them each $1,000 campaign contribution checks. At a later breakfast for lobbyists, he recruited them to make calls on his behalf to Democratic members of Congress. Gray also formed an LPAC and raised funds for it with a letter explicitly soliciting the funds to contest the leadership post. Gray's competitors were less enthused about lavishing funds and gifts on their colleagues. Gray won.

Meanwhile, Newt Gingrich (R-GA) formed GOPAC, an LPAC that supported Gingrich's efforts to identify, train, and assist promising GOP candidates at the state level. Unlike the leadership aspirants in the previous examples, Gingrich's campaign activity was not directed primarily at incumbents who could support him in leadership contests in a crude "pay-to-play" scheme. In fact, Gingrich gave only $3,000 to incumbent candidates in 1994 (1.5 percent of his total donations), while giving $181,000 (90.5 percent) to nonincumbents.[9]

Gingrich's donations were part of a broader, multipronged effort to win majority status for the GOP. Beyond recruiting and funding candidates, Gingrich sought to confront and delegitimize the majority Democratic Party by activities such as filing ethics charges against Speaker Jim Wright and fanning discontent over the 1992 House banking scandal. He further sought to clarify the ideological distinction between the congressional parties by refusing to cooperate with President Bush in 1991 in passing a budget that would raise taxes or with President Clinton on most major legislation. He then mobilized Republicans around an alternative policy agenda by crafting the Contract with America—the centerpiece of the 1994 GOP message. Gingrich's efforts paid off when a "farm team" of GOP candidates exploited President Clinton's declining popularity and rode an anti-Clinton tide into the House. With the GOP's sweeping electoral victory, Gingrich became the new Speaker of the House.

These examples show that during the 1980s and early 1990s, party leaders and a handful of highly ambitious members were redistributing significant sums of campaign money. A few members gained notoriety from their colleagues and the media for using campaign money as a prominent component of their leadership campaign. While such behavior was becoming more frequent and more elaborate, not until the 1990s would such practices become institutionalized among all members rather than just leadership aspirants with PACs. Gingrich's efforts would become a new model of party campaign leadership, with campaign money used not just to win friends and supporters but to win majorities.

Finding New Party Money, Part II: The Battle for
Majority Control

The 1990s was a decade of political upheaval, and the parties, seeking to exploit political opportunities and prevent losses, continued their seemingly relentless search for new sources of campaign money. The 1992 election—which brought 110 new members to the House (and a Democrat to the White House for first time in 12 years)—reinforced the need for party money to deal with electoral uncertainty. Most important, dramatic changes unfolded in Washington in 1994, as both parties (and the entire Washington power structure) responded to the GOP's stunning takeover of the U.S. House and Senate. Continued intense competition for control of the House motivated both parties to raise and spend substantially more money than they ever had.

The parties developed two primary approaches to fundraising and spending in the battle for majority status. The parties exploited uncapped soft money contributions from well-heeled individual and organizational donors to unprecedented heights. They also increasingly attempted to mobilize hard money contributions from their incumbents, who could redistribute funds from their ongoing hard money fundraising operations for their own campaigns and LPACs.

Incumbent participation in party funding became more institutionalized early in the decade. To help reduce the DCCC's debt, campaign committee chair Vic Fazio (D-CA) formally initiated the practice of soliciting contributions from members during the 1991–92 electoral cycle, levying a "suggested" dues of $5,000 for all Democratic incumbents (Sabato and Larson 2002). The NRCC followed suit during the 1993–94 election cycle, launching its own program to encourage incumbent financial support (Gimpel 1996, 10–11; Herrnson 1997, 108–9). For both parties, necessity seemed to be the mother of invention. As former NRCC chair Bill Paxon explained about the GOP push for incumbent dollars in 1994, "We did it because we were desperate. We didn't have any money" (quoted in Eilperin 2006, 21). The GOP could take advantage of its newfound majority status by tapping the wave of contributions that interest groups directed to members of the majority party (Cox and Magar 1999; Rudolph 1999), and it could use these funds to secure its majority. Like a franchise, the GOP would take a cut of the access-oriented money its members were receiving from donors seeking to influence legislation. The DCCC needed to replace access-oriented money that it was no longer receiving by mere virtue of being in the majority. It turned to its members to use their local fundraising networks to supplement its own national donor base.

Importantly, however, the increases in party spending that resulted from the battle for majority status following the 1994 election were not in the traditional forms of party expenditures—direct hard money contributions to candidates and coordinated expenditures on their behalf; rather, the parties explored new avenues for spending. Events in 1996 opened up those new avenues. First, President Bill Clinton's reelection campaign that year set a precedent for using soft money to pay for "issue advertising." Unambiguously designed to promote the election or defeat of a specific federal candidate, these ads fell just short of express advocacy because they avoided specific phrases (i.e., "vote for," "vote against") deemed by the Supreme Court in *Buckley* to be indicators of express advocacy. As a result, the parties were able to pay for such ads with a blend of hard and soft money. Other federal campaigns quickly followed the lead of the DNC/Clinton campaign. Since advertising is a substantial expense, using unlimited soft money contributions to pay for ads opened an unprecedented avenue for party involvement in congressional campaigns. Both parties, moreover, recognized that soft money could be effectively deployed for grassroots voter targeting and mobilization in competitive districts (Magleby 2000). Not surprisingly, the parties' recognition that they could use soft money more extensively than they had been doing created an intense party demand for soft money from wealthy individuals and deep-pocketed corporations and labor unions.

The second pivotal event of 1996 was the Supreme Court's ruling in *FEC v. Colorado Republican Federal Campaign Committee*. In this case, the Court ruled that parties could make unlimited hard money expenditures as long as such expenditures were made independently of the benefited candidate. Such expenditures allowed the parties to sidestep the existing caps on direct party contributions and coordinated expenditures and permitted the parties to concentrate large amounts of funds in a few particularly important races rather than disbursing them widely. Thus, just as spending on issue ads provided incentives for parties to raise more soft money, the opportunity to spend unlimited sums of hard money on independent expenditures motivated parties to raise more hard money. Of course, raising large sums of hard money, which must be gathered under restrictive federal guidelines, is far more difficult than raising large sums of soft money, which could be collected in unlimited sums from well-heeled donors.

Interest groups also responded to the shifting regulatory environment. No longer content merely to contribute to candidates directly through their PACs, groups increasingly made independent expenditures and used soft money to finance air and ground wars. The combined impact of outside money from parties and interest groups increased the uncertainty of candidates in targeted contests, as candidates no longer had ownership over the issue agenda of the campaigns. Indeed, in the most competitive contests, it became common for the spending of parties and interest groups to swamp candidate spending (Magleby 2000).

The regulatory shift that unfolded in the 1990s fueled an arms race in party funding (Krasno and Sorauf 2003). In a seemingly shrinking number of competitive congressional districts, each party spent primarily to offset the barrage of independent expenditures and issue advocacy campaigns financed by the other party and its allied interest groups. That the informational cacophony from such campaigns might overwhelm voters or cause them to tune out mattered little to the parties; as long as one party was spending heavily to try to win a congressional election, the other party viewed more spending as the only viable response. CCC officers would be heavily criticized if the party's candidate lost a "winnable" seat while the party provided little assistance. But if the party spent lavishly and their candidate was defeated, the blame could be shifted to the candidate's campaign, the national environment, or district-specific quirks rather than the party's efforts.

In such an environment, candidates can have difficulty raising sufficient funds to communicate with voters over the din of independent party and group campaigns. Nonincumbents, of course, are at a particularly severe disadvantage in such an environment. They typically lack the networks of local contributors enjoyed by incumbents. They are also usually unable to raise funds nationally from direct mail or via the Internet without the assistance of a party or interest groups, and they obviously lack the formal positions that enable incumbents to extract contributions from investor donors. To add to nonincumbents' woes, local party organizations usually lack the money and volunteers to be of much help in contests that attract intense outside involvement. With few available alternatives, nonincumbents turn to the national parties for assistance (Aldrich 1995; Parker 2008; Schlesinger 1985).

That resource-poor challengers and open-seat candidates would accept strong party involvement on their behalf is intuitive. But resource-rich incumbents are a different matter. This is particularly true when the CCC dues required by strong parties make incumbents poorer in the process. In an electoral environment in which even incumbents' capacity to raise money can be overwhelmed by outside interest groups and the opposing party or even a free-spending self-financed challenger, having an effective and well-financed CCC provides a reassuring backup to an incumbent's own campaign efforts. From the incumbent's perspective, paying CCC dues is like buying election insurance. The homeowner hopes to never have a fire but buys insurance just in case (and then hopes that the insurance company will pay up as the homeowner expects); the incumbent hopes to never have a tough election and can reasonably expect that the CCC will come to his or her aid if a competitive election occurs. But fundraising aggressively and paying one's dues helps to minimize the risks, at least psychologically. The CCCs encourage the expectation that members must have "sweat equity" in the joint member-CCC electoral efforts by establishing fundraising targets that members must meet for their own campaigns in order to be eligible for CCC assistance (Isenstadt and Hohmann 2010). If the CCC has a tough year fundraising, an endangered incumbent will draw on his or her past record as a team player in making his or her claims for limited resources from the CCC.

Faced with ever higher demands for funds to pour into competitive campaigns, parties generally opted for easier-to-finance soft money expenditures (e.g., issue ads) over hard money independent expenditures (Herrnson 2004, 116). Yet the parties still needed hard money. Parties had to pay for the so-called federal share of issue ads and all soft money expenditures with hard money (Corrado 1997). Hard money was also still necessary for direct contributions, coordinated expenditures, and independent expenditures. In fact, Parker (2008, 22–23) shows that as a percentage of candidate expenditures, party expenditures increased substantially in the 1990s. In response, the parties leaned even further on incumbents to redistribute their hard money funds to the CCCs and to needy party candidates.

From a fundraising perspective, turning to incumbents for hard money makes perfect sense for the parties. First, by tapping incumbents for money, parties save the high costs typically associated with direct mail and glitzy fundraising events. As former DCCC chairman (2003–4) Representative Robert Matsui (D-CA) remarked, "[M]oney from members is particularly important, because there [are] no costs of fundraising. . . . When a member gives a dollar, that entire dollar is spent on candidates, whereas with direct mail, there's the cost of stamps and printing" (quoted in Carney 2004, 2170). Second, through incumbents, parties reap the rewards of incumbent donor networks. Newly mandated disclosure of bundled contributions by lobbyists suggests that a nontrivial percentage of individual contributions raised by House incumbents may be bundled by lobbyists.[10] Indeed, seven months into the 2009–10 election cycle, Representative Roy Blunt (R-MO) had already raked in $310,534 in individual contributions bundled by lobbyists, while on the Democratic side, Barney Frank (D-MA) reported $133,575 in bundled contributions.[11] Fundraising events in Washington, D.C., allow parties to tap into incumbent connections with lobbyists, who might not otherwise give to parties (Heberlig et al. 2008). Finally—and perhaps most important—by providing incentives for incumbents to redistribute their campaign funds, parties reduce competition with incumbents for funds. Instead, taking advantage of incumbents' natural fundraising advantages, the parties need only encourage members to raise as much campaign money as possible and then take a "cut" to finance the parties' collective electoral efforts. The consequence is greater efficiency in fundraising, as incumbents with the capacity to raise money redirect it either to the party—which in turn spends it on the candidates who have the greatest need (Bedlington and Malbin 2003; Bianco 1999)—or directly to needy candidates themselves.

The result of this new fundraising relationship between members of Congress and the parties is that incumbents are essentially becoming "brokers" for their party committees (Sorauf 1988, 171). Brokers are common in large political fundraising enterprises (Brown, Powell, and Wilcox 1995, 57–62; Wright 1985), as each solicitor taps his or her own network of contacts and also asks those contacts to solicit from their friends and associates. When acting as brokers for the party, each member of Congress activates his or her fundraising network for the member's own campaign, with their own brokers and finance committees, working their own personal and professional networks. They raise funds in the traditional way for the member's own campaign but pass some of the money along to the party or to party candidates. The party now has access to a much more politically and geographically diverse contributor base than it is able to tap into on its own (Heberlig et al. 2008).

The arrangement whereby incumbents support the parties financially provides rewards for contributing incumbents and outside donors as well. By redistributing money to the party and its candidates, incumbents increase their likelihood of advancing in the party and committee leadership hierarchies (Heberlig 2003; Heberlig, Hetherington, and Larson 2006). By 2000, one senior GOP leadership aide put the new expectations of committee chairs in blunt terms as follows:

Fundraising for the party as a whole and members individually will pay a significant role in the selection of chairmen in the next Congress. You can't tell me that a Member who raises $1 million for the party and visits 50 districts is not going to have an advantage over someone who sits back and thinks he's entitled to a chairmanship. Those days are gone. (quoted in VandeHei 1999b, 34)

Moreover, by advancing to more powerful formal positions in the House, incumbents further increase their fundraising leverage over corporate and labor interests (Grier and Munger 1993). If consistent donations are a measure of approval, suppliers of funds to incumbents do not seem to oppose the arrangement either—despite the fact that their contributions end up in the campaign accounts of candidates they do not necessarily support. Investor PAC directors, who are sufficiently sophisticated to know that their contributions are redistributed by members, are likely fine with any arrangement that yields continuing access to incumbents.[12] In contrast, many individual donors may not know that their contributions to incumbents are redistributed to the parties and other candidates. Whereas anecdotes about members advancing because of campaign contributions were once reported because such an occurrence was unusual in an institution dominated by seniority and career ladders, Capitol Hill journalists increasingly reported links between fundraising and advancement, and political scientists increasingly supplied statistical evidence of a relationship (see chapter 6).

By the close of the 1990s, several trends had converged to motivate an unprecedented, substantial redistribution of incumbent campaign funds for the benefit of the party's collective electoral interests. First, there was an intense and ongoing battle for control of the House. With majority control up for grabs, more members were willing to part with large sums of campaign money, and few complained when leaders imposed five- and six-figure party "dues." Second and equally important, control of the House hinged on a few seats, meaning that most incumbents were safe. *CQ Weekly Report* listed only 46 House districts, on average, as competitive in the 1998–2004 period, compared to 118 districts, on average, in the 1990–96 and 2006–2008 periods (also see Oppenheimer 2005). Finally, the strong party leadership that developed in the postreform House (Rohde 1991; Sinclair 1995) was able to use its powers to ensure that members did not free ride on the efforts of others. Party leaders exerted greater influence over the party campaign committees, developing a big picture strategy with the CCC chair and advising the chair on how to spend the money that the leaders raised personally and mobilized through the contributions of members of their caucus (Cohen 2010).

The increased power of congressional party leaders over the last decade has produced a more centralized fundraising regime (Gierzynski 2000, 32–33). The congressional parties expect members to whom valuable positions are awarded to use their posts to raise campaign funds for the party and its candidates. Consistent with these expectations, Taylor (2003) finds that committee leaders extract party-oriented PAC contributions from interest groups with interests before their respective committees. Additionally, increased centralization of power places party leaders in a position to serve as the "enforcers" of the "contract" between the interest group and the members to whom they have contributed (McCarty and Rothenberg 2000). Party leaders would be particularly interested in enforcing the desires of organized interests when individual members are essentially serving as the conduit for money between interest groups and the parties.

The intersection of the trends toward more powerful congressional party leaders, intense party competition for majority status, and use of Congress's institutional power for leverage over donors reached its zenith in former majority leader Tom DeLay's K Street Strategy. The K Street Strategy was the core of the GOP's strategy for cementing their status as majority party following their dramatic victory in the 1994 election. DeLay's K Street Strategy focused on the Washington lobbying community, traditionally based on K Street.[13] Many of the firms—even those representing corporate interests and thus conservative in their ideology and Republican in their partisanship—had disproportionately Democratic lobbying teams to reflect the traditionally disproportionate Democratic membership of Congress. Likewise, PACs had given their contributions disproportionately to Democrats prior to the 104th Congress to gain access and influence among the Democratic majority. DeLay made known very publicly that now that the GOP was the majority, the lobbying community would need to reshape itself to reflect this new political reality. DeLay would pressure lobbying firms to hire Republican lobbyists and direct their PACs to contribute to GOP candidates and party organizations—and to cease contributing to Democratic candidates and party organizations—as conditions for access to the GOP leadership in Congress. Since lobbyists are a major source of campaign contributions to members of Congress, more GOP lobbyists would produce more contributions to GOP candidates. Increasing contributions from lobbyists and PACs would help provide Republican members of Congress with the resources to reinforce the traditional institutional advantages of incumbency, thus helping the Republican Party retain its majority.

Additionally, the Republican congressional leadership would integrate lobbyists into the process of policy development. Lobbyists would assist in writing the bills, thus presumably assuring that policies were written to maximize benefits to their clients. They were also essentially incorporated into the GOP whip organization, helping the party persuade its members to vote for the legislation. This strategy would include having lobbyists use their membership in the district of a member of Congress in grassroots lobbying campaigns to demonstrate constituent support for the legislation (and to send the message that there was constituency support for a primary challenge if the member failed to follow the party line). When the legislation passed, the implemented policies would provide a steady and lucrative stream of income to the beneficiary organizations. The grateful organizations would share the wealth with the munificent party in Congress and its members who passed the legislation, by generously supporting their campaigns. Simultaneously, Congress would pass policies that would undercut the financial pillars of the Democratic Party, such as trial lawyers, labor unions, and public employees. The result would be a substantial funding advantage for the GOP, allowing it to keep and expand its congressional majority (Hacker and Pierson 2005).

Washington Post columnist E. J. Dionne (2005) calls the K Street Strategy "an interlocking directorate of politicians, lobbyists, fundraisers, and interest groups." All worked together to provide benefits for the other. As long as the lobbyists and interest groups overwhelmingly directed campaign funds toward the GOP, the GOP would have the resources necessary to win elections and stay in the majority. As long as the GOP retained its majority, probusiness lobbyists and the interest groups got the policies they wanted. They also got the policies they would profit by, providing them substantial sums to share with their benefactors in Congress.

Although the K Street Strategy did not "work" in the sense of providing the GOP with sufficient funds to protect their congressional majorities indefinitely, it illustrates the link between parties, government institutions, and private donors that has been at the heart of parties' fundraising dilemmas since the heyday of the urban party machines at the turn of the twentieth century. To be sure, the relationships and behavior at the heart of the K Street Strategy do have similarities with traditional party machine behavior. Traditional party machines extracted resources from those dependent on government for their livelihoods: public employees, government suppliers and contractors, and businesses that needed government permits to expand. The K Street Strategy adapted traditional machine behavior relevant to the contemporary political environment by expanding the targets to industries dependent on government regulatory policy and lobbyists, whose access to powerful government officials and perceptions of their effectiveness are their livelihood.

The K Street Strategy is a colorful illustration of some of the recent activities of the congressional GOP leadership, but focusing on a few outlandish activities leads us to overlook more fundamental institutional behavior and its implications for understanding congressional parties. Democrats, as the minority party in Congress from 1995 to 2007, could not use the patronage or policy leverage that Republicans used to attempt to turn K Street into a subsidiary of the party. Yet when we look at their fundraising behavior and use of incentives within the House to reward members who redistribute campaign funds to the party and its candidates, we find that both parties behaved in similar ways. The real story is the important changes in the relationships between individual members of Congress and their parties, changes in the institutional operations of Congress to facilitate fundraising, and the consequent changes in fundraising by members of Congress.

Finding New Party Money, Part III: BCRA

In 2002, Congress passed the Bipartisan Campaign Finance Reform Act. Among other changes in federal campaign finance regulations, the law created a new category of regulated political speech called electioneering communications and—most important for our purposes—prohibited the national party and elected officeholders from raising soft money. The loss of soft money was hardly inconsequential for the CCCs. In 2002, the DCCC spent $54.4 million and the NRCC spent $69.7 million in soft money.[14] Replacing those sums would be no small task.

At the same time, however, BCRA increased the total hard money limits that an individual could contribute in aggregate to parties, candidates, and PACs from $50,000 per election cycle to $95,000 per election cycle (see Potter 2005). The limit was also indexed to inflation so that it rises every two years, as are all the aggregate sublimits to candidates, parties, and PACs. Moreover, BCRA limited an individual's total contributions to congressional candidates (at $2,000 per candidate per election) to $37,500. That meant that parties and interest groups could collect the remainder of an individual's $95,000 limit (i.e., $57,500) and that any individual who wanted to give the maximum possible amount in an election cycle would have to contribute to parties and interest groups. An individual's total PAC limit (at $5,000 per PAC per year) was $40,000. Thus, even if an individual maxed out on candidate and PAC contributions, he or she could still give $17,500 to party organizations. In short, although BCRA took away opportunities for unlimited soft money contributions to parties, it opened up the opportunity for larger—though limited—hard money contributions to the parties.

First implemented in 2004, BCRA's ban on party soft money caused parties to invest heavily in expanding their base of small donors through a variety of solicitation programs, using both low technology (direct mail, phone banks) and high technology (the Internet and the World Wide Web) (Dwyre and Kolodny 2006). The parties substantially increased giving by small donors ($200 or less), and the proportion of funds contributed by large donors ($20,000 or more) declined (Corrado and Varney 2007). The parties, particularly the Democrats, later took advantage of BCRA's provisions that allow individuals to contribute more to party committees than to candidates or PACs by increasing the amounts raised from "max-out" donors—that is, those who reach the $95,000 aggregate contribution limit (Magleby 2011).

BCRA also very much deepened the parties' reliance on incumbent dollars, as both parties scrambled for hard dollars to replace soft money banned by BCRA. Both the DCCC and NRCC increased member "dues" substantially in 2004, and both committees raked in record sums of incumbent money that year (Dwyre et al. 2006). Similarly, while the Senate CCCs had not established dues, Democratic senators nevertheless tripled their contributions to the Democratic Senatorial Campaign Committee (DSCC), and Republican senators doubled their contributions to the National Republican Senatorial Committee (NRSC).

Incumbents could also use their access to corporate campaign money to fund their contributions to the CCCs, as BCRA forced corporate soft money contributors to change their contribution strategies. Corporations that had traditionally given large soft money contributions to the parties now faced a decision regarding how to redirect their political spending. Certainly, they could increase their hard money giving and their lobbying expenditures. They could also contribute to the new party-allied 527 and 501(c) organizations that formed in response to BCRA to take the large soft money contributions that the party organizations themselves no longer could accept. These committees would use the funds to pay for issue ads promoting or attacking issue stances—and, by association, the candidates named and pictured in the ad who shared that position. But given the likelihood that 527 and 501(c) groups would serve as attack dogs who would push the boundaries of electoral discourse (because they are not directly accountable to voters as are candidates and parties), corporations might face a public image risk by underwriting these committees financially.[15] The safer route to get money to parties would be to give larger hard money contributions to safe incumbents (La Raja 2008b, 112), knowing that incumbents would redistribute a large proportion of the contribution to the party.

As a result of their efforts to change their fundraising strategies to adapt to BCRA, both the NRCC and the DCCC raised substantially more in hard money in 2004 than they had in 2002. The NRCC increased its hard money take by one-third, from $123.6 million to $185.7 million, while the DCCC increased its hard money by 50 percent, jumping from $46.4 to $93.2 million. To be sure, neither committee entirely replaced the sum of hard and soft money receipts from 2002 with only hard money donations in 2004. Their losses, though, were relatively modest: the NRCC's total receipts were down $7.6 million (3.9 percent); the DCCC was down $9.7 million (9.4 percent). Moreover, the 2004 total hard money fundraising of each party's national organizations was greater in 2004 than their sum of both hard and soft money in the previous presidential election cycle in 2000.[16] GOP organizations increased their take from $715.7 million in 2000 to $782.4 in 2004, and Democratic totals rose from $520.4 million to $678.89 million during the same period.[17]

The emphasis on incumbents as key to the parties' post-BCRA fundraising efforts continued in the 2006 election cycle, as incumbents set new records for giving to the CCCs. House Democrats redistributed $28,010,806 to the DCCC from their principal campaign committees and leadership PACs, and House Republicans transferred slightly less ($26,592,124) to the NRCC. House incumbents also continued to give generously from their principal campaign committees and LPACs directly to fellow party candidates. Incumbent contributions have been less important in the Senate than in the House, and the Senate CCCs have not levied formal party dues. Nevertheless, Senate incumbent contributions to the party campaign committees also increased significantly from 2002 to 2004 (Dwyre et al. 2006) and again in 2006.

The increased importance of incumbent fundraising to the House party campaign committees is illustrated in figure 2.1, which shows the proportion of total receipts provided by members of the House. Despite the Hill committees' substantially increased efforts and successes in expanding their donor bases and fundraising through the web, their reliance on incumbent redistribution continues to increase. Democratic incumbents provided 4 percent of the DCCC's funds in 1990, and this fell to 2.9 percent in the 1994 election cycles as the party lost its majority status in Congress. But by the 2000 election cycle, Democratic incumbents were supplying over 20 percent of the DCCC's funds. The NRCC depends less on incumbents for funds than do the Democrats, but the trend of increased reliance is clear there, too. GOP incumbents provided less than 1 percent of NRCC funds in the 1990 and 1992 election cycles. Starting in the 2000 election cycle, GOP House members provided between 10 and 15 percent of the NRCC's hard money in each cycle. By 2006, incumbents' principal campaign committees alone provided more money to the CCCs than individual contributions of $20,000 or more (Corrado and Varney 2007).

The Senate Hill committees are somewhat less dependent on their incumbents for funds than are their House counterparts, but the trends are similar (Dwyre et al. 2006). In the 2000 and 2002 election cycles, for example, Democratic senators provided less than 3 percent of the DSCC's funds. This jumped dramatically in 2004 as Democratic senators increased their giving eight-fold (from $1.8 million to $14.6 million), comprising 16.4 percent of the DSCC's funds. In 2006, the DSCC substantially increased its fundraising from individual donors, and its proportion of funds from senators fell to 9.7 percent. As with their House counterparts, the NRSC is less dependent on incumbents for funds than is the DSCC. The proportion of NRSC funds from GOP senators has hovered around 5 percent through the past several election cycles.[18]

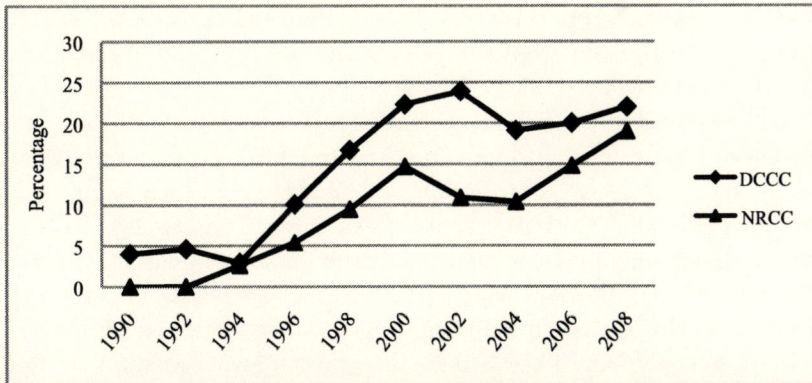

Fig. 2.1.   The percentage of CCC hard money from U.S. House members

The change in majority status following the 2006 elections did not result in a reassessment of fundraising practices. If anything, they intensified parties' efforts to mobilize incumbents to redistribute funds to ensure that the parties and their candidates would be competitive in 2008. Despite losing majority status, the House GOP levied substantial financial assessments on incumbents just one week into the 110th Congress, requiring each member to sign a pledge that he or she would raise the required sum (Zeller and Teitelbaum 2007). Meanwhile, the House's new Democratic majority enlisted its new committee chairs to fill the DCCC's coffers (Birnbaum and Solomon 2007). The parties' deepening reliance on incumbent financial support highlights an important reality of contemporary American political parties: that well-financed party organizations in the United States now necessarily depend on the presence and cooperation of powerful incumbents, who can use their leverage over well-heeled interests to finance not only their own reelections but the party's collective electoral efforts as well.

Senate Republicans, however, serve as an indicator that members' willingness to raise and fork out ever-increasing sums to the parties is not unlimited. After having lost majority status in the Senate in 2006 and facing expectations that they would lose even more seats in 2008, GOP senators cut their NRSC contributions by nearly half from 2006 to 2008, from $4.7 million to $2.8 million, while the majority Democrats nearly doubled their DSCC contributions, from $11.8 million to $20.6 million.[19] Without majority status at stake, GOP senators reverted to pre-1994 redistributive behavior and did not comply with party pressure to share their wealth. NRSC chair John Ensign publicly chastised his colleagues and took his frustrations to the media: "We've tried fear, we've tried positive reward, positive reinforcement, we've tried being a little harder on them, we use different things at different times—begging, we beg a lot" (quoted in Bolton 2008). All of this was to little avail.

House Republicans, like their Senate counterparts, were also not expected to regain the majority in 2008 and faced the likelihood of losing additional seats. Their contributions to the NRCC declined from $25.4 million in the 2006 election cycle to $22.8 in the 2008 election cycle. There were 29 fewer GOP members of the House in the 110th Congress, and two of the GOP's biggest givers were retiring, former Speaker Dennis Hastert and former NRCC chair Tom Reynolds. The decline in the average contributions per member to the NRCC thus appears less dramatic than the overall decline in funds: $131,000 per GOP House incumbent in 2006 versus $119,000 in 2008.

With majority status at serious risk in 2010, House Democratic leaders had some difficulty getting safe incumbents with substantial war chests to pay their party dues in a timely manner. A frustrated senior Democratic aide exclaimed, "The house is burning, and you have an opportunity to put out the fire, but you're across the street whistling. What are they holding out on?" (quoted in Isenstadt 2010). In the end, however, our preliminary analysis of the 2010 data shows that Democrats contributed slightly more to the Democratic Congressional Campaign Committee in 2010 than in 2008. The 83 Democratic incumbents who sought reelection in districts rated as competitive by *Congressional Quarterly* in 2010 did decrease their contributions to the Democratic Congressional Campaign Committee from 2008 (from $4.4 million to $1.5 million), but other safe Democratic incumbents contributed more to make up the difference. Similarly, total redistribution from Democrats was slightly higher ($3.4 million) in 2010 than 2008. Democratic leaders may have felt like they were pulling teeth, and perhaps did not achieve the increases in redistribution that they had planned, but they did raise more money in a much more difficult electoral environment.

The U.S. Supreme Court's ruling in *Citizens United v. FEC* (2010) is likely to heighten incumbents' and parties' anxieties about the need for ever-greater sums of money. The court ruled that the "free speech" rights of corporations (and, presumably, labor unions) could not be limited by congressional restrictions on the amounts of money they spend in elections to advocate for or against candidates. Such spending had been banned since 1907, and the Supreme Court had upheld the prohibition in *Austin v. Michigan Chamber of Commerce* (1990) and *McConnell v. Federal Election Commission* (2003).[20] Although the *Citizens United* case does not affect the amount of hard money that corporate PACs can give directly to candidates, allowing direct electoral spending by corporations obviously creates a new avenue for substantially greater flow of money into elections. Worse from the perspective of candidates and parties is that corporate spending is outside of their control and that they must raise and spend sufficient amounts of money to get their message heard and to counter potential corporate-backed attacks against them. With a new spending option open to them, corporations could potentially shift their political spending toward express advocacy rather than making PAC contributions to incumbents (who can then redistribute those funds to the parties).

One study of the 2010 congressional elections (Franz 2011) suggests that the Court's ruling undercutting BCRA's electioneering communication provisions in *Wisconsin Right to Life* may have had a more important impact on outside money than its ruling in *Citizens United*. But, as with Franz, we would hesitate to draw any conclusions based on only one election after the *Citizens United* ruling. Indeed, using *Citizens United* as precedent, a federal circuit court ruled (in *SpeechNow.org v. Federal Election Commission* in March 2010) that political committees that make independent expenditures could accept donations of unlimited size. This ruling has facilitated the emergence in 2011 of "Super PACs"—political committees raising unregulated funds from corporations, unions, and wealthy individuals to pay for independent express advocacy—indicating that the Court's ruling in *Citizens United* has begun to bring about fundamental changes to the congressional campaign finance system. How such PACs will influence the relationship between parties, officeholders, and interest groups is not yet entirely clear. But they certainly have the potential to destabilize the electoral environment that incumbents face by adding considerable uncertainty about the number and aggressiveness of groups that might emerge to oppose them.

Conclusion

As this chapter makes clear, the answer to the question of "who should pay to produce the collective good of the party organization" (Hopkin 2004, 632) has been the same throughout U.S. history: well-heeled private interests. Yet how parties have generated funds from private interests has changed significantly over time. In some ways, the current arrangement for funding the parties represents an amalgamation of past practices. Nineteenth-century parties were funded largely by elected officeholders and government workers with patronage jobs. As the American state expanded and became professionalized, progressive reformers removed government workers from the business of party fundraising, while newly emerging corporate (and, later, labor) interests assumed a prominent role in funding parties. In the early years of the twenty-first century, incumbents have once again assumed a significant role in funding the parties. Now, however, officeholders fund the parties not by kicking back a percentage of their official salaries but by redistributing funds they have extracted from well-heeled interests over which they enjoy significant leverage.

Driven by narrow party margins in Congress, fierce competition for funds with candidates and interest groups, and legal limitations on party fundraising capacity, the congressional parties have deputized their incumbents as the primary fundraising brokers for the party campaign effort.

Whereas their urban machine ancestors used control over nominations to induce financial contributions from their incumbents, contemporary congressional parties use their control over positions of institutional power in Congress to induce cooperation. Wary of becoming a defenseless target of free-spending interest groups, the opposing party, or self-financing challengers—and seeking to augment their own power by serving in powerful majority party positions—congressional incumbents now possess greater incentives than they once had to comply with the parties' fundraising demands. As such, they have increasingly mobilized their local and Washington fundraising networks for the purpose of funding the party and its candidates in competitive races. The rest of this book demonstrates how incumbent funding of the parties has shaped and is shaped by party organization in Congress.

Critics of the role of private money in politics, particularly from self-interested sources with business before government, will not be pleased with the evolution of party finance. Moving from a corrupt patronage system to one whereby politicians solicit private interests on behalf of the party is not a substantial improvement. Indeed, that the party now benefits from the relationship between the politician fundraiser and the donor may make the parties all the more attentive to donor's priorities. This seems particularly true given that party leaders are coordinating a substantial share of the fundraising for their party's electoral efforts. For reformers, there must be bitter irony in the recognition that congressional parties have responded to BCRA's ban on soft money by using their incumbents to extract hard money contributions from the same donors.

But for these critics, a campaign finance regime orchestrated by parties and held accountable through elected party leaders may well be preferable to the unlimited, unaccountable flow of money into campaigns from corporations and large organizational interests encouraged by the Supreme Court's *Citizens United* decision. A party-directed system at least serves a policy agenda that voters can respond to, and it channels a substantial proportion of the funds to nonincumbent candidates in competitive districts. As this chapter has shown, if there is a source of money available, parties tend, in time, to find an innovative way to tap and direct it for their purposes. It was not long ago, after all, that incumbents were seen as the overlords of campaign fundraising and that parties had little hope of playing a significant role in congressional campaigns.

3 | Majority Status and Institutional Power

Larson: The DCCC will ask people to contribute to others?
Democratic Member of Congress A: I have asked them to let me
know. . . . We all have finite resources and we want to put them into
races where they will make a difference. *I want to be in the leadership
. . . I mean the majority party,* and the way to do that is to make sure
we win enough races.[1]
          —Telephone interview by Larson, December 2, 1994 (italics added)

Representative A's slip of the tongue in the preceding comment illustrates
the link between individual ambition and campaign money that has often
been assumed to exist (e.g., R. Baker 1989). It would be easy to assert that
the initial, self-interested response was the true answer (Freudian analysts
that we are) and that the correction was the more politically correct response usually given for public consumption. Yet the bifurcated response,
we believe, is at the heart of the contemporary advancement structure in
the House of Representatives. One advances into powerful institutional
positions by redistributing campaign funds, but because the party controls
access to the positions, it can ensure that individuals direct their ambitions
toward advancing party goals. Now that majority status is the predominant goal of both congressional parties and now that the mobilization of
campaign funds from incumbents is a critical method of attaining majority status, redistribution advances the power goals of both the individual
member and the political party. As the rest of Representative A's answer indicates, winning the competitive districts on which majority status hinges
is the key for both the party and the ambitious member.

Whereas members of the U.S. House of Representatives redistributed
less than $3 million to candidates and party committees in 1990, they re-
distributed nearly $100 million by 2006. This rapid increase in campaign
contributions by members of Congress remains unexplained by and poses

challenges to the extant research on congressional parties, which has focused almost exclusively on the legislative efforts of the parties. While spelling out the logic of the congressional parties' increasingly coordinated legislative activities, scholars have all but missed their increasingly coordinated electoral activities. Not surprisingly, then, many questions about the steep rise in incumbent party-connected contributions have gone unanswered. Why has such a dramatic change in behavior occurred in a relatively limited period of time? How have parties suddenly been able to induce reelection-seeking members to make financial sacrifices for the collective electoral goals of the party? What impact have the new party fundraising expectations had on member career trajectories within the House and beyond? How have members adjusted their own fundraising strategies in order to comply with the new party fundraising expectations? What theoretical light does members' newfound generosity shed on the logic of contemporary congressional parties?

As Steven Smith (2007, 2) notes, the central question for scholars who study congressional parties is, "Why would members invent and tolerate parties that lead them to behave differently than they would otherwise?" Such scholars have spilled a great deal of ink attempting to answer this question as it relates to partisan legislative activities, but they have done little to answer it with respect to the parties' collective electoral efforts. This is a striking gap in light of the traditional characterization of American parties as electoral parties concerned with securing power (Downs 1957; Epstein 1986; Schattschneider 1942; Schumpeter 1950; Wright 2000).

On one hand, serving in the majority party enhances members' ability to achieve their individual goals (Cox and McCubbins 1993). Thus, it seems intuitively rational for members to assist other candidates to help their party attain majority status. On the other hand, there has traditionally been very little evidence of members of Congress acting collectively in elections. Instead, there is far more evidence of members putting their own electoral fortunes ahead of the party's (Jacobson 1985–86; Kolodny 1998).

Members' individual electoral interests, this evidence demonstrates, often undermined the party's collective electoral interests. So, why would members change their behavior from maximizing their own self-interests to greater collective action? We argue that close competition for majority status fundamentally alters the relationships between parties and their incumbents, providing opportunities for leaders to use their delegated powers to advance the party's collective electoral goals and giving rank-and-file members greater incentive to respond positively to the party's coordination and mobilization efforts. The probability of attaining majority status changes the ordering of priorities for congressional parties and their members.

The Collective Action Problems of Congressional Parties

Scholarly attempts to explain congressional behavior often start with the individual member and posit three member goals: reelection, policy, and power (e.g., Fenno 1973). Similarly, congressional parties have a number of potential goals: winning majority status, implementing a policy agenda, helping fellow partisans win control of other branches of government, and providing access to electoral coalition partners.[2] Nancy Pelosi has presented a tripartite formulation of the Speaker's job.

> I have almost three jobs. I'm the Speaker of the House, so I have a legislative job to do. I am the Democratic political leader in terms of making sure we win this election, and have the resources to do that, and travel the country constantly to do that. And I am a representative of San Francisco still in the Congress, proud to say. So I have to balance those challenges. (Quoted in Newmyer 2008)

Understanding how the goals of individual members, party caucuses, and party leaders interact is critical to explaining the behavior of each actor.

Individual party members presumably share their party's collective goal of attaining majority status (Jacobson 1985–86; Herrnson 2009; Kolodny 1998); after all, majority status helps them achieve their individual goals. Majority party members have advantages throughout the legislative process, their institutional positions are more powerful when serving in the majority, they can raise more campaign money in the majority, and their electoral chances increase if the party succeeds legislatively (Cox and McCubbins 1993, 2005; Cox and Magar 1999; Rudolph 1999). Policy is also likely to be closer to the ideal preferences of members of the majority party (Sinclair 2002).

Members are not likely to subscribe equally to all of the party's other collective goals, however. For example, members whose constituencies do not share the dominant ideology or agenda of the party may not be as fully invested in the party's collective policy goals. Nor is the ideologically outlying member likely to make sacrifices to promote the election of party members from other factions, even if doing so helps the party expand its hold on majority status. Likewise, a member is unlikely to prioritize the collective goal of providing access and policy or pecuniary benefits to groups in the party coalition if particular groups are not populous or popular in his or her own constituency. Thus, while sharing the goal of majority status, members may not share other collective legislative and electoral goals that, if achieved, would contribute to the attainment of majority status.

For much of the twentieth century, for example, conservative southern Democrats did not share the policy preferences of the majority of their party, nor did they share the similar constituencies; thus their individual policy goals were not necessarily advanced by their party status. The Democratic Party label, however, served their interest in getting reelected in a one-party region, and because Democrats were the majority party in the House, provided them opportunities to serve in institutional positions whose power is enhanced in the majority. In the late 1980s and early 1990s, numerous GOP moderates supported a more confrontational electoral strategy articulated by Newt Gingrich, while not necessarily supporting the conservative policy agenda favored by Gingrich and the bulk of the GOP caucus. By contrast, many ideologically conservative members favored a less aggressive electoral strategy (Connelly and Pitney 1994; Koopman 1996). A member may have different preferences regarding the party's policy and electoral aims and the strategies it deploys to accomplish them (Moscardelli, Haspel, and Wike 1998).

Moreover, because parties have multiple collective goals, party leaders must choose which goals to prioritize. While the majority party leadership can use its control of congressional organization and processes to minimize the trade-offs between electoral and policy goals members face in lawmaking (Sinclair 1995, 2006), leaders are likely to prioritize the goals that have the highest priority within the caucus and are the most achievable at that moment in time. A consequence of a party having multiple collective goals is that the party must potentially overcome collective action problems to address each of them, and the solutions to each may themselves conflict.

Even if a member will be better off individually if his or her party achieves its collective goals, the well-known collective action problem implies that members will resist contributing to efforts to achieve them (Olson 1965). Even when the collective goals are highly likely to be achieved, members have an incentive to free ride off the efforts of others. A member can enjoy the benefits of the collective good without diverting efforts from his or her own goals to achieve them. So, why would any rational member contribute?

Majority status is clearly a partisan collective good. As long as sufficient numbers of a member's copartisans win election, the member gains the benefits of majority party membership whether or not he or she helped the party obtain its collective goal. The incentive for members to make any individual sacrifices to achieve majority status, then, traditionally has been very limited. Parties were consistently unable to persuade members to contribute to collective party electoral efforts. Quite the contrary, members routinely requested even more assistance for their own election campaigns (Jacobson 1985–86).

Redistribution and Collective Action

The collective electoral challenges facing political parties are clear in the distribution of campaign funds. Since campaign money is raised largely by individual candidates, rather than by the parties, money disproportionately goes to members with the greatest willingness or ability to raise it—often senior members with positions who represent safe seats—rather than to competitive districts where it could make a difference in determining majority status. An efficient redistribution of party campaign money, from financially flush members in safe seats to needy candidates in competitive contests, would benefit all party members by maximizing the party's chances of winning a House majority (Bianco 1999). Thus, it would seem entirely reasonable for members to share some of their surplus funds with "needier" candidates. By helping those candidates win, they could help themselves by creating grateful allies and, should the party win majority status, increase their own power within the institution.

Traditionally, however, members ignored this logic. They spent more on their own reelection campaigns than objective observers would think was necessary for winning reelection (Herrnson 2004; Jacobson 1997). From an individual member's perspective, spending one's campaign funds on one's own election decreases the probability, however unlikely, that one will be defeated. While the party congressional campaign committees may act as an insurance policy and spend heavily if the incumbent does have a tough election, incumbents would prefer not to count on the party keeping its promises. An aide to Wisconsin representative James Sensenbrenner explains that were the congressman to get into electoral trouble, he would rather "have his money sitting in his own campaign account rather than over at the NRCC and having to beg to get it back" (quoted in Dennis and Whittington 2008).

Even without a significant electoral challenge prompting the need to spend substantial campaign funds, members are inclined to hoard funds. Although scholars have found little empirical evidence that large war chests deter strong challengers (Box-Steffensmeier 1996; Goodliffe 2001; Krasno and Green 1988; Ragsdale and Cook 1987; Squire 1989), incumbents act as if they do. A large war chest can also serve as "precautionary savings" in case a highly qualified challenger does emerge (Goodliffe 2004) or can be used to seek higher office in future election cycles. Either way, from a member's perspective, redistributing money to help the party achieve a majority risks jeopardizing the member's individual political goals. "Losers," as Jacobson (1985–86, 604) noted, "do not share the collective benefits of the party's victory."

When a change in majority control seems highly unlikely, members have every incentive to focus on their own individual electoral victory. Their efforts can have a large effect on their own campaign. Their ability to help other candidates win in other districts is much more limited, particularly when other incumbents are also focused on their own reelection and are not providing assistance to competitive party candidates. Furthermore, when majority control is out of reach, helping the party win a few seats is unlikely to do much to increase an incumbent's power on the Hill. In sum, a member's contribution will not significantly affect the amount of collective good that the party will produce. Focusing on their own electoral victory allows them to continue working to achieve their other goals in Congress.

Prior to 1994, nearly all members of Congress operated under the premise that, because of the Democratic Party's large majorities and incumbents' skill at using the perquisites of office to retain their seats, Democratic dominance in the House would continue for the foreseeable future. There was little incentive for Democrats to cooperate electorally. As long as incumbents continued deploying tried-and-tested reelection strategies, almost all of them would continue to win individually, which would cumulate into a continuation of the party's majority. Solving the electoral collective action problem was unnecessary for Democrats to achieve the collective partisan goal of majority status.

For most Republicans, seeking to overcome the Democratic Party's advantages must have seemed a futile endeavor. As members of the minority party, Republicans' policy or pork barrel achievements came at the sufferance of majority Democrats. Thus, there was an incentive for Republicans to cooperate with the Democrats rather than cooperate with each other to change the partisan status quo (Connelly and Pitney 1994). Republicans muddled through; they sought to retain office and achieve select personal and constituency goals in an institutional environment that was stacked against them. Sabato and Simpson's description of the House GOP prior to the 1994 election is instructive on this point.

> [T]he instinct for self-preservation among Republican incumbents undermined [Gingrich's efforts to challenge majority Democrats' sources of institutional power]. Time and again, whether the issue was eliminating the congressional frank, reforming campaign laws, or reducing congressional staff, Republicans who had become accustomed to or dependent upon these perquisites quietly opposed calls for their elimination. It is the rare human being who can resist the blandishments of power, because it is a rare human being who does not fear losing power. They were incumbents first, Republicans second, and thus partners in their own subjugation. (Sabato and Simpson 1996, 74)

Achievement of immediate individual goals is easily prioritized over collective goals, even when achievement of those collective goals would make a member better off individually. With the institutional deck stacked against them, collective action must have seemed largely pointless to Republicans.

Obviously, much has changed for members of both parties. Thus, a key theoretical task for scholars who study congressional parties has been to explain how, why, and when congressional parties are able to solve their collective action problems. This involves exploring the relationships between individual members of Congress, party leaders, and the political environment.

Theories of Congressional Parties

Conditional Party Government

As Rohde (1991) and Aldrich and Rohde (2001) argue, congressional parties increasingly solved their collective action problems to advance partisan legislative agendas in the 1980s and 1990s. The model of conditional party government (CPG) explains the revival in partisan strength in Congress as a function of a realignment of voters into party coalitions based on shared, ideological policy agendas. In what turned out to be a massive electoral sort, conservative southern voters bolted the Democratic Party and began identifying as Republicans, newly enfranchised African American voters in the South threw their support behind Democrats, and liberal Republican voters (largely in the northeast) gradually became Democrats. At both the elite and mass level—and especially in the congressional party caucuses—the result was greater ideological homogeneity within each party and greater ideological heterogeneity between the parties. Under these conditions, members of Congress are likely to vote with the party because they and their constituents share the dominant party philosophy. Members are far less cross-pressured by diverse constituencies than they were prior to the electoral sorting. Members of an ideologically cohesive caucus are now willing to delegate additional powers to the party leaders to ensure passage of the party agenda supported by caucus members and their constituents. This produces leaders who are increasingly assertive in articulating and publicly advocating a legislative agenda for the party, who use the rules of the House to facilitate the passage of the party agenda, and who become directly involved in legislative development (Rohde 1991; Sinclair 1995, 2006). Such leaders, in turn, divide the parties "beyond the preferences [members] bring with them into office" (S. Smith 2007, 120).

Yet even as the level of partisan legislative coordination increased during the 1980s and early 1990s, the level of partisan electoral coordination within Congress did not (Kolodny and Dwyre 1998; Sorauf 1992). The congressional campaign committees were able to shift more resources away from safe incumbents and toward competitive challengers and open-seat candidates (Herrnson 1988; Sorauf 1992), but the direct participation of members of Congress in the party's electoral efforts remained devoted to assuring their own reelections. The amount of funds contributed by members of Congress to party candidates remained largely stagnant throughout the 1980s and, if anything, dipped slightly in the early 1990s (Bedlington and Malbin 2003).

Parties had addressed their collective action problems legislatively, but they had not solved their collective action problems in elections. CPG theory provides no clear guidance to illuminate how and why members should act collectively to assist each other in elections or to assist their party in attaining majority status (see also S. Smith 2007, 121). Since parties in the United States have traditionally been understood primarily as electoral institutions rather than as governing institutions, the dichotomy between the congressional party's legislative and electoral actions poses a significant challenge to our understanding of congressional parties.

Parties as Individual Preferences

Krehbiel (1993, 1998, 2000) questions the influence of parties in the CPG model and argues instead that changes in congressional voting patterns and policy outputs can be explained by members' ideological preferences and the rules of the chamber alone, not by party leadership powers or activities. Krehbiel sees parties as a function of self-selection by candidates, based on the general fit between the party's policy agenda and their own individualistic policy preferences. If liberal candidates are increasingly self-selecting the Democratic Party and if conservative candidates are increasingly populating the Republican caucus, Krehbiel asks, why it is necessary to posit a role for leadership in producing policy outcomes? Members' preferences alone would explain policy outcomes. The difficulty of untangling homogenous member preferences from leadership effects in explaining increasing party cohesiveness has been a challenge for scholars who study congressional parties.

Analyzing the electoral activities of congressional parties and their members offers a different tack to addressing this conundrum of party influence. Whereas members and their parties' goals and interests are largely convergent in overcoming collective action problems to pass legislation when the caucuses are ideologically homogenous, there is greater conflict in reconciling individual and party goals in elections. Of course, members desire to serve in the majority and to enjoy the individual power benefits that result. However, to achieve this outcome, they must make financial sacrifices for the party and its candidates, sacrifices that increase, however marginally, their own electoral risk. Powerful leaders may not be necessary to help parties with homogenous preferences pass legislation, but they are necessary to coordinate and mobilize contributions to the party's collective electoral efforts and to overcome members' short-term self-interest in the process. In short, leadership influence should be easier to detect in members' fundraising behavior than in their legislative behavior.

The Electoral Model

Cox and McCubbins (1993, 2005) use the model of a cartel to describe the relationship between the political party in the House and its members. The party has its power through its ability to structure the legislative process in ways that facilitate members' abilities to achieve their individual goals. Two party powers are particularly critical: power over the legislative agenda and power over the internal advancement of members. These two powers are closely related, especially for the majority party. The party uses its control over valuable positions to ensure that those who advance are committed to the collective good of the party as exhibited by their support of the party agenda. Members delegate power to leaders to produce the most important collective good of the party, a positive brand name on which party members run for reelection. Delegation of power to party leaders is necessary to produce legislative accomplishments. Without accompanying legislative victories by the party, partisanship in voting increases members' electoral risks (Lebo, McGlynn, and Koger 2007).

However, the most critical power of party leaders—including committee chairs—is largely negative: they refuse to advance proposals that would divide the party coalition. Leaders will cooperate with the caucus and will refrain from pushing policies favored by only one faction of the party, because they risk losing power if they do otherwise. Promoting party-splitting proposals will make the party look ineffective to the electorate, thus risking its majority status. If the party loses majority status, the leaders lose their powerful positions.

Cox and McCubbins give a larger electoral role to party leaders than Krehbiel or Aldrich and Rohde. They emphasize that party leaders have the responsibility to pass a policy agenda that will give members a pleasing record of achievement on which to run. Local voters will then react positively to their local representative's accomplishments—with the party's collective legislative accomplishments as one component of the member's overall record—and vote to reelect the member, thus helping the party retain majority status. Yet even this electoral role for party leaders seems indirect and derivative of legislative leadership responsibilities.

Cox and McCubbins (2005, 22) admit to giving little attention to the process by which voters learn about the congressional party's accomplishments. Yet members of Congress and their parties do not just pass bills and deliver constituent services and expect voters to notice, care, and be appropriately grateful. They do not rely on the media to report their accomplishments to the electorate. The parties campaign aggressively—developing messages, mobilizing resources, identifying persuadable targets—to influence voters' perceptions of their records, individually as candidates and collectively as a party. They put substantial effort into controlling their message and its method of delivery to ensure correct frames and precise language. They target messages to the voters who are most likely to be affected by it. They attack the opposing parties' weaknesses as much or more than they promote their own merits. Candidates and parties cannot control events or media, but they do act to exert control over factors they can affect: campaign money, volunteers, message, home style.

In short, in Cox and McCubbins's party theory, parties are surprisingly inert—their powers are mostly negative, restricted to the majority party, and reliant on voters to notice and properly credit the party for its accomplishments. The institutional structure builds in advantages for the majority party, and the ability of leaders to block coalition-splitting issues from the agenda precludes the need for party loyalty voting or for efforts to create party discipline. In such an environment, there is little need for party leaders to mobilize members to overcome collective action problems.

Prior to the battle for majority status in the mid-1990s, the majority party did not have to be actively involved in elections, because its incumbents benefited from so many structural advantages: they could pass legislation benefiting their districts, raise far more funds than challengers, and use their offices to advertise themselves and provide services to constituents. Party leaders could minimize their overt contributions to the elections of individual members by protecting members from casting votes that would offend their constituents, providing a brand name and record of party accomplishments that would not hurt the member with constituents, and perhaps assisting directly with personal favors and fundraising (Sinclair 1983). Incumbents did not require party involvement, because they could tailor their messages and activities to the preferences of their local voters. Incumbents could contribute to the collective good of the party—retaining majority status—merely by assuring their own reelection.

As Cox and McCubbins (2005, 213) note, their structural theory of party power is only secondarily concerned with how parties use positive powers to overcome collective action problems. Thus, it is less able to address how the minority party mobilizes to achieve legislative or electoral goals. It is also less able to explain how majority parties can mobilize to defend their majority status when it is threatened.

The narrow margins of majority control and the parties' electoral mobilization since the mid-1990s offer a clear contrast. For an incumbent, focusing on one's own reelection may no longer be sufficient for achieving one's goals when one's power can be substantially altered by a change in majority status. Members can no longer contribute to the collective good of the party merely by refraining from taking actions that could hurt the party's brand name. Under threats from the other party or the external political environment, they must contribute proactively to the party's collective electoral efforts.

Willing Partisans

Lee (2009) poses a substantial challenge to much of the contemporary literature on congressional parties in at least two respects. First, she claims that congressional parties are driven by ideology far less than contemporary scholars studying congressional parties admit. Hearkening back to earlier scholarly perspectives on parties (Downs 1957; Schattschneider 1942; Schumpeter 1950), she argues that parties are teams motivated by power and held together by a sense of shared risk. Quoting Schattschneider (1942, 37), Lee (2009, 11) posits, "It is ridiculous to assume that men cannot collaborate to get power unless they are actuated by the same impulses. Possession of the vast resources of modern government, its authority, its organization, administrative establishment, and so on, will provide something for nearly everyone willing to join hands in the political enterprise."

Since our perspective does not require incumbents' ideological preferences to be the main cause of partisanship, our work has no trouble coexisting with Lee's claims about ideology. Posing more of a challenge to our perspective is Lee's claim that political scientists have exaggerated the collective action problems facing congressional parties. According to Lee, members are "willing" partisans happily engaged in teamwork in order to gain and maintain majority party control. Olson meant his theory to apply to large groups—far larger than congressional parties in either the House or the Senate. Caucuses are small enough for members to see the impact of their contributions and for leaders to use social pressure as a deterrent against free riding. Thus, it is misplaced, Lee argues, to organize all research about Congress around Olson's theory of public goods.

> For legislative parties, the logic of collective action may often be precisely opposite of that laid out by Olson. For most legislators most of the time, it may be beneficial to work with their parties, while only occasionally being costly. If this is the case, legislators will not require an affirmative reason to cooperate with their party in pursuit of collective goods; instead, they will need a specific reason to *defect*. (Lee 2009, 17)

In Lee's account (2009, 18), congressional party politics is "largely volun-taristic."

Lee's claims about collective action would seem to clash with the framework we employ, a framework in which parties provide selective incentives to induce otherwise unwilling members to support the party's collective electoral goals. But in reality, our approach has less difficulty co-existing with Lee's claims than one might initially suspect. First, Lee (2009, 14) notes that parties do in fact possess and deploy selective incentives in the form of attractive committee and party leadership positions—an implicit acknowledgment that congressional parties are indeed confronted by at least some collective action problems. (Why would parties possess and deploy selected incentives if collective action problems were not a threat?) Second, we agree that House party caucuses are small groups and that social pressure and group dynamics play an important role in generating compliance with group norms—once group expectations are established. But more important, Lee's argument is intended to apply mainly to legislative politics, in which, she claims, the costs are often low for siding with one's party.

> Once a legislator is going to vote at all, voting with the party need not be any more costly than voting against the party. Legislators often aren't doing anything "extra" by going along with their parties. Voting with one's party is not analogous to volunteering time or writing a check to underwrite a collective effort to achieve a public good. (Lee 2009, 16)

Regardless of whether one accepts Lee's claims about collective action problems as they relate to legislative politics, it seems clear that a member who cuts a five-figure check to the party congressional campaign committee is underwriting a costly collective effort—and that, indeed, doing so does impose a significant burden on the member. Willing partisans or not, most members would probably not redistribute money to the party if they could get away with not doing so. Raising campaign money is costly, time consuming, and (to many members) distasteful; giving money to the party means having less of it (or having to raise more of it) for one's own campaign. Finally, Lee's claim that collective action problems may not be as pervasive to legislative endeavors as commonly assumed actually underscores a central point of this book: if congressional scholars want a more complete understanding of how congressional parties operate, they need to examine fundraising behavior, not simply legislative behavior.

A Theory of Electoral Collective Action by Congressional Party Caucuses

All four major theories of congressional parties provide bricks in the foundation that we build on, but also, as we have noted, they do not adequately explain (or even attempt to explain) how congressional caucuses coordinate for electoral collective action. Our theory builds heavily on Cox and McCubbins's framework. We extend their theory to explain how the parties have expanded their cartel powers from the legislative to the fundraising sphere and how and why members have varied in their responses to the battle for majority status.

Institutions are solutions to collective action problems (March and Olson 1984). They provide structures, rules, and incentives to privilege certain options over others as individuals make choices. As human creations, institutions allow their creators to design a stable system of incentives that rewards cooperation toward common goals and collective goods. By rewarding behavior that advances a collective good, rather than individual interests, institutions can shape how individuals prioritize and pursue their individual goals. Congressional parties thus use their power over institutional organization to advance their electoral goals and to provide their members with incentives to contribute to the party's collective goals. Institutional leaders often become the key actors in solving collective action problems, as they are endowed with power to coerce or to offer incentives to induce cooperation among members (Bianco and Bates 1990). Institutions and their leaders succeed in overcoming collective action problems when they create structures in which the pursuit of individual self-interest simultaneously advances an organization's collective interests.

As we have seen, members of Congress often prioritize the achievement of their own individual goals over participation in efforts to achieve the party's collective good. As Schlesinger (1985) and Aldrich (1995) point out, individual candidates and incumbents are only likely to coordinate through parties when doing so helps them advance their individual goals. A critical challenge for congressional parties is that their influence over member goals is not uniform. Instead, party influence over member goals varies by the particular goal and over time, depending on the strength of the party. For most of the twentieth century, for example, the congressional party had minimal influence on a member's most important goal— reelection. Though their party's overall reputation can affect members' electoral margins (Cox and McCubbins 1993), incumbents could largely win reelection on their own by building strong relationships with their constituents, voting district preferences, performing constituency service, and developing their own networks of donors (Cain, Ferejohn, and Fiorina 1987; Fenno 1978).

Parties traditionally have had more (albeit still limited) power over members' ability to advance their policy goals. To pass their policy agendas, members must build coalitions. Although legislative coalitions are not necessarily partisan (e.g., Clausen 1973; Collie 1988; Sinclair 1982), a member's partisan colleagues often form an accessible base of like-minded coalition partners. Being a member of the majority party provides a member with substantial structural advantages in the legislative process (Cox and McCubbins 1993). At the same time, however, a member's association with his or her party's policy platform can be electorally costly if voters in the member's district are generally inclined to support the other party's agenda or if the member and/or his or her party are too partisan (Canes-Wrone, Brady, and Cogan 2002; Carson et al. 2010). Thus, individual members face the choice of how closely to tie themselves to their party's policy agenda and accomplishments.

Parties have arguably had the most influence on members' ability to achieve their power goals. Though parties allowed members essentially to self-select to policy and constituency committees that would advance their policy and reelection goals, the party retained control over appointments to the most powerful committees and sought to promote party loyalists to these critical posts (Shepsle 1978; Cox and McCubbins 1993; Maltzman 1997). Though seniority was the dominant route to committee leadership positions, the parties could intervene to replace those who threatened the majority coalition (Cox and McCubbins 1993). Party leaders could open opportunities for appointments in the extended leadership structure to give more members a stake in the party's decisions and to socialize them into the party (Sinclair 1983; Rohde 1991; Garand and Clayton 1986). For ambitious members, party appointments are valuable in their own right as well as stepping-stones to more powerful positions. As noted by Hall and Van Houweling (1995, 124), "Ascending to the seat of, say, committee chair or deputy whip may be mostly imperceptible to the people of Pougkeepsie, but such positions do mark important distinctions in the vicinity of the Potomac." Parties' control over the advancement system in Congress makes the party the gatekeeper to institutional power for individual members. Importantly and unlike control over the legislative process, both the majority and minority parties have cartel powers over the institutional advancement of their own members—thus giving each party leverage over members' ability to achieve their power goals.

A key to Cox and McCubbins's theory of legislative parties is the observation that some House members desire more than simply reelection to the House; they also want internal advancement within the House (see also Dodd 1977; Herrick and Moore 1993). As Hall and Van Houweling (1995, 124) put it, "[T]he assumption that one runs simply to run again (two years hence) is suitable only for a behavioral theory of pet gerbils on a cage-wheel." Positions of power give members the potential for considerable independent influence over strategic and policy decisions. They give members authority and resources that they can use as bargaining leverage to engage in exchanges with other members. Their positions give them a platform from which to forge connections with other members in powerful positions who can assist them. They are better positioned within the party's informational network to gather intelligence that will help them advance their goals. As ambitious members climb the "leadership ladder" or obtain multiple positions within the party and committee power structure, their potential for achieving their policy and constituency goals increases in increments relative to the power of the position.

As an outlet for members' desire for internal advancement, Cox and McCubbins (1993) argue, a party establishes attractive party leadership posts, which are made even more attractive by majority control. The power of such positions is necessary as an incentive for a member to undertake the challenges of coordinating and mobilizing members of the caucus to overcome the party's collective action problems, and the power of the positions attracts ambitious members to seek them. Because of the attractiveness of the positions, the number of members seeking positions of power outpaces the supply, giving the party control over who obtains the positions (Cox and McCubbins 1993; Kiewiet and McCubbins 1991; Shepsle 1978; Sinclair 1983, 1995). Parties still do not have much influence over whether members win election to Congress, but they do have considerable influence over the member's career advancement within the institution. As Sinclair (2006, 130–31) has observed, "Advancement within the chamber depends on a member's reputation with party peers and the party leadership, thus increasing the incentives to be a team player."

The literature on political ambition typically assumes that all politicians have a desire to advance and would take another position if they could do so without cost (e.g., Black 1972; Rohde 1979; Herrick and Moore 1993; Wawro 2000). As former Speaker Tom Foley said, "There may be some members who don't want to move up. . . . But most of the people around here are not like that" (quoted in Loomis 1988, 236). The congressional party, however, does not give everyone valuable leadership and committee positions. It imposes costs on ambitious members of the caucus to ensure that those who advance have demonstrated the intensity of their commitment to the collective good of the party.

Parties are rightly concerned that if a member is granted substantial power, he or she will use that power to advance his or her own individual goals—to shirk his or her responsibilities to the collective good of the caucus (Kiewiet and McCubbins 1991). Therefore, the caucus makes party leadership positions available only to members willing to serve the party's collective electoral interests. This requirement, for leaders and leadership aspirants, acts as a powerful selective incentive to "internalize" the party's collective goals. As Cox and McCubbins (1993, 133) put it, members who desire leadership positions are "*personally* motivated to pursue the *collective* interests" of the party (their italics). Or, as Jim Wilkinson, former communications director for the House Republicans noted, "It's time to see who's willing to pull the load. Once the dust settles, *who did the most for the team* is going to be a factor in all those decisions [regarding committee assignments and committee leadership posts]" (quoted in M. Allen 2000; italics added). The party, then, harnesses a member's individual ambition for advancement and puts it into the service of the party's collective good. Therefore, the foundation of our theory of party influence in Congress rests on the allocation of positions of power, because parties have the greatest influence over members' opportunities to achieve their power goals.

Attaining Positions

The question remains, however, how those with power over advancement (the party caucus and its leaders) can determine which members are sufficiently dedicated to serving the party's collective good and can therefore be trusted with power. Principal-agent theory notes that principals can ensure that their agents do not shirk by monitoring subordinate behavior constantly, but this method is extremely costly, as it absorbs the time and energy that the principal could use to pursue other goals (e.g., Brehm and Gates 1996; Kiewiet and McCubbins 1991). A better way to ensure the compliance of subordinates is to establish a selection process to ensure that the principals hire people who are unlikely to shirk and who therefore make it unnecessary to invest much time and effort to monitor them. The party caucus, then, faces a two-pronged challenge: first, to minimize the probability of shirking and maximize the probability of committed behavior by potential appointees; second, to minimize the search costs of the appointment process and of monitoring subordinate behavior after appointment, so they can focus on other competing responsibilities.

Party caucuses have thus traditionally promoted ideological "middlemen" to top leadership positions (Truman 1959; Kiewiet and McCubbins 1991). Middlemen are unlikely to shirk, because their personal preferences and the caucus's policy preferences are generally aligned. As centrists within the party caucus, they are well-positioned to deal fairly with all party factions, to promote legislation that reflects the preferences of the caucus, and to signal acceptable party policy stances to the electorate. To use their appointments strategically to retain power, they are likely to appoint members from all ideological factions. Distributing appointments broadly helps to keep peace within the family by giving all factions access to power within the caucus and by giving leaders information on the preferences and needs of such factions (Sinclair 1983). To the extent that leaders use their appointment powers to select ideological allies (Heberlig, Hetherington, and Larson 2006), middlemen will appoint centrists who are acceptable to the caucus for the same reasons that they themselves are acceptable to the caucus.

The caucus will not be equally concerned with all positions (Cox and McCubbins 1993, 2005). The positions with the most responsibility for delivering partisan collective goods, such as legislative accomplishments and a positive image to the public, will be most closely monitored by the caucus for the member's commitment to the party. Thus, elected party posts with primary responsibility for agenda setting, coordination, and making lower-level appointments will be the most scrutinized. Positions lower in the party hierarchy receive lower levels of scrutiny from the caucus, because these members individually can do limited damage to the party's collective goals and reputation. Additionally, lower-level appointees often work under the direction of and are supervised by elected party officers or more powerful party appointees (e.g., chief deputy whips or cochairs or vice chairs of party committees). Thus, the caucus will demand the most evidence of commitment to the party's collective good from members seeking the highest-ranking, more powerful posts. It will be more willing to allow compromises and trade-offs in less powerful posts, giving members appointed to these positions the opportunity to demonstrate their commitment to the party through their performance over time.

Although straightforward from the perspective of principal-agent theory, traditional congressional advancement practices present two critical inconsistencies with the theory. One of the key problems for congressional parties in preventing policy shirking is that the leadership positions responsible for the development of policy—the committee chairs—traditionally have been determined by seniority rather than by an explicit process allowing for party review (although party control over committee leadership posts has increased in both the post-1974 and post-1994 reform periods). The result is that committee chairs have at times been at odds with the policy priorities and preferences of a majority of the party caucus. The party more directly controls appointments to extended leadership positions and prestige committees.

Furthermore, while there are clear theoretical reasons for the party to appoint to these positions those committed to the collective good of the party, the evidence that the party caucus actually makes appointments on this basis has been mixed. Using party loyalty voting as the measure of a member's dedication to the party's collective interest, for example, has produced inconsistent results in explaining appointments to prestige committees (Cox and McCubbins 1993; Frisch and Kelly 2006; Maltzman 1997; Rohde and Shepsle 1973; Smith and Ray 1983;). The effect of party loyalty on appointments is weakened by the party's need to balance it with several other representational considerations, such as regional and ideological balance. Similarly, Sinclair's inclusion model (1983) notes that extended leadership appointments can serve a number of competing goals of party leaders. She emphasizes that the extended leadership structure serves an information-gathering function for legislative coalition building. If leaders need to hear from all factions of the caucus, it makes it less likely that these positions can be used to advance loyal members of the caucus. Moreover, Garand and Clayton (1986) argue that extended leadership positions can be used by the leadership to socialize members into the party. Rather than rewarding members for their loyalty, the positions are used to teach members to become more loyal.

These results suggest several problems with the parties' abilities to identify or reward loyalists. Perhaps the parties do a poor job of evaluating the qualifications of appointees. Perhaps parties' efforts to achieve the multiple goals simultaneously undercut the predominance of party loyalty as a criterion for promotion. Perhaps political scientists have not effectively conceptualized or measured how parties can evaluate their members' dedication to the party's collective good. Taking these results seriously begs the question of how clear a member's demonstration of commitment to the collective good of the party must be in order to advance. On another level, these unimpressive results lead us to ask, If parties go to the effort of establishing extensive whip systems to monitor the preferences of the caucus on votes for individual bills, why would they not devote similar effort to monitoring the aptitude of those to whom it will entrust discretionary powers—and who can have a much more permanent and serious impact on the party's collective success?

In fact, the caucuses have several methods to evaluate a member's dedication to the party's collective good. Given the importance to the caucus of selecting the right people to receive its delegation of power, it is unlikely to rely solely on one indicator but instead relies on multiple measures. We argue that parties evaluate members' existing service in extended leadership positions, party loyalty voting, and redistribution of campaign funds as measures of the member's willingness to serve the party's collective interests.[3] Which particular criterion receives the most emphasis depends in part on which collective goal is being prioritized by the party caucus at the time. Party loyalty voting will become more important when the party is prioritizing solutions to legislative collective action problems; the redistribution of campaign funds will become more important when the party is prioritizing solutions to electoral collective action problems. The extent of evidence demanded by the caucus will vary based on the position's power and ability to affect the party's production of collective goods.

Partisan Time Commitment. The first indicator of partisan commitment is the member's existing service in an extended leadership position. Such service can be seen as a measurement of willingness to devote limited time and effort to collective party activities rather than individualistic policy and constituency service activities. Representative David Price (2000, 173) observed that he and many of his competitors for the next available slots on the Appropriations Committee (un)coincidently found themselves serving together on many whip task forces as they sought to build relationships with senior party members. Incorporating many members into the extended leadership benefits the leadership by giving junior members valuable opportunities to participate and by giving leaders a means of gathering information about the preferences of various factions of the caucus (Sinclair 1983). But most important for our purposes, the extended leadership gives party leaders and the caucus the ability to gather information on the abilities of potential leaders.

Active participation in the extended leadership network also gives appointees the opportunity to interact with other members of the caucus and to demonstrate their abilities to the members who will ratify their future appointment or elect them to party offices. The literature on leadership ladders stresses that members advance by proving themselves to their colleagues. In particular, Canon (1989, 437) notes, "Well-developed leadership institutions reduce information costs by allowing the rank and file to gain a clear picture of the leadership style of the candidate who is attempting to climb the ladder. In these cases, promoting from within becomes the low-risk alternative." Although this observation has been made numerous times in the literature, there has been little empirical work evaluating how experiences in extended leadership positions affect advancement in Congress.

Party Loyalty Voting. A second means by which the party caucus can evaluate a member's dedication to the collective good is his or her support for the party's legislative agenda. As noted earlier, the literature on committee transfer has devoted substantial attention to party loyalty voting as a criterion for advancement, with mixed results. Still, there is a value to having party-voting loyalists in positions of power. Those who share the party's policy preferences are in a good position to send strong signals of the party's stances to colleagues as a voting cue or to the public. As the party caucuses have polarized and homogenized, for example, voting loyalists would be more valuable in the whip system, to send clear signals of the party position to members of the caucus on obscure, complex, or ideologically ambiguous legislation where a clear signal would help them vote their ideal preferences (Meinke 2008). Moreover, members who share the positions of the party caucus are unlikely to shirk from the caucus position when negotiating the contents of legislation. The effect of party loyalty voting on advancement has been limited, in part, by the party's recognition that members sometimes need to vote their constituencies in order to be reelected. Losing a member does little to advance the party's preeminent goal of securing majority status. As parties homogenized ideologically, however, party loyalty voting became a significant predictor of appointment to both parties' whip systems (Meinke 2008). Thus, all things equal, those who are more loyal to the party's policy agenda should be more likely to advance.

Campaign Contributions. Third, members who sacrifice campaign funds to help elect other party members, thereby expanding the caucus and increasing the probability of the party securing majority status, should be more likely to advance. Contributing to the congressional campaign committee, noted former DCCC chair Vic Fazio (D-CA), "is one way of determining how much effort you are willing to make for the greater whole, the sort of thing that moves people up in the committees and the leadership" (quote from Alston 1991, 2766). If raising campaign funds is generally an unpleasant task for members and since members have an incentive to spend money on their own reelection rather than accepting minimal additional risks by giving it to other candidates or the party, redistributing funds is a good measure of a member's willingness to make personal sacrifices on behalf of the team. In this scenario, a member who redistributes money is signaling to party leaders the intensity of his or her ambition for a coveted committee or leadership post (see Austen-Smith 1993 and 1995 on political action committees using contributions as signals). Providing funds is also a quantifiable measure of a member's partisan loyalties, one that leaders and the rest of the caucus can easily see in Federal Election Commission reports. When competition for majority status is fierce, the caucus is especially likely to value members who make financial sacrifices in support of the party's most important collective goal.

The literature typically views the relationship between campaign funds and advancement from an exchange perspective (R. Baker 1989; Brown and Peabody 1992; Cann 2008; Canon 1989; Currinder 2003; Green 2008; Green and Harris 2007; Kolodny 1998; Salmore and Salmore 1989, 268–70). The party caucus and the ambitious individual member of the caucus trade resources that are valuable to the other: the party receives campaign funds from the individual member; the individual member receives a powerful institutional post from the party. The exchange perspective subscribes to a basic "pay-to-play" scheme: if you pay those in a position to help you advance, then you are more likely to win powerful posts.

At one level, there is undeniably an exchange occurring: the party is exchanging selective incentives, the powerful positions it controls, for members' financial contribution to the collective electoral good of the party. But the signaling perspective, we believe, better captures the dynamics of what is occurring than does a crude pay-for-play exchange perspective. Members who redistribute generously are signaling their qualifications for leadership beyond just their willingness to sacrifice funds for the collective good of the party. They are demonstrating their ability to build organizational infrastructures to attract large coalitions of donors—just as party leaders must build legislative and electoral coalitions both within the caucus and outside of Congress—to achieve the party's collective goals. The member's success in fundraising and coalition building from a position of minor influence signals his or her potential to take maximum advantage of the position for the benefit of the party. If party leaders are increasingly expected to take the lead in providing and mobilizing campaign funds for the party, they are demonstrating that this is an aspect of the job that they can do. Fortunately, we believe there are ways to evaluate whether the signaling or pay-to-play perspective is correct, and we spell out our approach in detail in chapters 4, 5, and 6.

Although we are interested in testing the relationship between redistribution and advancement, it is important to emphasize that we view contributions as only one measure the party uses to assess incumbents' commitment to its collective good. Indeed, the Republican caucus rejected a proposal to allow the House Republican Steering Committee to block members from receiving valuable subcommittee assignments if their campaign contributions were deemed inadequate. House minority leader John Boehner (R-OH) reportedly told the caucus, "We are not going to get in the business of members buying seats" (quoted in O'Connor 2008). The fact that the proposal was openly discussed probably was a sufficient signal for ambitious members that their chances of advancement were much greater if they did contribute generously. Whether the party is evaluating members' voting records or campaign contributions, it is improbable that leaders or the caucus would choose one candidate over another based on a few dollars' difference in redistribution or a slightly different voting record. Indeed, reviewing the record of contested leadership and chairmanship contests shows that the candidate who redistributes more than his or her competitors for those positions does not always win, although the big giver does win a disproportionate percent of the time (Cann 2008; Heberlig, Hetherington, and Larson 2006). As one Democratic House leader has argued,

> I don't think [giving money] gets you votes. But it can hurt you if you don't have it. Not having it is a problem. It's not necessarily the amounts. Rather, it's a signal that I can help you. Your ability to help is important. (Quoted in Brown and Peabody 1992, 359)

A good fundraising record is necessary but insufficient for advancement (Wilcox 1989).

Though both party voting and campaign contributions are measures of commitment to the party's collective good, they are likely to work somewhat differently. Since parties feel pressure to represent all ideological factions and in order to keep peace within the family, the party has an incentive to represent partisan outliers to some extent (Sinclair 1983, 1995). There is little reason to suspect, however, that parties feel any pressure to represent the "noncontributor caucus." All members of the caucus would see the benefit of promoting those who contribute financially to the electoral success of the party and little reason to reward noncontributors to keep them loyal to the team. This is not to say that noncontributors will not advance. They may have other qualities that make them worthy of promotion, but their deficiencies in redistribution would be a hurdle that they would have to overcome with superior performance on other criteria.

There is also reason to hypothesize that these indicators of party loyalty will be weighted differently by the majority and minority parties (Frisch and Kelly 2006). The majority party seeks to deliver on its policy agenda in order to retain power. Thus, it has an incentive to weight member's ability to contribute to the party's collective legislative success more heavily when evaluating members for promotion. The majority party, therefore, is more likely than the minority party to promote members based on party loyalty voting. The minority party has little ability to promote its policy agenda, and the votes cast by its members will largely occur in response to proposals advanced by the majority party. The minority party's highest priority is increasing its share of seats or at least not losing even more seats, in order to become the majority party in the future. Therefore, when evaluating members' potential for advancement, the minority party has an incentive to weight a member's redistribution of campaign funds more heavily than party voting. In contrast, a member's performance in an existing party post should be equally relevant as a criterion for advancement in both the majority and minority parties.

Ambitious members will respond to incentive systems that facilitate their advancement, particularly if they perceive little risk to their own reelection in doing so. Moreover, they are likely to be monitoring leaders and the caucus for signals of the criteria for promotion. Balancing such criteria with the qualities a member must exhibit and tasks the member must undertake to achieve other constituency service, policy, and electoral goals, the member is likely to engage in behaviors that lead to their promotion. Isenstadt and Hohmann (2010) thus describe one member's devotion of hours per week to fundraising despite his distaste for it: "One freshman, who said he was contemplating a rise through his party's leadership ranks, said there was nothing worse than giving the impression to party bosses that he couldn't fend for himself financially or that he was somehow the financial weak link." The ambitious member will seek to identify effective methods of signaling his or her dedication to the collective good of the party—to show that he or she will be a faithful trustee of the power delegated by the party. Once an ambitious member perceives the criteria for advancement within the party, the member grooms himself or herself to take advantage of opportunities to advance (Herrick and Moore 1993). Many times, this means outright campaigning for party or committee posts based on these criteria, to demonstrate their qualifications to colleagues (Loomis 1984; Frisch and Kelly 2006). Archival research shows that members actively solicit appointments from party leaders, with some citing endorsement from other leaders, other evidence of loyalty, or promises of future loyalty (Meinke 2010).

In sum, parties use institutional positions in Congress as selective incentives to reward those members who demonstrate their ability to serve the collective good of the caucus. Members who seek to increase their personal power by obtaining positions in Congress must demonstrate their capacity for serving others besides themselves before the caucus entrusts them with significant power.

Retaining Positions

Once members have obtained positions of power, the caucus expects continued dedication to the party's collective good, whether or not the member sought additional promotions. Likewise, the caucus will be most concerned with the performance of members who serve in the most powerful positions. Traditionally, within the majority party, this was defined as voting loyally, especially on procedural motions (Froman and Ripley 1965), and facilitating the consideration of legislation on which there was a consensus within the party caucus (Cox and McCubbins 1993, 2005). Advancement structures and criteria were less systematic within the minority party (Canon 1989).

In an era of heated competition for majority status, caucuses expect members to leverage their positions in order to raise more money for the party. Party and committee leaders and prestige committee members have traditionally been able to attract substantial amounts of campaign contributions because of their leverage over policy outcomes about which interest groups care deeply (Grenzke 1989; Grier and Munger 1991; Romer and Snyder 1994). These positions are most valuable when serving in the majority (Cox and McCubbins 1993). Thus, for members who serve in these posts, the best way to augment one's power is to have one's party win a majority. Members with positions, then, should be the most responsive to the potential for change in majority status in their willingness to comply with party expectations for the redistribution of campaign funds (Heberlig and Larson 2005). Moreover, failure to comply with the party's fundraising expectations risks inviting a challenge from other ambitious members who promise more attentiveness to the collective interests of the caucus. Instituting term limits and "auditions" for party and committee leadership positions provides recurring opportunities for the party to exercise its leverage over members who desire to attain or retain positions.

In sum, the party can obtain campaign resources to help it achieve majority status by making such contributions an important criterion for attaining and holding positions of power. Achieving majority status is a party's most important collective goal, and providing campaign funds is a means by which all members can contribute directly to this goal in addition to their own reelection. In this way, parties can harness members' ambition for power within the institution in a way that benefits all members of the party. An unanswered question thus far is why this has been a recent phenomenon. We turn now to elaborating how and why the battle for majority status changes the ways in which parties seek to prioritize collective goals.

The Battle for Majority Status

Though congressional parties have collective goals and delegate responsibility for achieving those collective goals to party leaders, members' specific expectations of party leaders vary based on the context of the political environment (Cooper and Brady 1981; Rohde 1991). The political context helps to determine which collective goals are attainable and thus which ones receive priority from the party caucus at a particular moment in time. Changes in the political context can disturb the institutional equilibrium and provide opportunities for innovative party leaders to reframe the party's collective goals and develop strategies for overcoming collective action problems to achieve those goals (Greenstein 1987; Strahan 1992). Consensus within the party and an auspicious political environment lower the transaction costs for leaders undertaking the efforts of coordinating and mobilizing their caucus, thus increasing the likelihood that the leaders will devote their attention to addressing one collective goal rather than another that poses higher transaction costs and higher risks of failure.

We here present stylized descriptions of three recent eras in the House of Representatives to represent distinctive alignments of members' expectations and leadership power and activities: the individualistic era of the 1950s through the mid-1980s, the partisan legislative era from the mid-1980s to the GOP takeover of Congress in 1995, and the era of majority stakes government from 1995 through the present. In each era, party leaders and their caucuses make different trade-offs among or strike different balances between multiple collective goals. The trade-offs are based on the opportunities and obstacles presented by the political environment. Each era presents a different configuration of member expectations and leadership activities. The likelihood of a change in party control of the institution is a key variable in determining how congressional parties will prioritize their goals.

The Individualistic Era

The individualistic era was characterized by an electorally dominant yet ideologically heterogeneous majority party, the Democrats. Power in Congress was decentralized due to the ideological and constituency divisions within the parties. Party was a by-product of individual actions based on shared preferences (Krehbiel 1993, 1998, 2000). The caucus's central expectation of party leaders was that they refrained from taking actions that would interfere with individual members' goals of reelection, policy, and power (Cox and McCubbins 1993).

When majority status is at equilibrium and seems unlikely to change, parties can focus on facilitating individual members' reelections, because a collective electoral effort is unlikely to make a difference. As long as the incumbents in the majority party continue to be reelected and as long as the party holds a sufficient number of open seats, it will retain the majority. The minority party must reelect its incumbents and pick up enough seats to be subjectively "close" in order for collective action to make a difference. During the individualistic era, the party caucuses delegated collective electoral responsibilities to the congressional campaign committees, so that incumbents could focus on their own goals and would not need to take an active part (Kolodny 1998). Party leaders provided fundraising assistance to members (R. Baker 1989; Wilcox 1989; 1990) but did not coordinate a collective electoral effort. Each CCC could distribute its electoral resources broadly in order to maximize the number of incumbents it could keep happy, because targeting resources on a few marginal seats would not affect control of the chamber.

Legislatively, when a change in majority status is unlikely and the parties are ideologically heterogeneous, leaders can focus on "keeping peace within the family" and gathering information to determine areas of collective agreement around which an agenda can be built (Sinclair 1983). Both the transaction costs of attempting to mobilize majorities in a diverse caucus and the probability of failure would be high. Leaders who attempted and failed to mobilize the caucus would put their tenure in office in doubt. In this scenario, leadership will be personalistic and service oriented, as leaders facilitate members' ability to advance their own goals (Cooper and Brady 1981; Sinclair 1983). During the postreform era of the 1970s and 1980s, for example, as members demanded more opportunities to pursue their own goals, parties could decentralize power structures to facilitate members' individual ambitions (Dodd 1977; Loomis 1984; Sinclair 1983).

The Partisan Legislative Era

By the mid-1980s, the constituency and ideological divisions that had inhibited partisan legislative collective action had ebbed, and members delegated increased powers to party leaders (Rohde 1991). The partisan legislative era was marked by party leaders engaging in aggressive agenda setting and manipulation of institutional procedures to facilitate collective mobilization and coordination, to produce partisan behavior beyond what members would do merely out of own self-interest. Despite solving legislative collective action problems, partisan electoral coordination remained minimal. The Hill committees began playing an increasingly important service-oriented role in congressional campaigns (Herrnson 1988), but little was asked of individual incumbents.

When a change in majority status is unlikely and the parties are homogenous, leadership can become more agenda oriented and focus on mobilizing and coordinating members around a common agenda (Rohde 1991; Sinclair 1995). For the majority party, this means passing legislation; for the minority party, it means organizing a united front to communicate the party's objections clearly to the public. In the partisan legislative era, the transaction costs of coordinating and mobilizing the caucus around a collective legislative agenda for leaders decreased, thus giving them substantial incentive to devote their time and effort to collective legislative activities.

The conditional party government environment also allowed party leaders to exert more influence over the advancement structure in the House (Rohde 1991; Sinclair 1995, 2006). Elected party leaders were given additional appointment powers as well as more influence on the party steering committees. This allowed party leaders to increase the weight of party loyalty in the mix of qualities relevant to winning an appointment. Party leaders could not exercise these powers alone, of course; the caucus had to ratify their decisions. Sinclair (2006, 89, 136) notes that the party caucuses sometimes overturned a leadership appointment because members wanted a more loyal individual to get the post. A leadership aide quoted by Sinclair (2006, 137) reinforces this point: "You don't need to be beholden to the leadership so much as to the Conference at large." The clear implication is that leaders placed heavier emphasis on party loyalty as a criterion for advancement and had the clear support of their caucuses in doing so.

Because the electoral context remained at equilibrium with an asymmetric partisan advantage for the Democrats, party electoral goals were secondary to legislative goals. Though one of party leaders' responsibilities was to attain majority status, they were constrained by the caucus. Most redistribution activity was undertaken by party leaders themselves (R. Baker 1989; Wilcox 1989), and members resisted party leaders' infrequent suggestions to redistribute more (Kolodny and Dwyre 1998). Progress in securing majority status was only one of numerous qualifications considered by the caucus for retention of leaders and often was not the most important one (Canon 1989; Kolodny 1998; Peabody 1976). The transaction costs of electoral mobilization remained high, so leaders had an incentive to emphasize legislative activities where the costs were lower.

Members were able to accept that delegating increased legislative powers to leaders increased the probability of achieving their individual (and the party's collective) policy goals. But as long as the Democrats were the dominant majority party, members believed that increased electoral coordination would provide little payoff in terms of their own reelection or the party's collective electoral fortunes. This would change dramatically in 1994, as the stunning GOP takeover of the House introduced the era of majority stakes government. Achieving majority status became the dominant partisan goal, and leaders were expected to mobilize their caucuses to achieve it.

The Era of Majority Stakes Government

The GOP's unexpected takeover of majority status in the 1994 election upset the previous equilibrium. With majority status at stake, obtaining it became the predominant goal, and leaders and the caucuses reoriented their priorities. Under majority stakes government, the majority party has an incentive to organize the institution in ways that will enhance its ability to solve electoral collective action problems. The caucus shifts its delegation of power to allow party leaders to undertake more collective electoral mobilization activity (Moscardelli, Haspel, and Wike 1998). Facing lower transaction costs, leaders adapt their use of delegated powers to achieve collective electoral goals. Party leaders could develop programs to encourage incumbents to contribute to the party's election campaign efforts and to change institutional reward structures to advantage members who complied with the party's expectations of campaign support. Members are more willing to comply with leaders' efforts to coordinate and mobilize collective action when they believe that their efforts can make a difference in achieving the collective goal (Hardin 1982; Moe 1980).

The caucus reprioritizes its criteria for selecting and retaining leaders, putting greater emphasis on potential leaders' abilities to achieve the party's electoral goals (Heberlig, Hetherington, and Larson 2006). Savvy leaders will reorient their attention and energies accordingly. Just as leaders can use their powers of coordination and mobilization to secure the passage of legislation while minimizing electoral risks to individual members, they can use the same powers to ensure that safe incumbents do their fair share financially to advance the party's campaign for majority control. The parties' cartel powers over institutional advancement are now used to maximize their ability to capture campaign resources. Thus Pelosi biographer Vincent Bzdek (2008, 188) colorfully describes party leaders' contemporary fundraising responsibilities on behalf of their caucuses:

> The fundraising really never ends. It's a permanent campaign feeding a giant Jabba-the-Hutt bureaucracy with a life, appetite, and will of its own. Leading it, leading 435 leaders, is more a matter of keeping Jabba fed, watered, and happy than moving him anywhere meaningful.

Speaker Pelosi put such an emphasis on fundraising and electoral goals, for example, that *National Journal* reporter Richard Cohen (2010) dubbed her "the Campaign Boss." Legislative goals are still important in that they are one means of achieving electoral goals; a record of passing bills that does not lead to the retention of majority status, however, is unlikely to be rewarded.

The ideological polarization of the parties in the 1990s also raised the stakes of majority control in ways that it may not have in earlier, less polarized eras (Fiorina 2006). If policy is made by a cross-partisan band of moderates, the policy outcomes are likely to be similar regardless of which party holds majority status. But when parties are polarized, the powers of the majority party in the House allow that party's dominant ideological faction (the "majority of the majority," in Speaker Hastert's parlance [quoted in Babington 2004, A1]) to drive policy, and those outcomes will be far from the preferences of almost everyone in the minority party caucus. A polarized environment, then, makes majority status all the more valuable: the majority party receives not only the benefits of institutional positions but also the ability to achieve policy goals much closer to its ideal. All of this will increase the parties' emphases on electioneering: the majority seeks to retain its power, and the minority seeks to remove the "intolerable" burdens of its status (Fiorina 2006, 245).

Mobilizing campaign money also provides a means for party leaders to address potential trade-offs between the policy and electoral effects of collective party action on members from competitive districts in a polarized political environment (e.g., S. Smith 2007, 138). To the extent that the majority of caucus members and party activists desire policy outcomes that are more extreme than those desired by members and their constituents in more moderate districts, leaders may face a quandary in attempting to achieve collective policy and electoral goals simultaneously. Passing an "off-center" (Hacker and Pierson 2005) policy agenda may endanger party moderates. Increasing the role of safe incumbents in party fundraising efforts provides a means by which leaders can achieve both goals simultaneously. The leader mobilizes the party to pass its "ideal" party policy agenda and then mobilizes the resources from safe and policy-satisfied incumbents (and presumably satisfied donors and activists) to be directed to the members in the most competitive districts. If used effectively, the resources can help to frame the party's accomplishments in a way that is most pleasing to local voters and to mobilize party supporters in the district to turn out to help the incumbent. A leader who effectively secures the party's policy goals and majority status secures his or her own party office.

To solve electoral collective action problems, leaders must go beyond their exertions of power in earlier eras. They need to exert positive powers, not just block coalition-splitting legislative proposals. Their financial contributions to party candidates and personal fundraising assistance alone will be insufficient to impact election outcomes for individual candidates, let alone the party's aggregate share of seats. The party's ability to affect election outcomes depends on its ability to steer large numbers of hard money contributions to candidates in competitive districts and to the party congressional campaign committee so that it can make independent expenditures in these districts. For this strategy to succeed, however, the party must compel members to make financial sacrifices.

Party leaders play a critical role in overcoming collective action problems by coordinating the efforts of individual incumbents, by assuring them that their contributions will make a difference and that they will not be "suckers" if they participate (Bianco and Bates 1990; Moe 1980). Leaders monitor compliance with the parties' fundraising expectations and offer selective incentives to those who contribute to the party's collective efforts. In a highly polarized partisan environment, in which power is a zero-sum game and the power of one's group is at stake, party leaders frame their mobilization appeals to members as necessary for the "team" to succeed (Sinclair 2006). As we have seen in chapter 1, congressional leaders have gone to great lengths to establish programs for facilitating the redistribution of campaign funds and making clear their expectations for participation: establishing "dues," fundraising whip systems, tracking and publicizing contributions, and providing trinkets and rewards or petty threats to encourage compliance. If leaders are to be held accountable for the party's electoral performance by the caucus, institutionalizing a redistribution apparatus helps leaders monitor members' contributions to party's collective campaign efforts. Additionally, contributions to other candidates and to the party committees are on public record and thus are easy ways to measure and hold accountable the extent to which a member has been a "team player."

With the rise of the battle for majority status, party leaders could use the powers that had been delegated to them for legislative purposes to advance the party's electoral goals. The leadership could then reward party loyalty expressed legislatively, by helping to pass the party's policy agenda, or electorally, by redistributing campaign funds. Ambitious members seeking positions as selective incentives thus have a substantial incentive not only to support the party's legislative goals but also to comply with the party's demands for campaign funds.

Compliance by the Rank and File

Once leaders have established a party election mobilization strategy that members accept as consistent with the common good of the party and necessary for defeating the "out party," group dynamics kick in. Congressional party caucuses are small groups, where members can monitor and use social pressure to encourage one another to follow group expectations (Lee 2009; Olson 1965). Communication between leaders and members of the caucus and between the members themselves is reciprocal, so participants know each other's willingness to participate in collective action (Chwe 1999). Beyond giving generously through his own leadership PAC, for example, House Appropriations Committee chair Jerry Lewis (R-CA) directed his subcommittee chairs to form their own leadership PACs to redistribute funds to assist other GOP candidates (Eilperin 2006, 26). In situations in which social pressures are strong, a bandwagon effect can develop (Chong 1991). One's reputation within the party is a selective incentive about which members care deeply (Sinclair 2006, 135; S. Smith 2007, 56), and to maximize the effects of peer pressure, both parties have published lists of members delinquent in paying their party dues. Members take cues from others in their group rather than responding to the actual effects of their actions or even their own actual preferences (Jones and Baumgartner 2005, 140–42).

The result of such group dynamics is a pattern of redistribution that resembles an arms race, such as we have seen in figure 1.1. Once the bandwagon effects have started, members continue to contribute, regardless of the actual number of competitive seats or the actual probability of winning majority control. In chapter 2, we saw a similar arms race dynamic in CCC spending, when contributions and spending in competitive races becomes entirely unrelated to the actual probability that such spending will affect the outcome of the contest (Krasno and Sorauf 2003). More party spending and redistribution becomes necessary merely to offset the expected spending and redistribution by the other party and its members. Lebo, McGlynn, and Koger (2007) find similar dynamics in party unity voting, as members of each party adjust their levels of party voting in response to levels of party voting in the other party.

Responding positively to the pressure and selective incentives from their leaders and colleagues to contribute to collective action is more likely when members believe that their contributions to the collective effort can make a difference. Given the opportunity for members to make unlimited contributions to the CCCs, their perception that the congressional party can affect election results is critical. As we have detailed in chapter 2, CCCs only recently have become more active and influential participants than local parties in many congressional contests. Incumbents can see that their contributions are directed toward highly professionalized campaign activities that are effectively targeted to the districts on which majority status hinges, increasing their confidence in the efficacy of their participation.

Members are also more willing to contribute to collective action when the cost of doing so is low (Olson 1965). In the case of redistributing campaign contributions, the total financial cost may be considerable, but members are willing to contribute because doing so poses minimal risk to their own reelections. Although partisan margins are thin, creating a pitched battle for majority status, majority control hinges on a relatively small number of competitive seats. Meanwhile, most incumbents' electoral safety gives them substantial flexibility to redistribute funds. As detailed in chapter 2, if members desire to raise more money to comply with the demands of the party to share their wealth, networks of individuals and PACs are easily accessible sources of money for incumbents to tap for additional fundraising. Precisely how incumbents adjust their fundraising activities to meet their new partisan obligations will be analyzed in chapter 7.

It is important to emphasize that rank-and-file members still have the choice whether to comply with the party leadership's fundraising demands. Members who are uninterested in advancing or who are unconcerned with being viewed as a "team player" can continue traditional fundraising behavior and redistribute little or no funds to party candidates or committees. They also have the choice of how vigorously and quickly to comply and how to use the leadership's demands for funds as bargaining leverage. As Alex Isenstadt of *Politico* reports (2010),

> It's not unheard of for members to hold out on their party contributions until late in the election cycle. Some Democratic incumbents typically wait until just a few weeks before Election Day to cut their checks as a means of soliciting promises from party leaders, while others have been known to keep their wallets closed as a means of protesting the legislative agenda that was—or was not— pursued in the previous two years.

As we explain in the next chapter, there is good reason to expect that members will vary systematically in their responsiveness to the new party fundraising expectations, and we show evidence that in fact they do. To continue making their fundraising demands, leaders need only sufficient support for their own reelection within the caucus. As long as a plurality of the caucus perceives that these fundraising demands are consistent with the collective good of the party and do not undermine their own individual goals, leaders will continue to mobilize campaign funds from the caucus.

Conclusion

In the electoral arena, congressional parties are becoming increasingly coordinated, if not machinelike, because they are increasingly able to overcome collective action problems endemic to their structure. Leaders have aggressively mobilized members to assist the party and its needy candidates financially, and they have increasingly deployed congressional structures designed for legislative purposes to induce members to contribute to the party's collective electoral good. Members now support delegating such powers to leaders and complying with leaders' electoral mobilization efforts because of value of majority status, the likelihood that their party can attain it in the next election, and the increasing role of the national party in congressional elections. The congressional parties' literature, while recognizing the strengthening legislative powers of congressional party leaders and the increased legislative coordination of congressional parties, has not documented or explained the increased electoral mobilization of congressional parties.

The battle for majority status changes the relationship between party leaders and individual members of Congress. It gives leaders and members incentive to change their behavior and to adjust institutions to reflect the party's collective needs in a competitive electoral environment. When majority status is not at stake and members have little incentive to cooperate electorally, party leaders provide services to facilitate members' ability to achieve their individual goals. Though individual members certainly hope leaders can deliver majority status, their support for leaders is likely to rest on what the leader can do for them and whether the leader is keeping the party out of electoral trouble. When majority status is at stake, members expect their leaders to develop strategies for overcoming collective action problems to help the party achieve its collective electoral goals. Whether individual members participate or not is secondary to their expectation that party leaders use their powers assertively on behalf of the collective good. After all, members benefit individually from the collective good whether or not they contribute.

Yet when majority status is at stake, members also have an incentive to comply with the leadership's mobilization efforts on behalf of the party's collective electoral goals. For many members, particularly those who occupy (and aspire to occupy) positions of power, the difference in power that major party control makes is potentially so great that it overwhelms any advantage to going it alone and working only on achieving individual goals. Even for members without power ambitions, the difference in one's ability to pass legislation, block unfavorable legislation, and raise campaign funds is sufficiently large that one is likely to contribute when it is reasonable to think that cooperation is likely to make some difference in attaining majority status. In sum, members will cooperate with the party when doing so helps them achieve their own goals.

4 | The Growth of Member Giving

Bill Thomas (R-CA), the ranking Republican on the House Administration Committee, contributed $19,000 to GOP candidates in the 1990 election cycle. In the anti-incumbent political environment of the 1992 election cycle, he redistributed only $1,000. He did not contribute to the National Republican Congressional Committee in either cycle. In the 1994 election cycle, as Newt Gingrich mobilized senior GOP members to contribute for the party's push to take over majority status, Thomas contributed $21,000 to GOP candidates and $7,500 to the NRCC. With the GOP takeover of the House in 1995, Thomas became chair of the House Administration Committee and more than doubled his contributions in the 1996 election cycle, giving $49,000 to candidates and $32,500 to the NRCC. In the 1998 election cycle, Thomas formed a leadership PAC, the Congressional Majority Committee, but contributed only $5,000 to other candidates through it, though he also gave $48,000 to candidates through his principal campaign committee. His contributions to the NRCC, however, surged dramatically to $150,000.

At the end of the 2000 election cycle, Bill Archer was term limited out of the chairmanship of the Ways and Means Committee. Thomas's leadership PAC sprang into action, donating $183,000 to GOP candidates, with another $43,000 coming from his principal campaign committee. He also contributed $252,000 to the NRCC from his PCC. Thomas won the battle with Phil Crane for the chair of Ways and Means. Chairing a prestige committee gave Thomas more leverage over interest groups than he had as a rank-and-file member of the committee or as chair of the House Administration Committee. His redistribution doubled again in the 2002 election cycle, when he gave $335,500 from his LPAC and $500,000 from his PCC to the NRCC. In 2004, Thomas's contributions to candidates increased even further—he gave $520,000 and $67,000 to candidates from his LPAC and PCC, respectively—whereas his contributions to the NRCC decreased to $425,000.

In the 2006 election cycle, Thomas faced term limits as Ways and Means chair and announced his retirement from Congress. With the congressional party and his colleagues having limited influence over his future career, Thomas's contributions scaled back substantially: he gave $41,000 from his LPAC and $44,000 from his PCC to candidates and $330,000 from his PCC to the NRCC. Despite the hundreds of thousands of dollars in total campaign monies Thomas gave to federal candidates and party committees over the nine election cycles from 1990 to 2006, he gave nothing to the California Republican Party and an average of only $1,500 per election cycle to local party organizations. Thomas's career was oriented toward advancement in the House, and so, therefore, was his contribution activity.

Bill Thomas's contribution patterns exemplify several aggregate patterns that we will see in this chapter in the redistribution of campaign funds by House members. First, the total amounts of funds Thomas redistributed increased substantially over time. Second, Thomas dramatically increased the contributions from his PCC to the party congressional campaign committee; the increases in his contributions to candidates occurred more dramatically through his LPAC than through his PCC. Third, Thomas's contribution levels responded to his status in the institution: his redistribution activity was very low when he was a member of the minority party that had little hope of becoming the majority, he redistributed more actively when he became a committee chair, his contributions increased even further when opportunities for advancement became available, he redistributed substantial sums while he chaired a powerful committee, and his redistribution levels declined once he decided to leave the House. Finally, state and local parties receive financial assistance from House incumbents, but with little ability to affect House members' goals, they benefit much less from redistribution than do the congressional parties. Members of the House respond to party mobilization efforts, but their level of responsiveness varies based on their institutional position and career goals.

In this chapter, we document the variation in redistribution activity by members of the House. Redistribution activity has increased substantially over time, but it has increased more for some types of redistribution than for others. We argue that these variations are a function of several factors: campaign finance laws governing the methods by which members make contributions, the competition for majority control over time, the mobilization efforts of the parties, and the influence the party has over the career goals of the individual member.

The Rise in Redistribution

As illustrated in figure 4.1, all types of redistribution increased from the 1990 to the 2006 election cycles. Incumbent redistribution from both members' PCCs and their LPACs have grown, and contributions to both other candidates and party organizations have increased. Money has flowed increasingly from federal incumbents to state and local parties as well. The money spigots have been opened: nearly all House incumbents now contribute, and nearly all potential recipients benefit from such contributions.

The dramatic increases in redistribution have not occurred equally by method or by recipient. Campaign finance laws have played a critical role in directing the flow of campaign funds from House incumbents. Money flows more abundantly where legal barriers are less restrictive; increases in giving have been less dramatic where regulatory barriers exist. Members of Congress, like other political donors, take the easiest path to achieving their goals.

Donations to each party's House congressional campaign committee nicely illustrate the effect of contribution limits (see table 1.1 in chapter 1). Contributions from a member's PCC to the CCC are entirely unrestricted; members can and do give six- and even seven-figure contributions to the

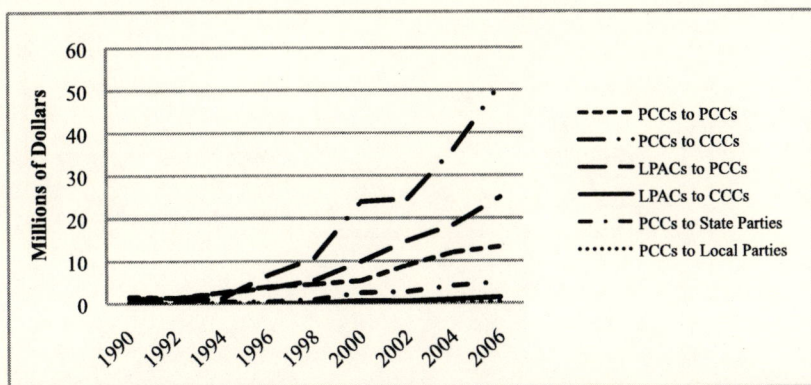

Fig. 4.1.   Increases in the redistribution of campaign funds by members of the U.S. House, 1990–2006

CCCs. In contrast, contributions from LPACs to national party committees are, like all PAC contributions to the national parties, capped at $15,000 per election. Members therefore do not need an LPAC to give generously to their party. Even members who sponsor LPACs have incentives—majority party control and the prodding of party leaders—to give unlimited contributions through their PCCs rather than restricted contributions through their LPACs. Not surprisingly, a dominance of PCC giving to CCCs is precisely what we see: members of the House contributed over $51 million from their PCCs to the House CCCs in 2006, compared to only $1.4 million from their LPACs. The effect of the restrictions is also plainly evident in how members responded to party mobilization efforts over the time period in our analysis: contributions from PCCs to CCCs increased by more than 13,000 percent during this period, whereas contributions from LPACs increased by less than 200 percent. Figure 4.2 shows the dramatic shift in PCC giving from candidates to the CCCs as the parties exploited the different contribution limits. In the 1990 election cycle, only 19 percent of PCC contributions went to the CCCs; since the 2000 election cycle, about 80 percent of PCC contributions have gone to the CCCs.

Variations in contribution limits also help to explain variations in contributions to candidates between PCCs and LPACs. Throughout most of the period of our study, incumbents could give up to $1,000 per candidate per election through their PCCs. While Congress left this limit in place when it passed the Bipartisan Campaign Reform Act in 2002, it increased the limit to $2,000 in the Consolidated Appropriations Act of 2005. Con-

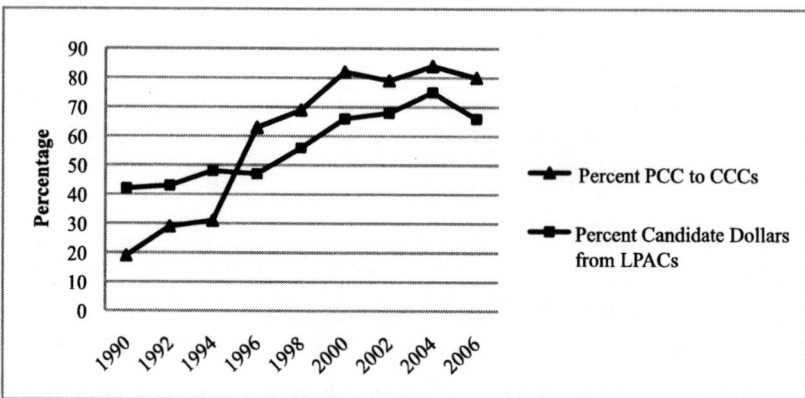

Fig. 4.2. Changes in contribution patterns by the PCCs and LPACs of U.S. House members, 1990–2006

gress did not, however, index the new limit to inflation, meaning that the limits will remain at $2,000 unless Congress acts again (Metzler 2006). LPAC contributions to candidates have a higher limit, before and after the 2005 adjustment for PCCs: $5,000 per candidate per election. Members with the capacity to sponsor an LPAC therefore have an incentive to route their contributions to candidates through it in order to increase the sums they can funnel to their favored recipients.

We see differences in contributions to candidates consistent with the different legal restrictions. In the 2006 election cycle, for example, LPACs contributed $24.9 million to candidates while PCCs contributed $13.3 million, despite the fact that less than half (36 percent) of House members who sought reelection had LPACs. Similarly, as the parties have mobilized more campaign assistance from incumbents, the financial support for candidates has increased more dramatically through LPACs, the less restrictive route. Between 1990 and 2006, contributions from LPACs to candidates grew by nearly 2000 percent, while contributions from PCCs to candidates increased by 731 percent. The same incentives have led more members to form LPACs over the past several election cycles: whereas 21 House members (5 percent) had an LPAC in 1990, 206 members (47 percent) sponsored an LPAC in 2006. Figure 4.2 shows that the proportion of total candidate giving has shifted heavily toward LPACs, from LPACs providing just over 40 percent of candidate contributions from incumbents in the 1990 election cycle to almost 75 percent in the 2004 election cycle. As incumbents shifted their PCC giving toward the CCCs, many of them also formed LPACs to give to candidates. We will explore this dynamic in more detail in chapter 7.

The absence of limits on contributions from PCCs to CCCs has allowed such contributions to grow at a substantially greater pace than more heavily regulated donations from PCCs and LPACs to candidates. Figure 4.1 shows that the total sums and amount of growth of contributions from PCCs to CCCs is much larger than either category of contributions to candidates. The greater growth in contributions to the CCCs also reflects the intense battle for majority control of the House that emerged in the mid-1990s. In 1990, Democrats had been the dominant majority party for 40 years, and few expected that status to change. Thus, candidates who were willing to share campaign funds had an incentive to contribute to other candidates rather than to the party (R. Baker 1989). Winning candidates recognized the incumbent donor's gift and would be in a position to return the favor by, for example, supporting the donor in a leadership election or assisting the donor with legislation. By contrast, incumbents had few incentives to give to the party CCC. Contributions to the CCC were unlikely to affect majority status, and because CCC spending in an individual candidate's campaign could not be traced to the original incumbent donor, the payoff (in terms of favors returned) would be impossible for contributing incumbents to collect. These expectations are clearly supported in the contribution patterns. In the 1990 election cycle, 88 percent of total incumbent giving was directed toward candidates (PCC + LPAC); total CCC contributions were less than $400,000.

Once majority control of the House was at stake in each election following 1994, members had much greater incentive to give unlimited amounts from their PCCs to the party CCCs. For an incumbent, winning membership in the majority party was more valuable than the favors he or she could earn from recipients of $1,000 or $5,000. In the 1996 election cycle, the first following the GOP takeover of the House, contributions from incumbents to the CCCs surged 82 percent from the previous election cycle (from $1.2 million to $6.7 million) and nearly equaled total PCC and LPAC contributions to candidates ($7.2 million). Contributions to the CCCs in 1996 encompassed nearly half, or 48 percent, of total incumbent giving. By the 2006 election cycle, incumbent contributions to the CCCs had clearly overtaken contributions to candidates, comprising 58 percent of total incumbent giving. With majority status at stake and party leaders pressuring members to support the party's campaign efforts, incumbents advanced their interests more by helping the party achieve its collective goals than by donating to individual candidates.

State and local parties have limited selective incentives to provide to House members in exchange for campaign funds. State and local party organizations provide some, though limited, assistance to members' election campaigns (Herrnson 2008) but have little to no effect on a member's goal achievement within the House. In terms of career advancement outside the House, incumbents' ambitions for statewide offices are relevant to their generosity to state parties, as we will see in chapter 8. Nevertheless, the party's mobilization of campaign funds by reelection-seeking incumbents seems to have had a spillover effect that has benefited state and local party organizations as well. Though state and local parties receive relatively limited sums of House incumbent support compared to CCCs and House candidates, they have increased their take over the past several election cycles.[1] House member contributions to state parties have grown from $228,876 in 1990 to almost $5 million in 2006—an increase of nearly 1,700 percent. Incumbent contributions to local party organizations have increased by almost 850 percent—from $31,450 to $298,405—over the same period, but such donations remain a very small part of the total re-distribution activity by members of Congress. House members have re-sponded to the battle for majority status, then, by increasing their contri-butions to federal candidates, the CCCs, and, to a lesser extent, state and local party organizations.

The post-1994 period has witnessed a surge of campaign money redis-tributed by House incumbents—from incumbents' PCCs and LPACs to all potential recipients. The rising tide has lifted all boats, though some have been lifted higher than others. Campaign finance laws have played a large role in routing the flow of campaign dollars redistributed by incum-bents; the CCCs have benefited substantially from the outpouring of in-cumbent financial support because members can transfer unlimited sums from their PCCs to the national party committees. The flow of LPAC money to federal candidates has increased substantially because limits on LPAC donations to candidates are higher than the limits on PCC contri-butions to candidates. Federal recipients have benefited disproportion-ately compared to state and local parties because congressional parties have greater influence over the goal achievement and career advancement of most House members. To understand further how and why the redis-tribution of incumbent campaign dollars has increased, we turn to an ex-amination of which members contribute and how their contribution pat-terns have changed over time.

Who Redistributes?

The substantial increase in campaign funds redistributed by House in-cumbents reflects a sharp growth in the number of incumbents making contributions as well as in the number of members giving larger amounts. Additionally, members who have the most to gain from majority status—those with institutional positions made more powerful by membership in the majority party—have been the most active in fueling the increase in redistribution.

The party has a number of types of positions with which it can reward members who serve the party's collective interests. Most obvious are the elected leadership positions: the Speaker, the majority/minority leader, the whip, the caucus chair and other caucus officers, and the heads of the party CCCs. These members are selected by the caucus for the purpose of coordinating and mobilizing members in support of the party's legislative and electoral goals. Party leaders who fail to help their party make progress toward securing majority status often lose their positions (Canon 1989; Peabody 1976). Elected leaders traditionally have done substantial fundraising on behalf of the party and its candidates (R. Baker 1989; Wilcox 1989, 1990). Because of their direct responsibility for the party's collective electoral success, we should observe fundraising behavior among the top leaders that advance the party goal of majority control, especially contributing to the party's candidates and to its CCC. In fact, "raising bundles" for redistribution has become an "unwritten part of the job" (Sherman 2010).

Other party posts have less responsibility for the achievement of collective party goals than the elected leaders but more responsibility than rank-and-file members. Party reforms imposed over the course of the past 30 years—for example, caucuswide votes on committee leaders and increased leadership influence in the committee assignment process—have induced members who occupy these posts to act as responsible partisans (Deering and Smith 1997; Rohde 1991; Sinclair 1995, 2006). Under former Speaker Newt Gingrich's leadership, House Republicans went even further in bringing committee leaders and members on prestige committees under party control (Aldrich and Rohde 1997–98; Smith and Lawrence 1997). The GOP increased its potential control over chairs by imposing term limits and requiring new chairs to "audition" and win the approval of the Steering Committee (Foerstel 2000; Hirschfield 2000). Additionally, chairs are members of the majority party. Thus, these members have a substantial personal incentive to help the party win majority status—they lose substantial power if their party becomes the minority. Ranking minority party members likewise have considerable incentive to help elect a majority from their party so that they can become the chair.

Party leaders also have appointment powers with which to reward members who serve the collective good of the party. These include positions in the extended party leadership (Sinclair 1983, 1995): the whip system, the steering committees, party policy committees, CCCs, research committees, and personnel committees. These positions give members the opportunity to participate in leadership decisions, and they serve as entry-level positions from which to advance up the leadership ladder (Canon 1989; Loomis 1984; Price 2000). Because members' appointments are dependent on the leadership, they are likely to direct their contributions in ways that advance the party leadership's most important collective goal: obtaining majority status.

The party steering committees also appoint members to standing committees. Party leaders traditionally have been most concerned with appointments to the prestige committees (Appropriations, Rules, and Ways and Means), since these committees have the most influence over the achievement of the party's agenda. Leaders are therefore concerned with appointing party loyalists more to prestige committees than to other committees (Cox and McCubbins 1993; Deering and Smith 1997). Prestige committee members are expected to support the party agenda. Because these committees are powerful, their members have the leverage to raise substantial funds from interest groups whose policy goals are affected by their committee's decisions (Grier and Munger 1993; Romer and Snyder 1994). Members on prestige committees thus have additional responsibilities to redistribute campaign funds to the party. As one GOP aide explained, "With A-committee assignments come A-committee responsibilities. There is a sense that these members are in a position to do more to help the team" (quoted in Isenstadt 2011). Much like committee chairs, moreover, the power enjoyed by members of prestige committees increases greatly when serving in the majority party, giving prestige committee members substantial incentive to help their party win majority status.

In contrast, rank-and-file members—those with no elective or appointive party posts—have more flexibility to develop their own idiosyncratic contribution networks. Although they gain somewhat more power by serving in the majority party, the differences in power are not as dramatic as those with official party or committee leadership posts. Moreover, if they do not have ambitions for elective or appointive party posts, they have limited incentive to make sacrifices to serve the party's collective goals. The voters in their districts are likely to have more power over the members' careers than has the congressional party. Rank-and-file members are therefore only likely to serve the party's collective interests to the extent that it does not interfere with their own personal priorities. They are likely to be the most individualistic in their contribution patterns and the least oriented toward helping the party achieve majority status.

Institutional Positions and Responsiveness in Redistribution

The increase in the redistribution of campaign money is explained in part by growth in the number of incumbents willing to share their campaign wealth. Figure 4.3 shows that the percentage of members participating has increased sharply between the 1990 and 2006 elections, though the increases vary by position. Elected party leaders contributed at unanimous or nearly unanimous levels throughout the nine election cycles. Committee leaders and members in the extended leadership have participation trends that are nearly identical, starting at two-thirds participation in 1990, rising rapidly in the 1996 election cycle (to nearly 80 percent) and 1998 election cycle (to nearly 90 percent), then reaching unanimous or nearly unanimous participation in the 2004 election cycle. Prestige committee members, who had higher levels of participation in 1990 than did chairs and members of the extended leadership, also responded quickly to party mobilization efforts, reaching near unanimous levels of redistribution (97 percent) by the 1998 election cycle. Rank-and-file members, defined as those holding none of the aforementioned positions, have consistently participated at lower rates. We expect lower participation rates among rank-and-file members; after all, unlike committee or party leaders, they have no direct responsibility to their colleagues in the party caucus. Yet while rank-and-file members did not respond as rapidly to the CCCs' calls for funds as did members holding leadership positions, rank-and-file members steadily increased their levels of support throughout the period. By 2004, the percentage for rank-and-file participation had grown to the mid-90s, nearly the percentage of members holding leadership positions.

The importance of positions is also evident in the amounts of campaign money redistributed by members. Figure 4.4 clearly illustrates the relationship between funds redistributed and the value and power of various leadership positions. Members occupying positions whose power depends most on majority party control give the largest median contributions. Figure 4.4 demonstrates the importance of party leaders in the

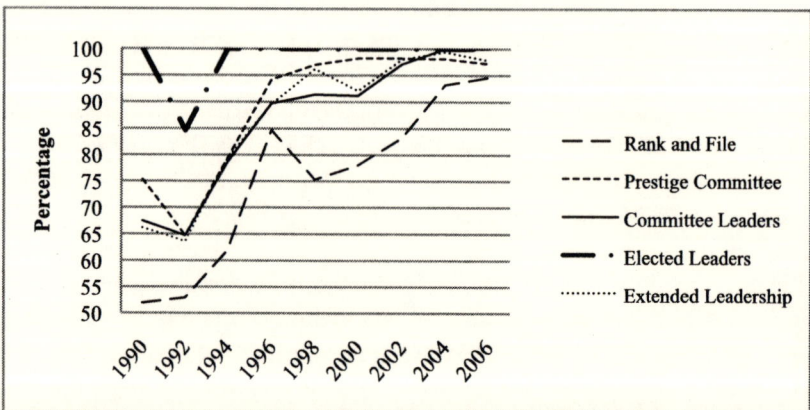

Fig. 4.3.   Increases in the percentage of House members redistributing, 1990–2006

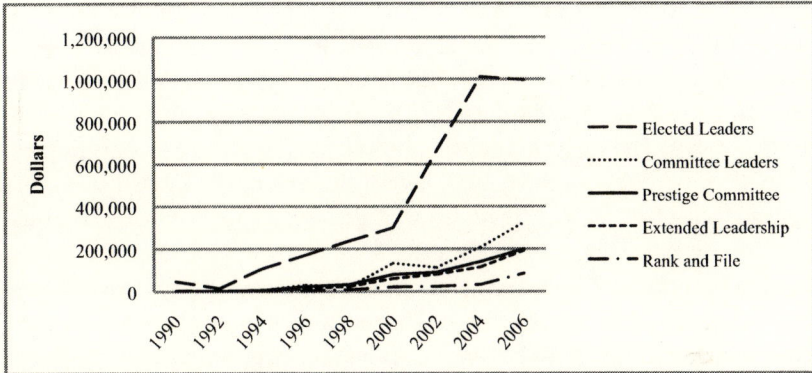

Fig. 4.4. Median dollars redistributed by position in the U.S. House,
1990–2006

redistribution process; across all nine election cycles, elected leaders gave substantially larger median contributions than members holding any other position.

Committee leaders generally rank second in contribution levels, though their median contribution level is usually only about one-third that of elected party leaders. Long-standing and newer committee leaders alike increased the sums they redistributed. Members who served as chairs or ranking members prior to the GOP takeover of Congress in 1995 redistributed an adjusted median of $25,885 in the 1990–94 election cycles. (See "Adjusted Campaign Contributions" in the appendix at the end of this chapter for an explanation of how we standardized contributions across election cycles.) In the three election cycles following the GOP takeover (1996–2000), these same members more than doubled their adjusted median level of redistribution to $55,750. Thus, "old-style" committee leaders got the message and responded to party mobilization efforts, and in doing so, they sought to preserve or enhance their own power by serving as chair rather than ranking member.

Members who first became chairs or ranking members during the 1996–2000 period were even more generous than were committee leaders held over from the Democratic majority era. The new committee leaders redistributed an adjusted median of $85,400 from 1996 to 2000, 50 percent higher than the continuing committee leaders. In fact, the "new" committee leaders had been more generous than the "old" committee leaders even prior to their promotion, giving an adjusted median of $39,990 in the

1990–94 period—also 50 percent higher than the old committee leaders during the same time frame. Both old and new committee leaders, then, increased their redistribution by just over 100 percent from 1990–94 to 1996–2000, but the new leaders were starting from a higher baseline of contributions. The surge in redistribution from committee leaders immediately before and after the GOP takeover was the result both of committee leaders increasing their giving and of the replacement of less generous leaders with more generous committee leaders.

Term limits on GOP committee chairs also affected member giving. Between the 1998 and 2000 election cycles, committee leaders' median contributions surged from $23,455 to $132,250, and this surge seems best explained by the GOP's term limits on chairs. The three-session term limit was instituted when the GOP gained a majority in the 104th Congress, and it was being implemented for the first time in 2000 (Foerstel 2000). Twelve chairs were term limited. Simultaneously, prospective chairs would have to appear before the Steering Committee to "audition" for their positions. Several term-limited GOP chairs, such as Bill Thomas (CA) and Henry Hyde (IL), sought to chair other committees on which they were senior members. These chairs presumably increased their giving in order to demonstrate to GOP Steering Committee members their commitment to the party's collective good and thus their qualifications to chair the new committee. Four members successfully completed this round of "musical chairs" and surrendered the chair of one committee for the chair of another.

Prestige committee members and members of the extended leadership structure gave similar sums of campaign funds, with prestige committee members usually contributing at slightly higher levels than members of the extended leadership. The median contribution level of these members increased at a similarly steady pace over the nine election cycles in our analysis—from about $3,000 in 1990, to approximately $30,000 in 1998, to just under $200,000 in 2006.

Rank-and-file members contributed fewer dollars per capita than those holding important committee and party positions, as figure 4.4 demonstrates. The median contribution of rank-and-file members is consistently less than half that of members of the extended leadership structure, the category of positions at the next lowest level in median contribution. Additionally, the median contribution of rank-and-file members increased by modest amounts compared to their colleagues with institutional posts, remaining relatively nominal until the most recent election cycles. By the 2006 election cycle, however, the median sum redistributed by rank-and-file members was $85,500, greater than the median redistributed by all members holding institutional positions in the election cycles preceding the GOP takeover.

It is also important to add that the median contribution levels of rank-and-file members are depressed by the fact that members who are the most generous redistributors of campaign funds are likely to become members of the extended leadership or prestige committees (Heberlig 2003; Heberlig and Larson 2010). By moving willing and successful redistributors into more powerful positions with the capacity to raise even more campaign funds, parties can reap even greater financial support from these members in the future. But once these members are promoted, their contributions no longer count toward the rank-and-file totals, leaving the rank-and-file category populated largely by junior members who have limited leverage for raising and redistributing large sums and by senior members who apparently do not desire party-controlled positions enough to comply with party demands for campaign funds.

While the congressional parties' efforts to extract campaign funds from their incumbents has yielded dramatic growth in member contributions over the past nine election cycles, a more subtle consequence of the parties' efforts has been a shift in the members who bear the primary burden of supporting the party and its candidates financially. As figure 4.5 illustrates, this burden is shared and has remained largely stable across an era of dramatic growth in redistribution. Yet one notable change is the decline in the proportion of total funds provided by elected party leaders. Even as the total funds provided by elected leaders have increased, the total funds provided by members in other institutional positions have increased even more dramatically. As figure 4.5 shows, elected leaders contributed nearly one-quarter of total party funds in the early 1990s; a decade later, they contributed just over one-tenth of the total funds. Meanwhile, committee leaders and prestige committee members, taken together, have increased their share of total member contributions by roughly the same amount as elected leaders' shares have fallen, with a 4 percent increase for committee leaders and a 6 percent increase for prestige committee members. The proportion of total funds contributed by extended leadership members has remained stable over time; the proportion of funds provided by the rank and file has fluctuated from one election cycle to the next, from slightly above to slightly below 10 percent of the total. The parties' mobilization efforts, then, have not diminished the importance of elected party leaders as resource providers, but such efforts have helped to spread the burden of raising resources more broadly, particularly to committee leaders and prestige committee members.

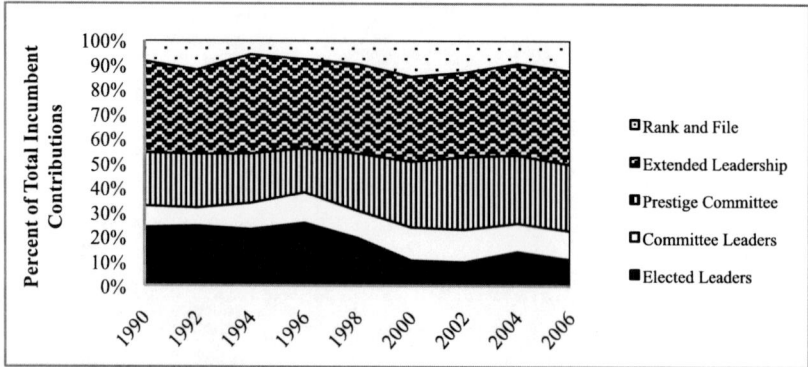

Fig. 4.5. Changes in the proportion of total funds redistribution by position within the U.S. House, 1990–2006

The practice of sharing campaign funds was a relatively uncommon activity in the early 1990s, and it was disproportionately undertaken by elected party leaders. Redistributing campaign funds is now common-place, and the failure to do so is the exception. Elected leaders still carry the heaviest load per capita and bear much of the responsibility for mobi-lizing and coordinating the redistribution activity within their caucuses, but they now have substantial assistance from the rest of the caucus, par-ticularly from other members with institution positions whose power is highly dependent on serving in the majority. Almost everyone in the cau-cus has joined the party's campaign fundraising efforts.

Redistribution and the Political Environment

In chapter 3, we argued that the increase in the redistribution of campaign funds by traditionally self-interested and electorally risk-averse members of Congress is due in large part to the intense battle for majority status. Figure 4.6 illustrates these dynamics by showing the proportion of funds redistributed by members of the majority party. Obviously, majority sta-tus matters: members of the majority party always redistribute more than their minority party counterparts, because of their ability to leverage their institutional status to get contributions from donors seeking access and influence over legislation. In the early 1990s, the Democrats had held ma-jority status since the 1950s, and since few expected a change, Republicans had few incentives to redistribute money. Thus, Democrats provided over 70 percent of redistributed funds. With the competitive 1994 election, however, both parties increased their redistribution, and the majority Democrats eked out an advantage of 52 percent in redistribution (though not in the election). Once the GOP held the majority, they held a consistent redistribution advantage—though never as large as the Democrats' early 1990s dominance. Parallel to 1994, the GOP's smallest advantage (55 percent) occurred in 2006, as the Democrats mounted their most serious and ultimately successful challenge. However, both parties increased their level of redistribution in 2006 to contest majority status. With the Democrats holding majority status in the 2008 election and expected to gain even more seats, Republican redistribution declined, redistribution from Democrats increased, and Democrats redistributed 61 percent of total funds. The 2010 elections were expected to favor Republicans and both parties increased their redistribution from 2008. Republicans were on the offense and increased their redistribution by more than the Democrats, thereby limiting the majority party's share of total redistribution to 55 percent—ironically, the same proportion as the GOP's in 2006 when they also lost majority control.

The implementation of the Bipartisan Campaign Finance Act also affected party CCC fundraising activities during this period (see chapter 2) in ways that have direct implications for the mobilization of campaign funds from incumbent members of Congress. In particular, BCRA eliminated soft money contributions—unlimited contributions from individuals and organizations for so-called party-building activities—to national

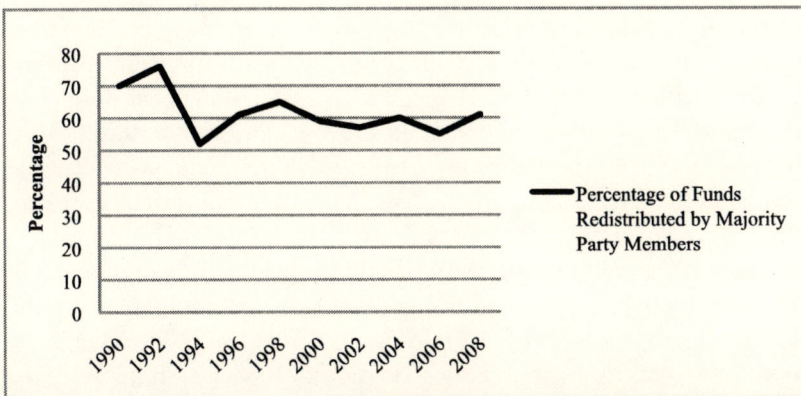

Fig. 4.6.   The proportion of redistribution by the majority party

party organizations. Parties would replace six-figure contributions from a few big contributors with capped hard money contributions from thousands of donors by tapping incumbents, who typically have large war chests, strong ties with the PAC community in Washington, D.C., and networks of individual donors in their districts (Dwyre et al. 2006). The most efficient way for the party to substitute hard money for soft money would be to mobilize members whose positions gave them significant fundraising leverage and required of them substantial responsibility to the party: elected party leaders, committee leaders, prestige committee members, and members of the extended leadership.

In earlier work (Heberlig and Larson 2005), we explained how the redistribution of campaign funds by members of Congress should vary by the method of redistribution (PCC contributions to candidates versus LPAC contributions to candidates versus PCC and LPAC contributions to CCCs) and by the political environment (especially the battle for majority status). Here, we extend those arguments and models to account for additional changes in the political environment brought about by the implementation of BCRA. Later in the chapter, we further extend our arguments to include members' contributions to state and local party organizations, where the incentives for redistribution are different than the incentives to contribute to federal candidates and party organizations.

Modeling Contributions

The descriptive data show who gives (especially in terms of institutional position) and how giving over time is affected by the political environment (particularly the level of competition for control of the House between the two parties). In describing models of contributions, we give special attention to the ways in which the characteristics of the donor and the political environment interact. These two factors are conditioned further by the different methods used to redistribute money. Our expectations are summarized in table 4.1. Measurements for all variables are provided in the appendix at the end of this chapter.

Members have three different methods for making contributions: contributing to other candidates through their principal campaign account, contributing to their party's CCC through their principal campaign account, and contributing to other candidates through an LPAC.[2] The methods members rely on are likely to tell us something about their goals and ambitions. Contributions to candidates, through a campaign account or an LPAC, allow the contributor to receive personal recognition by the recipient. That recipient, if elected, is then in a position to return the favor by voting for the contributor in a party caucus election for various positions. Thus, it is likely that contributions made through these methods are designed primarily to advance members' individual career ambitions, even if the indirect result also helps the party collectively. This is especially likely to be true for leadership PACs, as their name would imply.

TABLE 4.1. Summary of Hypotheses

	PCC Contributions to Candidates	PCC Contributions to Congressional Campaign Committees	Leadership PAC Contributions to Candidates
Position			
Party leader	+	+	+
Chair/RM	+	+	+
Contest for position	+	no relationship	+
Prestige committee	+	+	+
Subcommittee leader	+	no relationship	no relationship
Unelected party post	+	+	no relationship
Retiring	−	−	−
Seeking higher office	−	−	−
Partisanship			
Majority party	−	+	+
Party loyalty voting	+	+	+
Capacity to Contribute			
Electoral margin	+	+	no relationship
Cash on hand	+	+	n.a.
Grandfathered	−	−	n.a.
Responsiveness to Potential for Majority Status			
Party margin	−	−	−
Leader × party margin	−	−	no relationship
Chair × party margin	−	−	no relationship
Prestige × party margin	−	−	no relationship
Unelected party × margin	−	−	no relationship
Implementation of the Bipartisan Campaign Reform Act of 2002			
BCRA	+	+	n.a.
Leader × BCRA	+	+	n.a.
Chair × BCRA	+	+	n.a.
Prestige × BCRA	+	+	n.a.
Extended Leadership × BCRA	+	+	n.a.

Note: n.a. = not applicable.

Contributions to CCCs, however, allow the party to target the money and do not allow a direct connection between the contributor and the ultimate candidate recipient. The contributor gives to the CCC to please the person(s) making the contribution request and to help the party achieve its goal of majority control. Those who contribute to the CCCs, then, are likely to have some responsibility to the caucus or to party leaders.

Institutional Ambition. The descriptive data in the previous section and the theoretical discussion in chapter 3 show that members with all types of leadership posts redistribute more campaign funds than their colleagues without positions. We generally expect members holding leadership posts to redistribute larger sums of campaign money to candidates through both PCCs and LPACs and to CCCs through their PCCs. Likewise, we expect these members to be more responsive to the battle for majority status and to the implementation of BCRA. They should increase all types of giving as seat margins between the parties narrow and as both parties pressure their members for hard money contributions following the loss of soft money contributions in the 2004 and 2006 elections.

There are a few qualifications to these general hypotheses regarding positions, however. The first qualification pertains to members of the extended leadership. Although the number of members who sponsor leadership PACs has grown significantly during the past decade, it probably remains true that only the most powerful members can raise the additional money necessary to underwrite a large PAC (Wilcox 1990, 171–72). Similarly, members who occupy lower-level party posts owe their positions to elected party leaders and thus are likely to be especially responsive to appeals to contribute to the CCCs. (Indeed, the member may have been appointed to his or her party's CCC.) Thus, we expect that occupying an extended leadership post will be positively associated with contributions from a member's principal campaign committee, particularly to the CCCs, but not with leadership PAC contributions.

In the contemporary Congress, party leaders have always—regardless of party margins—been expected to raise funds for individual party candidates (R. Baker 1989; Brown and Peabody 1992; Wilcox 1989, 1990). In doing so, leaders fulfill members' expectations that leaders help them individually (Sinclair 1983, 1995), while also helping to build the party's legislative numbers. Thus, we expect that the effect of holding a party leadership post on contributing campaign money to individual candidates should be relatively stable across various levels of party margins. Yet in terms of power, the value of a party leader's post is inextricably linked to the party's collective electoral fortunes. Thus, we anticipate that contributions from party leaders to the congressional campaign committees should increase as party margins become smaller (and as majority party control thus becomes at stake).

Those competing for a top party or committee leadership post are also likely to redistribute substantial sums. Since the late 1970s, contributing campaign money to candidates appears to have become all but a requirement for members running for leadership slots (R. Baker 1989; Brown and Peabody 1992; Sabato and Larson 2002; Wilcox 1989, 1990)—whether or not majority party control is at stake. Although contributions alone probably are insufficient for winning a post, we anticipate that members running in contested party or committee leadership contests will contribute more than members not running in such contests. Moreover, the importance of getting direct credit for one's contributions implies that running in a leadership race will be associated primarily with contributions to candidates (from both leadership PACs and members' principal campaign committees) rather than contributions to the CCCs.

Each party also has numerous subcommittee positions to offer its members. However, we do not anticipate the same level of party fundraising activity from subcommittee leaders as we expect from committee leaders and prestige committee members. Subcommittee leaders are chosen by partisan committee colleagues rather than by party leaders or through caucuswide votes. Although the value of subcommittee leaders' positions is linked to the party's electoral fortunes, the relative absence of caucuswide influence over who occupies these posts means that members who occupy them are likely to be judged on how well they serve the committee's, rather than the party's, goals. Thus, subcommittee leaders' contributions are likely to go to individual members rather than to the party.

Members' ambitions within the committee system also are likely to affect their generosity in redistributing funds. Theriault (1998) and Hall and Van Houweling (1995) find that members whose likelihood of advancing in committee is "blocked" by a younger member with greater seniority are more likely to retire. Since members are likely to redistribute funds in response to the party's control over their advancement, members whose advancement is blocked by other members should redistribute less money, while those who are not blocked and have the greatest opportunity to advance should redistribute more funds. We coded a member's advancement as blocked when a younger member had more seniority on all the committees on which a member served.

Larson (2004) finds that retirees and members seeking higher office redistribute less money to the CCCs (see also Kolodny and Dwyre 2006).

Since retirees and members running for higher office are leaving the House, they face little incentive to please party leaders by giving money to the party. Giving to their colleagues or other party candidates would not facilitate achievement of their future career goals. While some retirees may contribute anyway to draw down the unneeded funds leftover in their campaign accounts, retirees have no incentive to raise more money for the sake of the party. Members engaged in a statewide campaign have an acute need for campaign funds and can transfer money from their House campaign accounts to their statewide election committees; contributing to House candidates and party organizations would do little to advance their future career goals. Thus, we expect that members who are retiring or running for higher office will redistribute fewer dollars than will members seeking re-election to the House.

Members' Policy Goals and Party Voting. Majority party control should be more important to members who typically support their party's positions than to members who typically defect from their party's positions. Thus, the more supportive a member is of his or her party on the floor, the more campaign money he or she will redistribute.

Members' Capacity to Raise Surplus Funds. Members' reelection goal should also affect their willingness to redistribute campaign money. As Jacobson (1985–86) argues, no incumbent would aid the party's collective electoral fortunes if doing so would endanger his or her own reelection prospects. Furthermore, parties do not want incumbents facing serious electoral threats to redistribute campaign funds, since an incumbent who loses reelection risks the party's goal of majority control. Thus, the more electorally secure members are in their districts, the more money they will redistribute through their principal campaign committees.[3] Cash on hand also plays a particularly crucial role as a control variable in our model. Given the fundraising advantages that members in formal positions of power enjoy (Grier and Munger 1993), they are likely to have larger campaign war chests than members without such posts. Including a cash-on-hand variable therefore ensures that any relationship found between holding a leadership post and redistributing campaign funds is actually due to holding a leadership post (and not to the fundraising advantages associated with holding a leadership position). Thus, the more campaign money with which a member begins the election cycle, the more campaign dollars he or she will redistribute.

By affording members an advantage in raising money from corporate and trade PACs (Cox and Magar 1999), membership in the majority party provides incumbents with an increased capacity to raise surplus campaign funds. These advantages leave majority party members particularly well positioned to take advantage of the less restrictive regulations associated with contributions to the congressional campaign committees through their principal campaign accounts and contributions to candidates through leadership PACs. As a result, we expect that members of the majority party will tend to channel greater sums of campaign money through the congressional campaign committees and leadership PACs, whereas members of the minority party will give more money directly to candidates from their principal campaign accounts.

Members' willingness to contribute to collective goals also is likely to be affected by campaign finance rules. The 96th Congress (1979–80) modified federal campaign finance laws to prohibit retiring members from converting excess campaign funds into personal funds, but members of that Congress "grandfathered" themselves from the prohibition. In 1989, Congress passed a law stating that after the 1992 elections, grandfathered members still serving in Congress would no longer be permitted to take advantage of the exemption (Fritz and Morris 1990, 83; Groseclose and Krehbiel 1994). Thus, through 1992, grandfathered members should be less likely than nongrandfathered members to redistribute campaign funds from their principal campaign accounts.

Political Environment. Finally, we anticipate that party margins will have an impact on members' redistribution activity. As margins narrow, the top party leaders should apply increasing pressure on all members to be more generous in supporting the party and its candidates financially. Members have good reasons to respond more generously, lest they fall out of favor with the leaders who can do much to influence their legislative careers. They also can more easily be persuaded that their contributions make a difference when margins are slim. Thus, in addition to the interactive effects we anticipate between party margins and various leadership positions, we expect that party margins will have an additive effect on all three types of redistribution activity. In particular, the smaller the margin between the two House parties, the more campaign funds each member will redistribute to the party and its candidates.

Regulatory changes should have implications for PCC contributions to candidates and the CCCs. First, the Consolidated Appropriations Act of 2005 raised the limit on members' PCC contributions to candidates from $1,000 to $2,000 per election. It is possible that the new limit, first implemented in the 2005–6 election cycle, would yield increases in contributions from House members' PCCs to other candidates' campaigns. However, $2,000 is still less than half the amount that members with LPACs can legally contribute to candidates. In earlier work (Heberlig and Larson 2005), we found that some members holding institutional positions had already shifted much of their candidate giving from PCCs to LPACs prior to the implementation of BCRA, to take advantage of the higher contribution limits for LPACs. Thus, while the implementation of higher limits for PCC-to-candidate giving is likely to increase such contributions for rank-and-file members, it is not likely to have an interactive effect on PCC-to-candidate giving for elected and extended party leaders, committee chairs, and prestige committee members.

BCRA also has clear consequences for contributions from PCCs to CCCs. By eliminating unlimited soft money contributions, BCRA forced parties to scramble to find hard money sources to replace it. Incumbent members of Congress, with their existing hard money fundraising networks and ability to transfer unlimited sums to the CCCs, provided an obvious target to help parties efficiently and rapidly collect additional hard money. Moreover, by increasing (and indexing for inflation) the limit on individual contributions to members from $1,000 to $2,000, BCRA presumably enhanced incumbents' fundraising capacities. Members holding party and committee leadership posts and prestige committee assignments provide the most likely target for parties to turn to for additional party fundraising assistance. They have leverage over the legislative process and thus leverage over major donors who can be tapped for additional funds. They also are dependent on the party caucus or elected leadership for their positions and thus have the greatest incentive to comply with party fundraising demands. The implementation of BCRA should thus have both additive and interactive effects (with positions), increasing the sums of campaign funds members transfer from their PCCs to the CCCs.

Model Results: Incumbent Contributions to Federal Candidates and the Congressional Campaign Committees

To test these expectations, we employ tobit regression, a type of multivariate regression analysis. Widely used by social scientists, multivariate regression is a powerful technique that permits analysts to estimate simultaneously the effect of each independent variable in a model on the dependent variable, isolated from the effects of the other independent variables in the model. To further illuminate the utility of the technique, consider a simple multivariate regression model with one dependent variable—the sum of money redistributed by a U.S. House member in a given election cycle—and two independent variables: the sum of campaign cash the member has on hand at the beginning of the cycle and whether or not the member holds a party leadership position. Both independent variables are likely to influence the sum of campaign money a House member redistributes. But since party leaders tend to keep more cash on hand than do non-leaders, the effect of holding a party leadership position on money redistributed will be intertwined with the effect of cash on hand—and thus we need a way to separate out, or untangle, these two effects. Multivariate regression offers such a way. In particular, it permits us to estimate (1) the effect of holding a leadership position on the sum of money a member redistributed, purged of the effect of the member's cash on hand; and (2) the effect of a member's cash on hand on the sum of money the member redistributed, purged of the effect of holding a leadership position. We use these types of statistical techniques consistently throughout the remaining chapters of the book to evaluate our hypotheses.

We present tobit analyses of the sums of contributions, adjusted for inflation, given by individual House members. We analyze three dependent variables corresponding to the preceding descriptive analysis: (1) contributions from a member's campaign committee to House candidates, (2) contributions from a member's campaign committee to his or her party's congressional campaign committee, and (3) contributions from a member's leadership PAC to House candidates. We use tobit as the analytic technique because contributions are censored at zero (Long 1997).

Table 4.2 reaffirms the importance of institutional positions in redistributing campaign funds.[4] Party and committee leaders and prestige committee members give significantly more money to other candidates and to their CCCs; they also give significantly more money through LPACs than do other members of Congress. Not surprisingly, the results are substantively strongest for the elected party leaders—on average, a $6,565 increase in campaign contributions from a leader's principal campaign committee to other candidates, a $171,483 increase in contributions from a leader's campaign committee to the party's CCC, and a $118,628 increase in contributions from a leader's PAC to other candidates. Leaders' positions in Congress give them the responsibility to help their party retain power and the leverage to extract money from donors; in the interest of maintaining their positions, they comply.

Other positions are related to giving as well. Committee leaders give significantly more to candidates through LPACs and more to the CCCs, and prestige committee members give more across the board. By contrast, the statistically insignificant extended leadership coefficients in all three

TABLE 4.2. Tobit Analysis of Federal Contributions by Members of the House of Representatives, 1990–2006 Election Cycles

	To Candidates from Incumbent PCCs	To CCCs from Incumbent PCCs	To Candidates from Incumbent LPACs
Position			
Party leader	6,565**	171,483***	118,628***
Committee leader	1,538	23,435**	21,989***
Prestige committee	3,908***	15,551**	20,355***
Unelected party post	1,424	4,154	710
Subcommittee leader	−124	−2,652	−3,434
Contest for position	7,015***	11,108***	29,949***
Blocked advancement	518	−4,571**	−10,572***
Retiring	−315	−19,995***	−8,835
Seeking higher office	−5,517***	−17,155***	−25,846***
Partisanship			
Majority party	−2,484***	1,745	16,068***
Party loyalty scores (z)	1,294***	3,145***	3,800**
Capacity to Contribute			
Electoral margin	105***	240**	107
Cash on hand	.004***	.022***	——
Grandfathered	−4,853**	−2,513	——
Responsiveness to Political Context			
BCRA	6,824***	42,287***	28,343***
Party margins	−109***	−565***	−594***
BCRA–Position Interactions			
Party leader × BCRA	9,292	41,111**	17,131
Committee leader × BCRA	2,404	35,945***	−2,919
Prestige committee × BCRA	−107	2,960	1,743
Extended leader × BCRA	5,897**	542	13,862*
Party Margin–Position Interactions			
Party leader × margin	113**	−1,049***	248
Extended leader × margin	39**	123*	133
Committee leader × margin	26	−267***	28
Prestige committee × margin	−21	−219***	−220*
Constant	−6,497*	−23,529	−407,946***
Ey at mean	28,246	89,575	120,150
$\Phi(z)$ at mean	.61	.50	.08
N	2,940	2,952	2,950
Likelihood ratio χ^2	699***	1,329***	787***

*$p < .10$; **$p < .05$; ***$p < .01$

equations demonstrate that members serving in the extended leadership redistribute no more than others to the CCCs or to other candidates.

The results in table 4.2 show that subcommittee leaders have no special responsibilities in redistributing campaign funds. Indeed, the coefficients for subcommittee leader are statistically indistinguishable from zero in all three regressions. Owing their responsibility to party caucuses on their committees (rather than to the full party caucus), subcommittee leaders appear to have escaped the fundraising responsibilities that now apply to full committee leaders.

Members running for top party and committee leadership posts contribute greater sums of campaign dollars to other candidates and to the CCCs through their principal campaign committees and more through their leadership PACs. Involvement in a leadership contest produces a modest $7,015 increase in campaign contributions to other candidates from a member's PCC, a larger $11,107 increase from the member's PCC to the CCCs, and a still larger $29,949 increase in contributions to candidates from the member's PAC. (Of course, a member running for a leadership post may well give through both types of committees.)

That leadership aspirants give significantly more than other members to the party CCCs was an unexpected finding. In earlier work analyzing the 1990–2000 election cycles (Heberlig and Larson 2005), we found that members vying for leadership positions preferred to give directly to individual candidates—who (if they won) would be part of the electorate in the leadership contest—and did not give significantly more to the parties. With the additional party mobilization during the 2002–6 election cycles, even members seeking party and committee leadership positions gave more to the CCCs. These findings imply that leadership aspirants now must demonstrate their financial commitment to the party's collective electoral efforts rather than merely contributing directly to caucus members who will form the electorate for leadership contests.

The effect of ambition also is apparent in the member's committee status. Members whose committee advancement is blocked by younger members with greater seniority redistribute significantly less to the CCCs and less to candidates through LPACs. For example, blocked members give $4,570 less to the CCCs than do members with open advancement routes. Blocked and unblocked members give similar amounts to other candidates through their PCCs, however, suggesting that LPACs are the primary outlet for advancement-oriented contributions to colleagues.

If members with powerful formal positions are likely to redistribute more money in response to party influence over their career aspirations,

members who are leaving the House through retirement or seeking another office no longer have to please the party or their colleagues. Table 4.2
shows that members who are leaving typically give less money through all
three methods. These results confirm that members give not for the pure
joy of generosity but to advance their career goals; once their immediate
career goals change, their redistribution activity declines forthwith.

Majority party control also affects contribution patterns. The evidence
in table 4.2 suggests that, as predicted, members of the majority party tend
to route larger sums of contributions through leadership PACs, while
members of the minority party give more money directly to candidates.
There is no difference in party status and contributions to the CCCs, as
the Democrats closed the GOP advantage from the 1996–2000 period (cf.
Heberlig and Larson 2005). Substantively, majority party membership has
the biggest influence on LPAC contributions; majority party incumbents
give through LPACs an average of $16,068 more than members of the mi-
nority party. As noted earlier, majority party members have greater capacity to raise money (Cox and Magar 1999) and can redistribute it through
the venues with the least restrictive contribution limits. Majority status
also confers the enhanced fundraising ability necessary to market an
LPAC successfully.

As expected, a member's support for party policy also influences contributions. In particular, the statistically significant estimates for party loyalty in all three equations indicate that the more a member supports his or
her party's majority on the House floor, the more campaign dollars that
member redistributes to other candidates and to the party's CCC. Substantively, the party loyalty estimates seem fairly modest. At the mean of the
sample, a one-unit increase in party loyalty produces an average increase of
just $1,294 in contributions from members' principal campaign commit-
tees to other candidates, $3,145 from members' campaign committees to
the party CCCs, and $3,800 from members' LPACs to other candidates.

A member's capacity to contribute also affects his or her contribution
behavior. The more campaign cash a member begins the election cycle
with, the more he or she gives to candidates and to the CCCs.[5] But even
relatively large increases in cash on hand spur only limited generosity
among incumbents. For example, we computed that a change from
$44,694 to $362,724 in cash on hand[6] led to an average increase of just
$7,125 in contributions to the party CCCs. Members involved in uncom-
petitive races are significantly more likely than members in competitive
contests to contribute through their principal campaign committees to
other candidates and to the CCCs. Conversely, no relationship exists be-

tween previous margin and giving through an LPAC. As predicted, members exempted from ethics laws prohibiting the conversion of campaign funds for personal use gave less to candidates through their principal campaign committees. But these members redistributed no more or less to the CCCs through their PCCs or to candidates via an LPAC.

Critically for our theory, members also respond to the level of competitiveness for the control of the institution. Incumbents give significantly more money using all three methods as the seat margin between the parties declines (as indicated by the negative coefficients). We computed that an increase in party margins from 23 to 55 seats (one standard deviation) led to an average decrease of $17,838 in contributions from members' principal campaign accounts to the party CCCs. This finding is consistent with our reasoning that party leaders will pressure members to be more generous as party margins tighten.

Just as members respond to the battle for majority status, they also responded to the implementation of BCRA. As predicted, all members increased their contributions to candidates and to CCCs in the election cycles governed by BCRA. Clearly, members responded to the increased party pressure to replace CCC soft money banned by BCRA and, in 2006, took advantage of the increased contribution limits governing contributions from members' PCCs to candidates. Indeed, members gave an average of $42,287 more from their principal campaign committees to the CCCs in the post-BCRA period than in the pre-BCRA period.

As predicted, the effect of several leadership variables on contributions is conditioned by party margins and the implementation of BCRA. In general, members responded to close margins and BCRA in their contributions to the CCCs—consistent with party mobilization activities—and were less responsive with contributions to candidates. Elected party leaders, chairs and ranking members, and prestige committee members all gave significantly less to their CCCs when seat margins widened. This finding supplies critical support for our theory that responsiveness to the party's collective electoral goals depends on the level of competition for majority control and the member's institutional level of responsibility to the party caucus. Similarly, elected party leaders and committee leaders contributed significantly more to the CCCs after the implementation of BCRA. Finally, members in the extended leadership organization gave more to candidates through both their principal campaign committees and LPACs in the post-BCRA era than they gave in the pre-BCRA period.

However, for the most part, PCC contributions to candidates by members with important formal positions tend to be only weakly related to party margins or BCRA. In fact, the top party leaders, as well as members in unelected party posts, appear to contribute slightly more campaign money from their PCCs to other candidates when party margins are larger than when they are smaller. Only members of the extended leadership redistributed significantly more from their PCCs to other candidates after BCRA than prior to it. These results demonstrate the party's success in persuading members with responsibility to the party to contribute to the party CCC rather than directly to individual candidates. Party mobilization allows the contributions to be directed in ways that benefit the party's collective electoral strategy rather than the individual goals of the incumbent donor.

Incumbent Contributions to State and Local Parties

The overall redistribution patterns in figure 4.1 show that the campaign funds given by members of Congress to state and local party organizations are minimal compared to the sums they contribute to the national party CCCs. The rise in contributions to state and party organizations also lags, in timing and amount, behind the rise in contributions to the CCCs. Most House members focus their giving entirely on the national level: of the House members who sought reelection and redistributed any campaign funds, over three-fourths (77.7 percent) gave only to federal candidates or CCCs and did not contribute to state or local party organizations. In contrast, a mere 2.4 percent of redistributors contributed only to state and/or local party organizations but not to federal candidates or parties. It is not surprising that House members are more likely to contribute at the federal level, where their careers are focused. But the dominant focus of redistribution to the federal level is quite dramatic.

To be sure, there has been an increase in redistribution activity by House members to state and local party organizations. We hypothesize that the increase in funding of state and local party organizations is largely a spillover effect of the parties' mobilization of redistribution at the national level. State and local parties have little power over the career advancement of members of Congress (perhaps with the exception of those seeking statewide office, a topic we will explore in chapter 8); members of Congress therefore have little reason to be responsive for their requests for money. There is also not much incentive for House members to increase the amounts they contribute to state and local party organizations over time. The battle for majority control of the House that has fueled incumbent contributions at the national level would be unlikely to fuel a similar increase in funds for state and local parties. In fact, the congressional parties' stepped-up demands for incumbent campaign money, combined with incumbents' risk aversion, may have the effect of making less incumbent money available for state and local party organizations. But we believe that members of Congress, increasingly socialized into sharing their campaign resources at the national level (Sinclair 2006, 141), have begun to extend such practices to the state and local sphere. We measure the spillover phenomenon by the amount of adjusted funds a member of Congress redistributed at the federal level in the previous election cycle.[7] If there is a spillover effect, a member's federal redistribution in the previous election cycle ($cycle_{t-1}$) should be positively related to their redistribution at the state and local level in the subsequent election cycle ($cycle_t$). Similarly, a member's redistribution to state parties in election $cycle_{t-1}$ will increase contributions to local organizations in the subsequent cycle.

The implementation of BCRA also has relevance for the redistribution of campaign money by members of Congress to state and local party organizations. Soft money transfers from national party organizations were a substantial source of revenue for state party organizations during the 1990s (Dwyre 1996; La Raja 2006). Legislation to prevent federal party organizations from collecting soft money contributions and to bar members of Congress from helping to raise it would thus have a substantial effect on state party finances. So, just as the CCCs turned to members of Congress for assistance in replacing soft money with hard money, state and local parties would be likely to do the same. Thus, redistribution to state and local parties should increase following the implementation of BCRA.

Unlike our model of contributions to the CCCs and federal candidates, however, we do not expect incumbent contributions to state and local parties to be a function of holding an influential party or committee leadership position in the House. Members who serve in positions of power in Congress are responsible to the caucus that elected them or the party leaders who appointed them, not to state or local party organizations. Thus, while party and committee leaders have ample reason to comply with demands for funds from the congressional party, they have no more reason than any other member to comply with requests for funds from state and local parties. Moreover, the national orientation of congressional leaders may well lead them to emphasize building and maintaining relationships more in Washington, D.C., than within their states and localities. To the extent that members with positions do give more to state and local parties, it is likely to be because their high-profile status and accompanying fundraising prowess make them likely targets for requests from such organizations. Controlling for the fact that these positions redistribute generously at the federal level—the spillover effect—may supersede any potential relationship between formal positions and contributions to state or local parties.

State and local political conditions also are likely to be relevant to explaining the redistribution of member campaign funds to state and local parties. First, members of Congress are likely to contribute to state parties when elections are competitive in their home state. One way of measuring competitiveness in a state is the Ranney index of interparty competition (Ranney 1976). It is based on three components: (1) the proportion of elections in which each party wins gubernatorial elections and the percentage of seats for each party in the state legislature, (2) the length of time each party controls the governorship and state legislature, and (3) the proportion of time the two parties split control of the governorship and legislature. Close competition for high-profile statewide offices in particular election cycles may attract contributions from members of Congress to state parties. The most competitive contests are typically open seats; thus open-seat gubernatorial or U.S. Senate campaigns may increase incumbent contributions to state parties. Of course, members of the House can also contribute directly to gubernatorial and/or Senate campaigns, and they may make such contributions in addition to or instead of contributions to the state party.

Second, the strength of party organizations may affect the level of redistribution from members of Congress. We have mixed expectations regarding the relationship between state party strength and incumbent contributions. On one hand, strong party organizations are likely to be more electorally effective than weak state parties, and the effectiveness with which a state party uses campaign funds may inspire incumbents to support it financially. On the other hand, members of Congress may give money to state or local parties to compensate for their weakness—with stronger state and local organizations in need of fewer dollars from incumbents to finance their activities and operations. In this latter perspective, incumbents know they must help finance state and local party activities, lest they cease to occur. Just as members of Congress use their office staff to supplement weak local party organizations (Monroe 2001), members may contribute to state and local parties in order to ensure that they have sufficient resources to assist their own campaign and other House candidates in the state. We use the measures of state and local party organizational strength by Cotter and others (1984). The specific values of their measures are factor scores of 12 resources and activities engaged in by state and local parties (including budgets, staffing, recruitment, programs, leadership, etc.), based on interviews and surveys of state and county party chairs in the late 1970s. Although these measures are dated, they are the most complete set of measures available of state party strength.

Third, a member of Congress's past political experience may be relevant to their contribution patterns. Members who have served in state government are more likely to have relationships with state party officials and thus may be more likely to contribute to state party organizations. We code experience in both state elective offices and state party organizations. Similarly, House members with experience in local elective offices and party posts should be more likely to contribute to local party organizations.

Fourth, a member's ambition for statewide office should influence his or her willingness to contribute to state party committees. Members seeking to build relationships with state officials to facilitate a statewide run may be more likely to contribute to state party coffers than will be members with static ambition. Brace (1984) and Rohde (1979) note that state size negatively impacts the probability that a House member will seek statewide office. Specifically, the greater the number of congressional districts in a state, the more difficult it is for a House member to gain a statewide following and the more competition he or she faces from other House members for higher office—thus decreasing the probability of a statewide run. Extending this logic, we expect state size to impact incumbent contributions to state and local parties as well. In particular, the larger the number of congressional districts in a state, the less likely the member is to have statewide ambition and, in turn, the fewer dollars the member will contribute to the state party. In contrast, the larger the state, the more important the local party organization should be to the member—hence increasing the sums of dollars members will redistribute to local parties. Indeed, Californian Bill Thomas's campaign contributions, highlighted at the start of this chapter, reflect precisely such a pattern. As a member of a large state delegation, Thomas gave nothing to the state Republican Party but made small contributions to local party organizations.

Several other variables in the regressions for federal campaign contributions remain in the state and local models: cash on hand, previous electoral margin, subcommittee chairs, party loyalty voting, majority party, "grandfathered" status, and retiring or seeking higher office. We expect they will perform similarly.

Results: The Redistribution of House Member Campaign Funds to State and Local Party Organizations

As with our models for incumbent contributions at the federal level, we use Tobit analysis to estimate incumbent contributions to state and local parties. Tobit accounts for the censoring of contributions at zero.

State Party Organizations

Table 4.3 shows similarities and differences between House members' contributions to state and national entities. The results also provide evidence for the interconnectedness of member giving: the more a member redistributes at the federal level in election cycle$_{t-1}$, the more he or she redistributes to his or her state party organization in the subsequent election cycle. As members are increasingly socialized to be team players at the national level, state party organizations benefit from the spillover effect.

We see, further, that BCRA's implementation had a positive and significant effect on incumbent redistribution to state parties. BCRA cut off federal and state party access to soft money, and both levels of party organization relied on incumbents to help them offset the loss. House members responded generously to state party organizations, just as they did to the national party CCCs. Since 2006, these trends have continued as House member giving to state parties has nearly tripled, rising to $9.7 million in 2008 and $14.7 million in 2010.

House members also respond to state political characteristics in making contribution decisions. They are likely to contribute to weak state party organizations more than to strong ones, as indicated by the statistically significant negative relationship between state party strength and contributions. Members of Congress apparently contribute generously out of their own self-interest; they provide resources to weak state party organizations that, without fundraising help, would be of little strategic use to incumbents or to the party's nonincumbent House candidates. In contrast, strong state parties can raise the funds to be strategically effective without being underwritten by an incumbent's campaign.

Open-seat gubernatorial contests also lead to larger incumbent contributions to state parties, though having a U.S. Senate seat on the ballot appears to have no effect. Presumably, should House members wish to contribute in Senate campaigns, they can give directly to their party's candidate and/or to the Senate Hill committees rather than to the state

TABLE 4.3.   Tobit Analysis of Contributions by Members of the House of Representatives to State and Local Party Organizations, 1990–2006 Election Cycles

	To State Party Organizations	To Local Party Organizations
Spillover Effects		
Federal contributions$_{t-1}$	.002***	−.001
State contributions$_{t-1}$	—	.003
State and Local Factors		
State office	1,031**	—
Local office	—	9.36
Party competition	1,059	−1,198
State party strength	−2,771**	—
Local party strength	—	25
Open gubernatorial seat	1,112**	32
Open senate seat	−792	−55
Size of House delegation	−147***	41***
Position		
Party leader	2	215
Unelected leader	−17	69
Committee leader	1,747**	256
Prestige committee	1,602***	284*
Subcommittee leader	−920**	111
Contest for position	1,254	−224
Blocked advancement	691	141
Retiring	−1,298	−11
Seeking higher office	−2,927**	−444
Partisanship		
Majority party	−2,944***	−177
Party loyalty scores (z)	−39	75
Capacity to Contribute		
Electoral margin	55***	6
Cash on hand	.003***	.001**
Grandfathered	−6,119***	−721
Implementation of BCRA		
BCRA	5,059***	494**
Constant	−36,064**	−24,461**
Ey at mean	22,158	5,581
$\Phi(z)$ at mean	.22	.05
N	2,950	2,938
Likelihood ratio χ^2	317***	159***

*$p < .10$; ** $p < .05$; ***$p < .01$

party. The absence of a relationship between the Ranney index and member contributions indicates that the level of state party competition outside of specific high-profile contests has no effect on House members' generosity to state parties.

As expected, House members who previously served in state government or in state party posts are significantly more likely to contribute to their state party organization than are House members with no statewide experience. Even after they have left for Washington, members continue to maintain relationships built in their precongressional political careers. A member's potential statewide ambitions are relevant to contributions to state parties as well. In particular, the larger the state and, thus, the less likely a House member is to seek statewide office, the fewer dollars he or she redistributes to state parties. Simply put, the less need incumbents have to build ties with state party officials, the fewer incumbent dollars state parties receive.

Apart from findings unique to our state party model, table 4.3 also presents results consistent with our findings at the federal level. First, a member's financial capacity to contribute makes for greater generosity. Members with larger stocks of cash on hand and safer districts give more to state party organizations than do their less financially and electorally secure colleagues. These members can afford to be generous; they can give at both the state and federal level without substantially increasing their own electoral risk.

Members' career paths also influence their contributions to state parties, in the same manner they impact their contributions at the federal level. Members grandfathered by 1970s campaign finance laws—those allowed to keep their campaign funds if they retired by 1992—were less likely to contribute to state party organizations. Retirees and members seeking higher office also appear to give less to state parties, although the estimate for retirees falls short of conventional levels of statistical significance. Retirees' career goals are no longer advanced by federal or state parties, lessening the need for retirees to maintain relationships with these organizations. Members seeking statewide office, in contrast, have a clear and immediate need for assistance from state party officials to achieve their career goals. However, they need substantial sums of money to run their statewide campaigns and are likely to transfer funds from their House campaign account to their Senate or (if allowed by state law) gubernatorial accounts rather than contributing to the state party.

Some institutional positions—but importantly not all—have similar contribution patterns at the federal and state levels. Committee leaders and members of prestige committees both contribute significantly more than their colleagues to state parties. Subcommittee leaders contribute significantly less to state parties. Elected and extended party leaders, however, do not give significantly more or less than their colleagues to state party organizations. The party activity of elected and extended leaders is focused on the House and does not extend to assisting home-state party organizations.[8] Members whose committee advancement is blocked in the House give less to the CCCs and to federal candidates through LPACs, but they appear to give no more or less to state party organizations.

Interestingly, members of the majority party contribute significantly less to state parties than do members of the minority party. Majority party members have their own power to defend in Washington and prioritize giving at the federal level in order to maintain their party's majority.

Local Party Organizations

Contributions from House members to local party organizations are not only relatively small in size and relatively rare; they are also, according to our results, somewhat idiosyncratic to the individual member of Congress. Only three variables are related to contributions to local party organizations at conventional levels of statistical significance ($p < .05$): cash on hand, the number of House seats in the state, and the implementation of BCRA. Still, our results show that at least some of the variables that explain incumbent contributions to state parties also account for incumbent contributions to local organizations. For one, just as House party and committee leaders were no more generous than their colleagues in giving to state parties, the top leaders exhibited no additional generosity in contributing to local parties. House members also gave more generously to local parties, as they did to federal and state parties, when they had large sums of cash on hand. Finally, members responded to BCRA by stepping up their assistance to local parties, presumably to offset the loss of soft money that local parties could no longer legally receive from the national party committees. Such assistance grew dramatically from the 2006 to the 2008 election cycles, jumping from $382,000 to $888,000. Contributions to local parties faded somewhat in 2010 to $528,000.

Table 4.3 demonstrates that incumbent contributions to local parties have some unique dynamics. As hypothesized, House members from larger states are less likely to contribute to state party organizations but are more likely to contribute to local party organizations. Because members' probability of advancement is inhibited in large states, they have less need to build relationships to state organizations and will instead solidify their relationships with local party organizations.

Modeling incumbent contributions to state and local parties separately from incumbent contributions to national political committees has allowed us to uncover systematic differences in the motivations incumbents have for redistributing campaign funds across various levels of the electoral system. While we find evidence for spillover effects—members' previous contributions to federal parties increases their probability of contributions to state parties—many of the variables that explain state-level contributions are unique to the political dynamics in the states. Moreover, compelling explanations for the redistribution of incumbent campaign funds to national committees do little to explain member contributions to local party organizations. Such results are encouraging, for they confirm that each party organization plays a different role in the careers and fulfills different types of political goals for members of the House.

Incumbents therefore respond accordingly. They direct most of their contributions to national candidates and parties, and they have responded to the battle for majority control and to the CCCs' loss of soft money. Members with formal positions whose power is most dependent on majority control have been the most responsive. State and local parties can do less to advance the careers of most House members; they therefore receive less assistance from incumbents than do national committees. But state and local parties have nevertheless benefited from the efforts of national parties to promote incumbent generosity. Finally, in making contribution decisions, House members are responsive to the needs of their respective state parties, and—for House members contemplating future statewide campaigns—the importance of ties to state party leaders.

Conclusion

Where there was once limited campaign giving by members of Congress—especially to the parties themselves—there is now substantial giving. Where once giving was done by only leaders or the highly ambitious, now almost everyone has joined the effort. Once the parties prioritized majority party control and mobilized members to contribute toward that goal, they began behaving like coherent, coordinated electoral organizations.

Institutions and institutional incentives matter. This chapter provides consistent evidence that giving by members of Congress is highly dependent on the institutional position of the donor, the institutional power stakes afforded by the political environment, and the parties' efforts to direct member contributions in ways that will advance the collective goal of majority status. When parties mobilized electorally and sought to tie institutional positions and power to a member's financial support for the party's electoral goals, they were able to overcome collective action dilemmas and entice self-interested incumbents to give generously. The parties have been particularly successful at exploiting campaign finance rules that permit members to give unlimited sums from their PCCs to the party CCCs—a development that has produced a massive shift in how members of Congress direct their campaign contributions. Additionally, members with partisan institutional positions—and thus the members with the most power at risk—are the most responsive to changes in partisan margins and to the campaign finance environment. At the same time, they are not particularly responsive to state and local party organizations, which hold no sway over their power.

Although individual members are increasingly responsive to the parties, they have not abandoned their individual goals. Rather, they have adapted how they achieve their individual goals to the new era of partisan competition on Capitol Hill. Members who are not dependent on the parties to achieve their power or policy goals or who have no interest in advancing in party and committee hierarchies can get away with contributing smaller sums.

The increase in redistribution to state and local parties suggests that members give for reasons other than advancing within the congressional party. Contributing to state or local parties provides little direct benefit to members of Congress. The spillover effect we document in this chapter suggests the role of experiential learning by members of Congress. Incumbents are mobilized to contribute by the congressional party, learn the efficacy of redistribution as a party-building activity, and extend their new redistributive habits to other party organizations. If redistribution is seen by members as an expected part of campaign activity, especially as new members of Congress are quickly socialized into the activity, redistribution could continue at high levels regardless of the party margins in Congress or the likelihood of a change in majority status in any given election cycle.

APPENDIX: VARIABLE MEASUREMENTS

Adjusted campaign contributions: the sum of a member's contributions from his or her principal campaign committee to other candidates' campaigns or the party congressional campaign committee. Incumbent contributions were calculated by the authors based on data obtained from the Federal Election Commission. To compare contributions across eight election cycles in which contributions escalated substantially, we set all contributions at their 2000 value. First, we divided that election cycle's total member contributions (EC_t) by the total member contributions in 2000 (EC_{2000}). That proportion was then inverted so that, when multiplied by EC_t, EC_t equals EC_{2000}. Each member's contribution for EC_t was then multiplied by the same proportion. Essentially, we are measuring each member's percentage of total contributions for that year and expressing it in terms of 2000 dollars. In this way, the effect of each year's contributions on advancement can be assessed on the same basis as every other year's (see also Heberlig 2003). In this chapter, adjusted campaign contributions are used only to present descriptive data. This measure is not used in any of the analyses.

Aggregate federal contributions$_{t-1}$: the sum of a member's PCC and LPAC contributions to candidates and the party CCC in the preceding election cycle.

BCRA: 1 = election cycle following the implementation of the Bipartisan Campaign Reform Act (2004, 2006); 0 = otherwise.

Blocked advancement: 1 = on all the committees on which a member serves, a younger member has greater seniority; 0 = on at least one committee, all representatives with greater seniority are older than the member.

Cash on hand: total dollars remaining in the incumbent's personal campaign committee at the end of the previous cycle.

Committee leaders: 1 = chair or ranking member of a standing committee; 0 = otherwise.

Contributions to candidates (dependent variable): total contributions from an incumbent's principal campaign committee to candidates of the incumbent's party in an election cycle, adjusted for inflation.

Contributions to local parties (dependent variable): total contributions from an incumbent's principal campaign committee to the incumbent's local party organizations in an election cycle, adjusted for inflation.

Contributions to state parties (dependent variable): total contributions from an incumbent's PCC to the incumbent's state party organization in an election cycle, adjusted for inflation.

Contributions to state parties$_{t-1}$: total contributions from an incumbent's PCC to the incumbent's state party organization in the previous election cycle, adjusted for inflation.

Contributions to the party congressional campaign committee (dependent variable): total contributions from an incumbent's PCC to the incumbent's party CCC in an election cycle, adjusted for inflation.

Elected leaders: 1 = Speaker, floor leader, whip, caucus/conference chair or other officer, or chair of party committee (e.g., CCC); 0 = otherwise.

Election margin: a member's percent of the vote in the previous election cycle.

Extended party leadership: 1 = member of whip system, Steering Committee, Policy Committee, or CCC; 0 = otherwise.

Governor open seat: 1 = no incumbent seeking reelection for governor in the incumbent's state in election cycle; 0 = otherwise.

Grandfathered: 1 = members first elected in the 96th Congress or before who were eligible to convert campaign funds for personal use if they retired during or before the 1992 election cycle; 0 = otherwise.

Leadership PAC contributions (dependent variable): total contributions from an incumbent's LPAC to candidates of the incumbent's party in an election cycle, adjusted for inflation.

Local office: 1 = member held an elective local office or was a local party official prior to election to Congress; 0 = otherwise. Coded based on information in members' biographies in Congressional Quarterly's *Politics in America*.

Local party strength: Cotter et al. 1984, 52–53, table 3.8. The specific values of Cotter et al.'s measure are factor scores of 12 resources and activities engaged in by state and local parties (including budgets, staffing, recruitment, programs, leadership, etc.), based on interviews and surveys of state and county party chairs in the late 1970s. A few state parties did not participate in Cotter et al.'s survey. We filled in the missing values for these state parties by averaging the party's scores in geographically contiguous states.

Majority party: 1 = member of the majority party; 0 = otherwise.

Number of House seats: number of House districts in the incumbent's state.

Party loyalty voting: the z-score of a member's Congressional Quarterly score in party loyalty voting (adjusted for attendance). The z-score is used to make the scores comparable across different sessions of Congress.

Party seat margin: difference between the number of seats held by the majority and minority parties during the current session of Congress.

Prestige committee member: 1 = member of Appropriations, Rules, or Ways and Means committee; 0 = otherwise.

Retiring: 1 = member announced his or her intention to retire during or at the end of the Congress and did not run for another elective office; 0 = otherwise.

Seeking higher office: 1 = member ran for a different elected office; 0 = otherwise.

Senate open seat: 1 = no incumbent seeking reelection for the U.S. Senate in the incumbent's state in election cycle; 0 = otherwise.

Sought party or committee leadership post: 1 = named by *CQ Weekly Report* as a contestant for an elected party leadership post or a committee chair/ranking member post; 0 = otherwise.

State office: 1 = member held an elective state office or was a state party official prior to election to Congress; 0 = otherwise. Coded based on information in members' biographies in Congressional Quarterly's *Politics in America*.

State party competition: Ranney (1976) index of interparty competition, based on (1) the proportion of elections in which each party wins gubernatorial elections and the percentage of seats for each party in the state legislature, (2) the length of time each party controls the governorship and state legislature, and (3) the proportion of time the two parties split control of the governorship and legislature. We use the values of the Ranney index for the corresponding election cycle as calculated in the relevant edition of Congressional Quarterly's *Politics in the American States.*

State party strength: Cotter et al. 1984, 28–29, table 2.4. The specific values of Cotter et al.'s measure are factor scores of 12 resources and activities engaged in by state and local parties (including budgets, staffing, recruitment, programs, leadership, etc.), based on interviews and surveys of state and county party chairs in the late 1970s. A few state parties did not participate in Cotter et al.'s survey. We filled in the missing values for these state parties by averaging the party's scores in geographically contiguous states.

Subcommittee leader: 1 = chair or ranking member of a subcommittee of a standing committee; 0 = otherwise.

5 | Brother, Can You Spare a Thousand? Who Gives to Whom?

One of the most popular ways to curry support is to buy it. It is an unspoken prerequisite that a [leadership] candidate has to be an aggressive fundraiser who has campaigned for GOP candidates and, more important, has directed tens of thousands of dollars to the campaign accounts of his or her colleagues.

—Jim VandeHei in the *Washington Post* (2006)

Traditionally, political scientists and media observers have believed that leadership aspirants contribute campaign funds to advance their own ambitions and that there is little collective benefit of their behavior for the party. In fact, purely self-interested behaviors by members of Congress often create less-than-optimal collective consequences for efficient or effective political parties, institutional operations, or public policy. By analyzing members' contribution strategies, this chapter seeks to understand how members use money—particularly contributions to candidates—to achieve their goals.

Traditional explanations for why members of Congress contribute and to whom they contribute emphasize that these contributions help members achieve their individual goals: winning leadership positions, building legislative coalitions, and assisting allies (R. Baker 1989; Currinder 2003; Heberlig 2003; Wilcox 1989). We distinguish between individualist and party-centered contribution strategies for achieving one's goals, with the former strategy aimed at building coalitions of loyal followers and the latter designed to maximize the party's number of seats. The extant research on member contributions to other candidates, which focuses almost exclusively on leadership PAC contributions, suggests that both individualistic and party-centered strategies are at work (e.g., Currinder 2003; Kanthak 2007; Wilcox 1989, 1990). Our task in this chapter is to measure how much of a role each plays and the extent to which the balance of these strategies has changed over time as parties have increased their mobilization efforts and as more members participate in the redistribution of campaign funds.

This chapter demonstrates that collective partisan objectives—targeting money to candidates in close races as a means of winning or maintaining majority status—overwhelm individual strategies in explaining the allocation of member contributions. We conclude that members still contribute to advance their own individual goals within the institution. But in an era of centralized congressional parties and tight party competition, members must serve their party's collective electoral needs if they want to advance their individual goals within the institution (Cox and McCubbins 1993, 2005). By controlling the structure of opportunities for institutional advancement, congressional parties harness members' individual goals of power and place them in the service of the party's own collective well-being.

Individualist versus Party-Centered Contribution Strategies

While members claim various reasons for making contributions to other candidates, we distinguish between individualist and party-centered contribution strategies for achieving one's goals. An incumbent employing an individualist strategy uses campaign money to build coalitions of loyal followers that can be mobilized in leadership races or legislative efforts. He or she responds to party pressures to redistribute money by contributing to candidates best positioned to return the favor—for example, safe incumbents (who form the bulk of the electorate in leadership contests), committee colleagues, and members from one's state delegation. Underlying the individualist strategy is an implicit quid pro quo arrangement. The member donor uses money to achieve his or her individual goals by cashing in chits accumulated from the dollars he or she redistributes.

By contrast, an incumbent employing a party-centered strategy contributes in order to serve the party's collective electoral interests. He or she responds to party calls for money by giving to candidates running in contests on which the party's numerical strength is most likely to hinge—for example, those in competitive campaigns (particularly nonincumbents). Underlying the party-centered strategy is that members advance their individual goals not primarily by exchanging dollars for votes in a pay-to-play system but, rather, by serving the party's collective electoral goals. By working to win a party majority, party-centered redistributors gain credit from rank-and-file members who appreciate their team efforts. In the process, donors increase the value of their own power by increasing the odds that their party will win a majority.

The individualistic perspective has clearly been the dominant perspective in thinking about member contributions to candidates from both principal campaign committees and LPACs, but especially the latter. Indeed, such a perspective drives nearly all of the thinking about member contributions among journalists and government reform organizations such as Common Cause (e.g., Drew 1999; Eilperin 2006; Jackson 1988). As with the VandeHei quote that opened this chapter, a 1994 editorial in the Capitol Hill newspaper *Roll Call* exemplifies this position, asserting that LPACs are "sophisticated vote-buying machines for leadership candidates, who use them to secure votes for internal races that should be decided not on the basis of money but on the ability to lead" (*Roll Call* 1994, 4). The fear is that members give to one another for self-interested reasons and that money has overshadowed other, presumably more meritorious attributes in selecting House leaders.

The individualistic perspective on LPACs has also been the dominant perspective, if perhaps less bluntly wielded, in the academic literature. While Ross Baker (1989), for example, characterizes member contribution activity prior to the late 1970s as mostly goodwill gestures by those who had ample campaign cash toward those who needed it, the process changed, he argues, with the rise of LPACs. Members formed such committees, Baker argues, to increase the sums they were able to give to colleagues as a means of building personal coalitions. Moreover, rather than helping the parties, LPACs would hurt them by allowing members to raise and spend even more funds independent of the party organizations. LPACs could also be expected to allocate funds in ways that advanced the personal ambitions of their sponsors at the expense of party unity. Even when the LPAC sponsor is a party leader, money from a member's LPAC inevitably buys loyalty to the individual leader, not to the party collectively.[1]

Much of the other academic literature on LPAC contributions to candidates highlights the individualistic framework as well.[2] Sorauf (1988), for example, refers to LPACs as "personal PACs," reflecting what he views as the individualistic nature of LPAC goals and contribution strategies. Similarly, Wilcox (1990, 177) quotes the staff member of a representative who sponsored an LPAC as saying, "The Congressman formed the PAC because he wanted to be a major player in the House. There is no question that he gets more respect because of it." Even some of the more recent literature on LPACs retains strong roots in the individualistic tradition. For example,

Pearson's analysis (2001) of members who sponsored LPACs in the 2000 election cycle highlights the finding that members who hold party and committee leadership posts and those who will likely compete for these posts in the next Congress were significantly more likely to have PACs.

The views of House members themselves also appear to support the conventional wisdom that money is used to advance members' intra-institutional ambitions. As Representative B put it, "Leaders [contribute to other candidates] to build a little bit of loyalty and support for their particular leadership roles. The Speaker and the majority leader, both of whom have contributed to my campaigns . . . , assume I will remember their largesse with a degree of favor when the time comes."[3] "I would never have any [other] reason for a PAC," noted Representative Charles Rangel (D-NY), one of the three candidates in the 1986 contest for Democratic majority whip (quoted in Benenson 1986, 1751).

Indeed, the connections between personal advancement and LPAC contributions are made remarkably explicit in a newsletter/fundraising solicitation distributed by Representative Bill McCollum's (R-FL) Countdown to Majority LPAC in the fall of 1994, when McCollum was campaigning for the top Republican whip post in the House.

> McCollum is in a tight three-way race for the number two job in the Republican leadership. An absolute majority is required for election, and a runoff is probable in this race. The election will be decided by the votes of those 40 or 50 or more freshman Republicans who will be elected for the first time in November. Countdown to Majority is recognized as Bill McCollum's PAC. To the degree that it is successful raising funds and making contributions to Republican candidates who are elected to Congress this fall it enhances McCollum's chances to be elected Whip. (Countdown to Majority Political Action Committee 1994, 1, 3)

The individualistic perspective, it is also worth noting, does not rule out that member contributions can yield collective partisan benefits (in terms of electing additional party candidates). But such benefits are viewed as the fortunate by-product of individualistic strategies rather than as the result of an explicit party-based contribution strategy (Brown and Peabody 1992; Canon 1989; Currinder 2003; Kolodny 1998; Salmore and Salmore 1989, 268–70).

More recently, some scholars have emphasized a party-centered perspective of member contributions. Paul Herrnson (2004, 103; 2009), for example, refers to LPAC and PCC contributions as "party-connected" money. He adopts this characterization because LPAC and PCC allocation patterns so closely mirror those of the congressional campaign committees. Herrnson notes that member contributions often follow the cues of party leaders as leaders attempt to coordinate the party's electoral activities. The point of the party's efforts to mobilize money from incumbents, after all, is to increase the resources devoted to winning the most competitive contests. Bedlington and Malbin (2003, 130, 133) explicitly question the individualistic perspective, noting, "[T]here are two problems with the standard explanation [that the intent of redistribution is to build coalitions of loyal followers]. First most of the . . . top givers were fairly secure in their party or committee leadership positions. They appeared not to be lobbying to change their relative positions *within* the party, but fighting to be part of the majority party" (their italics). Our analysis in the previous chapter confirms this: members contesting for positions are big givers, but members already holding positions are bigger givers.

We argue that contribution allocations will primarily follow party-centered patterns. Though contributions are undoubtedly made to help members advance their careers, member advancement just as surely occurs within an institutional context structured by the political parties. It is the party caucus that elects the top party leaders, and it is the top party leaders who make appointments to lower-level party posts. Parties also control assignments to committees and committee leadership posts. The party caucus expects that in exchange for power, members demonstrate their ability to serve the party's good (Cox and McCubbins 1993). If members use the redistribution of campaign funds to demonstrate their ability to serve the party's collective interests, it will be through giving in ways that help the party obtain and retain majority status, not simply by buying the votes of a minimum winning coalition of incumbents.

If redistributed campaign funds are designed to demonstrate a member's commitment to the collective good of the caucus, members' contributions should be allocated in a way that maximizes the party's number of seats; that is, member dollars should flow predominantly to contests that help the party electorally, rather than to incumbents, who will be the primary recipients if contributions are little more than bribes to colleagues in exchange for votes in leadership contests. Here we develop a model of member contributions to evaluate what motivates contributions and the extent to which allocation decisions change over time in response to the intensity of the battle for majority control and coordination by party leaders (see also Heberlig and Larson 2010).

Regardless of the party's effort to mobilize and coordinate contributions, individual incumbents must decide to whom to contribute and how much to contribute to each. As Representative B (a Democrat) explained, the information provided by the Democratic Congressional Campaign Committee "does not automatically trigger the response of sending campaign funds to these people." Rather, he noted, the information provided by the party committee serves mostly as a catalyst for discussion among members themselves.

> Then what happens is there is usually an informal communication process that takes place on the floor or committee or wherever, and a member will say, "I see you are on the list of the top ten endangered Democrats—anything I can do to help you?" And if you say, "Yeah, I'm likely to need some money," they will send some.[4]

Our task is to explain why some members contribute to some candidates and not to others.

The Effects of Party Mobilization

Although incumbents decide individually to whom to contribute, the political environment in which they make such decisions varies from election cycle to election cycle. The increase in power of congressional party leaders (e.g., Rohde 1991) and their increased role in coordinating party electoral activities (Kolodny and Dwyre 1998; Dwyre et al. 2006) are likely to be a critical influence on members' contribution patterns. In the absence of significant party pressure, contributing members would use their own criteria to decide who received their contributions. If they wanted to contribute to candidates in competitive races, they could; if they wanted to advance their own legislative or advancement goals, they could. But as the battle for majority status intensifies and party leaders take a more active role in mobilizing and coordinating contributions, contributions should become more party-centered (Buchler 2004). While members still make their own decisions about whether to contribute and to whom to give, members increasingly make contributions in response to demands from party leaders and will increasingly take cues from party leaders. We have already seen evidence of this trend in chapter 4 as members dramatically increased their giving to party congressional campaign committees. Did party coordination efforts also affect the distribution of funds from incumbents to other party candidates?

One way to assess this question is to divide the contributions by their recipient. We use three recipient categories: (1) a challenger or open-seat candidate, (2) an incumbent in a competitive race (as rated by *CQ Weekly Report*), and (3) a safe incumbent. Contributions from a member's principal campaign committee and LPAC are combined. To see the shift in giving over time in response to the battle for majority status and the increased efforts of party leaders to mobilize campaign money, we use the 1996 election cycle as the divider. Prior to 1996, the parties did little to mobilize contributions from incumbents; after 1996, their efforts were aggressive and institutionalized. Table 5.1 shows the changes in the proportion of total funds donated to each of the three types of recipients.

Democrats shifted their contributions to candidates substantially. Prior to 1996, Democrats split their contributions rather evenly between challengers/open-seat candidates and incumbents in competitive elections (just over 40 percent for each). After 1996, they shifted their contributions toward challengers and open-seat candidates (nearly 60 percent of all candidate giving) and away from competitive incumbents (nearly 30 percent) as they sought to increase the number of Democrats in the House to regain majority status. Democrats' contributions to safe incumbents declined slightly from 14.5 to 11.5 percent of candidate donations.

Republicans shifted their contributions away from challengers and open-seat candidates (56.6 percent of contributions in 1990–94 to 44.9 percent in 1996–2006), while maintaining their giving to competitive incumbents at just under 40 percent of contributions. As the new majority party, they needed to hold their existing seats to maintain majority status and could risk investing less money in challengers and open-seat candidates to expand their number of seats. More remarkably, Republicans tripled their proportion of giving to safe incumbents once they became the majority, from 5.2 to 15.5 percent of candidate contributions. GOP members of all categories of institutional position (elected leaders, extended party leaders, committee chairs, prestige committee members,

TABLE 5.1. Distribution of Member Giving Based on the Competitiveness of the Election, 1990–2006 (%)

	Republicans		Democrats	
	Pre-1996	Post-1996	Pre-1996	Post-1996
Challengers/Open seat	56.6	44.9	44.8	59.3
Competitive incumbents	38.2	39.6	40.7	29.2
Safe incumbents	5.2	15.5	14.5	11.5

rank-and-file members) tripled their proportion of giving to safe incumbents (to a high of 17.7 percent of total giving for elected leaders and a low of 14.8 percent for members of the extended party leadership). Since the *Congressional Quarterly* election competition ratings occur at the end of the election cycle, it may be that early contributions from other GOP incumbents helped to ward off competitive challenges to their incumbents, which would at least partially explain the big boost of giving to safe Republicans. Regardless, the fact that all categories of members with the Republican caucus shifted their giving toward safe incumbents indicates that this strategy was seen as broadly acceptable, if not encouraged.

Responsibility to the Party Caucus

While all members are likely to shift toward more party-oriented contribution strategies over time, some members are more likely than others to do so. Our theory predicts that elected party leaders are likely to employ contribution strategies that are most oriented toward competitive contests, because of their direct responsibility for the party's collective electoral success. Other party posts have less responsibility for the collective goals of the party than do elected leaders, but they have more responsibility for party goals than do rank-and-file members. Members holding appointments are dependent on the leadership, thus they are likely to direct their contributions in ways that advance the party leadership's most important collective goal: obtaining majority status. Furthermore, the power of committee chairs and prestige committee members increases greatly when serving in the majority party, giving them substantial incentive to help their party win majority status. Members with these party positions are likely to employ contribution strategies that, in their orientation toward competitive contests, fall between those of elected party leaders and rank-and-file members. Rank-and-file members, by contrast, have the least accountability to leaders and the caucus; they are thus likely to employ the most individualistic contribution strategies, as they exercise the flexibility to contribute to candidates who help them advance their own goals.

Contribution Strategies

Currinder (2003), Kanthak (2007), and Wilcox (1989) argue that both individualistic and collective partisan goals play a role in members' contribution strategies. Likewise, Herrnson (2009, 1215) argues that "Most party members use their party-connected committees to pursue both collective and private benefits." Our model largely incorporates the variables Wilcox described as related to member contributions. Broadly speaking, however, our goal is to evaluate the relative effects of individualistic versus collective party-centered goals on member-to-member contributions. We do this by evaluating (1) the extent to which member contribution networks vary over time as party mobilization and coordination increases and (2) the extent to which, cross-sectionally, the party orientation of a member's contribution strategy is a function of his or her level of responsibility to the party as measured by institutional position.[5]

Party-Centered Strategies

The central collective goal of the congressional party is to attain majority status (Jacobson 1985–86; Kolodny 1998). Contributors oriented toward this goal will build networks primarily in competitive districts in which their party could potentially gain or lose seats, thus affecting the party's ability to achieve a majority. To help target contributions to the most competitive races, the parties develop target lists of incumbents and non-incumbents to solicit contributions from all types of donors.

In terms of coordinating contributions from members of Congress, the informational role played by the committees is more important to generating contributions for nonincumbents. This is because members are likely to know less about the electoral fortunes of nonincumbents than they know about the electoral fortunes of their colleagues. Members do not need a lot of additional information about which of their colleagues are in trouble. As one high-level official of the Democratic Congressional Campaign Committee explained,

> It's pretty self-evident who the people are who need [campaign support]. It becomes very obvious to the people in this political scene to know who is in trouble. They're reading the same stuff you are reading, and they know every marginal there is. And there is camaraderie; members who are in trouble talk to other members. Obviously, everyone knows each other.[6]

Adds Representative B, "By the time you get into September and October, the word is well out who the members in need are. The [campaign committee] doesn't particularly have to generate a whole lot of information."[7]

Beyond cloakroom discussions and lists compiled by congressional campaign committees, there are a number of quantifiable indicators that can be used to identify competitive contests and that should increase the probability of a contribution, particularly from incumbents with party positions: the party candidate's electoral margin in the previous election, open seats, the presence of quality candidates,[8] and "split-ticket" districts that vote for a House member of one party and a presidential candidate of the other. (See the appendix at the end of this chapter for measurements.) We include two measures of quality candidates. The first is whether the party's nonincumbent candidate is considered a "quality" candidate; the second is whether the party's candidate is opposed by a quality candidate. Either situation should increase the probability of a contribution. Challengers who have not held elective office have a low probability of winning (Canon 1990; Jacobson and Kernell 1983) and thus are less likely to receive contributions than other candidates. Open-seat candidates, quality candidates, and challengers are all dummy variables; incumbents are the excluded category. We also control for the districts in Texas that were redistricted outside of the normal decennial pattern in order to make reelection more difficult for several incumbent Democrats by substantially changing their constituencies. Conversely, a candidate running unopposed indicates a decided lack of competition and should decrease the probability of a contribution.

These party-centered variables are likely to influence the probability of contributions from all incumbents to candidates. We expect, however, that these variables will have their largest substantive effect on the contributions of elected party leaders and their least substantive effect on rank-and-file members, with committee leaders, prestige committee members, and members appointed to the extended party leadership structure falling in between.

Individualistic Strategies

Incumbents are also likely to build contribution networks based on their own preexisting networks of personal relationships. Additionally, they are likely to contribute to candidates who help them advance their own policy goals (Wilcox 1989).

Within Congress, members have contact with many colleagues, but their personal networks are structured especially by their committee assignments. Members spend substantial time in committee and thus have greater opportunity to build relationships with their committee colleagues than with other members of Congress. When made aware that a committee colleague needs funds (whether through the press, party leaders, or a direct request from the colleague), a member is more likely to be responsive because of those relationships. Representative C noted, "[W]hen I have colleagues who are particularly close friends or people I work with on committee, and I know they are in a tough race, I sometimes just offer to help them."[9] Committee colleagues also are mutually dependent in helping one another achieve their legislative goals.

Party networks are particularly likely to facilitate connections between candidates from the same state. Contributing to home-state candidates indicates a desire to participate actively in the party network in the state, perhaps in response to direct requests from those candidates and/or state party officials. State delegations in Congress also can mobilize contributions. "The state delegations focus members' attention on districts we can win and urge other members to contribute to these people," observes Representative B.[10]

Members of Congress are also connected through ideological networks, which members frequently use to take cues when deciding how to vote on legislation (Kingdon 1989). Members could seek to promote their policy agenda by contributing to candidates who share their ideology or build coalitions for leadership races based on ideological allies (Kanthak 2007). *Congressional Quarterly* and *Roll Call* reporter Kathleen Hunter (2010) found that several congressional Democrats "said that they don't want their campaign dollars funding Democrats who have blocked progress on an overhaul [of their priority issues]." For a discussion of how we address the challenges of measuring nonincumbent candidate ideology, see the appendix at the end of this chapter.

Finally, incumbents' own electoral self-interest will affect their contributions to other candidates. Those in competitive races need more resources for their own campaigns and will be less likely to contribute to other candidates. We measure incumbents' need for campaign resources by their electoral margin in the previous election cycle and their amount of cash on hand left over from the previous cycle.

Our dependent variable is whether or not a contribution was made from each returning member of the House of Representatives to each congressional candidate from the incumbent's party in the 1990, 1998, and 2004 election cycles. Each case is a dyad, a matched pair of the characteristics of one incumbent with the characteristics of one candidate, repeated for each incumbent and each candidate of the incumbent's party. We examine each party and year separately to allow for differences based on party strategy and/or majority versus minority status.

We chose 1990, 1998, and 2004 as relatively equidistant election cycles representing the changes in the mobilization of congressional party fundraising over time: 1990 was prior to intense party efforts; 1998 was near the beginning of intense party efforts; and by 2004, party mobilization efforts were institutionalized, and expectations of members were clear.[11] Each of these election cycles has the additional advantage of being relatively evenly contested between the parties; a one-sided election would likely result in disproportionate giving by the favored party's incumbents to challengers and by the disfavored party's incumbents to incumbents.

Dyad Analysis

In 2004, the election cycle in which the most contributions were made of the three cycles we analyze in this chapter, GOP incumbents made 5,084 contributions to 404 candidates (contributions in 6.1 percent of the total opportunities); Democrats made 3,764 contributions to 397 candidates (contributions in 5.2 percent of the total opportunities). A contribution from any one incumbent to any other candidate is the exceptional outcome rather than the norm of no contribution. We thus use rare events logit as the estimation procedure.[12] Rare events logit corrects for the underestimation of probability of unusual events in traditional statistical estimation methods (King and Zeng 2001). This technique is particularly useful for our purposes, because it allows us to compute valid estimations of the magnitude of the effect of variables on the probability of contributions and to compare the substantive effects between members holding different positions.[13] Calculating the substantive effects of the independent variables is critical to testing our hypotheses that the party orientation of the contribution network will vary based on the member's position within the institution. We focus on the magnitude of the effects, because most coefficients are likely to attain traditional levels of statistical significance with our large number of cases.

Attempting to examine the results for each of the variables for each of the positions in each of the election cycles as discussed in our specific hypotheses results in informational overload. Moreover, the results for each variable are not important for the broader patterns of contributions we wish to evaluate in this chapter. Thus, we present the estimated values of the substantive effects for individual variables in the appendix at the end of this chapter and focus on the party orientation of contribution networks here.

Positions and Partisan Orientation of Contribution Networks

To compare the party orientation of contribution networks, we calculated the ratio of the substantive effects of the party-centered versus individualistic variables for each of the position categories (see also Heberlig and Larson 2010). First, we estimated the change in probability of a contribution for all of the party-centered variables, simultaneously changing one standard deviation around the mean and, for dichotomous variables, their minimum to maximum values, while holding the individualistic variables constant at the means or at the minimum value for dichotomous variables. This produced a cumulative effect score for the party-centered variables. Substantively, the score represents the probability of a contribution being made if a candidate has all the characteristics of being highly competitive (e.g., a quality open-seat candidate, running against a quality opponent in a district that was very close in the last election yet won by the presidential candidate of the opposing party). We then changed all the individualistic variables while holding the party-centered variables at their means (or minimums for dichotomous variables), to produce a cumulative effect score for the individualistic variables. The individualistic score is the probability of a contribution being made if the incumbent has high levels of personal connections to the candidate and can easily make financial sacrifices (e.g., an ideological allied committee colleague, from the same state, when the incumbent is safe and is flush with funds).[14] These scores are presented in table 5.2 for each party.

We then calculate the ratio of the party-centered to individualistic scores for each position. We label this score the party-orientation ratio because it shows the strength of party-centered variables relative to individualistic network variables. This allows us to assess the relative effects of each category of variables on the probability of a contribution while accounting for the fact that members holding each type of position have different probabilities of making contributions. In this way, the relative party orientation of rank-and-file members, who give few contributions, can be fairly compared to elected party leaders, who give many contributions. Similarly, it allows us to compare the relative magnitude of effects of different categories of variables across election cycles in which the total number of incumbent contributions is increasing.

For all positions, the scores for party-centered effects are considerably

TABLE 5.2. Party Orientation of Contribution Networks

Year	Elected Leader			Extended Leader			Committee Leader			Prestige Committee			Rank and File		
	1990	1998	2004	1990	1998	2004	1990	1998	2004	1990	1998	2004	1990	1998	2004
Republicans															
Party-centered variables	.132	.555	.826	.105	.334	.267	.054	.299	.691	.091	.312	.285	.066	.287	.138
Individualistic variables	.010	.069	.001	.064	.073	.033	.058	.166	.176	.003	.062	.024	.102	.124	.090
Ratio	13.20	8.04	826.0	1.64	4.58	8.01	0.93	1.80	3.93	30.33	5.03	12.12	0.65	2.31	1.55
Democrats															
Party-centered variables	.296	.573	.932	.075	.380	.763	.034	.370	.819	.106	.438	.740	.039	.256	.724
Individualistic variables	.001	.034	.014	.032	.064	.031	.043	.136	.011	.033	.099	.022	.087	.152	.070
Ratio	296.0	16.85	67.07	2.34	5.94	24.61	0.79	2.72	75.11	3.21	4.42	33.94	0.45	1.68	10.31

higher than the scores for individualistic effects, leading to party orientation contribution ratios consistently greater than 1. The exceptions are in the earliest election cycle, 1990, when party mobilization is lowest. Committee leaders and rank-and-file members of both parties had party-orientation ratios of less than 1 because individualistic variables had larger effects on their contributions than party-centered variables. As we see, the ratios become positive in later election cycles as party mobilization efforts increase.

The differences in the party-orientation ratio are generally as we predict. For each position, the party-orientation ratio generally increases between each election cycle as the battle for majority status intensifies and as party mobilization efforts increase. The party orientation increases in each of the three election cycles for 6 of the 10 position categories. Figures 5.1 and 5.2 show these trends for all positions except for elected party leaders (which we exclude because their scores are magnitudes larger than other scores in some election cycles and change more dramatically). We use a line graph to connect the changes in party-orientation ratios for each position across the three election cycles we analyze. The lines are not meant to imply that there would be continuous, linear evolution of the ratios in the intervening election cycles.

Figure 5.1 shows that Democratic scores increase marginally from 1990 to 1998 but then jump dramatically in a party-oriented direction in 2004. Democratic committee leaders show the pattern most dramatically, increasing their party-orientation ratio from less than 1 (0.79) in 1990 (meaning that they were slightly more likely to contribute based on indi-

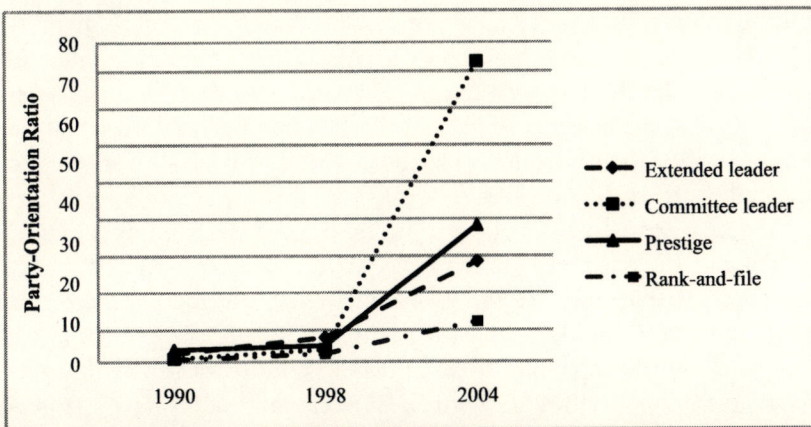

Fig. 5.1. Party-orientation ratios for Democrats

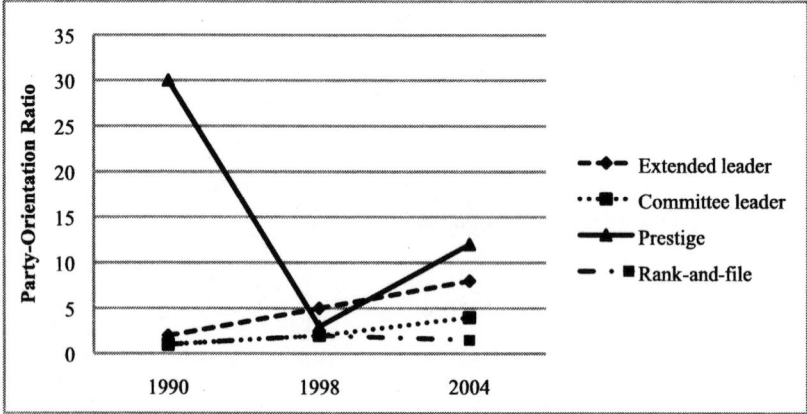

Fig. 5.2. Party-orientation ratios for Republicans

vidualistic rather than partisan goals), to a ratio of 2.72 in 1998 (meaning that as party mobilization started, they were almost three times as likely to contribute to competitive candidates than to those who could help them achieve personal goals), to a ratio of 75.11 in 2004. Once party expectations were clear and Democratic ranking members could become chairs if the party won majority status, they were 75 times more likely to contribute to candidates who would affect majority status than to candidates who could most help them achieve other individualistic goals.

Figure 5.2 shows a steady rise in party-orientation ratios for Republicans in contrast to Democrats' late surge. The clear exception is GOP prestige committee members who had very high party-orientation ratios in 1990 (due to low individualistic scores), whose scores dropped in 1998 before rising again in 2004. Rank-and-file Republicans' party-orientation ratios dropped slightly from 1998 to 2004 (from 2.31 to 1.55) but are high in none of the three election cycles.

We see a clearer picture of contribution trends by examining the components of the party-orientation ratio. With few exceptions, the party-centered variables increase the probability of a contribution from one election cycle to the next for each position. Elected leaders, committee leaders, and prestige committee members in both parties show this pattern most dramatically. For example, GOP elected leaders have a 13 percent probability of contributing to a candidate in the most competitive races in 1990, a 55 percent probability in 1998, and an 83 percent probability in 2004. For Democratic elected leaders, the probability of contributions to competitive candidates is even higher: 30 percent in 1990, 57 percent in 1998, and 93 percent in 2004.

The individualistic variables show a somewhat different pattern. Between 1990 and 1998, the impacts of individualistic variables increase, though not as substantially as the effects of the party-centered variables. Averaged across the institutional positions, the effects of the individualistic variables increase from .043 in 1990 to .098 in 1998. But between 1998 and 2004, individualistic variables decrease in importance, from .098 in 1998 to .047 in 2004 when averaged across positions, while the impacts of party-centered variables generally continue to increase. In 1998, members may have heard the message "Give." By 2004, party campaign committees were increasingly targeting their funds to competitive districts (Krasno and Dowling 2006; McGhee and LaRaja 2006). Thus, their coordination efforts were likely more refined, causing members to focus more precisely on competitive districts. The cumulative result is that the party-orientation ratios become larger in each election cycle as party-centered variables become increasingly more important than individualistic variables in predicting contributions.

Even the exceptions to this pattern are instructive. The elected leaders of both parties are examples. Elected leaders consistently have party-orientation ratios greater than 1, but the magnitudes of the ratios dip in 1998 before rising again in 2004. The change is due to the slight increase in the effect of individualistic variables in 1998. The effect of party-centered variables, however, continues to increase in each election cycle. Party leaders are clearly very oriented toward the collective electoral good of their parties in their contribution patterns.

In fact, consistent with our hypotheses, party leaders generally are more party-centered than other members in their contribution patterns, as demonstrated by their larger party-orientation ratios in each election cycle. The single exception is that Democratic committee leaders have higher ratios than elected party leaders in 2004, a year in which many elected leaders were attempting to attain and secure their positions in the wake of longtime Democratic leader Richard Gephardt's midterm decision to resign his post to seek the presidency. We will return to this issue in chapter 6. Otherwise, elected leaders consistently are more party-centered than lower-level leaders (extended party leaders, committee leaders, and prestige committee members) and are substantially more party-centered than the rank-and-file in each election cycle.

Similarly, lower-level leaders are more party-centered in their contribution patterns than are rank-and-file members in each election cycle, as illustrated in figures 5.1 and 5.2. For Democrats, the average party-orientation ratio of lower-level leaders is more than four times greater than that of rank-and-file members (17.0 versus 4.15). The gap is even larger for Republicans, though their overall ratios are lower than Democrats' ratios: lower-level leaders have party-orientation ratios six times the size of rank-and-file members (9.1 versus 1.5). The gaps in party-orientation ratio between lower-level leaders and rank-and-file members are present for every position in all three election cycles for both parties. Ambitious lower-level leaders may have an incentive to contribute to incumbents who they know are returning and who will be able to return the favor to help them advance. The evidence here suggests that the push of the party to contribute to competitive candidates is even stronger. Members who have shown some evidence of institutional ambition by obtaining a position (Currinder 2003; Herrick and Moore 1993) are even more likely than rank-and-file members to direct their contributions toward candidates who will help to advance the party's collective electoral good.

Conclusion

Members of Congress are increasingly acting as a team, both to pass legislation (Rohde 1991; Sinclair 1995) and to elect party candidates (Dwyre et al. 2006). While the candidate-centered era was characterized by members assembling their own individualistic networks (Fiorina 1989; Mayhew 1974), members now increasingly coordinate their activities through the party. Despite these trends, the extent to which members prioritize individual versus collective party goals in their attempts to cooperate has been unclear.

Members who seek leadership positions traditionally have given substantial sums of campaign contributions to fellow incumbents and party candidates (R. Baker 1989; Wilcox 1989, 1990). Thus, in the context of analyzing the outcome of individual contests, it is easy to track the amounts that the winners (and losers) have given to their colleagues and to conclude that contestants are trying to build personal coalitions by buying the support of other members. If contributions are primarily a means of advancing individual ambitions, it is easy to infer that individual goals trump collective partisan goals. Indeed, some have argued that incumbent contributions weaken the party—which contributes very little directly to members' campaigns—by making members loyal to individual incumbent contributors rather than to the party collectively (e.g., R. Baker 1989).

Yet parties in Congress create incentive structures to ensure that they delegate power to those who responsibly serve the collective interests of the caucus (Cox and McCubbins 1993). Parties reward members who demonstrate their commitment to serving the party caucus over those who would seek to advance their institutional ambition using a more individualistic approach. Our evidence strongly supports this perspective. First, we show that contributions from all types of members are predominately given to the candidates who are most likely to help the party achieve its goal of majority status. Second, we show that members with party positions are more likely to contribute in ways that advance collective goals than are rank-and-file members. Third, we show that the party orientation of contribution patterns has increased as the parties have increased their mobilization efforts to achieve majority status. Ambitious members may indeed contribute to advance their own career and power goals, but the party ensures that these contributions advance the interests of the entire party caucus. By controlling the structure of opportunities for institutional advancement, parties organize themselves to guarantee that members advance their own personal goals and the party's collective goals simultaneously.

APPENDIX

Variable Measurements

Cash on hand: total dollars remaining in the incumbent's personal campaign committee at the end of the previous cycle.

Challenger: 1 = nonincumbent candidate who is running against an incumbent; 0 = otherwise.

Committee colleague: 1 = candidate serves on the same congressional committee as the incumbent; 0 = otherwise.

Contribution (dependent variable): 1 = campaign contribution from a personal campaign committee or LPAC of a member of the House of Representatives to a House candidate from the incumbent's party in the 1990, 1998, and 2004 election cycles; 0 = no contribution.

Ideological proximity: for incumbents, the difference between their DW-NOMINATE scores. For nonincumbents, see "Measuring Nonincumbent Ideology" in this appendix.

Incumbent's electoral margin: incumbent percentage of the vote in the previous election cycle.

Open seat: 1 = district in which no incumbent seeks reelection; 0 = otherwise.

Opposing party quality candidate: 1 = the nonincumbent candidate of the opposing party has held elective public office; 0 = has not held elective office.

Party candidate's electoral margin: the absolute value of 50 percent minus the party candidate's share of the vote in the previous election (Gierzynski 1992).

Quality candidate: 1 = the nonincumbent candidate of the incumbent's party has held elective public office; 0 = has not held elective office.

Redistricted: 1 = candidates from Texas in 2004 in districts whose boundaries were substantially redrawn; 0 = otherwise.

Same state: 1 = candidate is from the same state as the incumbent; 0 = otherwise.

Split-ticket district: 1 = candidate in a district in which a plurality of voters selected a presidential candidate from one party in the most recent presidential election and a candidate from the other party in the most recent congressional election; 0 = otherwise.

Unopposed: 1 = incumbent has no major party opponent; 0 = otherwise.

Measuring Nonincumbent Ideology

Measuring the ideology of nonincumbent congressional candidates is a challenge, as they have not systematically revealed their preferences on legislative votes, the basis for calculating most measures of representatives' ideology. The major studies of member-to-member giving (Currinder 2003; Kanthak 2007; Wilcox 1989) avoid the problem by limiting their analysis of ideology to incumbents. We use incumbents' ideological scores, first-dimension DW-NOMINATE scores, to estimate the ideological scores of nonincumbent candidates.

Similar to Damore and Hansford (1999) and to Lowry, Potoski, and Talbert (2003), we model incumbents' DW-NOMINATE scores based on a vector of independent variables measuring the characteristics of the incumbents and their districts: party identification and gender of member, the district's Democratic presidential vote in the most recent past election, northeastern state, southern state, percentage of unionization in the district, and dummies for each election cycle (1990 is excluded as the baseline).[15] The unionization variable is calculated by multiplying the proportion of unionized workers in the state with the proportion of urban residents of the district (both pieces of data were obtained from Adler 2003). This procedure accounts for the variation in unionization across districts. Urbanization is used to create a district-level measure of unionization because unions are more densely organized and are more politically mobilized in urban areas (Asher et al. 2001). The model was estimated with ordinary least squares regression, with robust standard errors to account for the multiple observations of individual cases (members of Congress serving in multiple sessions). The model predicts DW-NOMINATE scores very successfully: the model chi-square is highly significant, and the adjusted R^2 is .885. The results of the model can be found in table 5.3.

We include both parties in the same model to decrease the problem of pre-

TABLE 5.3. Predicting Nonincumbents' Ideology (DW-NOMINATE scores), OLS with Robust Standard Errors

Variable	b	S.E.	Beta	p-value
Party identification	.645	.010	.740	.00
Democratic presidential vote	−.008	.001	−.268	.00
Northeastern state	−.042	.011	−.037	.00
Southern state	.039	.013	.040	.00
Unionization (× 100)	−.002	.001	−.033	.01
Female	−.050	.014	−.034	.00
1998 election cycle	.046	.011	.049	.00
2004 election cycle	.050	.010	.054	.00
Constant	.108	.024		.00

$N = 1,308$
Model $F = 1,119$ ($p < .001$)
Adjusted $R^2 = .885$

Note: S.E. = standard error.

dicting beyond the range of the data. There are few Democrats representing districts with very Republican characteristics, and vice versa. Thus, using a Democrats-only model to predict candidates' ideologies in districts not typically represented by Democratic incumbents would be highly fraught with error. Estimating DW-NOMINATE scores with both party members and a range of district characteristics allows us to account for variation within and between parties.

We use the model to predict ideology scores of nonincumbent candidates by entering the values of the candidates and their districts for each of the independent variables. Obviously, there is still considerable error; we offer a more in-depth discussion of the liabilities of this measure elsewhere (Heberlig and Larson 2010, 469).

Results of Rare Events Logit Estimations of Probabilities of a Contribution to a Candidate

The full results of the rare event logit models are presented in tables 5.4 and 5.5 for Republicans and Democrats, respectively. As the results demonstrate, most of the independent variables are significantly related to contributions in the predicted direction. It is especially noteworthy that the party-centered variables are more consistently related to contributions than the individualistic variables, particularly for Democrats. Most results of the party-centered variables are consistently statistically significant across the party and position of the incumbent and the election cycle: a "safer" district for the party decreases the

TABLE 5.4. Rare Events Logit Analysis of Contributions to Party Candidates by Incumbents, Estimated by Party Position and by Election Cycle: Republicans

	Elected Leader			Extended Leader			Committee Leader			Prestige Committee			Rank and File		
Year	1990	1998	2004	1990	1998	2004	1990	1998	2004	1990	1998	2004	1990	1998	2004
Challenger	-.003*	.003*	-.022*	-.004*	.002*	-.020*	-.009*	.002*	-.026*	-.004	.001*	-.021*	-.004*	.002*	-.020*
Party's previous margin	-.001*	-.007*	-.018*	-.001*	-.006*	-.010*	-.003*	-.005*	-.044*	-.012*	-.008*	-.044*	-.009*	-.004*	-.024*
Open seat	.007	.013*	.121*	.001	.011*	.041*	-.001	.009*	.034*	.003	.012*	.042*	-.000	.012*	.020*
Redistricting	n.a.	n.a.	.151*	n.a.	n.a.	.055*	n.a.	n.a.	.072*	n.a.	n.a.	.059*	n.a.	n.a.	.045*
Quality candidate	.015*	.001*	.051*	.019*	.000	.032*	.025	.000	.070*	.017*	.000	.038*	.005	-.000	.024*
Opposing a quality candidate	.007*	.002*	.033*	.007*	.002*	.051*	.023*	.002*	.038*	.004*	.002*	.047*	.016*	.003*	.057*
Split ticket district	.004	.001	.053*	.003	.000	.041*	.005	.001	.036*	.002	.001*	.040*	.004	.002*	.037*
Unopposed	-.002	-.0001	-.017*	-.003*	-.0002	-.012*	-.004	-.000	.016	-.002	-.001	-.013*	-.002	-.001*	-.011*
Same committee	-.000	.002	-.018*	.004	.002*	.002	.008	.002*	.016	-.002	-.001	-.011*	.019*	.003*	.019*
Same state	.012*	.002	.018	.033*	.006*	.064*	.042*	.005*	.055*	.019*	.010*	.062*	.052*	.008*	.100*
Incumbent's electoral margin	-.004*	.006*	-.052	.004*	.001*	-.025	-.036	.001*	-.013	-.014	.001	.005	.003	-.001	.021*
Cash on hand	.006*	-.001*	.018*	.001	.001	.025*	-.007	.000	.028*	.001	.001*	.040*	.004*	.001	.022
Ideological proximity	-.005*	-.002*	-.024*	.001	-.002*	-.017*	-.005	-.002*	-.025*	-.005	.001	-.012*	.004*	-.003*	-.021*
N	569	1,290	1,381	4,017	10,913	12,502	990	1,965	2,402	1,780	6,676	7,219	2,163	7,254	8,704

Note: Values are the predicted probabilities of a two-standard-deviation change (one standard deviation above the mean, one below it) in the independent variable for continuous variables and a 0 to 1 change in a dichotomous variable. n.a. = not applicable.

*p < .05

TABLE 5.5. Rare Events Logit Analysis of Contributions to Party Candidates by Incumbents, Estimated by Party Position and by Election Cycle: Democrats

	Elected Leader			Extended Leader			Committee Leader			Prestige Committee			Rank and File		
Year	1990	1998	2004	1990	1998	2004	1990	1998	2004	1990	1998	2004	1990	1998	2004
Challenger	-.001*	-.012*	.001	-.003*	-.003*	-.008*	-.003*	-.003*	-.006*	-.003*	-.003*	-.007	-.005*	-.003*	-.004
Party's previous margin	-.006*	-.038*	-.044*	-.012*	-.013*	-.045*	-.004	-.012	-.053*	-.009*	-.012*	-.047*	-.008*	-.012	-.023*
Open seat	.015*	.024	.206*	-.0001	.005*	.054*	-.003	.001*	.069*	.002	.004*	.067*	-.001	.002*	.045*
Redistricting	n.a.	n.a.	.029	n.a.	n.a.	.033*	n.a.	n.a.	.049*	n.a.	n.a.	.031*	n.a.	n.a.	.056*
Quality candidate	.008*	.034*	.032*	.008*	.007*	.062*	.006	.006*	.068*	.011*	.010*	.060*	.006	.005*	.062*
Opposing a quality candidate	.013*	.020*	.040*	.007*	.004*	.049*	.007*	.005*	.062*	.007*	.005*	.061*	.006*	.004*	.049*
Split ticket district	.003	.017	.042*	.001	.001*	.068*	.002	.002*	.102*	.001	.002*	.070*	.002	.0001	.056*
Unopposed	-.001	-.010	.026*	-.003*	-.004	-.007	-.001	-.003*	.033*	-.002*	-.004*	.008	-.004*	-.006*	-.014
Same committee	.002	.000	-.001	.001	-.000	.009*	.004	.001	-.002	.005*	.002	-.002	.005*	.001	.009*
Same state	.002	.003	-.006*	.017*	.014	.064*	.011*	.007*	.048*	.010*	.016*	.068*	.015*	.020*	.091*
Incumbent's electoral margin	-.007	.132	.033*	.0003	.001	.001	.001	.012*	.009*	.002	.0002	.003	.004*	-.002	.005*
Cash on hand	-.002	-.019	.048	.005*	.002	.003	-.004*	.004	.003	.004*	.002	-.004	.003*	.003	.008
Ideological proximity	-.0003	-.009	-.004	-.0002	.001	.003	-.002	.001	.004	.002	.003	-.005	-.002*	-.003*	-.008
N	439	342	867	6,767	6,218	12,067	1,170	1,152	2,537	3,416	2,961	6,939	3,783	5,120	9,203

Note: Values are the predicted probabilities of a two-standard-deviation change (one standard deviation above the mean, one below it) in the independent variable for continuous variables and a 0 to 1 change in a dichotomous variable. n.a. = not applicable.

*$p < .05$

probability of a contribution from incumbents, while open districts, redrawn districts, and quality candidates of the incumbent's party or the opposing party all increase the probability of contributions. Among the individualistic variables, only contributing to home-state candidates produces consistent statistically significant results. The relationships also generally strengthen as contributions become more frequent in the later election cycles, as we would expect.

6 | Getting Ahead by Giving a Lot: Party Goals and Advancement in the House

We opened chapter 1 with the story of Collin Peterson's bumpy ascent to the post of ranking Democrat on the Agriculture Committee. Despite his seniority on the committee, Peterson had to promise the party that he would increase his financial assistance to the party after obtaining the post, and he has. Still, he obtained his committee leadership position without a prior record of supporting the party or its candidates financially.

Peterson's promotion contrasts to a great degree with media stories of advancement on Capitol Hill over the past decade. News coverage of these contests has highlighted spirited contests for committee and party leadership positions in which members' redistribution of campaign funds was a central element. In the committee system, these include the contest for chairmanships of the Energy and Commerce Committee in 2000 (Mike Oxley versus Billy Tauzin), the Ways and Means Committee the same year (Phil Crane versus Bill Thomas), and the Appropriations Committee in 2004 (Jerry Lewis versus Ralph Regula and Hal Rogers) (see Krawzak 2004a, 2004b; Pianan 2000; Schatz 2005). In the party leadership hierarchy, the contests include the race between John Boehner and Roy Blunt to replace Tom DeLay as majority leader in 2006 and the three-year epic battle ending in 2001 between Steny Hoyer and Nancy Pelosi for the Democratic Party whip post (see Foerstel 2001; Ota 2006; VandeHei 2006). Except for the Boehner-Blunt contest for the GOP majority leader's post, all of the contests were won by the candidate who redistributed the most money. The contests for chair were particularly notable since chairmanships were traditionally given to the most senior member of the majority party on the committee.

The Tauzin-Oxley contest for the Energy and Commerce Committee chair was even more unique. With both candidates possessing high party loyalty scores and with each redistributing generously, the GOP awarded the chairmanship to Tauzin but created another committee, Financial Services, for Oxley to chair. He was awarded the chair over the more senior member of the former Banking Committee, Marge Roukema, who had a much less loyal voting record and gave little money to the party and GOP candidates in the 2000 election cycle.

Republican Party leaders have made the role of campaign money more central to the selection of committee chairs by formally ending the seniority rule and requiring that chair candidates "audition" before the GOP Steering Committee to demonstrate their leadership abilities and commitment to the party "team." Not only do members have to commit to helping to pass the party legislative agenda, but they also have to show their ability to help the GOP win majority control by redistributing campaign funds. One Republican staff member describes the process as follows:

> Since the seniority system is gone, candidates have to interview for chairmanships. They provide a statement about their philosophy and their position on bills. But that's not what matters. When they are interviewed by the leadership, around this horseshoe table, everyone has the [philosophy] statement. But they also have a book sitting on the table. It lists the money they raised and how much they contributed to other campaigns.... They actually flip through the book as they question you. (Quoted in Dubose and Reid 2004, 272)

One Republican member of Congress we interviewed confirmed that members have to toe the line in their voting and their campaign contributions: "The sad thing is, it's all about money. They are given figures that they have to raise—hundreds of thousands of dollars. I've [also] had a number of members tell me, 'I'd like to vote a certain way, but I want to become chair.' Anyone who wants to become chair has to compromise."[1]

The same is true on the Democratic side of the aisle. Democratic whip Jim Clyburn (SC) notes the importance of the leadership in selecting new committee chairs: "Anytime you've got openings, and seniority is just one element [in determining the new chairman], it gives power to the process" of the Speaker-dominated Steering and Policy Committee choosing the new chair (quoted in Allen 2010). In making this selection, the Steering and Policy Committee "weighs seniority but also party loyalty, legislative ability, fundraising prowess and other factors" (Allen 2010).

Campaign money has also played an increasingly open role in party leadership contests. Biographies of Nancy Pelosi (Bzdek 2008; Sandalow 2008) trace the importance of her ability to raise and disburse campaign funds at every stage of her political career: from her fundraising for candidates as a citizen activist to the tremendous financial assistance she has provided to Democrats as Speaker (and every step in between). As recounted by Marc Sandalow (2008, 176), Pelosi's fundraising efforts were both an impetus for her to seek an elected party leadership position and a reason why she was victorious: "It was the money that ultimately convinced Pelosi to run for a leadership position. . . . Pelosi was increasingly asked, 'What are you getting out of this?' . . . So if Pelosi was raising the money, why wasn't she calling the shots?"

Similarly, on the Republican side, considerable attention has been paid to the role of campaign money in the leadership careers of Newt Gingrich and Tom DeLay. Newt Gingrich developed GOPAC, a leadership PAC dedicated to identifying, training, and assisting promising GOP candidates to lift the Republicans from minority status in the House. Following Gingrich's example, DeLay used his LPAC, campaign travels, and ability to mobilize contributions from lobbyists to candidates as an asset in his 1994 race for GOP whip (Dubose and Reid 2004, 87). DeLay's PAC offered not only direct contributions to candidates but in-kind donations (e.g., political consulting assistance) as well. As majority whip, he developed the ROMP (Retain Our Majority Program) to channel early contributions to vulnerable Republican incumbents to help them deter quality challengers, and he mobilized his whip team to contribute $3,000 apiece to these candidates (Corrado 2000; VandeHei 1999). He also organized the K Street Project, an effort to steer campaign funds from the Washington lobbying community to Republican Party organizations and candidates (see chapter 2). In the view of biographers Dubose and Reid (2004, 270), "Everything Tom DeLay has achieved in leadership derives from the tens of millions of dollars he raised and then contributed to Republican House races." Moreover, DeLay's success made his tactics all the more prominent: "His take-no-prisoners style of fundraising—in which the classic unstated bargain of access for contributions is made explicitly and without apology—has been adopted by both parties in Congress" (Birnbaum and VandeHei 2005).

Anecdotes, however, are insufficient to demonstrate the influence of money on the advancement system in Congress, and the influence of campaign money is not limited to elected party leader posts and committee chairmanships. To illustrate the effect of redistribution on advancement, we present, in table 6.1, adjusted campaign funds for members who obtained selected new positions in the House. The adjusted campaign funds are set to equal the value of redistributed contributions in the 2000 election cycle, so that, despite the substantial increase in total redistribution from 1990 to 2006, the values for each year are comparable. (See the measurement labeled *campaign contributions* in the appendix at the end of this chapter.) We present the median adjusted contribution for each position, so that values are not skewed by a few exceptionally large donors. The numbers are presented separately by party and before and after the 105th Congress (the 1996 election cycle), when each party's mobilization of campaign funds intensified.

Table 6.1 shows that in nearly all cases, members who attained new positions in the 105th–110th Congresses redistributed substantially more funds than those who attained them before the 105th Congress. The median adjusted contribution of new elected Democratic Party leaders, for example, is almost 73 times the size of new Democratic leaders prior to the 105th Congress. (Indeed, the median adjusted contribution of elected Democratic leaders after the 104th Congress is even substantially larger than the largest sum [$135,000] redistributed by a new Democratic leader prior to the 105th Congress.) Similarly, the financial effect of the GOP's decreasing reliance on seniority and of its encouragement of bidding wars can be seen in the tripling of median contributions of new committee chairs. By contrast, Democrats largely stuck with the seniority system for promoting committee leaders and saw the adjusted value of the median contribution from their new chairs decline slightly.[2] The median contributions of members who transferred to prestige committees tripled in both parties, while the contributions of new extended leadership appointees nearly doubled in both parties. Other than Democratic commit-

TABLE 6.1. Median Adjusted Redistributed Campaign Funds and New Positions

	Republicans		Democrats	
	101st–104th	105th–110th	101st–104th	105th–110th
New elected party leader	$390,590 (13)	$144,956 (17)	$3,000 (3)	$218,240 (19)
New chair/ ranking member	$34,750 (27)	$121,084 (46)	$71,600 (32)	$64,278 (30)
New extended leadership	$34,875 (168)	$53,360 (187)	$29,428 (214)	$58,540 (190)
New prestige committee	$19,600 (43)	$59,868 (46)	$21,280 (53)	$69,876 (63)
No institutional position	$9,300 (147)	$23,000 (272)	$6,950 (196)	$16,330 (255)

Note: The number of members in each category appears in parentheses following the amount of campaign contributions.

tee leaders, Republican elected leaders were the only group for whom median contributions declined, and this is a result of the adjustment
process.[3] GOP elected leaders and new leaders gave a substantial proportion of total GOP funds prior to the 105th Congress (45 percent).[4] The actual median contribution of new GOP leaders prior to the 105th Congress
was $79,594, while after the 104th, it was $183,000.

Money was not the only factor in the outcomes of leadership contests
discussed in recent media reports. Though the money angle was often
the hook, the stories told by journalists typically mentioned other factors as well, among them the contestants' personalities, level of state delegation support, working relationships with other members, policy differences with the party leadership, representation of continuity versus
reform in caucus or committee business, and other factors relevant to
the specific contest. Because of the number and variety of factors involved in a single contest, however, the journalists rarely offered any
conclusions about which factors were most important to the final outcome, let alone how the results might generalize into an understanding
of advancement in the House.

Similarly, Peabody's classic *Leadership in Congress* (1976) chronicled
the fascinating game of "inside baseball" in party leadership contests during the 1960s and early 1970s. Peabody listed 20 variables to explain the dynamics of nine case studies explored in the book, but not the redistribution of campaign funds. Historically, money mattered in the rise of
Lyndon Johnson (Caro 1983) and a few other top party leaders, but it did
not seem to play a systematic role (R. Baker 1989; Kolodny 1998).

While political scientists enjoy reading about these battles for promotion and using them as anecdotal evidence, we have had difficulty generalizing about advancement within the House (Wawro 2000, 116). More
fundamentally, we have not been able to integrate these high-profile contests for a few top positions into a broader structure for understanding career development. Many members have opportunities to advance within
the House, but few compete for these top positions. A theory of advancement and the role of political parties in creating the institutional structure
and incentives for advancement must account for the opportunities that
are available and relevant to most members of the caucus.

The rapid rise in the sums of campaign money redistributed by congressional incumbents has stimulated research on the role of money in
advancement. Indeed, political scientists have found that campaign contributions now play a significant role in determining whether members
obtain a variety of institutional posts: elected party leadership positions

(Green 2008; Green and Harris 2007), party leadership appointments (Heberlig, Hetherington, and Larson 2006; Heberlig and Larson 2007), prestige committee assignments (Heberlig 2003), and committee and prestige subcommittee leadership posts (Cann 2008; Deering and Wahlbeck 2006).

Although this approach moves us away from a focus on the personal skills or the campaign strategies of the contestants, it remains limited by a focus on the specific process for contesting each type of position. Members are unlikely to see their career advancement in Congress as a series of isolated positions. Instead, they are likely to seek a position portfolio that maximizes not only their power goals but, through these positions, their ability to advance their policy, constituency, service, and reelection goals. Indeed, a member may both transfer to a prestige committee and join the whip system in the same session of Congress, or a member may accept a position both on the party steering committee and the party campaign committee in the same session of Congress. Any combination of position changes could dramatically increase a member's power and influence within Congress in a single session.

Examining movement into separate and distinct positions is misleading from the parties' standpoint as well. The literature emphasizes the desire of the party caucus to promote party loyalists—those members who are dedicated to the collective good of the caucus. Presumably, the caucus would be monitoring members to assess their abilities, efforts, and successes in serving the caucus's collective good. The caucus would want to ensure not only that the best qualified members advanced into the most powerful positions but that dedicated members serve in multiple capacities within the party structure. An ambitious member would need to exhibit party leadership qualities across several domains (e.g., politics and policy) to demonstrate his or her worth to the party caucus—and thus to deserve additional appointments or a promotion in the hierarchy.[5] Rather than identifying many loyal members who could serve adequately in different positions, the caucus would save time and effort by placing members who have demonstrated their reliability and trustworthiness in multiple positions. Once the party identified an up-and-coming partisan star, the caucus would put his or her talents to use legislatively, on key committees; politically, in devising electoral strategies with the party's congressional campaign committee; organizationally, in screening other members' loyalty and skills as a member of the party steering committee; and so on. As party leaders must be effective on multiple fronts, the party caucus should seek evidence of such multiple talents in members who aspire to the leadership roles.

Additionally, as we have argued in chapter 3, the parties have an incentive to vary the weight they place on members' fealty to the party's collective electoral fortunes as the competition for majority status changes. When party control is stable, the majority party has an incentive to weight members' voting loyalty most heavily. But when majority status is up for grabs, both parties—but particularly the minority party—have an incentive to weight financial contributions to the party's electoral success more heavily. Recent studies have provided evidence that money is now an important explanation of member advancement. What they have not told us is whether money matters because it serves the party's collective good or because it has been contributed to the safe incumbents who choose which colleagues fill the posts.

Knowing why members of Congress advance is important because of the implications for how Congress operates. Party and committee leaders especially have substantial influence over agenda setting and developing legislative responses to the pressing policy issues of the day. If members who advance to powerful positions have demonstrated their proficiency at legislative craftsmanship or expertise on policy issues, the public can be reassured that, to the extent there are legislative solutions to particular policy problems, congressional leaders have the skills to develop laws to address them. If, however, members of Congress advance for nonlegislative reasons, there would be more reason to doubt whether congressional leaders are capable of effectively developing legislative solutions to public problems. Raising funds and helping one's colleagues win election is surely a useful skill for parties seeking to attain power, but it is a less certain credential for developing expertise, crafting compromises, building and holding together legislative coalitions, negotiating with the president or the Senate, and other facets of House leaders' responsibilities. Knowing that money or legislative skills vary in their relative importance to one another over time would mean that parties adapt their priorities for leadership skills depending on which collective goal has the highest priority in a particular political environment.

If redistributing campaign funds matters in advancement, knowing how it matters tells us something important about the nature of parties and leaders in the contemporary House. If members advance by following a party-centered strategy—targeting their contributions to candidates in close races on which majority control hinges—it shows that parties reward members for making sacrifices for the collective good of the party. If members advance by following an individualistic strategy—targeting their contributions to safe incumbents in exchange for support in leadership contests—it shows that advancement depends more on what leadership aspirants can do for individual members than on what they can do for the party collectively.

Advancement in Congress is based on a mix of member ambition, recruitment by party leaders, and the assent of the party caucus. We need a systematic way to gauge the relative influences of experience, party loyalty voting, and the redistribution of campaign funds on members' advancement in the House. Theoretically and empirically, institutional advancement by members must be placed within the structures created and operated by the congressional parties. Elaborating on Cox and McCubbins's (1993) observation that parties use positions as selective incentives, we develop a supply-side measure of position value to show how parties ensure that members who advance demonstrate their dedication to the party's collective good.

The Institutional Structure of Advancement

In his study of the effects of legislative entrepreneurialism, Wawro (2000, 116) noted that except for studies of committee transfers, there has been little study of advancement within Congress. To the extent that there has been any ability to generalize about advancement in the House, the most basic generalization has been the leadership ladder (Peabody 1976; Canon 1989). Members obtained appointments to positions of relatively limited power early in their careers and, through their efforts to prove their skills to other leaders and their colleagues, rose into more powerful positions over time. The most ambitious might compete for an elected position after serving in several other positions in the extended leadership structure. Similarly, advancement in the committee system was based on putting in your time and gaining experience. Through the traditional seniority system, promotions to committee leadership positions based on time served became nearly automatic. Requirements that committee leaders be approved by a vote of the caucus, as well as the more recent application of this requirement to subcommittee chairs of prestige committees, added a measure of merit review similar to the party leadership's ladder. The advancement system seemed to be based on principles articulated in the

Gospel of Mark (4:25): "To whoever has, to him more shall be given" (New American Standard Bible).

Political scientists studying the career ladder have observed that it is hardly a linear climb for most members; instead, the key rungs could vary by party and over time (Canon 1989; Nelson 1977). Hibbing (1993, 120–21), in particular, discussed the difficulty of generalizing about career paths in the House. Some members obtain a post early in their career and never leave it to take another. Other members shift positions frequently. The examples Hibbing uses, however, are telling. James Delaney (D-NY) and Edward Patten (D-NJ) exhibit very stable career patterns. Both obtained prestige committee appointments early in their careers. With valuable positions, they would not need to seek other posts to achieve their power goals. In contrast, Olin Teague (D-TX) transferred committees several times, became chair of two different committees, was elected to a party leadership post, and, when forced to step down by caucus rules, served on the ethics committee. The difference between the peripatetic Teague and the stable Delaney and Patten was that Teague's committee assignments and chairmanships—Veterans Affairs, District of Columbia, Science— were not highly desirable assignments. To build his power, Teague needed to obtain additional assignments and to seek party posts when the opportunities arose. The broader lesson of these examples is that in generalizing about career advancement in the House, we should not necessarily expect all members to obtain similar positions in a similar order. We should, however, expect ambitious members to behave similarly in terms of party-regarding behavior, because the parties provide the structures and expectations that regulate how members advance.

Position Portfolios

A primary difficulty of studying institutional advancement is that the leadership "ladder" in Congress is shaped more like a triangle than a construction ladder with two parallel, vertical sidepieces and many horizontal rungs. There are hierarchies of positions within the committee system and party leadership structure, and a variety of positions within each of those structures are available simultaneously. One can advance hierarchically within the committee system by moving from rank-and-file status to being a subcommittee chair or by transferring from a policy committee to a prestige committee. Similarly, within the party leadership structure, one can advance from being an assistant whip to being a chief deputy whip or by moving from vice chair of the congressional campaign committee to its chair. But one can also increase one's power through "lateral" movements, for example, by adding an appointment to the party steering committee to one's existing responsibilities or by adding a party position to one's existing committee assignments. In choosing to undertake new positions, members will have to consider the appropriate balance of the demands of their new responsibilities in addition to their existing responsibilities and electoral needs. Examining the attainment of positions in isolation ignores the potential tradeoffs between them and does not allow us to explore the dynamics of the career ladder in Congress in which experiences in one position affect the probability of advancing to other positions.

Hibbing (1991) comes closest to our conception of advancement dynamics, by developing a measure of a member's position portfolio. Describing a position portfolio in the House as consisting of the combined power rankings of the variety of positions in which a member serves, he explores how the value of a member's portfolio changes over time based on his or her seniority. He recognizes that members' opportunities to enhance their portfolios are limited by the opportunity structure and by the number of positions the party makes available (see also Wawro 2000).

Hibbing measures the value of a member's position portfolio by creating a power score for a variety of positions within the House. The great difficulty, of course, lies in developing a quantitative measure of the "power" of a given position. Hibbing creates his measure by surveying selected political scientists, journalists, and congressional staffers to provide their subjective power ratings, on a 1–100 scale, for an array of positions. He then averages his respondents' rankings to create a score for each position. (See table 6.2 later in this chapter for Hibbing's scores.) Using these scores, he sums the ratings of positions held by each member to create overall scores of members' position portfolios.

Although we are attempting to measure a similar construct as Hibbing, we develop a different measure. Several reasons inform our decision. First, while Hibbing rates 15 specific party and committee positions, he excludes several party positions that are prime selective incentives for both senior and junior members. Parties have created numerous institutional positions whose major responsibilities lie outside of legislative development and coalition building. Examples of such positions excluded by Hibbing are conference vice chair and secretary, chairs of various party committees (e.g., the congressional campaign committees, party policy committees, and party communication committees), and an array of positions in the extended party leadership structure (e.g., membership on the congressional campaign committees) that provide important opportunities for junior members to involve themselves in party affairs (Loomis 1984; Price 2004; Sinclair 1983). For our purposes, another problem with Hibbing's index is that summing the values for members who hold multiple committee and party positions can result in scores that surpass those of the Speaker and the floor leaders.[6] Hibbing (1991, 187 n. 5) solves this problem by capping members' total scores at 100 so that they do not surpass the Speaker's score. The result is that a number of members end up with scores equal to the Speaker and the majority leader. Likewise, because they serve on only one committee, members and subcommittee leaders of the prestige committees often have lower scores than their colleagues.

A second reason we decided to create our own measure is that Hibbing rates only positions in the majority party, yet institutional and party positions are valuable selective incentives in both parties. In fact, party positions may be more valuable for members of the minority party than for members of the majority party, since minority party members have more limited opportunities to serve on powerful committees (Connelly and Pitney 1994, 46; Frisch and Kelly 2006, 216–17). The "power" of positions in the minority party, however, is clearly less than the same positions in the majority party, so it would be inappropriate merely to apply Hibbing's measures to the minority party. Thus, we seek to develop a specific score for positions in the minority party as well as for positions in the majority.

Positions as Selective Incentives: A Supply-Side Measure of Position Value

We are interested in the value of a position as a selective incentive rather than in the position's institutional power per se. Obviously, individual members will "value" particular positions within the institution differently, depending on the extent to which a position allows them to advance their personal goals (Herrick and Moore 1993). From this perspective, it becomes difficult to measure the value of positions, since we do not have measures of members' ambitions. But examining positions from the party's perspective—as selective incentives they can offer members who are committed to advancing the collective good of the party (Cox and McCubbins 1993)—makes a viable measurement strategy possible.

Essentially, we develop a supply-side measurement of position value. Our approach relies on the fact that positions are limited. We assume that the number of positions is less than the demand for those positions (Shepsle 1978; Sinclair 1983; Loomis 1984; Kiewiet and McCubbins 1991; Cox and McCubbins 1993), thus giving party leaders the ability to select who obtains the position. Like scholars of progressive ambition (e.g., Black 1972; Rohde 1979) and intra-institutional ambition (e.g., Herrick and Moore 1993; Maltzman 1997; Wawro 2000), we assume that all members seek to advance and would accept more valuable positions if they could obtain them without cost. Positions for which there is limited demand from members (e.g., an Ethics Committee assignment) are not used by the parties as selective incentives. The "value" of the position, then, is determined by its status and its scarcity rather than by the demand for it.

Munger (1988) and Wawro (2000, 112–13) note the inverse relationship between the number of positions available and the value of a position: when fewer positions are available, a position is more valuable, and when more positions are available, a position is less valuable. Scott Meinke's (2010) archival research reveals that party leaders are aware of the trade-offs between accommodating the demand by members for more positions and the risk of "diluting" the value of the positions. The value of holding a position rests in the fact that it has powers and ability to exchange benefits that individuals without the position do not have. Members who seek to take actions or receive benefits must go to the person(s) with the positions of authority to help them achieve their goals. The more people there are with the authority to assist a member, the less reliant members will be on any single person holding that position, which lowers the level of benefits that the position holder can extract in the exchange.

A position can be offered as a selective incentive if the party caucus or party officers exert control over the selection of members to these positions. The method of selection varies by position, but all require either election by members of the caucus or appointment by elected party officers or party committees (e.g., the steering committees). While many positions require pro forma approval by the party caucus and are obtained through some level of review by the party steering committee, selection to the posts viewed as selective incentives require close review by party officials or committees. Those making the selection place considerable weight on the member's ability to serve the collective party interest, rather than merely having expertise that would make them productive committee members or allow them to serve their constituents more effectively.

New positions within the committee system are defined as selective incentives when the party defines them as exclusive assignments—that is, appointment to this committee becomes the member's only committee assignment (Cox and McCubbins 1993). The party is thus limiting the individual member's other opportunities for goal achievement on other committees in exchange for the power of this particular committee assignment. In making an assignment exclusive, the party signals that it is closely screening members' qualifications for the assignment.

Our list of positions that parties use as selective incentives largely follows the literature's list of elected leadership and extended leadership posts, committee chairmanships, and prestige committee assignments. Elected positions include the Speaker, floor leaders, whips, and caucus officers. Extended leadership positions include chairs, vice chairs, and members of party committees (the steering committees, the congressional campaign committees, and the policy and research committees). The "party-controlled" committee assignments follow Deering and Smith's (1997) classification and include the Appropriations, Budget, Rules, and Ways and Means committees. (In the appendix at the end of this chapter, we offer an extended analysis and defense of treating the Budget Committee as a partisan selective incentive.) Consistent with changes in each party's rules, we also include the Energy and Commerce Committee as an exclusive committee for Democrats after the 104th Congress and for Republicans after the 107th Congress. Committee leadership posts and the Appropriations Committee's subcommittee leadership posts are also treated as selective incentives, because they are subject to vote by the caucus and because both leaders are increasingly expected to act as party leaders (Rohde 1991; Sinclair 2006).

The method of selection varies across these offices. Some are obtained via appointment by various elected leaders or the party steering committee; others are achieved directly via caucus election; still others are ratified by the caucus. Some have traditionally been secured mostly by seniority, and some have a considerable level of self-selection involved. Although the literature has documented differences in advancement across these positions, we here seek a generalizable account of advancement in the House, regardless of the specific method of selection for each position. Underlying all methods of selection is an acceptance of the new position holder by the party caucus. Appointers, then, must anticipate what the caucus is willing to support, and members who advance must offer evidence of their ability to serve the party's collective good.

Position Values

Based on the preceding logic, our measurement strategy is based on two elements: the position's "rank" in the status hierarchy and the number of positions available within the party. We measure the value of most positions in the extended leadership and committee leadership as the inverse ratio of the number of positions available within a party. This also allows us to account for the fact that the number and thus the value of those positions varies over time and by party across our period of study. For example, in the 105th Congress, there were 26 members on the National Republican Congressional Committee, so the value of this position to an individual is 1/26, or .038. By contrast, there were 37 positions available on the GOP Policy Committee in the 105th Congress. Since more positions were available, they were easier to obtain and hence worth less—1/37, or .027.

Where there are obvious hierarchical differences within a position category (e.g, deputy whips versus assistant or regional whips), we count the number of positions separately and assign each position its own score. We follow the same logic in calculating the value of committee chairs and ranking members (calculated separately by prestige, policy, and constituency/ undesirable committees) and the value of memberships on prestige committees.[7] Only the Appropriations Committee's subcommittee chairs need to be approved by the caucus; they are therefore the only subcommittee chairs counted as selective incentives.

An additional value of our measure is that it allows us to account for changes in the advancement structure made by the parties over time. As parties expand the number of positions to allow more members to participate in leadership activities, the value of the positions declines, but presumably the party can be less concerned with the partisan commitment of these members. Rather, it can give additional positions to "marginally" qualified members and use their performance in these posts to determine whether they are worthy of promotion to rarer, higher-valued posts as they become available.

We do not use the number of positions as the sole measure for all positions. For the top, elected leadership positions, there is only one position per party. A measure based on only the number of positions—a constant—would thus fail to account for the hierarchical nature of the partisan advancement structure in Congress. A move from whip to floor leader would not be counted as a move up, when, in reality, this is a significant advancement. Parties clearly value these positions differently based on their level of responsibility to the party and on the sequential nature in which members typically advance from one position to the other. Thus, for elected party leaders, we use a position's ranking in the party hierarchy as the denominator.

Positions are ranked when the party elects the post or includes the appointee in its "core" decision-making council (Sinclair 1983), defined by whether the position receives ex officio status on party committees (e.g., the steering committees, congressional campaign committees, or policy committees). Our hierarchical rankings are based on the following logic. First, positions that are elected by the party caucus rank above party appointive posts. So, caucus vice chair and caucus secretaries are ranked above CCC chairs and chief deputy whips. Second, we follow the traditional line of succession (e.g., Canon 1989) and traditional understandings of a position's level of responsibility to the caucus (e.g., Hibbing 1991). As a consequence, "ranked" leaders who hold the same position with the majority and minority parties have the same score. This result obviously discounts the difference in institutional power between leaders in the majority and minority parties, but it is consistent with our attempt to measure the value of the position within the party's arsenal of selective incentives.

We believe that this combined method produces scores that reasonably, albeit crudely, rank the value of positions in the House. We multiply the scores by 100 to allow them to be squared to account for the diminishing effects that holding highly valuable posts is likely to have on a member's advancement into additional positions. The values of all positions, which, for clarity of exhibition, we have averaged across our eight sessions of Congress (101st to 109th), are listed in table 6.2. A detailed comparison of our scores to Hibbing's scores is presented in the appendix at the end of this chapter.

Elected party leaders have the highest scores in order of their hierarchical rankings within the party structure. Chair positions range from prestige committee chairs, valued at 25 (equivalent to the party caucus chairs), to undesirable committee chairs prior to the GOP takeover, valued at 9.1. Using Deering and Smith's (1997) categorization, policy committee chairs score 14.3—equivalent to party CCC/policy committee chairs, while constituency committee chairs score 12.5—equivalent to chief deputy whips.

Scores for party and committee appointments are generally lower than elected leaders' and committee chairs' scores. While there is some variation across the scores of one appointment to another, none of the other scores are dramatically different from one another, with the exception of the Rules Committee.[8] Similarly, despite being calculated separately by party, the scores for like positions are quite similar when averaged over our eight

TABLE 6.2. Average Position Values, 101st–110th Congresses

Ranked Positions (1/rank) × 100	Our Ratings	Hibbing's Ratings
Speaker	100	100
Floor leader	50.0	80
Whip	33.3	59
Conference chair	25.0	39
Conference vice chair	20.0	0
Conference secretary	16.7	0
Chair of a party committee (e.g., CCC)	14.3	0
Chief deputy whip	12.5	34
Vice chair of party committee	11.1	0

Positions Based on Number of Members of Each Caucus Serving
(1/number within each party) × 100

	Our Ratings, GOP	Our Ratings, Democrat	Hibbing
Extended Leadership Positions			
Deputy whip	8.8	8.5	34
Other whip	5.1	2.3	0
Steering committee	4.1	2.6	30
Party policy committee	3.3	8.3	0
Party research committee (101st–103rd)	4.5	n.a.	0
CCC	2.7	2.4	0
Committee Positions			
Chair/Ranking member			
Prestige committee	25.0	25.0	72
Policy committee	14.3	14.3	59
Constituency committee	12.5	12.5	59
Less desirable committee	9.1	9.1	34
Subcommittee chair/Ranking member			
Appropriations/prestige[a]	5.0	5.0	56
Policy/Constituency	0	0	40
Less desirable	0	0	17
Prestige committee membership			34
Appropriations	3.4	3.3	
Budget	5.2	5.0	
Rules	16.6	19.4	
Ways and Means	5.4	5.4	
Commerce[b]	3.4	4.8	
Financial Services[c]	0	2.8	
Policy/constituency membership	0	0	17
Less desirable membership	0	0	1

Note: n.a. = not applicable.

[a]We only code subcommittee leaders of the Appropriations Committee because the party caucuses confirm those appointments. Hibbing codes subcommittee chairmanships on all prestige committees.

[b]Commerce was an exclusive assignment for the Democrats starting the in the 105th Congress, for the Republicans starting in the 108th.

[c]Financial Services became an exclusive assignment for Democrats starting in the 109th Congress.

sessions of Congress. This is especially the case for each prestige committee's values, the result of both parties having served in the majority and minority and thus being overrepresented and underrepresented on these committees at different points in time during this period. The differences in average scores between the parties, such as the GOP's higher scores for whips and Steering Committee members, are a result of the Republicans generally appointing fewer members to these positions. We reiterate that members are given a position's score for their party in each Congress in our statistical equations rather than the averages presented here.[9]

It is also important to note that we exclude a number of committee positions, such as memberships and subcommittee chairmanships on policy and constituency committees, which are obviously valuable to individual members' career portfolios (e.g., Groseclose and Stewart 1998) but are not valued by the party caucuses as selective incentives (Cox and McCubbins 1993; Maltzman 1997; Rohde 1991; Shepsle 1978). As such, these committee positions are of limited value in helping us understanding the interactions between parties and members as parties attempt to identify and promote individuals dedicated to the party's collective good and as members seek to signal their qualifications for such posts.

An individual member's *position portfolio score*, then, is based on the sum of the scores of all the party-incentive positions held by the member in a given Congress.[10] When we analyze why members advance at varying rates, we use the total value of new positions a member has obtained in a given Congress as the dependent variable. Members who receive multiple new appointments receive a score representing the sum total of all their new positions in the new Congress. Most members did not receive any new appointments in a particular session of Congress and thus have a score of zero for the dependent variable.

Collective Goods and Advancement

As we argue in chapter 3, parties establish a system of institutional advancement and use positions of power as selective incentives to reward those who signal their ability to advance the party's collective good. We further argued that there are three key criteria on which parties could evaluate members' contributions to the collective good: (1) partisan time commitment, (2) party loyalty voting, and (3) redistribution of campaign funds to help the party win majority status. Partisan time commitment indicates a member's willingness to work in lower-level party posts to help the party achieve its collective goals. Service in lower-level posts provides the opportunity for party leaders and the caucus to evaluate the member's skills and dedication in challenging circumstances. A member's level of party loyalty voting indicates the member's support for the party's legislative agenda. A member's redistribution of campaign funds provides the financial resources to promote the party's collective electoral goal of majority status.

Crucial to our theory is whether the importance of each indicator of a member's commitment to the party's collective good shifts over time based on the political environment. First, the indicators of party loyalty are likely to be weighted differently by the majority and minority parties (Frisch and Kelly 2006). The majority party seeks to deliver on its policy agenda in order to retain power. Thus, it has an incentive to weight a member's ability to contribute to the party's collective legislative success more heavily than the minority party when evaluating members for promotion. The majority party, therefore, is more likely than the minority party to promote members based on party loyalty voting. By contrast, the minority party's highest priority is increasing its share of seats or at least not losing seats, in order to become the majority party in the future. Therefore, it has an incentive to weight a member's redistribution of campaign funds more heavily than party voting when evaluating the member's potential for advancement. In particular, party-oriented campaign contributions—those to candidates in competitive elections and to the party's congressional campaign committee—should be weighted more heavily by a party seeking to attain majority status. In contrast, a member's performance in an existing party post should be equally relevant as a criterion for advancement in both the majority and minority parties.

The redistribution of campaign funds should become a more important criterion for advancement in both parties following the 104th Congress, as the parties engage in the new battle for majority status. Prior to the 104th Congress, members, particularly those of the majority party, would be unlikely to consent to a promotion system that heavily weighted contributions to the party's collective electoral campaign when majority party control was unlikely to change. This changed after the GOP takeover of the House majority in the 1994 election, when narrow margins and uncertainty about which party would control the majority in the next Congress became the norm. Suddenly, parties had an incentive to compete aggressively for majority status by raising funds from incumbents for their collective campaign efforts. Parties also had the motivation to use selective incentives at their disposal, such as powerful institutional positions, to reward members who contributed to the party's efforts to attain majority status. As criterion for advancement, a member's redistribution of campaign funds is likely to be weighted more heavily when majority status is up for grabs. This was true for both parties after 1996.

Therefore, we hypothesize the following specific differences across time and party: (1) the importance of campaign funds as a determinant of advancement will increase for both parties following the GOP takeover in the 104th Congress; (2) campaign funds will be a more important determinant of advancement for the minority party than for the majority party; (3) party-oriented contribution strategies—contributions to congressional campaign committees and to candidates in competitive contests—will be more important criteria for advancement after the 104th Congress and for the minority party; and (4) party voting will be a more important determinant of advancement for the majority party than for the minority party.

To test our hypotheses that advancement patterns will vary by party and time, we estimate separate equations for each party. We interact voting loyalty and adjusted campaign contributions with a dummy variable for sessions of Congress before and after the 105th, with the 102nd Congress through the 104th in the early period and with the 105th through the 108th in the later period, to test our hypotheses that the relative weight given to party voting and campaign contributions will change as majority status changes and the battle for majority control intensify.[11] Party voting should be more heavily weighted for advancement for the majority party (Democrats in the pre-105th period, Republicans in the post-105th period); adjusted campaign contributions should increase their influence on advancement in both parties after the 105th Congress but should have a larger influence on advancement in the minority party in both eras. (See the appendix at the end of this chapter for variable measurements.)

The dependent variable is the change in the individual member's position portfolio score. We use the total value of the new positions obtained by a member in a given Congress. Temporally speaking, our dependent variable measures advancement to a new position in the current Congress, whereas our independent variables capture member behavior and characteristics in the previous Congress. We estimate the model using tobit, since 69 percent of the cases have a dependent variable with a value of zero. The results are displayed in table 6.3.[12]

Partisan Time Commitment. We use two variables to assess the effect of members' previous offices on their advancement. First is the total value of their position portfolio in the preceding Congress (the linear term). We also include the square of their portfolio score. Together, the two variables account for the diminishing marginal effect of a member's current portfolio on his or her future probability of advancement.

The results in table 6.3 show that members already serving in a party-controlled position are significantly more likely to obtain new positions (the positively signed linear term). However, as the negatively signed squared term shows, the probability of attaining valuable new positions declines significantly as one reaches the higher-valued positions (and there are fewer opportunities to advance).

Experience leads to advancement because it decreases the uncertainty for the party regarding the member's skills and dedication to the party's collective good. The party caucus can delegate power yet simultaneously minimize its risk that the power will be abused. Even assignments that have not traditionally been viewed as terribly valuable from the perspectives of reelection or policy impact, such as the Budget Committee or service as a regional whip, can help members advance by putting them in positions where they are visible to party leaders. By putting junior members in contact with powerful senior colleagues, novices have the opportunity to learn party norms and expectations that can help them advance further. As the number of positions decline on the higher rungs of the leadership ladder and as the chances of improving one's portfolio diminish, having

TABLE 6.3. Increases in Position Portfolios, 101st–110th Congresses (tobit)

	Republicans			Democrats		
	Coefficient	S.E.	p-value	Coefficient	S.E.	p-value
Position score$_{t-1}$	.646	.129	.00	.244	.082	.00
Position score$^2_{t-1}$	−.016	.004	.00	−.003	.002	.06
Party voting	1.84	.717	.01	1.60	.627	.01
Campaign funds (× 1,000)	.010	.003	.00	.002	.002	.33
Seniority	−0.94	.176	.00	−.546	.115	.00
Blocked advancement	−1.36	1.10	.21	−.497	.874	.57
$ × post-104th (× 1,000)	.009	.004	.02	.014	.003	.00
Voting × post-104th	−.236	1.04	.82	−.895	.837	.28
Constant	−2.67	1.80	.14	−6.51	1.35	.00
	$N = 1,612$			$N = 1,749$		
	Model $\chi^2 = 135$***			Model $\chi^2 = 109$***		
	Log likelihood = −2,555			Log likelihood = −2,723		

Note: Dummy variable controls for individual sessions of Congress are not displayed. S.E. = standard error.

***$p < .01$

proved oneself to one's colleagues and earned their trust becomes a powerful asset for ambitious members seeking the few available posts.

Party Loyalty Voting. The main effects coefficient for party loyalty shows that higher levels of party voting are significantly associated with advancement for both parties prior to the 105th Congress. However, the interactive terms for party voting are unrelated to advancement for either party, demonstrating that the importance of party voting does not substantially change after the 105th Congress. Each party consistently requires its members to support the party's legislative agenda before they can win promotions.

Campaign Funds. The relationship between campaign contributions and advancement is consistent with our hypotheses regarding party status. For Republicans, the main effects term for contributions shows that campaign donations were significantly related to advancement in the pre-105th period. Moreover, the statistically significant and positive coefficient for the interactive term in the GOP regression demonstrates that the effect of money on advancement increased within the GOP conference in the post-104th period. As predicted, the story is somewhat different for House Democrats. In the regression for Democrats, the main effects term for contributions is statistically insignificant, indicating that the effect of contributions on advancement in the pre-104th period (when Democrats were the majority party) was statistically indistinguishable from zero. However, as shown by the positive and statistically significant interactive term for Democrats, money did have an effect on advancement within the House Democratic caucus in the post-104th period.

The tobit coefficients presented in table 6.3 tell us little about the substantive effect of contributions on the expected actual change in the value of a member's position portfolio. We compute these effects and plot them in figure 6.1, which displays the average change in the value of a member's position portfolio—during both the post-104th and prior periods—at various levels of redistribution.[13] We do not compute expected values for Democrats in the pre-105th period, because the main effects coefficient for that period was statistically insignificant.

The changes displayed in figure 6.1 demonstrate several points. First, members get more (in terms of advancement payoff) in the post-104th period than in the prior period. The graph lines for Republicans and Democrats in the post-104th period are considerably steeper than the graph line for the GOP in the 101st–104th period. Second, it is expensive to move up. For example, in the post-104th period, an increase in redistribution from $0 to $2 million would add 20.70 points to a GOP incumbent's

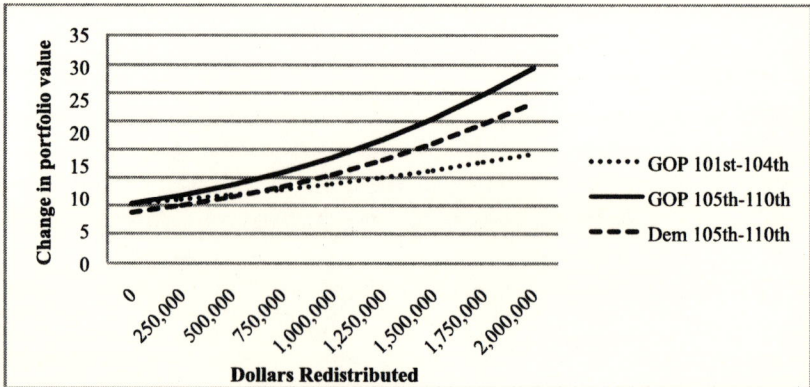

Fig. 6.1. Expected change in position portfolio value at various levels of redistribution

position portfolio score. With respect to position values, that is roughly equal to a conference vice chair post. Third, the changes are nonlinear. In terms of advancement, the more members continue to give, the bigger the payoff they receive for each dollar they redistribute. For example, in the post-104th period, an increase from $0 to $250,000 in contributions would add only 1.29 points to a GOP member's portfolio value. An identical $250,000 increase—from $1.5 to $1.75 million—would add 3.65 points to a member's position portfolio. So, there seems to be something of a threshold that members need to reach before donations begin having a more influential impact.

Besides partisan time commitment, party loyalty voting, and campaign money, we control for several independent variables that also could affect a member's attainment of new positions. Specifically, we control for the member's seniority and the session of Congress. Seniority should be negatively related to advancement—that is, junior members should be more likely to advance—and this is exactly what we find. With the exception of committee chairs and ranking members, the more senior a member is, the more likely he or she is to have already moved up in the party system (Hibbing 1991). Junior members can easily attain many of the low-value positions (e.g., in the whip system). The party has substantial incentive to give junior members the opportunity to participate, since such participation socializes them into partisanship (Garand and Clayton 1986) and vets them for future leadership opportunities.

This evidence provides strong confirmation regarding the criteria that parties use to evaluate members' commitment to the party's collective good for advancement: prior experience, party loyalty voting, and the redistribution of campaign funds to the party and its candidates. These criteria also are weighted by the political environment. Our evidence suggests that the minority party weights a member's ability to redistribute campaign funds more heavily than the majority party. Without picking up seats to win majority control, the ability of minority party members to achieve their other policy and power goals are limited. Our evidence does not support the hypothesis that the majority party will weight party voting more heavily than the minority party, as the effects of party voting seem to be stable for both parties across the time period.

Do Contributing and Voting Improve Position Portfolios?

Logically, it is easy to expect that if parties value voting and financial loyalty, members who combine both these qualities would be even more likely to advance than their colleagues who excelled on only one of these dimensions. Alternatively, it is possible that some members redistribute to compensate for a poor legislative loyalty record. We interacted members' levels of adjusted contributions with their voting loyalty scores to test these possibilities and ran the models separately by party and by time period (101st–104th and 105th–110th). We consistently found that the interaction (the combined effect) of voting and redistribution was not significantly related to advancement for either party, in either time period, or for elective or appointive positions (results not shown). Voting and redistribution, then, appear to be independent routes to promotion in Congress. When parties shift their priority from one collective goal to another (legislation to majority status), they promote members who can help them achieve that goal rather than members who can help them achieve both goals simultaneously.[14]

Campaign Contribution Strategies

Left unanswered by the previous analysis is how campaign contributions matter in the advancement of members of the House. The results we have just presented show that the aggregate amounts members contribute increase the value of their position portfolio, especially when the parties are competing for majority status. But we do not know whether the way in which the contributions were distributed to candidates and party committees affects advancement. Do parties reward members who follow an individualistic contribution strategy—that is, a strategy of giving to candidates (usually safe incumbents) who are most likely to help them achieve their personal advancement goals? Or do parties reward members who follow a party-oriented strategy of helping the party expand its number of seats by contributing to challengers and open-seat candidates? As our third hypothesis presented earlier states, parties should reward party-oriented strategies more when majority party control is up for grabs.

If the parties promote members who have donated primarily to safe incumbents (who vote in caucus elections), we have evidence of a "pay-to-play" system. The donor is simply exchanging campaign funds for the institutional position, and the parties are essentially auctioning positions to the highest bidder. There is no collective party goal advanced, other than that the members who received the contributions have more money in their war chests and that the parties have put their most motivated fundraisers in position to extract even more from contributors. Generously bequeathing funds to safe incumbents does little to help the party expand its number of seats or win majority control.

If, however, the parties promote members who contribute primarily to candidates in competitive contests, to nonincumbents, or to the congressional campaign committees, we have evidence that the parties are concerned about the donor's ability to provide for the collective electoral good of the party. Members who follow party-oriented contribution strategies have not only signaled their ability to organize substantial donor coalitions; they have also targeted their campaign funds in a fashion necessary to win majority control.

Chapter 5 showed that contribution strategies have shifted in a party-oriented direction. This shift is due in part to the party's greater efforts at mobilizing and coordinating contributions from its incumbents. But it also no doubt reflects the changing incentive structure when partisan margins narrow. As majority status becomes the parties' highest-priority collective good, the parties should be expected to allocate positions to lawmakers who employ party-oriented contribution strategies over those who employ individualistic contribution strategies. Here we examine members' contribution strategies as a way to assess this expectation.

In our conceptualization, incumbents can contribute campaign money to party candidates in four ways, which have varying potential to ingratiate themselves with the ultimate candidate beneficiary. The four categories are contributions to challengers and open-seat candidates, contributions to competitive incumbents, contributions to the member's party CCC, and contributions to safe incumbents. Contributions to challengers, open-seat candidates, and incumbents in competitive contests (as rated by *Congressional Quarterly*) all involve the seats on which majority status is likely to hinge. Contributions to candidates in these campaigns demonstrate a member's commitment to helping his or her party win majority control. There are reasons, however, to distinguish between them as contribution strategies. Contributions to challengers and open-seat candidates primarily help to expand the party's number of seats, whereas contributions to competitive incumbents help the party retain the seats it already holds. Contributions to challengers and open-seat candidates are therefore a higher strategic objective for the minority party, while contributions to competitive incumbents are a higher priority for the majority party (Currinder 2003).

Thus, parties are likely to reward incumbents who contribute to the specific kinds of candidates who help them achieve majority status. The majority party will reward members who contribute to competitive incumbents who protect their ability to hold the majority; the minority party will reward members who contribute to challengers and open-seat candidates who will help them become the majority. Moreover, given that incumbents are consistently more likely to win than challengers, members who contribute to challengers—and, to a lesser extent, to open-seat candidates—signal their ability to take greater risks in support of the party. If the party, particularly the minority party, seeks to reward those who serve its collective electoral good, it should reward those who take personal risks on behalf of the party's collective good.

Contributions to the CCCs also advance the party goal of majority control. A member's donations to the CCC allow the party to target the money to the contests on which majority control will hinge. The critical difference between the strategies oriented around collective goods is that giving directly to candidates allows the contributor to be identified by the recipient and thus allows for the potential repayment of the favor at a later time (e.g., in the form of votes in caucus leadership elections),[15] whereas contributing to the CCC severs the link between the incumbent donor and the ultimate recipient of the money. Party leaders and the caucus may be able to reward the CCC donor for his or her contributions to the team, but there can be no direct repayment of favors from the candidates who benefit from the contribution. Generous, party-oriented contributions of either variety should increase the donor's advancement, as these kinds of contributions demonstrate a member's sacrifice for the collective good of the party.

Contributions to safe incumbents, the fourth and final contribution category, are unlikely to affect collective electoral outcomes, because safe members are highly likely to win anyway. Donors presumably give to electorally secure colleagues largely to advance their own individualistic goals, such as building legislative or ideological coalitions, doing personal favors for acquaintances, or building chits that can be called in to win promotions in the House. Thus, a donation to a safe incumbent is essentially an exchange of selective goods—individual electoral assistance for individual institutional assistance. Given the high likelihood that safe members will be reelected, contributing to them is a low-risk strategy for members who are investing in colleagues who can return favors in the future. If members indeed reward colleagues who contribute to them with votes in leadership elections, there will be a positive relationship between contributions to safe contributions and advancement. Indeed, Matthew Green (2008; see also Green and Harris 2007) has produced evidence that members are significantly more likely to pledge public support to leadership candidates who have made LPAC contributions to their campaigns.

There is one way in which contributing to safe colleagues may have collective benefits. To the extent that receiving contributions from party leaders entices members to vote more consistently with the party (Cann 2008), contributions can produce collective legislative goods for the party. Still, it seems more likely that the primary reason for making contributions to electorally secure colleagues, especially for most members who are not top elected leaders, is to advance individualistic goals.

Contributions to safe incumbents may generate the breadth of support across the caucus necessary to win an elective leadership contest, and they may help incumbent party leaders generate votes for legislation. Thus, there is an incentive for party leaders and those competing for elected leadership posts to contribute to safe incumbents. But for members seeking appointive positions, it seems highly unlikely that party leaders or the party caucus would see contributing to safe colleagues as service to the party's collective good. Thus, our expectations for the relationship between contributions to safe incumbents and advancement are mixed: positive for elective positions but no relationship or a negative one for appointive positions.

We thus will analyze advancement in three forms: (1) increases in members' *position portfolios* (the dependent variable used in the previous section), (2) the increase in value of *elected positions* in the member's portfolio (elected party leadership positions, committee chairs, and the Appropriations Committee's subcommittee chairs), and (3) the increase in value of *appointed positions* (extended leadership positions and commit-tee transfers).[16] To avoid cumbersome interaction terms between party loyalty voting and four categories of contributions between the period preceding the 105th Congress and the post-105th period, we analyze the time periods separately to assess changes over time in the party's advance-ment structures. Tobit is again used as the estimation procedure. We pres-ent only results of the contribution strategy variables; the other indepen-dent variables produce the same results as they do in table 6.3, so there is no need to discuss them again here.

Table 6.4 shows that prior to the 105th Congress, both parties were significantly more likely to promote members who contributed more gen-erously to the party's challengers and open-seat candidates. This was the only category of contribution that was rewarded during this era. Demo-crats who contributed to safe incumbents were actually significantly less likely than their colleagues to advance.[17] Interestingly, table 6.3 shows that aggregate contributions from Democrats were unrelated to advancement prior to the 105th Congress; here we see that how campaign money was targeted was more important to advancement than the total amount re-distributed.

After the 104th Congress, the types of contributions that led to promo-tion shifted in both parties. Republicans now promoted those who con-tributed to competitive incumbents and to the National Republican Con-gressional Committee. With the majority in hand, the GOP only had to retain its incumbents to retain power. Party leaders also rewarded mem-bers with appointments who contributed generously directly to the party CCC. Democrats continued to promote members who contributed sub-stantial sums to challengers and open-seat candidates. What differed for Democrats after the 104th Congress was that members who targeted their contributions to competitive incumbents were significantly less likely to advance, while those who contributed to safe incumbents were more likely to advance. The explanation for this pattern becomes evident when elected and appointed positions are analyzed separately.

Looking at the column in table 6.4 for elected positions in the 105th–110th Congresses, we see that Democrats who contributed to safe incumbents as well as to challenger and open-seat candidates were more likely to be promoted to elected leadership positions. The members who sought elected positions in this era (especially Nancy Pelosi and Steny Hoyer) contributed munificently to a large number of candidates—non-incumbents and safe incumbents alike—in hopes of winning majority status and winning the votes of their colleagues for leadership posts.

TABLE 6.4. Contribution Strategies and Advancement, by Parties and Session of Congress (tobit)

| | Republicans | | | | | | Democrats | | | | | |
| | 101st–104th | | | 105th–110th | | | 101st–104th | | | 105th–110th | | |
	All	Elected	Appted.	All	Elected	Appted.	All	Elected	Appted.	All	Elected	Appted.
Challenger/Open seat	.35**	.76**	.07	-.11	-.20	.03	.24*	1.1**	.26**	1.1**	1.6*	.18
Competitive incumbent	-.31	-.93	.28	1.1**	3.0**	.48*	.10	.02	-.03	-1.2*	-2.7	.37
Safe incumbent	-2.2	-4.8	.27	-.06	-.24	-.07	-.34*	-.10	-.24	1.2*	2.6*	-.63
Party CCC	.10	.41	.07	.21*	.22	.13*	-.01	-.11	.04	-.09	-.08	.28**

*p < .05; **p < .01

Democrats in elected leadership posts gave, on average, $93,850 in contributions to safe incumbents during this era, which amounted to 7 percent of the total funds redistributed by Democratic elected leaders. By contrast, Democrats without elected leadership positions gave only 4 percent of their donations to safe incumbents during this period.[18] We get a different picture of the relationship between contribution strategies and advancement for appointed positions for Democrats in the 105th–110th Congresses, one that squares more neatly with our hypothesis that the minority will reward members who follow party-oriented contribution strategies: Democrats who contributed liberally to the Democratic Congressional Campaign Committee were significantly more likely to win appointments from party leaders.

In sum, the results, particularly for the Democrats, show that those seeking elective party office have an incentive to contribute directly to incumbents who serve as the electorate in leadership contests. If those seeking elective office gave to the party CCC, they would lose the opportunity to earn the personal gratitude of the recipients. Conversely, members who seek appointment to positions of power have an incentive to please party leaders by contributing generously to the party. Members seeking appointive posts do not need the personal loyalty of large numbers of recipients in the caucus to achieve their advancement goals; they do need to catch the eye of party leaders and demonstrate for them their dedication to the collective electoral fortunes of the party. These findings are consistent with the contribution patterns of members who hold and seek positions, where the evidence shows that members who sought elective party or committee leadership positions gave significantly more from their principal campaign committees and LPACs directly to candidates, whereas current elected leaders and members of the extended leadership gave significantly more to the CCCs (see chapter 4).

These results also align with findings that the minority party's advancement structures have traditionally been more open and entrepreneurial than those of the majority party (Canon 1989; Peabody 1976). The minority party caucus is open to insurgents willing to take elective positions of limited institutional power, pledging to try something new to lead the party into the promised land of majority status. Apparently, for minority party Democrats, this meant that leadership aspirants had to show their ability to raise and redistribute campaign funds, but it did not mean that they had to target their contributions only in ways that would maximize the party's collective electoral success.

Freshman Appointments

The preceding analysis demonstrates the importance of having a low-level, appointive position as a means of demonstrating one's abilities, building relationships with elected leaders, and impressing members of the caucus who can help one advance up additional rungs on the leadership ladder. Many members, 189 of those elected between 1990 and 2006, obtained their initial appointment as freshmen in Congress. For these members, our analysis thus far evaluates their success in obtaining additional appointments and has left open the question of whether the party evaluates and rewards freshmen seeking party posts in the same ways as it does experienced members. We argue that the party uses the same basic approach.

Still, incoming freshmen have not had opportunities to build relationships with members of the leadership or the caucus, nor have they participated in mobilizations to pass legislation through writing or whipping or voting. Thus, the caucus cannot use the same exact criteria as it does for returning members. Nor can we use the same measures. Instead, we measure the freshmen's legislative experience based on whether the member served in the state legislature.

The caucus is likely to value the state legislative experience of freshmen in deciding who to choose for positions of power. State legislative service also gives the freshmen a reputation among state party leaders, other state legislators, state-level interest groups and media, and so on, to whom members of Congress can turn for information about the skills and performance of a freshmen. Freshmen who have not served in the state legislature may have adequate political skills, but there is likely to be greater uncertainty about their abilities until they have had the chance to demonstrate them in a legislative context. All things being equal, former state legislators should be more likely to win extended leadership or prestige committee appointments as freshmen. From the 106th Congress to the 110th, freshmen have a high level of state legislative experience: 134 (59.3 percent) have served in the state legislature.

Freshmen can also contribute campaign funds to party candidates and their party's CCC to demonstrate their commitment to the party's collective electoral good. However, freshmen members, by definition, do not have the advantages of incumbency and usually face very competitive elections. They are likely to need their campaign funds for their own campaigns and are unlikely to have much flexibility to redirect funds to the party and fellow party candidates. Moreover, the party is also likely to prefer that they devote their efforts to winning the seat for the party rather than increasing their risk by redistributing campaign funds. Nevertheless, freshmen who do provide campaign assistance to the party's candidates are likely to increase their probability of winning valuable positions upon attaining office, because they have demonstrated their ability to make personal sacrifices on behalf of the party's collective electoral effort. Between 1998 and 2006, almost one-half of freshmen (46.9 percent) contributed to the party or party candidates in the election cycle in which they were initially elected to the House. In these five election cycles, freshmen contributed a total of $3.3 million in adjusted campaign funds (adjusted to values in the 2000 election cycle).

As with incumbents, freshmen who help to advance the party's legislative agenda are more likely to gain party posts. Cox and McCubbins (1993, 183–86) find that freshmen who vote loyally with the party are more likely to obtain prestige committee assignments. Obviously, we cannot measure freshmen party loyalty voting prior to their service in Congress, so, following Cox and McCubbins, we use freshmen party loyalty scores at the end of their freshmen term. This measurement strategy limits our ability to make causal inferences, because the experience of serving in party posts may affect a member's voting behavior during his or her freshman year (Garand and Clayton 1986).

Finally, younger members may be more likely to win party posts, as they will have more years to advance prior to reaching normal retirement ages. Party leaders have an incentive to recruit younger members into the leadership, because if the member has the requisite skills and commitment to the party, the party can benefit from his or her service for longer periods of time.

We also control for a freshman's electoral margin and political party. Parties may be more willing to appoint members with safe seats to party posts (Peabody 1976), because these members face less potential conflict between their party and constituency responsibilities. Additionally, because members who win comfortably are more able to afford redistribution, controlling for the member's margin of victory ensures that the member's commitment to the party (as expressed by redistribution), rather than his or her electoral safety, explains an appointment. We also control for political party because one party or the other may be more receptive to having freshmen in leadership positions during this era.

We analyze freshmen appointments from the 106th–110th Congresses. We include only newly elected members and exclude members who are elected to their first full term but served a partial term in the previous

Congress because of a special election victory.[19] In this time period, 50 freshmen (22.1 percent) received extended leadership organization appointments, and 6 (2.7 percent) received prestige committee appointments.

We analyze freshmen appointments using a logit model. Our dependent variable is whether the freshman received an appointment to the extended leadership structure or a prestige committee. The results are presented in table 6.5.

All three of our three key independent variables of party advancement criteria are signed correctly (positively). Only contributions, however, are related to appointments at a statistically significant level; state legislative experience and party voting are unrelated to promotion as a freshman. Younger members ($p < .07$) and Republicans ($p < .06$) are also more likely to receive appointments at marginal levels of significance.

The more campaign money a newly elected member redistributes to the party and its candidates, the more likely it is that the member will be able to take an initial step onto the leadership ladder in his or her first Congress. To estimate the effect of contributions on the probability of receiving an appointment, we changed the value of adjusted contributions from zero to one standard deviation above the mean ($53,700), while holding other variables at their mean or, for dichotomous variables, at their minimum. The probability of a Democratic freshman receiving an

TABLE 6.5. Appointment of Freshmen Members of Congress to a Party Position, 106th–110th Congresses (logit)

	Coefficient	S.E.	p-value
State legislative experience	.163	.352	.64
Party loyalty voting	.293	.204	.17
Campaign funds (× 1,000)	.155	.057	.01
Age	−.037	.020	.07
Electoral margin	−.003	.018	.84
Republican Party	.686	.357	.06
Constant	−.348	1.53	.82

$N = 225$
Model $\chi^2 = 27.5$ ($p < .01$)
Log likelihood = 220
Pseudo $R^2 = .11$

Note: S.E. = standard error.

appointment nearly doubles from 12.3 to 24.4 percent when contributions increase by this amount; for Republican freshmen, redistributing this sum increased the probability of receiving an appointment by 17 percentage points (from 22.1 to 39.1 percent). In contrast, increasing a hypothetical freshman's age from one standard deviation below the mean (40) to one standard deviation above the mean (57) decreases the probability of receiving an appointment by 8 percentage points (from 19.7 to 11.7 percent) for Democrats and by 12 percentage points (from 33.1 to 21.1 percent) for Republicans. Freshmen members who accept the considerable risk of contributing to the party and its candidates in their initial campaign signal their willingness to serve the party's collective good.

That campaign funds are the only variable associated with freshmen promotion reflects the clarity of money as a signal. Months before the start of a new Congress, party leaders and caucuses have a clear, quantifiable record of an incoming member's contributions; they also have knowledge of the member's electoral circumstances—and thus of the extent to which redistribution was a sacrifice for the new member. By contrast, at the same point in time, a freshman's legislative skills and willingness to vote with the party are much more uncertain. Understandably, leaders and the caucus will rely heavily—if not exclusively—on the more certain indicator of a freshman's commitment to the party's collective good. This finding also aligns with our finding that redistribution played a particularly important role in the advancement of returning members during this time period. In that sense, the parties are promoting freshmen and nonfreshmen on similar criteria.[20]

To be sure, redistributing campaign funds does not ensure a freshman an extended leadership post, nor does a failure to redistribute funds definitely exclude a freshman from attaining an appointment. Indeed, 17 freshmen who contributed nothing (14.2 percent of noncontributors) received an appointment, and 69 members (65.1 percent of contributors) who contributed failed to receive an appointment. Still, contributors were significantly more likely than noncontributors to obtain an extended leadership post, and redistribution was more reliable as a predictor of securing a post than were state legislative experience or party loyalty voting. Thus, redistributing early (and often) helps members gain an initial foothold into the leadership. From there, as our earlier analysis indicates, continued redistribution, effective service in the position, and loyal voting help one persuade the caucus to support one's continued advancement into more powerful positions.

Conclusion

Congressional advancement has long been a topic that has fascinated congressional scholars and journalists alike. Academic studies of advancement have tended to be oriented around case studies (e.g., Peabody 1976), focused on the environment or structures of advancement (Canon 1989; Nelson 1977; Polsby 1968), or focused on particular kinds of positions (e.g., the literature on committee transfers). The reason for the disjointed nature of the study of advancement is the lack of a common metric by which different positions with different methods of selection can be compared.

In this chapter, we have provided an integrated analysis of advancement in the House. We developed a party-based supply-side measure of position portfolios in the House, enabling us to link principal-agent theories and ambition theories to empirical, quantitative analysis of member advancement in the House. We found that experience, party voting, and generosity in providing campaign funds are key indicators of congressional advancement for both political parties. We also found that parties are sensitive to the political environment and adjust the weights of their criteria based on the ongoing battle for majority status. As majority status becomes a priority, providing campaign funding becomes more important, and parties seem to place greater emphasis on party-oriented contributions, especially for appointed positions.

We have shown that there are systematic patterns of advancement in the House of Representatives. The parties have rational means of evaluating potential leaders' skills and dedication. Advancement is a result not only of individual ambition but also of context and the institutional structures developed by the congressional party. The party requires evidence of a demonstration of commitment to the party's collective good to delegate power to individual members; our evidence shows that they receive it.

Democrats and Republicans who followed party-oriented contribution strategies increased the value of their position portfolios through appointive positions. Republicans who advanced to elective leadership posts targeted their contributions to the embattled incumbents who, if they won, would protect the party's majority. On the whole, then, our evidence shows that parties structure the advancement process to reward members who financially support the party's collective electoral fortunes. Still, some evidence of a pay-to-play system exists. Democrats who gave to safe incumbents after the 104th Congress were more likely to win powerful elected leadership posts. But these same Democrats also gave significantly higher sums to Democratic challengers and open-seat candidates whose victories would be necessary for the party to regain its majority. In short, Democrats who advanced to elective party posts followed mixed (or all-of-the-above) contribution strategies.

Our finding that money affects advancement in Congress raises potentially troubling normative concerns, even if the money helps the party collectively. Citizens expect congressional leaders to be effective legislators and managers of governing institutions rather than fundraisers. Our finding shows that congressional leaders wear two hats simultaneously: that of a legislative leader and that of a party fundraiser. They are responsible both for articulating and passing a party issue agenda and for generating resources and public support to help their colleagues win office. That they excel at fundraising nevertheless raises the concern that they give more attention to electioneering than to legislating. These activities, though, are interdependent. Likewise, the skills necessary to attract support from a large number of donors is not dissimilar to the skills necessary to build coalitions to pass legislation. Indeed, self-funding candidates frequently fail because they are unable to articulate a message attractive to voters, since they never have to develop one attractive to potential donors (Steen 2006). The real problem arises if the agenda necessary to attract support from donors differs from the public interest (or even from the preferences of the party's mass adherents). Similarly, the political gamesmanship oriented toward clarifying the differences between the parties and mobilizing the party bases and party donors may conflict with the need to work collaboratively to address public problems. If these concerns are correct, the battle for majority status, while giving the public more "control" over which party organizes Congress, may end up actually giving the public no more control over policy outcomes.

APPENDIX

The Budget Committee

Despite its status as a party control committee (Deering and Smith 1997; Sinclair 1983, 107–8), the Budget Committee has not traditionally been identified in the literature as a particularly valuable assignment for members. In part, this is due to the fact that Budget Committee appointments are term limited: one cannot gain power and expertise through seniority on that committee in a manner similar to other committees. The Budget Committee has also not traditionally been identified as a meaningful rung on the leadership ladder, one that ambitious members might use to promote future advancement.[21] Thus, we believe it is important to justify our decision to count Budget Committee appointments as selective party incentives and as positions in members' leadership portfolios.

We followed the careers of members elected in 1988 or after and who served in at least two sessions of Congress and therefore had the opportunity to advance. Using our data set, we coded the advancement of all members but divided them into three categories: (1) members whose initial appointment was to the Budget Committee (including members who simultaneously were appointed to an extended leadership position),[22] (2) members whose initial appointment was to an extended leadership position, and (3) members who received neither Budget Committee nor extended leadership appointments. We coded advancement when a member obtained a higher-status position in the elected or extended leadership than the one they obtained as a freshman, received a prestige committee assignment, or sought another office (governor, U.S. Senate). Having nothing in the literature on which to base our expectations, our intuitive guess was that members with extended leadership appointments would be the most likely to advance, members with neither extended leadership nor Budget Committee appointments would be the least likely to advance, and Budget Committee members would fall somewhere in between.

The results were therefore surprising and strongly support classifying Budget Committee assignments as stepping-stones in congressional advancement and therefore as valuable selective incentives controlled by the parties. Of the 78 junior members who were appointed to the Budget Committee from 1990 to 2004 and who served more than one Congress, 54 (69 percent) later advanced. The Budget Committee member's rate of advancement is extremely similar to—and, in fact, slightly higher than—members of the extended leadership. Of the 272 members appointed to the extended leadership, 176 (65 percent) later advanced. In contrast, members who obtained neither Budget Committee nor extended leadership positions were much less likely to advance: 43 of 145 (30 percent) did so.

Consistent with our theory of advancement, service on the Budget Committee gives party leaders and the caucus the opportunity to evaluate a member's performance on high-priority items on the party agenda. Much like service in the extended leadership, this visibility and opportunity to work with other members in party positions gives ambitious Budget Committee members an additional advantage in identifying and taking advantage of opportunities for promotion.

Comparison of the Position Portfolio Scores to Hibbing's Institutional Power Scores

The key difference between our measures and Hibbing's is that Hibbing assigns values to all subcommittee chairmanships and all committee memberships, whereas we ignore these positions on policy and constituency committees. Our measure is more heavily oriented toward extended party leadership positions; Hibbing's is more oriented toward committee positions. Additionally, we assign values to members of both parties, whereas Hibbing codes only the majority party. To facilitate comparisons between our measures, however, we apply Hibbing's majority party values to the members of the minority party who hold the same positions. We present a comparison between our values and Hibbing's scores for the 102nd and 103rd Congresses and for the 105th Congress. With the abolishment of almost all of Hibbing's "undesirable" committees starting in the 104th Congress, the range of his scale is limited thereafter, making comparison of scores before and after the 104th Congress difficult. We present the correlations separately by party. For the GOP, our score and Hibbing's correlate at .443; for the Democrats, the correlation is higher, at .553. Since Hibbing was rating the power of positions under the Democrats, it is not surprising that our measures are more closely related for them.

As a second approach to our comparison, we remove the values of committee positions that Hibbing includes but we do not (policy, constituency, and "less desirable" committee subcommittee chairs and memberships). Naturally, the correlation between our measure and Hibbing's increases for both parties, since we are now basing the comparison on the same set of positions: for the GOP, the correlation increases to .57, while for the Democrats, the correlation is .76. With this modification of Hibbing's measure, his measure gives values of greater than zero to three members that we score zero, while we give scores to 97 members that Hibbing scores zero (85 of these members have scores of less than 10).

Variable Measurements

Blocked committee advancement: 1 = on all the committees on which a member serves, a younger member has greater seniority; 0 = on at least one committee, all representatives with greater seniority are older than the member.

Campaign contributions: the sum of the three types of member contributions: contributions from a member's principal campaign committee to other candidates' campaigns, contributions from a member's PCC to the party congressional campaign committee, and contributions from a member's leadership PAC to other candidates. Incumbent contributions were calculated by the authors based on data obtained from the Federal Election Commission. To compare contributions across eight election cycles in which contributions escalated substantially, we set all contributions at their 2000 value. First, we divided an election cycle's total member contributions (EC_x) by the total member contributions in 2000 (EC_{2000}). That proportion was then inverted so that, when multiplied by EC_x, EC_x equals EC_{2000}. Each member's contribution for EC_x was then multiplied by the same proportion.

Essentially, we are measuring each member's percentage of total contributions for a given year and expressing it in terms of 2000 dollars. In this way, the effect of each year's contributions on advancement can be evaluated on the same basis as every other year's (see also Heberlig 2003).

Partisan time commitment: the value of a member's position portfolio score—the total value of the all the positions the member held—in the previous Congress. The effect of a member's existing portfolio should be subject to diminishing marginal returns; therefore, we include a member's preceding position portfolio score squared. The squared term accounts for the increasing difficulty of obtaining additional and more valuable positions the higher one has already risen in the leadership structure.

Party loyalty voting: the z-score of a member's *Congressional Quarterly* score in party loyalty voting (adjusted for attendance). The z-score is used to make the scores comparable across different sessions of Congress. Party leaders anecdotally use Congressional Quarterly scores as a voting loyalty measure in their evaluation of candidates for appointments (Barry 1989; Cann 2008; Deering and Smith 1997; Rohde 1991; Sinclair 1983).

Seniority: the number of years a member has served at the time of the Congress under consideration. With the exception of committee chairs and ranking members, the more senior a member is, the more likely he or she is to have already moved up in the party system (Hibbing 1991). Party leaders also have an incentive to appoint junior members to party posts to socialize them into the party (Garand and Clayton 1986).

Session of Congress: a dummy variable for each session of Congress to control for variations in opportunities to attain new positions.

7 | Leveraging Funds to Pay for the New Party Fundraising Expectations

In the contemporary era, fundraising has surely always seemed like a Sisyphusian task to officeholders: they are always raising money, and new demands for more funds are always present. Campaign staff need money for one more mailing, media consultants press for one more television ad, pollsters recommend conducting one more expensive poll, the campaign automobile needs yet another repair, and there is always another consultant or staffer to pay. Fundraising burdens are especially acute for House members, whose brief two-year term compels most to begin raising funds for the next campaign as soon as the last one is over. Even during the first few months of a new Congress—by most accounts, the best window of opportunity for serious lawmaking—producing a solid first-quarter fundraising report remains a strategic imperative. Enough is never enough. Like the ill-fated rock roller of Greek mythology, House members must feel like they never reach the fundraising pinnacle, where they can stop and do something less onerous.

To be ever pressed by party leaders to raise more money for the party and its candidates makes the money chase even more burdensome. As previous chapters have shown, the increased power of congressional party leaders over the last decade has produced a more centralized fundraising regime in the U.S. House. Party leaders increasingly control the career advancement of individual legislators within the institution. With party control on the line, leaders have used their power to reward incumbents willing to provide finance assistance to the party congressional campaign committees and fellow party candidates. Clearly, congressional party norms have changed radically from 25 years ago, when House incumbents—even those with substantial war chests—routinely refused to share their campaign money with the party CCCs (Jacobson 1985–86).

In this chapter, we explore the effects of the party's tremendous new fundraising expectations on incumbent fundraising behavior. In particular, we develop and test La Raja's (2008b, 217) speculation that "as incumbents give more to the party, they feel the need to replace this money by raising more for their campaign committees." The evidence we present confirms La Raja's speculation and demonstrates that the new party fundraising expectations have indeed had a substantial effect on lawmakers' fundraising behavior. In particular, the more a member's spending on party-connected campaign contributions "crowds out" his or her spending on reelection activities in a given cycle, the more that member increases his or her principal campaign committee's receipts from large individual donors and business PACs in the next cycle, and the more likely he or she is to form a new leadership PAC in the next cycle. We also show that these trends are more pronounced in the post-BCRA period, as congressional party leaders leaned increasingly harder on incumbents to help offset the loss of party soft money banned by BCRA (Dwyre et al. 2006).

Financing Contributions to the Party and Its Candidates

In theory, members have at least four ways of paying for the growing sums of campaign money they redistribute to the party CCC and party candidates. First, they can divert money they would normally save for their own war chests. Second, they can divert money they would ordinarily spend on their own reelections. Third, they can raise additional sums of campaign money for their principal campaign committees. Fourth, they can form a leadership PAC.

Most of what we know about incumbents suggests that they would prefer to pay for party-connected contributions without cutting into spending for their own campaigns or into the savings in their war chests. As Jacobson (2009, 100) points out, incumbents are a highly risk-averse lot who "tend to exaggerate electoral threats and overact to them" by spending beyond what is objectively necessary to win (also see Mann 1978). But spending excessive sums and building large war chests can also be viewed as a rational effort by incumbents to maximize certainty in what they perceive as a politically uncertain environment. Although most House members are safe most of the time, every member knows a colleague who was unexpectedly picked off by a challenger.[1]

Compounding electoral uncertainty for incumbents has been the rapid and dramatic increase in issue advertising by interest groups and political parties (Boatright et al. 2006; Herrnson 2008; Magleby 2000). Incumbents must be prepared to defend themselves against outside forces willing to spend millions in their district to undercut their reputation. Raising and spending money is a hedge against this uncertainty. Indeed, as Jacobson (2009, 98) writes, incumbents "now spend increasing amounts of money preemptively in order to inoculate voters against anticipated attacks." Similarly, incumbents likely perceive spending and saving, which they can control, as protection against unpredictable twists and turns in the political environment (e.g., negative national partisan trends), which they cannot control (Box-Steffensmeier 1996). Writing about the 2010 midterm elections, Newmyer (2010) underscores the tension for House Democrats between redistribution and spending on one's own reelection: "Facing stiff political headwinds this cycle, a number of members eyeing potentially tough re-election fights for the first time in years are holding on to their reserves." Finally, a large war chest can potentially help reduce incumbent uncertainty by potentially deterring would-be challengers (Box-Steffensmeier 1996) and—in the (unlikely) event that a strong challenger does emerge—by serving as "precautionary savings" (Goodliffe 2004; Sorauf 1988).[2]

To be sure, at a certain point, the steep costs of raising additional dollars may persuade members to finance at least some of their party-connected contributions by spending less on their own campaign activities or by saving less in their war chests. Raising campaign money is not free, and the costs climb for each additional dollar raised (Goodliffe 2004). Moreover, dollars spent on reelection activities, as well as those deployed to discourage the opposition, provide diminishing marginal returns (Box-Steffensmeier 1996; Jacobson 1997). Many lawmakers also claim to detest fundraising (Herrnson 2004, 165; Sorauf 1992, 72). As one House freshman asserted, "How much do I like doing [fundraising]? I hate it. It's the worst. I hate fundraising. I make no bones about it. . . . I don't know many people who like it. And if they do like it, there is probably something wrong with them" (quoted in Isenstadt and Hohmann 2010).[3] For members who dislike fundraising, doing more of it merely to turn over the funds to the party cannot be an appealing prospect. Nevertheless, incumbent anxiety looms large, implying that on the whole, members would prefer to finance their party-connected contributions by raising additional sums than by cutting into money budgeted for their own campaigns.[4]

In figure 7.1, we present data on a measure we call "crowding," the percentage of total incumbent campaign expenditures made up by party-connected campaign contributions. As figure 7.1 makes clear, party-connected contributions have grown significantly as a percentage of a member's overall campaign expenditure budget. For example, the typical

House Democrat redistributed 3 percent ($17,380) of his or her overall campaign expenditures to the Democratic Congressional Campaign Committee and to fellow House Democratic candidates in 1996 and 22 percent ($215,782) in 2006. For Republicans, the trend is less pronounced but still significant: in 1996, the typical Republican incumbent redistributed 4 percent ($29,706) of his or her overall campaign expenditures to the party and its candidates; by contrast, this redistribution figure was 11 percent ($170,445) in 2006. To be sure, the increasing percentage of incumbent campaign expenditures accounted for by funds redistributed to the party and its candidates has hardly left incumbents unable to finance their reelection activities. Even as party-connected contributions have made up a growing percentage of total incumbent campaign expenditures, the dollars spent by incumbents on reelection activities (i.e., total campaign expenditures minus party-connected contributions) have grown substantially. Nevertheless, the growing percentage of incumbent expenditures devoted to party-connected contributions represents campaign funds that, we can assume, members would have preferred to spend on their own reelections or to save in their war chests.

Incumbents have two ways to ensure that spending on redistribution does not crowd out spending on their own reelections. First, they can increase the sums they raise for their principal campaign committees, allowing them to redistribute sufficient funds to the party and its candidates without unduly cutting into the dollars they budget for their own reelections. Second, members can form a leadership PAC from which to redistribute money, allowing them to solicit donors who have given to their

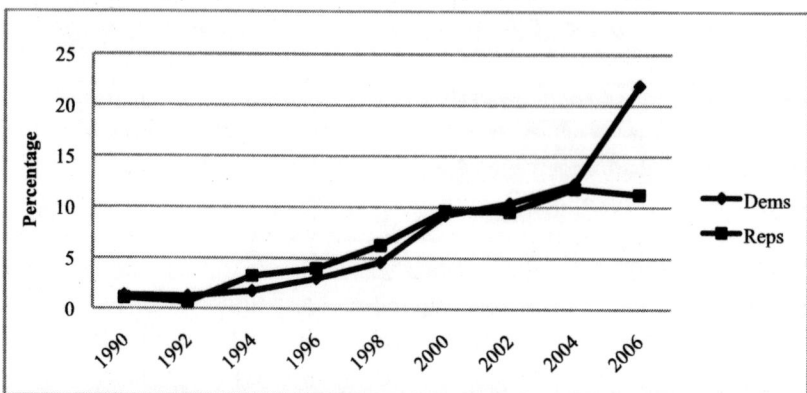

Fig. 7.1. Mean crowding (redistribution as a percentage of campaign spending), 1990–2006

PCCs for donations to an entirely separate committee. These two strategies generate two broad hypotheses about how members will prevent redistribution from crowding out spending on their own reelections. The first is that the greater the percentage of total spending a member devotes to redistribution from his or her PCC in a given election cycle (i.e., the more redistribution crowds out the incumbent's reelection spending), the more the member will increase his or her PCC's receipts in the following cycle. (In the next section of this chapter, we elaborate on the types of donors we expect members to tap to increase their receipts.) The second is that the greater the percentage of total spending a member devotes to redistribution from his or her PCC in a given election cycle, the more likely he or she will be to form a leadership PAC in the following cycle. In the following sections of this chapter, we develop these hypotheses and test them empirically, beginning with the PCC hypothesis.

Access-Oriented Donors versus Electorally Oriented Donors

In raising money to alleviate the tension between redistribution and reelection spending, incumbents will seek to maximize efficiency by soliciting donors who are most likely to respond positively. Doing so requires incumbents to be mindful of donors' strategic considerations. Well informed and unlikely to be fooled by the appeals of candidates (e.g., Biersack, Herrnson, and Wilcox 1994; Francia et al. 2003), donors will avoid wasting their resources on candidates who will not help them achieve their political goals.

All candidates must help potential donors overcome a collective action dilemma: a donor benefits from the collective good of his or her preferred candidate's victory regardless of whether the donor contributed to the candidate (Jacobson 1980, 57). Overcoming the collective action dilemma can be particularly onerous for electorally secure incumbents, because donors are not motivated to contribute to them by the fear of losing an ally (Mutz 1995). In these contests, donors know that their gifts are unnecessary for their favored candidate to win. In theory, the absence of such an inducement could make raising money to redistribute to the party's coffers difficult for the safe members most heavily leaned on by party leaders for funds. As one Democratic campaign strategist said about some of his electorally secure clients, "It's just difficult for them to [raise money for redistribution] because it's hard to raise money because everybody thinks they are in safe seats" (quoted in Hunter 2010).

However, not all donors have the same goals, nor do they employ the same contribution strategies. Donors generally follow either an electorally oriented or an access-oriented contribution strategy (Herrnson 2008; Sorauf 1988; Wright 1985). Donors that employ electoral strategies contribute primarily to help elect ideological or partisan allies to Congress. They are motivated by altering the overall partisan or ideological composition of Congress in a way that advances their partisan, ideological, or policy preferences. Because helping candidates or parties win elections is the primary goal of electorally oriented donors, they tend to contribute to ideological or partisan allies in close races, where their contributions are likely to have the largest electoral impact. These donors are likely to resist requests for campaign donations from safe incumbents, since giving to safe members leaves less money for defending endangered allies or electing new ones. Electorally oriented donors are thus unlikely to be a prime target for incumbents seeking to raise for funds for redistributive purposes.

Incumbents are instead more likely to turn to access-oriented donors, who contribute not to alter the composition of Congress but, rather, to pave the way for lobbying efforts (Biersack, Herrnson, and Wilcox 1994; Herrnson 2008). Access-oriented donors tend to give to incumbents, because, as overwhelming favorites to win, incumbents offer the least risk for donors seeking a payoff on their investment. Since the goal of access-oriented donors is to stay on good terms with incumbents, they may well contribute to an incumbent who requests money even if he or she is not in a tough reelection battle (Herrnson 2008). Indeed, the mere fact that the incumbent requests money may well be sufficient for many access-oriented donors with business before a member's committee to respond positively (Keim and Zardhooki 1988; McChesney 1997).[5] This makes access-oriented donors a rich source for incumbents looking to raise extra money to funnel to the party.[6]

There are four major sources of campaign funds for House incumbents: business PACs,[7] nonconnected PACs, labor PACs, and individual donors. To test the expectation that House members will reduce the tension between redistribution and reelection by raising additional sums from access-oriented donors, we must first categorize the major sources of donations as either access oriented or electorally oriented.

While recognizing the diversity in the universe of corporations and trade groups, scholars largely define corporate and trade PACs as access-oriented donors (Cox and Magar 1999; Grier and Munger 1993; Herrnson 2008; Rudolph 1999; Sorauf 1992; Wright 1985). These committees, which contribute the bulk of PAC money in the system, give an overwhelming portion of their contributions to (often safe) incumbents who sit on committees with jurisdictions relevant to the donor (Grier and Munger 1993; Romer and Snyder 1994). Although majority party incumbents can typically extract more business PAC money than minority party members (Cox and Magar 1999; Rudolph 1999), even minority party members have access to substantial business PAC money (Jacobson 2009). Moreover, since business PACs often give less than they are capable of, they are especially well positioned to respond to pressure from incumbents seeking to increase their receipts (Ansolabehere, de Figueiredo, and Snyder 2003, 109; McChesney 1997, 163). The bottom line is that business PACs, which tend to give regardless of the competitiveness of a contest, are a rich source of campaign funds for incumbents (Democrats and Republicans alike) seeking to subsidize their party-connected contributions. As such, we expect crowding caused by redistribution in a given election cycle to have a positive impact on business PAC dollars raised by the member in the next election cycle. Additionally, since majority party members enjoy greater fundraising leverage over business PACs than do minority party members (Cox and Magar 1999; Rudolph 1999), we expect that majority party members (Republicans for the years we examine) will subsidize their party-connected contributions with business PAC money to a greater extent than will minority party members (Democrats).

Scholars view nonconnected PACs, which have no parent organization, as the main electorally oriented donors in the PAC system (Biersack, Herrnson, and Wilcox 1994; Gais 1996; Herrnson 2008). Less able than PACs with parent organizations to overcome the collective action problems associated with mobilizing donors (Gais 1996), nonconnected PACs account for a relatively small portion of the campaign dollars raised by House incumbents. Since these PACs are typically uninterested in access, they are able to resist pressure from incumbents, leaving them free to allocate the bulk of their resources to ideologically compatible candidates in close races. Accordingly, we expect crowding caused by redistribution to have no causal effect on nonconnected PAC dollars raised by the member.

Labor PACs have been characterized by some scholars as electorally oriented (Rudolph 1999; Wright 1985), but in truth, these committees are probably better conceptualized as employing a "mixed" contribution strategy (Herrnson 2008). Most pertinent for our purposes, labor PACs seem clearly willing to give to safe incumbents, as long as they are Democrats supportive of labor (Herrnson 2008).[8] Thus, while labor PACs may be a reliable source of money for Democrats seeking to subsidize their party-connected contributions, they will likely be of little help for Republicans.

Individual donors account for the biggest portion of funds raised by congressional incumbents, but unlike PACs, they are less easily placed into the conventional categories of access-oriented and electorally oriented donors. Many individual donors appear to be motivated by ideological or partisan concerns, implying an electoral orientation (Francia et al. 2003, 49, 51, 103; Gimpel, Lee, and Pearson-Merkowitz 2008). Yet there is also compelling evidence that some individual contributors are access-oriented donors motivated by business concerns (Francia et al. 2003; Gimpel, Lee, and Pearson-Merkowitz 2008).[9] For our purposes, the problem is in distinguishing between contributions made by access-oriented individuals and those made by electorally oriented individual donors. The state-level findings of Joe and others (2008, 10–12) are helpful here. In particular, they found that compared to small individual donors, large individual donors were more likely to give out of concern for their own industry or business. Instructively, they also found that large individual donors were more likely than small donors to contact state lawmakers about business concerns. Thus, we think it is reasonable to view large contributions (defined here as $750 or more) made by individuals as access oriented and to view smaller contributions (less than $750) made by individuals as electorally oriented.[10] We also therefore expect crowding caused by redistribution to have a positive causal effect on large, but not small, individual contributions raised by members.

BCRA

Incumbent contributions were on the rise long before BCRA was passed. But for several reasons, BCRA likely increased the extent to which incumbents would try to reduce the tension between reelection and redistribution spending. First, the potential for such tension increased significantly in the post-BCRA period, as party leaders looked to incumbents to help offset the loss of party soft money. As former DCCC chair Representative Martin Frost (D-TX) noted, "[BCRA] has changed the world. It has required members to raise more money for themselves and for the party committee, and give more money to the party committee, than they've ever done" (quoted in Carney 2004). "We do expect significantly more from the members in this cycle than we did in prior cycles," added Representative Robert Matsui (D-CA), DCCC chair during the first post-BCRA election cycle (2003–4) (quoted in Carney 2004). Second, BCRA increased the capacity for incumbents to reduce the tension between redistribution and reelection spending by doubling the limits (and indexing them to inflation) on contributions from individual donors to candidates.[11] In sum, BCRA put more pressure on members to redistribute, while also giving them a greater capacity to do so without unduly cutting into their own campaign budgets.

Modeling the Fundraising Impact of the New Party Fundraising Expectations

To test the hypothesis previously spelled out, we use data from five election cycles: 1997–98, 1999–2000, 2001–2, 2003–4, and 2005–6. For each election cycle, the observations are all of U.S. House incumbents who ran for reelection consecutively in at least two of the five cycles.[12] We pool the observations for each election cycle, adding dummy variables for the 1999–2000, 2001–2, 2003–4, and 2005–6 cycles and using the 1997–98 cycle as our baseline. Our independent variable of primary interest, crowding, is simply the percentage of a member's total campaign spending in election cycle$_{t-1}$ allocated to party-connected contributions.[13] Per the preceding discussion, the higher a member's level of crowding is in election cycle$_{t-1}$, the more we expect his or her receipts from the relevant various donor categories to increase in cycle$_t$ relative to what he or she raised from those donor categories in cycle$_{t-1}$. Thus, while the independent variables are static, the dependent variables measure change (from cycle$_{t-1}$ to cycle$_t$) in the sum of dollars incumbents raise from, respectively, business PACs, labor PACs, nonconnected PACs, and four categories of individual donors ($750 plus, $500–749, $200–499, and $1–200).[14] All of the regression models incorporate fixed effects and use robust standard errors.[15] The following section describes the regression models' other independent variables that are expected to affect changes in a lawmaker's fundraising. Measurements for all variables are included in the appendix at the end of this chapter.

Variables Expected to Have a Direct Impact on Incumbent Receipts

We expect an array of factors other than crowding to directly influence incumbent fundraising. First, raising money is costly in terms of time and effort, and many members apparently do not enjoy the task. Thus, we expect that the more campaign cash a member begins election cycle$_t$ with, the less that member will increase his or her receipts from all sources in that cycle. Second, incumbents who are less electorally secure tend to raise more campaign money than incumbents who are more electorally secure (Grier and Munger 1993). We therefore expect electoral security to be negatively related to changes in campaign receipts. Third, party and committee leadership posts can help incumbents extract more campaign dollars from contributors, especially from those with an access orientation (Francia et al. 2003; Grier and Munger 1993; Romer and Snyder 1994). Accordingly, we anticipate a positive relationship between positions of power and changes in incumbent receipts for access-oriented donors but not for electorally oriented donors.[16] Fourth, members of the majority have a distinct advantage in raising money from access-oriented donors (Cox and Magar 1999; Francia et al. 2003; Rudolph 1999). As a result, we anticipate a positive association between majority party membership and changes in receipts from access-oriented donors. Fifth, since senior members can more easily provide services to access-oriented donors (Grier and Munger 1993), they should be able to leverage more campaign dollars from such donors than can their less senior colleagues. Yet, as with positions of power, seniority is likely to be more important in explaining changes in receipts from access-oriented donors than in explaining changes in receipts from electorally oriented donors. Finally, the sum of money a member raised from a particular source in cycle$_{t-1}$ may influence the extent to which he or she can increase the sums raised from that source in cycle$_t$. The expectation, however, could cut either way. On one hand, raising significant sums from a source may indicate that a member has a strong relationship with the source, implying that the member could tap the source for even more campaign money in the next cycle. On the other hand, if a member reached his or her limits in raising money from a particular source in an election cycle, that member's ability to raise additional money from that source in the next cycle would be limited.

Variables Expected to Have a Conditioning Effect on Incumbent Receipts

Although we expect crowding to affect a member's fundraising directly, we also anticipate that the influence of crowding will depend on other variables. First, as noted earlier in the chapter, BCRA put more pressure on members to redistribute, while also giving them a greater capacity to do so without unduly cutting into their own campaign budgets. We therefore expect the relationship between crowding in election cycle$_{t-1}$ and changes in a member's receipts between $cycle_{t-1}$ and $cycle_t$ to be stronger in the post-BCRA period than in the pre-BCRA period. Second, having a leadership PAC may lessen the tension between redistribution and reelection spending, because members can use LPACs to make party-connected contributions. Thus, we expect the relationship between crowding in $cycle_{t-1}$ and changes in receipts in $cycle_t$ to be smaller for members who sponsor an LPAC than for members who do not sponsor one. Third, since majority party members enjoy greater fundraising leverage with access-oriented donors than do minority party members (Cox and Magar 1999; Rudolph 1999), the former should be able to reduce crowding by increasing their campaign receipts more easily than the latter. Accordingly, we expect the relationship between crowding in $cycle_{t-1}$ and changes in receipts in $cycle_t$ to be larger for majority party members than for minority party members. Fourth, members who begin an election cycle with a large reserve of cash on hand confront less tension between redistribution and reelection spending. Thus, we expect that the more cash on hand a member has at the beginning of $cycle_t$, the smaller effect crowding in $cycle_{t-1}$ should have on changes in receipts between $cycle_{t-1}$ and $cycle_t$. Finally, members in competitive districts confront heightened tension between redistribution and reelection spending, because, from a career perspective, these members can least afford to have redistribution crowd out reelection spending. We therefore anticipate that the greater a member's electoral security, the less impact crowding in $cycle_{t-1}$ should have on changes in the member's receipts between $cycle_{t-1}$ and $cycle_t$. We evaluate each of these conditional effects by including relevant interactive terms in the regression models.

Model Results

To avoid barraging the reader with a blizzard of regression coefficients, we present coefficients only for the independent variables of primary interest. (Readers can locate the coefficients for the other variables in tables 7.4 and 7.5, in the appendix at the end of this chapter.) To evaluate the effect of crowding on changes in PAC receipts, we turn to the regression results in table 7.1.[17] For the business PAC regression, the coefficient for crowding is positively and statistically significant, demonstrating that the more campaign expenditures a member devoted to redistribution in election $cycle_{t-1}$, the more that member increased his or her receipts from business PACs in the subsequent cycle. This is evidence that members increase their receipts from business PACs when spending on redistribution begins to compete with spending on their own reelection.

The coefficients for the interactive terms represent the extent to which the effect of crowding on changes in business PAC receipts depends on other variables. The statistically insignificant coefficients for crowding* BCRA, crowding*LPAC, and crowding*cash on hand show that the effect of crowding on changes in business PAC receipts is, respectively, no different in the pre- and post-BCRA period, does not depend on whether a member sponsors an LPAC, and is not conditioned by the sum of money a member has on hand. By contrast, the positive and statistically significant coefficient for crowding*party demonstrates that the effect of crowding on changes in business PAC receipts is greater for majority party Republicans than for minority party Democrats. This may suggest that majority party members are better able than minority party members to reduce the tension between redistribution and reelection spending by increasing their receipts from business PACs. But it may also be an indication that business PACs have greater ideological affinity with Republicans than with Democrats.

Because of the presence of interactive terms, care must be taken in assigning substantive meaning to the combined results for crowding and crowding*party. Interpretation of the coefficient for crowding is straightforward: it tells us the average effect of crowding on changes in business PAC receipts for House Democrats. Thus, each one-percentage point increase in crowding in election cycle$_{t-1}$ caused House Democrats to in-

TABLE 7.1.   The Effect of Redistribution Crowding on Changes in PAC Receipts (fixed effects regression with robust standard errors)

	Change in Business PAC Receipts	Change in Labor PAC Receipts	Change in Nonconnected PAC Receipts
Crowding	5,676.57**	202.49	2,498.31**
	(2,490.93)	(415.01)	(920.46)
Crowding × BCRA	837.91	203.84	204.88
	(748.60)	(131.69)	(257.50)
Crowding × LPAC	1,128.44	98.21	722.63**
	(850.28)	(134.27)	(311.59)
Crowding × party	1,635.53*	−553.76***	875.25**
	(920.37)	(148.77)	(333.27)
Crowding × cash on hand	−.001	−.001	−.0005*
	(.001)	(.001)	(.0003)

Note: See table 7.4 for control variable coefficients.
*p < .10; **p < .05; ***p < .01

crease their business PAC receipts by, on average, $5,676 in the following election cycle. For House Republicans, the total effect of crowding on changes in business PAC receipts can be computed by adding the coefficient for crowding and the coefficient for the interactive term, crowding*party (Jaccard, Turrisi, and Wan 1990).[18] Doing so reveals that House GOP incumbents increased their business PAC dollars in cycle$_t$ by an average of $7,312 for each one percentage point increase in crowding in the prior cycle. Using simple multiplication allows us to illuminate more fully the advantage enjoyed by majority party Republicans. Based on the coefficients, a House Democrat who devoted 12 percent (the mean for members in our data set) of his or her total expenditures to redistribution in cycle$_{t-1}$ increased his or her business PAC receipts by an average of $68,076 in the subsequent cycle.[19] By contrast, a House Republican who allocated 12 percent of his or her campaign expenditures to redistribution in cycle$_{t-1}$ increased his or her business PAC receipts by an average of $87,696 in the subsequent cycle. Clearly, then, members of both parties have relied on business PACs to reduce the extent to which spending on redistribution crowds out and competes with spending on their own re-elections. But by exploiting the majority party's leverage over access-oriented donors, House Republicans were able to subsidize their party-connected contributions with business PAC money to an even greater extent than Democrats.

The results for nonconnected PACs in table 7.1 demonstrate that incumbents target more than just access-oriented donors in seeking to reduce the tension between redistribution and reelection spending. In particular, the statistically significant coefficient for crowding in the nonconnected PAC regression shows that for House Democrats, each one-percentage point increase in total campaign expenditures devoted to redistribution in election cycle$_{t-1}$ led to an average increase of $2,498 in nonconnected PAC receipts in cycle$_t$. Moreover, by summing the coefficient for crowding and the statistically significant coefficient for crowding*party, we see that crowding in cycle$_{t-1}$ caused House Republicans to increase their nonconnected PAC receipts by even more (an average of $3,373) than did House Democrats.[20] That nonconnected PACs help incumbents subsidize their party-connected contributions suggests that these committees may give to incumbents based on the knowledge that incumbents will redistribute the money to the party and its competitive candidates. Indeed, Herrnson (2008, 153–54) offers this as a possible explanation for the contributions made by some liberal nonconnected PACs to safe Democratic incumbents in the 2005–6 election cycle.

The coefficient for crowding in the labor PAC regression in table 7.1 is small and statistically insignificant, demonstrating that House Democrats generally do not turn to labor PACs to reduce the tension between redistribution and reelection spending. Yet the negative and statistically significant coefficient for crowding*party in the labor PAC regression demonstrates that Republicans have even less luck than do Democrats in raising labor PAC money to finance their party-connected contributions. These findings reflect the reality that labor PAC money comprises only a very small portion of funds in the congressional campaign finance system. As a result, even House Democrats, who are long-standing allies of labor, cannot turn to labor PACs for help in financing their party-connected contributions.

Table 7.2 presents the regression results for receipts from individual donors. The large, positive, and statistically significant coefficient for crowding in the first regression shows that members substantially increase their receipts from large individual donors to help reduce the tension between redistribution and reelection spending. Importantly, the statistically significant coefficient for crowding*BCRA demonstrates that, as predicted, the effect of crowding on large individual donations is significantly greater in the post-BCRA period than in the pre-BCRA period. This strongly suggests that BCRA's increased individual contribution limits may be helping incumbents to finance the growing sums of party-connected contributions party leaders expect from them

TABLE 7.2. The Effect of Redistribution Crowding on Changes in Receipts from Individual Donors (fixed effects regression with robust standard errors)

	Change in Ind ≥ $750	Change in Ind $500–749	Change in Ind $200–499	Change in Ind < $200
Crowding	10,499.29**	1,024.45	−16.01	3,106.05*
	(5,128.42)	(687.64)	(650.67)	(1,771.55)
Crowding × BCRA	3,714.13**	186.26	−79.61	443.12
	(1,455.04)	(189.76)	(177.77)	(552.87)
Crowding × LPAC	357.54	461.27	−62.63	−657.92
	(1,560.32)	(295.68)	(172.25)	(552.33)
Crowding × party	693.34	211.16	−93.79	598.15
	(2,056.58)	(255.70)	(193.22)	(542.34)
Crowding × cash on hand	−.001	−.001	.001	.001
	(.003)	(.001)	(.001)	(.001)

Note: See table 7.5 for control variable coefficients.
$*p < .10; **p < .05; ***p < .01$

in the post-BCRA era. Moreover, the effect of crowding on changes in large individual donations is no different for Democrats and Republicans, as shown by the statistically insignificant coefficient for crowding*party in the regression. Finally, the effect of crowding on changes in smaller contributions is mostly statistically insignificant. Donations of less than $200 ($p < .10$) are the exception.

The coefficients can help us highlight the size of the BCRA effect. The coefficient for *crowding* demonstrates that in the pre-BCRA period, each one percentage point increase in crowding in election cycle$_{t-1}$ caused a member to increase his or her receipts from large individual donors by an average of $10,499. In the post-BCRA period, the figure is $14,213.[21] When we multiply out, we find that in the pre-BCRA period, an incumbent who devoted 12 percent of his or her total expenditures to redistribution in cycle$_{t-1}$ (again, the mean for House members in the sample) would increase his or her receipts from large individual donors by an average of $125,988 in the following cycle. By contrast, in the post-BCRA period, this level of crowding would lead a member to increase his or her receipts from large individual donors by, on average, $170,556. Thus, in the post-BCRA period, House members of both parties have increasingly relied on large individual donors to reduce the tension between redistribution and reelection spending.

It is also important to recognize that BCRA has had an indirect effect on the trends we outline for large individual donors. In addition to members raising more from large individual donors for each one percentage point increase in crowding, the mean level of crowding is itself considerably higher in the post-BCRA period than in the pre-BCRA period.[22] The pressure put on incumbents by party leaders in the post-BCRA period has clearly increased the tension between redistribution and reelection spending.

Are members who increase the sums they raise successful at reducing the extent to which spending on redistribution crowds out spending on their own reelections? Although a full-blown analysis of this question is beyond the scope of this chapter, the short answer appears to be yes. A simple bivariate regression (results not presented) demonstrates that the more a member increases his or her total receipts from election cycle$_{t-1}$ to election cycle$_t$, the more that member reduces the percentage of overall campaign expenditures devoted to redistribution between those two cycles ($p < .01$). Not surprisingly, raising more money helps members reduce the extent to which spending on redistribution competes with and crowds out spending on reelection.

Leadership PAC Formation

Raising more funds for their principal campaign committees is not the only option for members seeking to prevent redistribution spending from crowding out reelection spending. Members can also form a leadership PAC from which to redistribute money. These committees afford several advantages to members. First, donors may legally contribute $5,000 per election cycle to a member's LPAC but are limited to smaller sums to the member's PCC. Second, an LPAC allows a member of Congress to solicit from a donor twice: once for the member's PCC and again for his or her LPAC. If generating a list of responsive donors is one of the critical challenges of campaign fundraising, forming an LPAC allows a member to increase his or her total fundraising without having to identify and persuade new donors. Finally, an LPAC permits a member to focus his or her efforts on Washington lobbyists, PACs, and other access-oriented insiders, who are happy to give to safe incumbents and who understand that incumbents will likely redistribute the funds.

An LPAC is not a particularly effective way to collect funds to pay party dues. Whereas contributions from one's PCC to the party congressional campaign committees are uncapped, contributions from LPACs to the party CCCs are limited to $15,000 per election cycle. But by using an LPAC to give to candidates, a member can free up his or her PCC funds to pay CCC dues. We expect LPACs to have become an increasingly attractive option in the post-BCRA period, as party leaders pressured members to give growing sums to the party CCCs to offset the loss of soft money.

Congressional leaders and leadership aspirants have been sponsoring LPACs since the early days of the Federal Election Campaign Act, and the incentives for sponsoring such committees have only grown for these members as the struggle for majority control intensified. As figure 7.2 shows, LPACs have become more popular among members outside of the top leadership rungs.[23] By 2006, almost half the members of the House were affiliated with a PAC.

In this section, we analyze the impact of crowding on LPAC formation. We expect that the greater the percentage of spending a member allocates to redistribution from his or her PCC in a given election cycle, the more likely the member will be to form an LPAC in the following cycle. As one chief of staff noted about the member for whom he worked, "Members are absolutely asked to give money to other members, and that was the reason he decided to set up a PAC. It was really taking a toll on his

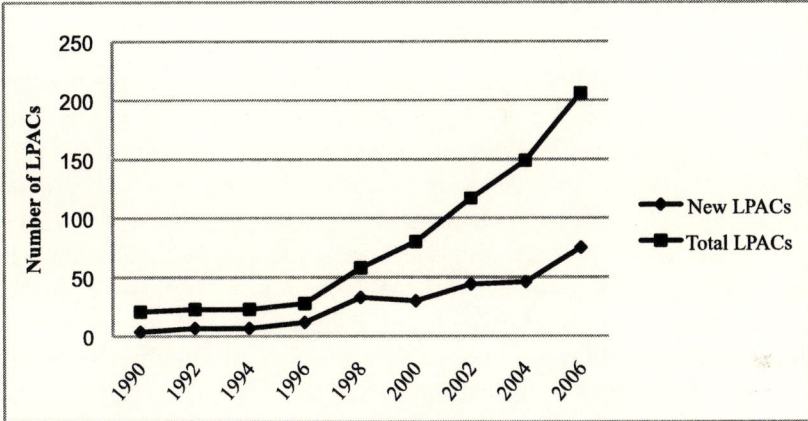

Fig. 7.2.   Increase in the number of LPACs, 1990–2006

personal campaign account to keep giving out of that" (quoted in Currinder 2009, 142).

Modeling Leadership PAC Formation

To estimate the effect of crowding on leadership PAC formation, we use logistic regression with robust standard errors. When we analyze data from the 1998–2006 election cycles, the cases are identical to those used in the analysis of members' PCCs except that we exclude members who had already established LPACs in previous election cycles. Our dependent variable is coded 1 if a member formed a new LPAC in election cycle$_t$, o otherwise. Our independent variable of primary interest, crowding, is the same as we used in the preceding analysis. With a few exceptions, the interactive terms, control variables, and expectations in the LPAC formation regression are largely the same as in the preceding receipts regressions.[24] The exceptions are as follows: First, in the LPAC regressions, we add a variable, contest, indicating whether a member was reported as a contestant for an elected party or committee leadership post. We expect this variable to be positively related to LPAC formation. Second, instead of including a measure of funds raised from a specific donor category in election cycle$_{t-1}$, we include the total receipts raised by a member in cycle$_{t-1}$. We expect that members with a greater fundraising capacity will be more likely to form an LPAC.

Model Results

The logistic regression results presented in table 7.3 confirm our expectations.[25] (Readers can locate the coefficients for the control variables in table 7.6, in the appendix at the end of this chapter.) The positive and statistically significant coefficient for crowding shows that higher levels of crowding in election cycle$_{t-1}$ increase the probability that a member will form a leadership PAC in the subsequent election cycle. Setting the control variables at their means, a change in crowding from the twenty-fifth to the seventy-fifth percentile increases the probability that a member will form an LPAC by .17. However, as the coefficient for crowding*party shows, crowding has a slightly smaller impact on the probability of forming an LPAC for Republicans than for Democrats, despite the fact that the GOP incumbents are (as indicated by the coefficient for party) more likely than Democrats to form new LPACs. Thus, while Republicans are more likely than Democrats to form LPACs, they are less likely to do so as a response to crowding. LPAC formation among Republicans during this period may instead simply be an attempt to exploit more fully the fundraising advantages associated with majority party control.

Two other results in table 7.3 are noteworthy. First, as the statistically significant coefficient for contest demonstrates, members continue to use LPACs to help them secure leadership positions. Indeed, running for a

TABLE 7.3. The Effect of Redistribution Crowding on Leadership PAC Formation (logistic regression with robust standard errors)

	Leadership PAC Formation	Change in Probability (change in x)
Crowding	.135**	.17
	(.049)	(25th, 75th percentile)
Crowding × BCRA	.008	—
	(.016)	
Crowding × Party	−.029**	−.02
	(.015)	(25th, 75th percentile)
Crowding × cash on hand	−7.17e-09	—
	(1.67e-08)	
Contest	1.169***	.17
	(.280)	(0,1)
Party	.910***	.09
	(.229)	(0,1)

Note: See table 7.6 for control variable coefficients. Change in x is with all other variables set at their respective means. Standard errors in parentheses.
$^{*}p < .10; ^{**}p < .05; ^{***}p < .01$

leadership post increases by .17 the probability that a member will form a new LPAC. Second, the direct effect of crowding on LPAC formation is no different in the pre- and post-BCRA eras. Instead, members have used LPACs as a strategy for reducing crowding in both periods. But as with the increasing dollars members have raised for their PCCs, BCRA has had an indirect effect on LPAC formation by increasing the level of crowding, which itself induces members to form LPACs.

Conclusion

The tremendous new party fundraising expectations of House incumbents have intensified the tension between members' reelection and redistribution spending. In this chapter, we presented evidence confirming that these tensions have had a major impact on lawmakers' fundraising behavior. In particular, we found that the more a member's redistribution spending crowded out his or her reelection spending in a given election cycle, the more campaign money the member raised from large individual donors and business PACs in the next cycle. Higher levels of crowding, we found, also made members more likely to form a leadership PAC. Finally, we presented evidence that BCRA amplified some of these trends by increasing party leadership pressure on members to redistribute and by giving members an increased capacity to do so.

This chapter's findings help illuminate how House incumbents, induced by the partisan selective incentives described in prior chapters, increasingly serve as campaign money conduits between interested donors and the congressional parties—which have themselves become like cartels seeking to monopolize campaign funds. To be sure, donors contribute to advance their own political goals, whether it is to elect like-minded officials or to gain access and favors from officials. But incumbents are not at the mercy of self-interested donors trying to buy favors. Instead, they are able to use their leverage over public policy to pull more money from access-oriented donors into the system (Malbin 2003). Incumbents then turn around and redistribute some of these funds to the party and its candidates, simultaneously advancing the party's collective electoral fortunes and their own individual stature within the congressional party. Intended or not, BCRA's soft money ban has only made these trends more pronounced.

The evolving relationship this chapter documents between centralized congressional parties, incumbents, and interests has significant normative implications for the campaign finance system. On the positive side, our results highlight the genuine redistributive character of members' party-connected contributions. Money originally contributed to safe incumbents for the purposes of gaining access ends up being redistributed largely to nonincumbent candidates in a way that enhances electoral competition.

The normative implications are not entirely positive, however. First, the need to support the party campaign at greater levels has intensified the money chase among incumbents. Members have felt intense pressure to raise money not only for their own reelection campaigns but also to support the party's collective electoral goals. Those who decline to participate greatly limit their chances for institutional advancement. It is a safe bet that nobody would think this is a healthy development. Relatedly, there is a danger that congressional leaders will have even stronger obligations to interested donors (McCarty and Rothenberg 2000). To be sure, the evidence that campaign donors receive anything for their contributions to incumbents is mixed (Baumgartner and Leech 1998). But an increase of interested money in the political system can only diminish the public's already dwindling trust in government (Hibbing and Theiss-Morse 2002, 93–102).

The combination of strong party leaders and fierce competition for control of Congress has produced an increasingly centralized fundraising regime in the U.S. House. Intended or not, moreover, BCRA's soft money ban left incumbents with even greater responsibility for supporting the party's collective electoral goals. The next chapter evaluates the extent to which these developments have influenced members' perceptions about the value of serving in the House.

APPENDIX

Variable Measurements

Dependent Variables

Change in business PAC receipts: business PAC funds raised by a member in election cycle t minus business PAC funds raised by the member in cycle$_{t-1}$.

Change in individual contributions between $500 and $749: individual contributions between $500 and $749 raised by a member in election cycle$_t$ minus individual contributions between $500 and $749 raised by the member in cycle$_{t-1}$.

Change in individual contributions between $200 and $499: individual contributions between $200 and $499 raised by a member in election cycle t minus individual contributions between $200 and $499 raised by the member in cycle$_{t-1}$.

Change in individual contributions less than or equal to $750: individual contributions less than or equal to $750 raised by a member in election cycle$_t$ minus individual contributions less than or equal to $750 raised by the member in cycle$_{t-1}$.

Change in individual contributions less than $200: individual contributions of less than $200 raised by a member in election cycle$_t$ minus individual contributions of less than $200 raised by the member in cycle$_{t-1}$.

Change in labor PAC receipts: labor PAC funds raised by a member in election cycle$_t$ minus labor PAC funds raised by the member in cycle$_{t-1}$.

Change in nonconnected PAC receipts: nonconnected PAC funds raised by a member in election cycle$_t$ minus nonconnected PAC funds raised by the member in cycle$_{t-1}$.

Leadership PAC formation: 1 = a member formed a leadership PAC in election cycle$_t$; 0 = otherwise.

Independent Variables Measuring Direct Effects

Beginning cash on hand$_t$: the sum of cash with which a member began election cycle$_t$.

Business PAC receipts$_{t-1}$: business PAC funds raised by a member in election cycle$_{t-1}$.

Committee leader: 1 = chair or ranking member of a standing committee; 0 = otherwise.

Contest: 1 = named by *CQ Weekly Report* as a contestant for an elected party leadership post or a committee chair/ranking member post; 0 = otherwise.

Crowding$_{t-1}$: the total dollars redistributed by an incumbent in election cycle$_{t-1}$ divided by the incumbent's total campaign spending in cycle$_{t-1}$.

Elected party leader: 1 = Speaker, floor leader, whip, caucus/conference chair or other officer, chair of party committee (e.g., CCC); 0 = otherwise.

Election cycle: 0/1 dummy variables for the 1999–2000, 2001–2, 2003–4, and 2005–6 election cycles. The 1997–98 election cycle is our baseline.

Extended party leadership: 1 = member of whip system, Steering Committee, Policy Committee, or CCC; 0 = otherwise.

Individual contributions between $500 and 749_{t-1}$: individual contributions between $500 and $749 raised by a member in election cycle$_{t-1}$.

Individual contributions between $200 and 499_{t-1}$: individual contributions between $200 and $499 raised by a member in election cycle$_{t-1}$.

Individual contributions greater than or equal to 750_{t-1}$: individual contributions greater than or equal to $750 raised by a member in election cycle$_{t-1}$.

Individual contributions less than 200_{t-1}$: individual contributions of less than $200 raised by a member in election cycle$_{t-1}$.

Labor PAC receipts$_{t-1}$: labor PAC funds raised by a member in election cycle$_{t-1}$.

Leadership PAC$_{t-1}$: 1 = member sponsored an LPAC in election cycle$_{t-1}$; 0 = otherwise.

Majority party: 1 = member of the majority party; 0 = otherwise.

Nonconnected PAC receipts$_{t-1}$: nonconnected PAC funds raised by a member in election cycle$_{t-1}$.

Post-BCRA: 1 = election cycle following the implementation of the Bipartisan Campaign Reform Act (2004, 2006); 0 = otherwise.

Prestige committee member: 1 = member of Appropriations, Rules, or Ways and Means committee; 0 = otherwise.

Previous margin: a member's percent of the vote in the previous election cycle.

Seniority: the number of years served by an incumbent.

Total receipts$_{t-1}$: the sum of campaign funds raised by a member in election cycle$_{t-1}$.

Independent Variables Measuring Conditional Effects

Crowding*beginning cash on hand
Crowding*leadership PAC sponsorship
Crowding*majority party
Crowding*post-BCRA
Crowding*previous margin

TABLE 7.4. Coefficients for the Control Variables in the PAC Regressions

	Change in Business PAC Receipts	Change in Labor PAC Receipts	Change in Nonconnected PAC Receipts
Elected party leader	108,379.10***	20,651.72**	7,682.14
Extended party leadership	3,247.12	508.46	−2,305.98
Committee leader	67,243.71***	5,805.13	10,196.85
Prestige committee member	−38,578.98*	−7,699.45	6,407.45
Seniority	2,936.66	622.80	1,617.23*
2000 election cycle	36,443.97***	5,835.71**	6,080.09
2002 election cycle	35,989.55***	9,916.75***	1,379.18
2004 election cycle	60,402.49***	10,448.90**	−1,348.16
2006 election cycle	130,566.00***	7,595.31	12,991.24
Business PAC receipts$_{t-1}$	−.55***	—	—
Labor PAC receipts$_{t-1}$	—	−.72***	—
Nonconnected PAC receipts$_{t-1}$	—	—	−11,697.38***
Previous margin	1,580.15**	−136.29	384.81**
Crowding × previous margin	−79.81**	2.02	−33.29***
Beginning cash on hand$_t$	−.01	−.01	.01
Constant	−11,399.72	53,837.06***	453.92
	$N = 1,604$	$N = 1,604$	$N = 1,604$
	$F = 12.96$***	$F = 15.24$***	$F = 6.24$***
	R^2 within = .27	R^2 within = .39	R^2 within = .22

Note: — = not applicable.
*$p < .10$; **$p < .05$; ***$p < .01$

TABLE 7.5. Coefficients for the Control Variables in the Individual Donor Regressions

	Change in Ind ≥ $750	Change in Ind $500–749	Change in Ind $200–499	Change in Ind < $200
Elected party leader	−24,426.55	−6,558.18	−12,822.65	−3,715.47
Extended party leadership	−13,574.23	−4,890.90	−1,438.54	−4,255.77
Committee leader	24,992.60	3,278.49	5,780.54	10,857.29
Prestige committee member	188.63	172.64	−5,855.38	6,881.78
Seniority	−6,445.24	−1,118.29	−1,318.57	−1,792.42
2000 election cycle	57,895.41***	11,574.69**	7,381.66**	15,671.51
2002 election cycle	76,873.06***	16,593.45**	6,635.79	3,208.02
2004 election cycle	156,146.40***	22,818.23**	15,073.52**	3,782.73
2006 election cycle	167,740.10***	26,832.57**	14,876.62**	5,981.59
Ind$ ≥ 750_{t-1}$	−8,949.15***	—	—	—
Ind$ 500–749$_{t-1}$	—	−1.013***	—	—
Ind$ 200–499$_{t-1}$	—	—	−.95***	—
Ind$ < 200_{t-1}$	—	—	—	−1.06***
Previous margin	1,935.81**	−13.59	−5.10	−709.01
Crowding × previous margin	−117.77*	−10.26	1.39	33.02*
Beginning cash on hand$_t$	−.21*	−.019	−.01	−.04***
Constant	79,542.76	76,980.07***	56,517.89***	179,023.00***
	$N = 1,604$	$N = 1,604$	$N = 1,604$	$N = 1,604$
	$F = 9.38***$	$F = 27.48***$	$F = 30.95***$	$F = 18.73***$
	R^2 within = .19	R^2 within = .48	R^2 within = .44	R^2 within = .51

Note: — = not applicable.
*$p < .10$; **$p < .05$; ***$p < .01$

TABLE 7.6. Coefficients for the Control Variables in the Leadership PAC Formation Regression

Variable	Coefficient
Elected party leader	−.37
Extended party leadership	.30*
Committee leader	.44
Prestige committee member	.15
Seniority	−.02
2000 election cycle	−.10
2002 election cycle	.18
2004 election cycle	−.16
2006 election cycle	.47
Previous margin	.01**
Crowding × previous margin	−.01
Beginning cash on hand$_t$ (× 1,000)	.004
Total receipts$_{t-1}$ (× 1,000)	.007
Constant	−4.25

$N = 1,315$
Log likelihood ratio $= -460.21$
Wald $= 90.32$***

*$p < .10$; **$p < .05$; ***$p < .01$

8 | Redistribution and the Value of a House Career

As the 108th Congress approached, Representative Jim Leach (R-IA) would be stepping down as chair of the House Banking Committee due to the six-year term limits imposed on committee chairs by the Republican caucus starting in the 105th Congress. The next most senior member of the committee and thus the person traditionally in line for the chair was Marge Roukema (R-NJ). Roukema was a moderate with little record of redistributing funds to the National Republican Congressional Committee or to GOP candidates. In 2000, she was forced to spend campaign funds defending herself against a very competitive primary challenge from Scott Garrett, a more conservative candidate. The chair of the Banking Committee was awarded to Mike Oxley (R-OH) rather than Roukema. Oxley was a conservative who had redistributed actively. Originally competing for the chair of the Energy and Commerce Committee, he was given the Banking Committee chair as a consolation prize and as a clear signal to the rest of the GOP caucus regarding expectations for aspirants to committee leadership positions. Roukema, denied advancement to the chair and facing another primary challenge from Garrett, decided to retire rather than seek reelection in 2002. On her decision to retire, Roukema commented, "I suppose it had to do with money" (quoted in Dubose and Reid 2004, 273). At least in Roukema's case, the current party fundraising expectations and the barriers they created to advancement made it easier to leave than to try to adapt to the new regime.

Our primary concern in this book is the effect of the battle for majority status on congressional parties' abilities to solve their electoral collective action problems and the parties' use of advancement structures in Congress to reward those who serve the parties' collective interests. The new partisan organization imposes opportunity costs on members, particularly for those, like Marge Roukema, whose advancement is impeded by the new party expectations and for those who find it difficult to raise sufficient funds to achieve their goals. Here, we explore whether these changes impose sufficient costs to affect members' decisions to seek reelection to the House. Is Roukema an exception or a new reality of disadvantaged and disaffected members of Congress?

In previous chapters, we have made several arguments that have a direct bearing on members' career decisions regarding whether and how to leave the House. First, we have argued that members respond to party mobilization of financial resources because the party has power over their goals. If a member's goals can no longer be met by the congressional parties, or the party inhibits the member's goal achievement (thus raising the personal costs of continued service), the member seems likely to resist compliance with party fundraising demands and more likely to leave for greener pastures. Second, we have argued that campaign funds increasingly serve as a signal of members' ambitions for advancement to positions of power within the House. By the same logic, it seems likely that members whose progressive ambition lies outside the House—for example, in running statewide for governor or U.S. Senate—would signal their desires for these posts by redistributing campaign funds to their state parties. If their goal is statewide office, it is the state parties, not the House congressional campaign committee, that can help them achieve their career goals. Members who are ambitious to advance within the House, however, have less incentive to divert campaign funds to state parties when these funds could be used to promote their higher-priority goals.

Our logic in developing these hypotheses is based on the evidence that members with progressive ambition behave differently than those with intra-institutional ambition and that those who plan to leave the institution behave differently than those who plan to seek reelection. Herrick and Moore (1993), for example, find that members who seek higher office introduce more bills, participate more actively on the floor, have more specialized legislative agendas, and have more staff than other members. All these behaviors are likely to help members attract the media attention to raise their profiles for a run for higher office. Similarly, members who seek higher office adapt their voting behavior away from the preferences of voters in their district and toward the preferences of voters for the office to which they aspire (Hibbing 1986; Rothenberg and Sanders 2000; Schlesinger 1966). Retiring members, for their part, are less likely to vote according to their constituents' preferences.

How congressional parties are organized and what they expect of their members can have an impact on the extent to which members view the House as an institution in which it is worth building a long-term legislative career. In *Federalist* Nos. 53 and 57, James Madison explained that Congress would need to attract and retain quality lawmakers in order to be an effective institution and that institutional design was critical to attracting and retaining able lawmakers. Thus, for example, Madison opposed term limits for House members because he believed they would deny Congress the benefits of seasoned lawmakers. Similarly, Mann and Ornstein (2006) cite partisanship and the permanent campaign for majority status, including the fundraising practices it engenders, as reasons why the contemporary Congress is "broken." If Marge Roukema's decision is generalizable and the new party fundraising expectations are prompting exit from the House, particularly by members with the greatest legislative acumen, such expectations have the potential to undermine the House's effectiveness as a lawmaking and representative institution.

Career Decisions

The literature on the career choices of members of Congress is quite extensive (e.g., Brace 1984; Copeland 1989; Groseclose and Krehbiel 1994; Hall and Van Houweling 1995; Kiewiet and Zeng 1993; Moore and Hibbing 1992, 1998; Rohde 1979; Schlesinger 1966). Numerous studies have plumbed the nuances of the decisions of members of Congress to run for reelection, retire, or seek another office. Most theoretical accounts tally up the costs and benefits of continued service for the legislator at that point in his or her individual career as well as the opportunities (or lack thereof) and risks afforded by the political environment (e.g., Black 1972; Rohde 1979). Simply put, when the benefits of an opportunity to attain another office are higher than the benefits of continuing in their current posts and when the risks in seeking to obtain the new position are relatively low, legislators are more likely to surrender their current post to seek the new one. When the costs of attempting to retain the current position are higher than the benefits of retaining it, they retire.

Several studies have closely examined the "cost" side of the equation, specifically seeking systematic evidence for anecdotal assertions that members retire due to "disaffection" with the institution (especially Hall and Van Houweling 1995; Moore and Hibbing 1992; Theriault 1998). These studies generally find little support for the notion that gridlock, workload, budget problems, polarization, lack of comity, and media and constituent pressure, which are the primary causes of disaffection in the anecdotal accounts, are related to retirements. (The exception is Binder [2003], who finds that legislative gridlock is positively related to retirement rates in the House.) These factors either remain relatively constant or on a continuous trend while retirements rise and fall independently. Thus, the disaffection hypothesis has not been highly regarded in the retirement literature.

Throughout this book, we have argued that members make career choices within specific political contexts and that political contexts change over time. In the aftermath of the 1970s reform era, Frantzich (1978) and Cooper and West (1981) noted the claims of retiring members that changes in the House environment made them less comfortable and contributed to their decisions to retire. The normative concern was that the most experienced and most effective members would leave because of changes in the institutional or political environment. It seems plausible and at least worth exploring whether new party pressures to raise and redistribute campaign funds and new organizational arrangements to entice compliance might lead to disaffection—particularly among specific groups of members who, in one way or another, are disadvantaged under the new redistribution regime—and thus increase the probability that these discouraged members will retire.

The pressure on members to raise and redistribute funds to the party and its candidates is high, forcing members to make trade-offs in how best to raise the funds to meet party expectations: raise more or accept greater electoral risk by drawing down cash on hand or spending less on their own reelections. Does dealing with such pressures to redistribute on top of other career pressures increase the likelihood of retirement? Do visions of higher office and the attendant need to preserve campaign cash help one resist the blandishments of party leaders?

Retirement

The early literature on retirement decisions suggests that frustration with the money chase may well compel members to leave Congress. Cooper and West (1981) and Hibbing (1982) document weariness with the never-ending need to raise money as a reason members of Congress cite when retiring. One member quoted by Hibbing (1982, 58–59) placed the blame for his retirement predominantly on fundraising fatigue: "The thing I hated most of all was fundraising. . . . I never enjoyed fundraising—not one minute—and I was good at it. . . . If I could put my finger on one thing that drove me out of office, it would be fundraising." Senator Evan Bayh (D-IN) also claimed that the exhaustion of fundraising was one of the reasons for his 2010 retirement.

It's miserable. It is not uncommon to have a fundraiser for break-fast, for lunch, for dinner, and if you have spare time in between, you go to an office off Capitol Hill and you dial for dollars. Then the weekend rolls around and you get on a plane and travel to the countryside with a tin cup in your hand. And it gets worse each cy-cle. (Quoted in Klein 2010)

Studies have found that changes in the legality of using campaign funds for personal expenses have had an effect on retirement decisions (An-solabehere and Snyder 2000). Indeed, a major explanation for the large number of retirement decisions in 1992 was the fact that it was the last election cycle in which some senior members could convert leftover money in their campaign accounts to personal use (see especially Grose-close and Krehbiel 1994; Hall and Van Houweling 1995). Nevertheless, de-spite rhetorical complaints from some retirees about fundraising pres-sures, there is little empirical evidence that it has driven many members into retirement. Moore and Hibbing (1992, 825) note that retirement lev-els declined in the 1980s (and 1990s) despite the fact that campaign costs and the pressures of fundraising continued to climb.

A straightforward application of the disaffection hypothesis to party fundraising demands would state that the pressure for members to raise increasingly large sums of money for the party and its candidates would lead to party fundraising burnout. Members would tire of the fundraising rat race and of being constantly asked for campaign money by other can-didates and their party's congressional campaign committee. Rather than continue, members would retire to do something more enjoyable and ed-ifying. Our theory of institutional ambition, however, leads us to doubt the formulation that increasing party fundraising expectations per se leads to retirement. There are, after all, substantial institutional benefits to generous support of the party. If those who redistribute dollars generously are the most likely to advance (as discussed in chapter 6), the redistribu-tion of campaign funds probably is worth the cost for most of the mem-bers who put the most effort into doing it. To the extent that redistribu-tion imposes costs on members, the costs are most likely to be felt by members who have difficulty achieving their power goals under the new regime of institutional advancement.

Another reason to be skeptical that redistribution burnout leads to re-tirement is that incumbents seem to have little difficulty raising substan-tial sums for their campaign activities (Ansolabehere and Snyder 2000; Herrnson 2008; Jacobson 2009; Krasno, Green, and Cowden 1994; Sorauf

1992). Though the party's redistribution expectations have raised the costs of continuing to seek reelection and advancing within the chamber, members seem to have adjusted their savings and reelection spending to accommodate redistribution expenditures, as we saw in chapter 7. Even members with low cash on hand have been able to raise more funds from the donors who are most likely to have liquidity to respond to the appeals of safe and ideologically compatible incumbents: business PACs, large individual donors, and, to a lesser extent, nonconnected PACs. Over the nine election cycles in our data, the median level of cash on hand is $91,860, substantially more than the median dollars redistributed, $16,710. Even in election cycles since 1996, when the party mobilization efforts began in earnest and levels of redistribution increased rapidly (see chapter 4), the median level of cash on hand is more than twice the amount of the median level of redistribution: $127,505 in cash on hand compared to $57,000 in redistribution. For most members, it seems highly unlikely that disaffection from pressure to raise funds for redistribution alone increases their probability of retirement.

It is likely, then, that the members most disaffected with the current party expectations are members who are generally lackadaisical fundraisers and who therefore would be unenthused about the additional efforts necessary to redistribute. These reluctant fundraisers consequently would find their ability to advance imperiled by their unwillingness to "pay to play." If this circumstance is true, members with lower levels of redistribution should be most likely to retire.

Although we will test the general relationship between redistributing campaign funds and retirement, our theory of institutional advancement leads us to propose two circumstances in which disaffection with the pressure to redistribute funds is most likely to occur. First, members who have low levels of cash on hand but who seek to redistribute prolifically—and who thus experience what we label "budget strain"—are likely to feel the stress of redistribution more acutely than their financially flush colleagues. They must believe that their power goals are at risk unless they overcome their present financial limitations. They must accept greater risk to their reelection by depleting their war chests even further, must spend less on reelection-oriented activities, and/or must increase their fundraising to cover the increased demands of redistribution while preserving their traditional levels of campaign spending and savings. As we saw in chapter 7, members with low cash on hand are more likely to change their fundraising behaviors to meet the party's redistribution expectations. We expect that members who are experiencing budget strain and who therefore must exert more fundraising effort than their colleagues to redistribute large sums will be more likely to quit rather than divert greater effort to fundraising.

We measure budget strain as the difference between the member's beginning level of cash on hand in election cycle$_t$ and the amount of funds he or she redistributed in the previous election cycle (cycle$_{t-1}$). Both measures include funds from the member's principal campaign committee only and exclude any leadership PAC activity. The relationship between budget strain and retirement should be negative: the less cash on hand a member has relative to his or her redistribution activity, the more effort he or she would have to exert to continue to redistribute profligately, and the more likely it is that he or she will retire. Simply put, the members with the least financial flexibility should be most likely to retire their position in response to the party's demands for more of their campaign cash.

The second condition under which members are likely to become disaffected with the pressures of redistribution occurs when members face barriers to advancement. Though redistribution provides an alternative route to advancement from traditional criteria such as seniority, party loyalty, and ideological centrism within the party (Cann 2008; Heberlig 2003; Heberlig, Hetherington, and Larson 2006), members who redistribute yet still fail to advance surely face substantial frustration. The story of Marge Roukema presented at the opening of this chapter illustrates this point. Why should members continue to divert time and resources to fundraising for the party when the party cannot reward their efforts? At this point, members face the choice of increasing their redistribution activity further in hopes that still greater levels of compliance with the party will be rewarded, remaining content with their current status in the House, or leaving since their opportunities to advance appear to be limited.

Our logic is based on the work of Theriault (1998) and Hall and Van Houweling (1995), who demonstrate that members whose committee advancement is blocked are more likely to retire. Specifically, they find that the traditional method of committee advancement through seniority disadvantages members who have younger colleagues ahead of them in the seniority queue. Their outlooks of attaining the most powerful committee positions are therefore dim, blocked by the likelihood that members ahead of them in seniority will attain the chair first and outlast them in Congress. If institutional impediments limit one's ability to achieve both one's power goals and whatever other policy and constituency goals come with institutional powers, one is more likely to leave and find fulfillment elsewhere. Thus, when Roukema was blocked as Financial Services Committee chair by the transfer of Mike Oxley to the committee, she left.

We posit that redistributive pressures exacerbate the tendency of blocked members to retire, because the costs of staying have increased while one's probability of advancement remains limited: one must resist the party's pressure to redistribute or divert one's energy from working on other goals to fundraise—with no attendant payoff for one's efforts. We coded a member's advancement to be blocked when a younger member had more seniority on all the committees on which the member served, thus lowering the probability that the member could realistically hope to become chair.[1] We interact members who are blocked with the adjusted sums they redistributed in the previous election cycle. We expect a positive relationship with retirement: members who redistribute generously yet have younger members ahead of them in the committee hierarchy will be more likely to retire.

Seeking Higher Office

Redistribution may also have implications for progressive ambition. House members who intend to seek higher office must make decisions anticipating the potential campaign requirements of a statewide run. We have already noted that members adapt their legislative behavior to appeal to a new constituency when seeking another office. They also adapt their fundraising behavior. Copeland (1989) finds that those who run for the Senate tend to be successful fundraisers. Ansolabehere and Snyder (2000) find that those who seek higher office build their savings over several election cycles, but their cash on hand is especially large in the cycle prior to their statewide campaign. A large bankroll in a House campaign account provides a solid foundation for additional fundraising efforts for the statewide campaign.

A need for funds for an expensive statewide race would seemingly give members an incentive to save their money rather than redistribute to House candidates and party committees (Larson 2004). After all, if the member runs statewide, win or lose, his or her House party leaders and colleagues will have little influence over his or her career, unless the ex-member becomes a Washington lobbyist. Thus, a failure to redistribute funds to party candidates or the congressional campaign committees when it is expected would seem to be an intuitive signal of a member's career intentions.

Likewise, redistribution of campaign funds to the state party could also be a signal of a member's career plans. Contributing money to a particular source is a sign of how much a donor values the recipient. The incumbent is sacrificing from a limited pool of funds that could be used for other purposes or must raise money to afford the additional expenditures. If the recipient has the ability to help the incumbent achieve his or her goals, the likelihood of a contribution increases. If the recipient cannot help the incumbent achieve his or her goals, there is little point in making a financial sacrifice to support them. Members who are anticipating a statewide run for office are building new and expanded electoral coalitions. They need to show their interest in state-level political activity and to build relationships with those who are politically active in the state (Fenno 2007, 261). Providing campaign funds is a signal of the intensity of one's interest and desire to build relationships (e.g., Austen-Smith 1993, 1995). Members who are anticipating retirement have little need for assistance from state or national party officials and thus little incentive to make sacrifices on their behalf (Larson 2004).

Nevertheless, there are also reasons to be skeptical that the redistribution of campaign funds signals future career decisions. First, there is reason to doubt that members of Congress would need to contribute to state party organizations as a means of gaining attention or building a relationship. Experienced politicians are obviously prized nominees for statewide positions, and state parties are likely to recruit proven vote-getters regardless of the legislator's past financial support. The ability of a member of Congress to win a statewide office is likely to depend largely on that member's ability to raise money to spend on the campaign, on his or her ability to find an attractive message, and on the national or state economic and political conditions—not on the state party's effectiveness (Abramowitz 1988; Atkeson and Partin 1995; Morehouse 1998; Simon, Ostrom, and Marra 1991). Thus, ambitious members have a substantial incentive to save their campaign funds for use in a statewide campaign rather than redistributing them to state or federal candidates and party organizations.[2] Likewise, as we saw in chapter 4, the amount of money contributed to state parties by members of Congress is extremely small (even by those who do seek statewide office), which suggests that the benefits to the member of Congress in making such contributions are limited (see table 8.1, in the next section of this chapter). Nevertheless, it is plausible that members with ambition for statewide office are more likely to make such contributions—even if the contributions are mostly small, goodwill gestures—than are members whose ambitions lie elsewhere.

In truth, we know very little about the relationships between members of Congress and state and local parties; thus, we know little about how important such a relationship would be for ambitious members of Congress. The party may be able to help to dissuade other potential candidates from entering the contest, though parties are usually reluctant to side openly with one candidate in a contested primary for fear of damaging their relationship with the eventual nominee. Local parties are important sources of volunteers for congressional campaigns, though the national parties are more important sources of expertise and money (Herrnson 2008). The importance of state parties seems to vary in Senate campaigns, though state parties are consistently supporting casts at best in a contest between candidates, national party organizations, and national interest groups (e.g., Magleby, Monson, and Patterson 2007).

One important limitation to our analysis of the relationship between incumbents' contributions to state parties and their career choices is our measurement of contributions to state parties. Contributions to federal candidates or party organizations and expenditures on behalf of federal candidates are required to be reported to the Federal Election Commission. Thus, we are measuring contributions from House members to the federal accounts of state parties. We do not examine the nonfederal transactions of state leadership PACs that some members had apparently formed prior to BCRA (Bresnahan 1998, 3; Chappie 1995). The obstacle to analyzing nonfederal transactions is that they are not subject to disclosure at the federal level. Instead, such activity is governed exclusively (if at all) by state laws that vary tremendously from state to state (Thompson and Moncrief 1998).

Congressional Career Decisions

Between 1992 and 2006, our data set contains 239 retirements (5.8 percent of cases) and 133 members (3.2 percent of cases) who sought statewide office.[3] These data were obtained from relevant editions of *CQ Almanac,* the *Congressional Staff Directory,* and the *Biographical Directory of the United States Congress* (http://bioguide.congress.gov).

We adjust the total of redistributed campaign funds at the state and federal level to their value in the 2000 election cycle, just as we did for federal contributions in chapter 6. We adjust the values so that the dollar amounts are comparable across election cycles despite the fact that the total amounts redistributed to state and federal organizations increased dramatically from 1990 to 2006. (For more detail, see the variable measurements in the appendix at the end of this chapter.)

We also present the values of members' redistribution in the election cycle in which they make their career decision, which we call the "current election cycle" (cycle$_t$), as well as in the preceding election cycle (cycle$_{t-1}$). We analyze both sums because the amounts of money redistributed in each cycle are not independent of a member's career decision. Members may redistribute little in the cycle in which they are retiring, not because of ambivalence about fundraising or disaffection with the link between fundraising and advancement, but because they do not need to raise money or please party leaders if they are retiring. The better indicator of their willingness to redistribute comes from an election cycle prior to their retirement decision. Similarly, contributions to state parties during an election cycle in which a member is campaigning for statewide office are likely a campaign expense. Contributions prior to their campaign are more likely to be a signal of their attempts to build relationships with state officials in anticipation of a campaign.

Table 8.1 compares the adjusted amounts of redistributed state and federal campaign funds, in the current and previous election cycles, by House members seeking higher office, retirees, and incumbents seeking reelection.[4] Members who seek statewide office redistributed, on average, $11,294 to state parties in the election cycle prior to running for office. Their contributions to state parties are more than twice the mean of retirees or members seeking reelection in the previous election cycle. The effect of running for office is also clear during the year in which members are actually running: their mean contributions to state parties drop dramatically during the cycle to $2,999, about one-quarter the amount of the previous cycle—presumably because they are prioritizing their spending on their own campaigns. In contrast, retirees' mean contributions to state parties decrease only slightly, and the mean contributions of members seeking reelection increase slightly in the current cycle. Similar patterns are apparent in the proportion of members who contribute to state parties: 30.9 percent of members seeking statewide office contribute to state parties in the previous cycle, compared to 19.6 percent of retirees and 24.4 percent of members seeking reelection to the House. In the current cycle, the proportion of members seeking higher office who contribute to state parties drops to 19.5 percent, the behavior of retirees remains relatively consistent (19.2 percent), and reelection seekers contribute in proportions equivalent to those seeking higher office in the previous election cycle (30.6 percent).

TABLE 8.1.   Adjusted Federal and State Party Organization Redistribution by Retirees, Members Seeking Reelection, and Members Seeking Higher Office, 1992–2006

	Seeking Higher Office		Retiring		Seeking Reelection	
	Mean Contributions	Percentage Contributing	Mean Contributions	Percentage Contributing	Mean Contributions	Percentage Contributing
State party (current cycle)	2,999	19.5	4,420	19.2	6,065	30.6
State party (previous cycle)	11,294	30.9	4,911	19.6	5,090	24.4
Federal (current cycle)	28,053	50.4	53,661	70.3	100,870	87.0
Federal (previous cycle)	57,347	87.9	120,594	74.9	87,468	72.8
Beginning cash on hand	363,437		237,652		185,515	

There are a few members who retired from the House without seeking another office in the same election cycle (and thus are counted as retirees in our data) who subsequently sought statewide office in a later election cycle. Several of these members also contributed to state parties: Tom Coburn (R-OK), Asa Hutchinson (R-AR), Bill Richardson (D-NM), and Matt Salmon (R-AZ); others did not, such as Blanche Lincoln (D-AR) and Mark Sanford (R-SC). The mean contribution of such members is $34,140 in adjusted funds to their state party in the previous cycle and a mean of $3,643 in the cycle in which they retired. Although their numbers are too few to generalize, the contribution patterns of these retirees parallels the patterns of members who leave the House to run for another office.

Likewise, a few House members run for local office (e.g., mayor of a big city), and some of these contribute to local parties in the election cycle preceding their run. For example, Representatives Robert Brady and Chaka Fattah ran for mayor of Philadelphia in the 2007 Democratic primary. Fattah had never contributed to local party organizations in six terms in Congress yet suddenly contributed $25,000 in the 2006 election cycle. Brady contributed to local parties every other election cycle (1998, 2000, 2006)—always the cycle preceding the mayoral race—and he gave a total of $95,000 across the three election cycles. Neither Fattah nor Brady has contributed any money to the state Democratic Party. When a member wants to be mayor, local party organizations are more helpful than the state party organization; local parties are thus the logical recipient of members' financial generosity. By contrast, Bobby Rush and Xavier Becerra made no contributions to local party organizations when they abortively sought the mayor's office (perhaps, especially in Rush's case, because the local party organizations were controlled by their opponents). Neither has ever contributed to their respective state or local party organizations in any other election cycle either.

Table 8.1 also includes data on members' adjusted contributions to federal candidates and their party's congressional campaign committee in the same cycles. Again, members who seek statewide office behave differently. They redistribute less money on average in both the current and the previous election cycles, and compared to retirees and colleagues seeking re-election, a higher proportion give nothing at all. Their ambition is focused outside the House, so they are less willing than others to make sacrifices to colleagues who will be of limited assistance in helping them to achieve their own career goals. It is clear that they have the capacity to redistribute but choose not to do so: table 8.1 shows that members seeking higher office have the highest mean levels of cash on hand, $363,437. These members are clearly saving their campaign funds to spend on their impending statewide campaigns.

Retirees redistribute substantial sums ($120,594) in the previous cycle, even higher than members who continue careers in the House. Presumably, this is because many of them are senior members with institutional posts, thus making them well positioned to raise funds and to receive party pressure to redistribute. Likewise, the proportion of retirees who redistribute in the previous cycle is nearly identical to continuing members (74.9 percent versus 72.8 percent). These data, then, do not suggest that members who are disaffected with the pressure to redistribute funds are more likely to retire. Apparently, members who dislike fundraising for this purpose either get over their doubts and do it anyway or are willing to accept the risk that noncompliance with party demands restricts their ability to advance within the House.

Once members have decided to retire, the congressional party no longer wields substantial power over their career, and redistribution activity declines substantially. Retirees redistribute only half the amount they did in the preceding election cycle, though most (70.3 percent) continue to participate at some level. Their redistribution activity falls despite the fact that they have substantial cash on hand after their final campaign ($237,652 on average) and no purpose for saving it. Members who run for reelection and plan to continue their careers in the House, by contrast, substantially increase the size of their adjusted contributions from the preceding to the current cycles, from a mean of $87,468 to $100,870, even though the adjustment process means that the sum of total contributions does not increase from one election cycle to the next. These findings are consistent with Larson's (2004) finding that House retirees give fewer dollars to the party congressional campaign committees than do their reelection-seeking colleagues.

The proportion of members contributing to state parties and the sums contributed are relatively small, especially in comparison to members' redistribution at the national level, so it is important not to overstate the strength of this signal of ambition. Nevertheless, these data provide evidence that members who intend to seek statewide office use their campaign funds differently than those who do not. They maintain higher levels of cash on hand than their colleagues, redistributing substantially less than others to federal candidates and party organizations. They do, however, redistribute more to their state parties than to their colleagues. Building relationships with state parties will help them advance their career goals more than will continued relationship building with colleagues in the House.

Multivariate Analysis

We model a member's career decision as a choice between three options in each election cycle: to run for reelection, to seek another office, or to retire. Following Kiewiet and Zeng (1993), we use multinomial logit to model the choice between these three unranked possibilities.[5] We estimate using robust standard errors clustered on the individual member to account for the fact that individual members are included in the data in multiple election cycles.

The key variables we add to standard models of career decisions are two variables measuring members' adjusted redistribution of campaign funds: to state parties in the previous election cycle ($cycle_{t-1}$), and total redistribution to federal candidates and congressional campaign committees in election $cycle_{t-1}$. We also include the member's cash on hand at the beginning of election $cycle_t$. Members with large amounts of cash on hand should be more likely to seek statewide office (e.g., Ansolabehere and Snyder 2000; Copeland 1989).

Our model includes numerous control variables that have become standards in the literature on career decisions. (See the appendix at the end of this chapter for measurements.) The higher the member's seniority and age are, the more likely it is that a member will retire. However, members are more likely to seek another office at lower levels of seniority and younger ages, as they will be giving up less power in the House and will have longer times to serve in another office (unless it is term limited) until reaching normal retirement ages. Members who are redistricted or who face ethical scandals are more likely to retire, given the increased costs of seeking reelection under more difficult circumstances. Members who are redistricted may seek to continue their political careers by seeking another office. Members whose policy preferences are out of step with their party are more likely to retire. Similarly, members who win by narrow electoral margins in the preceding election cycle are more likely to retire rather than undertake another difficult campaign. We also control for the value of a member's positions within the House. Those with more valuable positions—such as elected leaders, chairs or ranking members of committees, and prestige committee members—should be less likely to retire or seek another office. Being in the extended leadership may be a sign of a member's ambition (see chapter 3); if so, they may be more likely to seek statewide office. As Republicans are more likely to leave the House than Democrats, even when they are in the majority, we control for party identification (Murakami 2009).

We also control for the political context, as the availability of opportunities is especially likely to affect members' willingness to seek statewide office (Brace 1984; Copeland 1989; Schlesinger 1991). We code whether there is a gubernatorial and Senate race in the member's state in that election cycle and whether there is an open-seat race for those positions. House members are most likely to seek another office when the risk is lowest, which is when no incumbent is running and the seat is open. Also, we control for the number of House seats in the state (Brace 1984; Rohde 1979). The smaller the number of House seats is, the greater the overlap is between the member's House district and the statewide constituency to whom the member must appeal to win the gubernatorial or Senate campaign. Also, fewer House seats means less competition from House colleagues for the same statewide positions. Thus, we expect a negative relationship between the state's number of House seats and seeking statewide office: the larger the number of congressional representatives is, the lower the probability is of running statewide.

Many of the key hypotheses for seeking higher office are supported by the results presented in table 8.2, but the hypotheses regarding retirements are not. We will focus first on members' decisions to seek higher office, recorded in the right-hand column of table 8.2. Importantly, members who contribute significantly larger sums of campaign funds to state party organizations in the preceding election cycle ($cycle_{t-1}$) are significantly more likely to seek statewide office. While noteworthy, this result obscures a substantial change in members' behavior across the period of our study. We ran the regression model separately for the period prior to the 1996 election cycle, before redistribution was widespread among rank-and-file members, and for the 1996 election cycle and thereafter, when redistribution was commonplace (results not shown). Prior to 1996, members who ran for statewide office actually contributed significantly less than their colleagues to state party organizations. After 1996, when redistribution to both federal and state parties increased, the relationship between redistribution and seeking statewide office is positive and significant. This provides evidence that once members start to use campaign funds to advance their career ambitions, they use campaign funds to build relationships with state party officials as a means of facilitating a statewide campaign for office.

At the same time, members anticipating a run for statewide office in the next election cycle appear to redistribute less money at the federal level, though the estimate does not achieve conventional levels of statistical significance ($p < .08$).[6] Again, the relationship is stronger once members start to redistribute large sums of money starting in 1996; thus, those who plan to seek statewide office have an incentive to redistribute less to

TABLE 8.2. Decisions to Run for Reelection, Run for Statewide Office, or Retire, 1992–2006 (multinomial logit)

	Retire			Statewide Office		
	MLE	Robust S.E.	p-value	MLE	Robust S.E.	p-value
Adjusted State$_{t-1 \,(\times 1,000)}$	−.0021	.007	.98	.050	.022	.02
Adj. Federal $_{t-1 \,(\times 1,000)}$	−.00043	.0027	.88	−.012	.007	.08
Cash on hand$_{t-1}$	.003	.003	.30	.001	.0003	.00
Age	.029	.017	.09	−.034	.020	.08
Seniority	.170	.041	.00	−.011	.064	.86
Ethics	1.23	.365	.00	−.268	.862	.76
Blocked advancement	.609	.287	.01	.211	.344	.54
Redistricted	1.06	.416	.01	.872	.647	.18
Extended party leadership	−.101	.211	.61	.303	.235	.20
Elected party leadership	.534	.554	.34	.467	.884	.60
Subcommittee leader	.213	.256	.40	−.241	.368	.51
Committee leader	−.044	.339	.90	−.218	.037	.74
Prestige committee	−.803	.246	.00	−1.01	.377	.01
Electoral margin$_{t-1}$	−.004	.008	.60	.0008	.001	.93
Party voting	.025	.094	.79	.093	.122	.44
Majority party	−.137	.147	.35	−.118	.199	.55
Party identification (GOP)	.608	.154	.00	.578	.215	.01
Governor's race	.489	.298	.11	.179	.297	.54
Open seat governor	.126	.283	.66	.726	.338	.03
Senate race	.277	.239	.25	.896	.377	.02
Open seat U.S. Senate	.123	.283	.63	1.24	.257	.00
Number of House seats	−.011	.007	.14	−.063	.018	.00
Constant	−7.11	1.12	.00	−3.13	1.03	.00

$N = 3,450$
Log likelihood = 1,628
Model $\chi^2 = 289.17 \,(< .00)$
Pseudo $R^2 = .14$

Note: MLE = maximum likelihood estimate.

federal sources than their colleagues, in order to save more for their statewide campaigns (results not shown). Also, members with significantly higher levels of cash on hand are more likely to seek higher office. They can use their large war chests as seed money for an expensive statewide campaign. Collectively, these results provide clear evidence that members align their campaign money with their career goals: when anticipating a run for statewide office, members save their cash (in part by redistributing less) and give more to state party organizations who can be helpful in the upcoming campaign.

As expected, the opportunity structure also is an important explanation of members' decisions to seek higher offices. House members are significantly more likely to run statewide in election cycles in which there is a U.S. Senate campaign and when the U.S. Senate and/or governor's mansion is not being contested by an incumbent. Members of large House delegations are less likely to run than their colleagues from small delegations. The cost of becoming known statewide and the competition from other politicians is much greater for House members from large states than for members from small states.

The results of the model are largely supportive of our hypotheses regarding the relationship between redistributing campaign money to state parties and seeking higher office, but they do not support the variations of the "disaffection hypotheses" between redistribution and retirement. We examine the overall levels of federal redistribution in the previous election cycle (cycle$_{t-1}$) first, as shown in table 8.2. The coefficient for federal redistribution in cycle$_{t-1}$ is negatively signed but is not statistically related to retirement in the next election cycle. Members retire for reasons other than their disaffection with contemporary redistributive pressures and practices.[7]

Other variables perform largely as expected in explaining retirement decisions. Older and more senior members are more likely to retire, as are Republicans. Members who are redistricted, who face ethical scandals, or whose committee advancement is blocked are significantly more likely to retire. Prestige committee members are unlikely to give up their valuable posts through either retirement or seeking other offices. The redistribution of funds to state parties, however, is not related to members' decisions to retire or seek reelection, as state parties have little role to play in the continuation of a member's career in the House.

We also hypothesized that two categories of members should be most likely to become disaffected with contemporary pressures to raise substantial sums for redistribution. Neither of these groups of members is more likely to retire. We separately included these variables in the place of adjusted aggregate redistribution cash in the model presented in table 8.2. Since the results of all the other variables in the model remain stable, we present the coefficients for only these two variables in table 8.3.

Budget strain measures the difference between the member's cash on hand and the total amount the member redistributed from his or her principal campaign committee in the previous election cycle. It represents the amount of effort the member will have to devote to fundraising to attain previous levels of redistribution. We hypothesized that members facing budget strain should be more likely to retire in order to avoid such fundraising exertions. We find that budget strain is unrelated to retirement. Cash-poor members who seek to comply with party redistribution expectations apparently can adjust their fundraising activities to meet the party's demands with little difficulty (see chapter 7) or are content to continue their service regardless of whether they comply with the party's expectations.

The second kind of member most likely to become disaffected is the member who redistributes generously but whose advancement is blocked by younger members who are more senior in the committee seniority queue. Table 8.2 shows that members who are blocked by younger colleagues are more likely to retire, replicating the findings of Theriault (1998) and Hall and Van Houweling (1995). Table 8.3 shows, however, that "disaffected" members who redistribute generously and are blocked are no more likely to retire than anyone else. Generous members may believe that their redistribution will help their advancement goals when the opportunities arise. With seniority playing a less important role in the past promotions to committee leadership posts (Cann 2008; Deering and Wahlbeck 2006), they may believe that their generosity will help them to pass more senior colleagues. It also may help them to advance in party positions outside of the committee seniority queues. Additionally, there are likely to be high levels of uncertainty about future advancement prospects in the House, because members decide every two years whether to seek re-

TABLE 8.3.   Members Most Likely to Retire Based on Pressure to Redistribute

	MLE	S.E.	p-value
Budget strain	−.0037	.006	.54
Interaction between redistribution and blocked advancement			
Adjusted federal $\$_{t-1\ (\times 1000)}$	−.0002	.0003	.53
Blocked advancement	.683	.303	.02
Interaction	−.0007	.0005	.16

Note: MLE = maximum likelihood estimator. S.E. = standard error.

election, run for another office, or retire. Younger members ahead in the seniority line may seek other offices, may retire to become lobbyists, or may be defeated. There is no guarantee that being "blocked" today means that one will be blocked in the next session, so it is best to put oneself in the best possible position to advance, regardless of the specific political context or the decisions made by one's colleagues.

The evidence that retiring members do not differ from their colleagues in the sums they redistribute during the election cycle prior to their last term in Congress suggests that whatever the rigors of fundraising and pressures of redistribution are, they are not sufficient to compel ordinary members to leave Congress. Members who engage in minimal redistribution are not more likely to retire than those who do so energetically. Even members who seem most likely to be disaffected by the new party fundraising expectations—those who must exert the most effort to raise the funds because of low levels of cash on hand and those who redistribute generously but whose committee advancement is blocked by younger but more senior colleagues—do not retire more often than their colleagues based on their frustrations. Most members accept the need to raise and redistribute money for the party and adjust their campaign budgeting accordingly, as we show in chapter 7, or accept the risk that their advancement may be inhibited. Many members continue to redistribute funds even as they have announced their retirement.

Importantly, the evidence offers some reassurance for those concerned that pressure to redistribute finds would drive out the most active and successful legislators. The most active legislators—those with institutional posts (Hall 1996; Hibbing 1991)—who, as we have shown in chapter 4, are also the most active redistributors, are no or more less likely to leave than any other member. Those who find fundraising distasteful—skilled legislators included—are also no more or less likely to leave. If the best legislators were most likely to leave, this would indeed be a serious liability of the current fundraising regime. While additional investigation would be worthwhile, our current evidence suggests that this is not a primary consequence of the changes in party fundraising practices in Congress.

Freshmen and the Redistribution of Campaign Money

As a final approach to gaining some leverage on the consequences of the pressures to redistribute, we examine the members least likely to be aware of—and therefore to be frustrated by—party pressure to raise and redistribute campaign funds: newly elected members. Those engaged in their first election campaign to Congress are typically in competitive elections (at least more competitive than their incumbent colleagues) and do not face party dues requisitions or mobilization efforts to get them to redistribute funds. Their focus is on winning the seat for their party. As GOP chief deputy whip and NRCC recruitment chair Kevin McCarthy, who gave generously while first seeking election to the House, advised other nonincumbents, "If you're in a tight race, the number one thing you can do is win your election. That's why I don't advise everybody to [redistribute campaign funds]" (quoted in Miller 2010). If freshmen contribute prior to winning office—during their initial race for Congress—it suggests that they understand their party's fundraising expectations and arrive in Congress prepared to continue engaging in such activities. If they understand and accept these expectations from the beginning, they are unlikely to leave due to their disaffection with expectations of redistribution.

We start with the class of 1998, a period when member contribution activity was quickly becoming institutionalized by the parties. Fifteen percent of freshman contributed. Ernie Fletcher (R-KY), however, redistributed nearly $190,000, thus skewing that class's total contribution ($232,000) and mean contribution ($7,500). For the class of 2000, we find a percentage of redistributors (14.3 percent) similar to the class of 1998. In the aggregate, the class of 2000 redistributed $180,920, a mean of $4,300 per freshman. Apart from the single 1998 outlier, we see relatively similar redistributive behavior from freshmen in 1998 and 2000.

If redistribution is becoming a more widely understood and accepted expectation among prospective members of Congress, redistribution should increase among freshmen. It does in the classes of 2002 and 2004. Nearly half (48.8 percent) of the class of 2004 redistributed some campaign funds before being sworn into office. Indeed, the class of 2004 gave nearly $350,000—a mean of nearly $8,900 per freshman—which constitutes a substantial increase over giving by the freshmen class in prior election cycles. However, the class of 2006 does not approach the totals of the three preceding classes, perhaps because the new freshmen, several of whom won as Democratic challengers in Republican-leaning districts, needed every dollar they could raise for their own campaigns. The class gift totaled $104,000, with 29 percent of freshmen contributing. The mean contribution was $2,000. Of course, even a $2,000 contribution to the party would have been highly unusual for a nonincumbent (and indeed for many incumbents) as recently as 1990. The class of 2006 may be an anomaly, however, as the class of 2008—with a similar number of freshmen Democrats winning in competitive districts—returned to similar levels of giving as previous classes, with a participation rate of 45 percent, just over $400,000 in contributions, and a mean of $7,806 per freshman. The Republican-heavy class of 2010 also posts redistribution records on par or superior to the classes of the early 2000s. Forty-three percent of freshman contributed to produce a class gift of over $680,000, an average of just over $7,000 per freshman.

Given our finding that even veteran members of Congress have adapted to the new party fundraising expectations, there is even less chance, it would seem, that newer members, who arrive with an understanding of party expectations, will eventually leave out of frustration with them. To be sure, this could change if party fundraising expectations increased in order of magnitudes. New members increasingly know what they are getting into and come anyway, kicking in a few dollars on the way. Of course, our findings could also mean that Congress is increasingly attracting members who enjoy and excel at fundraising—which itself could have significant implications for the institution.

Conclusion

Prior to the mid-1990s, the congressional parties did not exert substantial pressure on their members to participate in solving the parties' financial collective action problems. Presumably, party leaders did not press their colleagues because they knew that their individualistic colleagues were unlikely to comply. The leader would then have wasted his or her effort, potentially undermined other goals, or—in a worst-case scenario—risked a challenge to his or her leadership by caucus members who resented the pressure.

That party leaders are now successfully mobilizing substantial campaign dollars from members shows that such efforts now pose little risk to leaders' job security. But some risk to the party remains if a minority of members who are disaffected with contemporary party fundraising expectations choose to leave rather than pay the piper. Retiring members create more open seats for the party to defend, potentially making it more difficult for the party to attain majority status, depending on the partisan composition of their districts. Additionally, the party risks losing members who are constructive on other dimensions—such as policy expertise, legislative skill, or voting loyalty—simply because they are less able or willing to fundraise.

The results of this chapter should allay those fears. Our results produce no evidence that members leave systematically due to the pressures to redistribute their campaign funds to the party and its candidates. Members have found ways to comply with the expectations while minimizing their own personal electoral risks (see chapter 7). The parties have not pushed their redistributive demands so high that they have burned out their most generous members. Nor have their demands pushed out members who find fundraising to be a distasteful and arduous task and who refuse to do more than the minimal amount necessary to secure their own reelection. Members who have resisted the party appeals have apparently accepted whatever diminished prospects of advancement may result from noncompliance. In short, there is no evidence that heightened party fundraising expectations have produced disaffection among the rank-and-file members or that disaffection has manifested itself through members voting with their feet by leaving the institution. Thus, we offer some reassurance that Congress is not suffering as a legislative institution because of the increased pressures to redistribute by the parties.

Our findings, then, reinforce the findings of many of the other studies cited in this chapter: there is little support for the disaffection hypothesis. Though we examine only one potential source of disaffection among members of the House, it is an area in which the potential source of disaffection (party pressure to redistribute funds) has clearly changed over time. Additionally, our theory is more specific than those offered in the extant research in that it specifically predicts which type of members are likely to be most disaffected by party fundraising pressures. Yet we still find no evidence that the members most vulnerable to disaffection are significantly more likely to retire.

If party fundraising pressure does not predict retirement, it does send signals of ambition for higher office. The spending and saving patterns of members who seek higher office are significantly different than those of their colleagues in a number of ways. First, these members are significantly less likely than their colleagues to redistribute campaign funds to their party and it candidates. Their ambitions do not lie in the House, making it safe (and indeed logical) for them to rebuff leaders' requests for campaign funds. Second, members who seek statewide office have significantly higher levels of cash on hand than their colleagues (see also Copeland 1989). Rather than redistributing these dollars to the party and its candidates, members with progressive ambition save their campaign funds for their impending statewide races. Third, members with progressive ambition do in fact redistribute campaign money. But compared to their colleagues, they redistribute relatively more dollars to state than to federal party organizations. Their future ambitions are advanced by building good relationships with state party leaders, and they use campaign funds as one method to cultivate such relationships (Schwartz 1990).

The evidence in this chapter, then, demonstrates that members use campaign funds in ways that are entirely consistent with their career ambitions. If a member is planning retirement, he or she has little need to please party leaders by generously supporting the party and its candidates. Accordingly, retiring members redistribute substantially fewer dollars to party concerns than do their reelection-seeking colleagues. If a member's ambitions lie at the state level, he or she is significantly more likely to direct campaign cash to state parties than to the House congressional campaign committees and federal party candidates (see chapter 4).

APPENDIX: VARIABLE MEASUREMENTS

Age: the member's age in the year of the election.

Blocked advancement: 1 = on all the committees on which a member serves, a younger member has greater seniority; 0 = on at least one committee, all representatives with greater seniority are older than the member.

Budget strain: the difference between the member's cash on hand and the total amount the member redistributed from his or her principal campaign committee in the previous election cycle.

Cash on hand: total dollars remaining in the incumbent's personal campaign committee at the end of the previous cycle.

Committee leaders: 1 = chair or ranking member of a standing committee; 0 = otherwise.

Elected leaders: 1 = Speaker, floor leader, whip, caucus/conference chair or other officer, or chair of party committee (e.g., congressional campaign committee); 0 = otherwise.

Electoral margin: the incumbent's percentage of the vote in the preceding election cycle.

Extended party leadership: 1 = member of whip system, Steering Committee, Policy Committee, or congressional campaign committee; 0 = otherwise.

Federal campaign contributions: the sum of the member's contributions from his or her principal campaign committee to other candidates' campaigns or the party congressional campaign committee. Incumbent contributions were calculated by the authors based on data obtained from the Federal Election Commission.

To compare contributions across eight election cycles in which contributions escalated substantially, we set all contributions at their 2000 value. First, we divided that election cycle's total member contributions (EC_x) by the total member contributions in 2000 (EC_{2000}). That proportion was then inverted so that, when multiplied by EC_x, EC_x equals EC_{2000}. Each member's contribution for EC_x was then multiplied by the same proportion. Essentially, we are measuring each member's percentage of total contributions for that year and expressing it in terms of 2000 dollars. In this way, the effect of each year's contributions on advancement can be assessed on the same basis as every other year's (see also Heberlig 2003).

Governor open seat: 1 = no incumbent seeking reelection for governor in the incumbent's state in election cycle; 0 = otherwise.

Governor's race: 1 = governor's race in incumbent's state in election cycle; 0 = otherwise.

Number of House seats: number of House districts in the incumbent's state.

Party identification: 1 = Republican; 0 = Democrat.

Policy preference/party voting loyalty: the *z*-score of a member's *Congressional Quarterly* score in party loyalty voting (adjusted to account for variations in the scores and the party agendas across sessions of Congress).

Prestige committee member: 1 = member of Appropriations, Rules, or Ways and Means committee; 0 = otherwise.

Redistricting: 1 = incumbents whose districts were combined in a redistricting process; 0 = otherwise.

Scandal: 1 = member against whom ethics charges were brought before the House Committee on Standards of Official Conduct prior to 1998, who was listed in an index search of *CQ Weekly Reports* as facing ethics charges, or who bounced more than 100 checks in the 1992 House banking scandal (1992 *CQ Almanac*, 17-A); 0 = otherwise.

Senate open seat: 1 = no incumbent seeking reelection for the U.S. Senate in the incumbent's state in election cycle; 0 = otherwise.

Senate race: 1 = U.S. Senate race in incumbent's state in election cycle; 0 = otherwise.

Seniority: the number of years a member has served at the time of the Congress under consideration.

State campaign contributions: total contributions from the incumbent's personal campaign committee to the state political party. State contributions were set to their value in the 2000 election cycle, following the same procedure as that already described for federal campaign contributions.

9 | Beyond Legislating

> Day and night, I am relentlessly raising money, starting early in the
> morning and ending late at night and on weekends.
> —Speaker Nancy Pelosi in an interview with *National Journal* (2010)

In the U.S. House, the contemporary battle for majority party control has
transformed congressional party leaders from legislative leaders, whose
primary job was to facilitate the passage of legislation important to party
members, into party leaders, whose responsibility for coordinating the
campaign for majority control is now every bit as important as their responsibility for passing legislation. Additionally, party loyalty among
members of Congress, once defined by the party caucus largely in terms of
voting the party line, is now defined as much in terms of redistributing
campaign money to the party. In short, the contemporary fight for majority party control that began in 1994 has fundamentally reshaped congressional parties and congressional party leadership.

Until this book, the transformation in the role of congressional parties
and leaders had gone largely unexplored by scholars who study congressional parties. The most prominent theories of congressional parties, even
those that characterize congressional party goals as primarily electoral
(Cox and McCubbins 1993, 2005), have focused exclusively on partisan
influence in the legislative process. As such, the extant research on congressional parties has had little to say about party influence over incumbent fundraising, and it has ignored a key component of party leaders'
jobs: coordinating the campaign for majority party control. A 2006 story
in the *New York Times* highlights the extent to which such party fundraising efforts have become an integral part of the day-to-day activities of
congressional party leaders.

Last weekend, Ms. Pelosi made more than 50 telephone calls to members of her caucus, chiding them to pay their [party] dues. Representative Rahm Emanuel, Democrat of Illinois and chairman of the Congressional Campaign Committee, has barred Democrats from using the telephones at party headquarters if they had not paid at least some of what they owed. "This is not my job," said Mr. Emanuel, recalling the message he repeats again and again to fellow Democrats. "This is our job." Strong-arm techniques, though, can backfire. So last week, in the final Democratic caucus before the recess, both Ms. Pelosi and Mr. Emanuel softened their language. Still, they distributed a spreadsheet, laying out for everyone to see how much—or how little—members had given to the party.... The delinquency statements that Democrats sent via overnight delivery to representatives' homes throughout the year have been supplanted by telephone calls or personal visits from party leaders. (Zeleny 2006)

Similarly, Peters and Rosenthal (2010, 117) note that Nancy Pelosi, as Speaker, "regarded it as both her responsibility and her opportunity to retain control of the House Democrats' campaign strategy and organization." Yet one would look in vain to the leading theoretical accounts of congressional parties for even a clue of the central importance of party fundraising and campaigning in the contemporary House.

To be sure, the congressional parties' increasingly centralized fundraising efforts have been studied by several scholars of party campaign finance (Dwyre et al. 2006; Franz 2008; Herrnson 1988; Kolodny 1998; La Raja 2008a, 2008b). But the important and empirically rich work produced by these scholars has generally not been guided by the theoretical work on congressional parties—which, in our view, is vital for understanding how and why congressional parties have wielded increasing influence over incumbent campaign money in the battle for majority control. Thus, by incorporating new party fundraising developments into current theoretical perspectives on congressional parties, our book has built a long-overdue bridge between the literature on party campaigning and the literature on congressional party organization.

In doing so, we build on the important opening moves in this direction by Cann (2008) and Currinder (2009). Beyond documenting recent relationships between redistribution and advancement, our contribution is to situate congressional party fundraising more squarely within current theories of congressional parties. We then use these theoretical accounts to derive and test predictions about which incumbents have incentives to redistribute, who gives to whom, the manner in which incumbents have financed the new party fundraising expectations, how such expectations have shaped House incumbents' career decisions, and how the battle for majority party control and centralization of congressional party fundraising efforts have altered member contribution strategies and patterns of incumbent institutional advancement in the House.

Theoretical Considerations

Congressional Party Theory

Our chief theoretical contribution has been to extend a variant of Cox and McCubbins' (1993, 2005) cartel theory—which states that congressional parties organize to help solve collective legislative dilemmas—to the realm of congressional party fundraising. Cox and McCubbins posit that the majority party uses its control over organization and process to protect members' electoral interests by passing legislation that enhances the party reputation (1993) and by keeping issues off of the floor that would split the party and present electoral difficulties for party members (2005). Yet despite the centrality of majority party control to their theory, Cox and McCubbins pay surprisingly little attention to how parties induce members to work for majority party control (S. Smith 2007). In particular—and as with other theories of congressional parties—cartel theory has nothing to say about nonlegislative party activities designed to advance majority status, as if solving collective legislative dilemmas would be sufficient, by itself, to guarantee a party continued control of the legislature. In reality, an impressive party legislative record would do little to advance majority party control without the financial resources necessary to communicate that record to voters. Moreover, as Lee (2009, 9) points out, undermining the opposition party record—a task that also requires formidable financial resources—is likely to be just as important to gaining and retaining majority control as is establishing a favorable record for one's own party. Thus, in our view, understanding how congressional parties solve collective party fund raising dilemmas is every bit as important as understanding how they solve collective legislative dilemmas. Congressional parties, we posit, seek to monopolize not only legislative agenda-setting powers but campaign cash as well. Cornering the political money market is essential, and the parties increasingly accomplish this by harnessing incumbent power.

Our book also heeds Rohde's exhortation (2010, 338) that scholars who study congressional parties give more sustained attention to the continuous battle for majority control of the House ushered in by the 1994 election. Toward this end, we demonstrate that the parties have adapted at least some of the institutional developments of the earlier (pre-1994) postreform House period (i.e., the extended leadership organization) toward the goal of winning majority control. Nothing underscores this point better than the evolution of the House whip organizations. Originally designed by Democrats to include rank-and-file members in the leadership's lawmaking and coalition-building efforts (Sinclair 1983), the House GOP whip organization in 2009 was charged with the task of prodding Republican incumbents to meet their party fundraising goals for the 2009–10 election cycle (O'Connor 2009). "We want to lead by example," said GOP deputy whip Kevin O. McCarthy (R-CA). "The way to help and grow back is to have a strong core whip team" (quoted in O'Connor 2009). Clearly, the parties use agenda-setting offices not only to monopolize legislative power but also to monopolize campaign funds.

We obviously share Rohde's belief that congressional party theorists need to continue to study more fully the impact of the battle for majority control on congressional politics. To guide their efforts, researchers ought to start with Steven Smith's (2007) insight that congressional party leaders are no doubt often confronted with the task of balancing multiple collective party goals. Trade-offs among such goals, says Smith (2007, 206), are likely "central to leaders' everyday activities." In terms of party fundraising, then, how do congressional parties balance the need for a favorable party reputation with the requirement of raising money from donors who push narrow interests over the public interest? Additionally, are party incumbents perhaps willing to live with less-than-ideal policy outcomes in order to finance the party's campaign for majority control? Similarly, do party fundraising imperatives compete with policy concerns when parties make organizational changes in the House (Wright 2000)? Heberlig, Hetherington, and Larson (2006) explore one such trade-off, demonstrating that House incumbents are willing to select leaders who are not ideological middlemen if they have a demonstrated record of party fundraising. But more can be done. In short, while our book illuminates the importance of party fundraising to congressional politics, future research should zero in on how parties balance the multiple collective goals of policy, reputation, fundraising, and electoral success.

The Textbook Tripartite Party

In bringing congressional party fundraising into the theoretical fold hitherto reserved for lawmaking, our book also forces a reconsideration of the textbook view of American parties as tripartite entities: parties in the electorate, party organizations, and parties in the government (Beck 1996; Hershey 2008). This conceptual categorization may have outlived its usefulness. Taking seriously Salmore and Salmore's (1989) exhortation to pay greater attention to the electioneering functions of the party-in-the-government, we demonstrate that the congressional parties are far more than simply legislative parties whose leaders are charged with advancing legislation important to the party. Instead, the congressional parties now occupy the central role in mobilizing and coordinating the sprawling party fundraising networks so critical to each party's electoral success. Simply put, the party organization and party in government are no longer distinct. The party in government is now doing many of the functions formerly attributed to the party organization. Even in a more ideological, policy-driven era, parties are still concerned first and foremost with winning. Majority control of the House is a necessary condition for advancing the party's most important policy objectives or providing policy and funding rewards to its coalition partners. Moreover, we specify how the majority and minority parties should behave differently in terms of redistribution and institutional reward structures in order to maintain or achieve majority status.

Paying to Play?

Our theory and findings also challenge the conventional wisdom, within both the media and in political science, that campaign contributions essentially buy votes (or buy off the officials making appointments) to help the contributor advance—that is, that ambitious politicians must "pay to play." We dispute the dominant characterization of this process as a straightforward exchange of money for advancement, and we argue instead that contributors must show their commitment to the party's dominant collective goal in order to advance. When the party's dominant goal is policy, campaign money may not be important to advancement. But even when the party's dominant goal is electoral (majority status), the party does not merely reward those who provide lots of money. Instead, it rewards incumbents who provide the money to the candidates who help it achieve majority status. For the majority party, that means protecting endangered incumbents; for the minority party, that means promoting challengers and open-seat candidates. Incumbents who allocate their contributions in ways that help the party achieve party status, thus signaling their willingness to serve the party's collective interests, are most likely to advance. We certainly argue that money matters, but how it matters is conditional, and those conditions are shaped by the parties and by the political environment in which they are competing.

Incumbents as Self-Interested Rational Actors

It should be clear that the rise in incumbent party-connected contributions does little to undercut the self-interested, rational actor thesis outlined by Jacobson (1985–86). Members of Congress have not suddenly become risk-taking altruists dedicated to their party's shared electoral purposes. To the contrary, the trends we document in this book demonstrate that members' individual political goals shape both the manner in which and the extent to which they comply with party fundraising expectations. First, congressional incumbents redistribute far more campaign money to the House congressional campaign committees and congressional candidates than they do to state and local parties. This is because congressional parties have substantial ability to affect members' individual career goals, whereas state and local parties do not. Second, members with powerful institutional positions engage in party fundraising efforts much more than do members with less ambition to climb the leadership ladder. This is because the party's collective electoral interests and the personal interests of members seeking power are highly interdependent: the power of members' institutional positions (and hence members' personal power) is maximized when their party is in the majority. Third, incumbents in difficult electoral circumstances redistribute fewer campaign dollars than do incumbents facing easy reelections. For incumbents facing difficult reelection contests, the first priority remains saving their careers. The parties, moreover, are not seeking martyrs; jeopardizing an incumbent's seat to improve the chance of picking up an additional seat makes little sense. Fourth, House members who are retiring or seeking another office decrease the sum of dollars they redistribute, because their goals are no longer advanced by pleasing a legislative party caucus they will soon be leaving.

We will add that the rise in incumbent party-connected contributions has almost surely been facilitated by the structure of contemporary partisan competition, which makes it relatively easy for most incumbents to redistribute funds. In particular, the post-1994 period has witnessed fierce competition for partisan control of the House but very little competition in most individual House races—with partisan control of the House typically hinging on a handful of competitive districts. If majority control was up for grabs but many incumbents had competitive races, members would almost certainly not be redistributing as much money as they are now. In short, we are currently seeing optimal conditions for incumbent party-connected contributions: a combination of intense partisan competition for control of the House with very little electoral competition in most members' districts.

Thus, the increase in incumbent party fundraising should not, by any means, be interpreted as philanthropy. Nor does it signal the end of incumbent self-interest. Rather, it demonstrates the parties' success, in a political environment characterized by fierce competition for majority control, in structuring institutions that harness incumbents' individual desire for power in the service of the party's collective electoral needs. Members are willing to finance the collective good of majority party control only because they have a personal stake in the party's collective electoral fate (Cox and McCubbins 1993).

How Long Can It Last?

It is reasonable to ask how long these arrangements will last. To us, the critical variable is whether competition for control of the House will continue to exist in its current form—that is, with thin partisan margins and with control hinging on a relatively small number of seats. As long as the margins between the congressional parties remain close, most members are safe, and each party has a reasonable chance at retaking the majority, members clearly have a strong incentive to redistribute large sums of campaign money. Given the relatively even partisan split in the electorate and between states (Brewer and Stonecash 2009), there is little reason to believe that this political context will change any time soon, absent an unforeseen exogenous electoral shock such as an economic collapse or an international security crisis.

One interesting question is whether incumbents would continue to redistribute campaign funds even if one party were to be electorally dominant again, as the Democrats were between 1954 and 1994. On one hand, the incentives to redistribute money would seem to be significantly lower if there was little chance of a shift in majority control. Moreover, incumbents may well resist efforts by party leaders to get them to share their wealth under such conditions, as they did during the 1954–94 period. On the other hand, the practice of redistributing campaign money may be a new norm within the congressional parties—an expectation that would persist regardless of the level of competition for control of the House. This would be the likely result predicted by a variant of path-dependent models, which imply that some processes, "once introduced, can be virtually impossible to reverse" (Pierson 2000). Certainly, party leaders seeking to mobilize incumbent money could make the case that a larger party is preferable to a smaller one and that member contributions can help maximize the number of party seats even if a takeover of the chamber is unlikely. If newly elected members of Congress seek their seats knowing full well the expectations of redistribution and attendant demands of fundraising, they are likely to continue the practice regardless of the electoral conditions. Moreover, as long as party leaders and party caucuses maintain the linkage between redistribution and advancement, ambitious members have a strong incentive to redistribute to achieve their own goals. In still another scenario, it may be that one-party domination of the House would return the practice of redistribution to its more individually oriented, less party-regarding roots, with incumbents giving to candidates who could help them in leadership contests and/or in building legislative coalitions (Wilcox 1989). Either way, it seems clear that as long as congressional campaigns continue to have insatiable appetites for campaign money, ambitious House incumbents seeking to advance their political goals will deploy campaign money in a fashion that helps them achieve their ends.

Party Competition and the Battle for Majority Status

The central claim of this book is that when majority control is on the line, fundraising is as much a part of the job of contemporary congressional party leaders as is passing legislation. As party leaders have enlisted incumbents to help support the party's collective financial needs, redistributing funds to the party now rivals fealty on the floor as a key indicator of party loyalty for leaders and nonleaders alike. Acting as political cartels, the congressional parties have attempted to corner the market on campaign cash by working through incumbents. A key concern, then, is the extent to which this trend has affected the House's ability to function as a governing institution.

Raising a concern about partisan competition for majority status is noteworthy because electoral competition (whether between candidates or between political parties) is traditionally taken to be an unalloyed positive for democracy (e.g., Schumpeter 1942; American Political Science Association 1950). Competitive elections boost voter interest and turnout and attract quality candidates to run to provide legitimate choices to voters. Competition constrains politicians from taking actions their constituents would oppose. Most fundamentally, competition between parties allows voters to control the policy decisions of government. Downs (1957) specifically argues that in a winner-take-all electoral system like that in the United States, competition produces party platforms and policy outcomes close to the preferences of the median voter.

The behavior of the parties in Congress since competition for control of the House tightened in the mid-1990s raises questions about whether the positive consequences of partisan competition are inevitable. It also raises the possibility of some less edifying consequences. It would be easy to argue, for example, that parties prioritize short-term electioneering over long-term policy development in such an environment, but that dichotomy is too simple. Party activists and their interest group allies certainly expect policy commitments to be fulfilled, and incumbents want a record of accomplishments on which to seek reelection. Rather, the issue is how parties develop and articulate policies in a competitive environment.

Contrary to Downs's prediction that party competition produces policy moderation, both parties' rhetoric and policy priorities have not seemed particularly slavish to moderate general election voters since 1995 (e.g., Fiorina, Abrams, and Pope 2005). The parties seem to be quite willing to set priorities that entail electoral risk. The GOP's impeachment of President Clinton and emphasis on large tax cuts disproportionately weighted to high-income taxpayers and the Democrat's push for health care reform are the most prominent examples.

The battle for majority control has led both parties to seek opportunities to "clarify the differences" between the parties. Emphasizing differences certainly is a way to mobilize the party base, and ideologically committed public officials seem consistently certain that emphasizing the party's stances on issues it "owns" (Petrocik 1996) and framing its policy stances with the right language (as tested through polls and focus groups) will persuade sufficient swing voters to support them (Jacobs and Shapiro 2000). Rhetorically, this approach has meant criticizing policies, procedures, and presidential actions taken by the opposition party that seem similar to those taken by one's own party when it held power (Lee 2009). Legislatively, it has meant restraining party members from cooperating in developing legislation promoted by members of the other party or even from voting for it to preserve the distinction between the parties. Consistently voting no has the additional partisan benefit of forcing the majority party to provide all the votes to pass their legislation. The majority must cajole its members who represent swing districts—predominately moderates—to cast potentially controversial votes and to vote a high percentage of times with the rest of their party. The minority party then uses the voting records of these members as campaign fodder in the next election to cast them as "too extreme" or "out of touch" with their constituents.

The parties serve their ideologically extreme "policy-demanding" activists and donors and expect that the party's accomplishments will motivate activists to turn out on election day and donate the resources required to sell the party's message to swing voters. This logic is particularly necessary to explain how and why the majority party believes it can push an agenda more ideologically extreme than the preferences of constituents in many swing districts—on which the retention of majority control hinges. The party presumes that its monetary advantage, fueled partly by the fundraising advantage of incumbents in marginal districts and the redistribution efforts of its safe incumbents, will be sufficient to protect representatives in swing districts from voter backlash against the tough votes these members must take to advance the party's legislative agenda. Long-term policy development and short-term electoral tactics, then, are not necessarily inconsistent. The problem is that off-center majority parties require tremendous sums of campaign money to remain in the majority, and raising these sums imposes a number of costs on the parties and Congress institutionally. The empirical findings of this book speak directly to the potential institutional liabilities of the new partisan fundraising regime.

One of the primary costs, as we see it, is the further entanglement of moneyed interests with the congressional parties. Because institutional advancement now requires a member to provide significant sums of campaign money to the party, members with established ties to large donors enjoy a distinct advantage in capturing and holding powerful leadership offices (Currinder 2009, 200; La Raja 2008b, 217). The result is that agenda-setting positions are now nearly always populated by members with the strongest ties to moneyed interests.

A specific consequence of these trends is that ideologically extreme members of Congress have used campaign funds to open a new route to power in the House (Heberlig, Hetherington, and Larson 2006). Extreme leaders can then use their appointment powers, agenda setting powers, and bargaining leverage to move policy deliberations in the House in their preferred direction, thereby exacerbating the dynamics of polarization we have discussed in the preceding paragraphs. Advances in fundraising through the Internet and social media, which provide easily accessible niche markets primed to be mobilized with the inflammatory rhetoric that has traditionally been a staple of political fundraising (Godwin 1988), suggest that this avenue to the leadership is likely to widen for ambitious ideologues.

Moreover, this trend not only affects the top echelon of leaders; it influences the behavior of anyone interested in moving up in Congress. As Herrick and Moore (1993) demonstrate, new members entering the institution begin grooming themselves early on for advancement, and in doing so, they no doubt pay close attention to how existing leaders have moved up. What they currently see is that campaign money matters a lot and that if they want to get ahead in party circles, they need to begin early on building a donor base that can help them subsidize contributions to the party and its candidates.

In terms of moving up, the edge enjoyed by members with deep ties to moneyed interests is exemplified by the 2004 contest for Appropriations Committee chair. The contest featured three candidates: Jerry Lewis (R-CA), Hal Rogers (R-KY), and—the most senior of the three—Ralph Regula (R-OH). Regula was at a distinct disadvantage in the competition because he refused PAC donations for much of his career and, consequently, never assembled a donor list sufficiently large to help him compile a record of party fundraising. Recognizing his weakness, Regula attempted to repair it, as recounted by Krawzak (2004b).

> Regula suffered from never having done much fund-raising for the party. His rivals for the post, Reps. Harold Rogers, R-Ky., and Jerry Lewis, R-Calif., have been raising money for other candidates for more than a decade. Regula realized he couldn't raise big money without tapping into PAC contributions. . . . [Thus,] on top of creating the leadership PAC, Regula opened his regular re-election fund to special interest donations in response to increasing 'pressure' to contribute more to the National Republican Congressional Committee (NRCC), which helps finance Republican House candidates.

Lewis and Rogers also tapped moneyed interests, as recounted by Mann and Ornstein (2006, 237–38).

We watched [the candidates] scramble to raise hundreds of thousands of dollars, turning to everyone they knew and everyone with
business before the committee. It was wrenching. Subsequently,
news reports suggested that the winner, Jerry Lewis, altered his view
on a defense program soon after attending a fund raiser for his
leadership PAC run by an investment firm in New York that
benefited handsomely from the policy change.

The fundraiser netted $110,000 for Lewis's leadership PAC and kept intact
a defense project worth $160 million, in which the firm had a stake (Mann
and Ornstein 2006, 255 n. 15; Kelley 2006). In the end, Lewis won, with
Speaker Hastert viewing him "as the candidate who had done the most for
the party over the long haul, especially given his connections in the defense industry" (Schatz 2005, 71).

The Lewis case depicts a party leadership concerned with monopolizing campaign funds for the party. It demonstrates that with majority control on the line, party leaders prefer to allocate agenda-setting offices to
members who have deep ties to moneyed interests and who are willing to
tap these ties to help fill the party's coffers. Moreover, the dynamics at play
in a contest such as this one would no doubt reverberate within the party.
Observing this competition unfold, new members grooming themselves
for advancement would learn from Regula's failure and move quickly to
forge relationships with moneyed interests that could help them underwrite a solid record of fundraising for the party and its candidates. In
short, the use of fundraising as criteria for allocating positions of
influence sends a signal to junior members that one can hardly hope to
advance within the party without the kind of deep ties to donors that
Lewis had. The notion that new members are socialized early into party-
regarding contribution behavior is reinforced by our finding in chapter 8
that the redistribution of campaign funds has increased substantially
among incoming members of Congress.

Critics of Republican rule of the House between 1994 and 2006 might
be tempted to believe that such practices are not as stark among House
Democrats. Indeed, as the opening vignette for this book recounts,
Speaker Pelosi endorsed Colin Peterson (DFL-MN) to chair the Agriculture Committee in 2006 despite the fact that Peterson had done little to
help the Democratic Congressional Campaign Committee since his election to Congress. But as the opening narrative also recounts, Peterson had
to promise to change his ways before Pelosi would endorse him for the

chairmanship; and change he did, by forming a leadership PAC and redistributing six-figure sums to the DCCC from his principal campaign committee. Notably, Peterson subsidized his newfound generosity by increasing his receipts from agricultural interests.[1] Ultimately, write Peters and Rosenthal (2010, 115), "the difference between the Republican pay-to-play approach and Pelosi's may not be readily discernable. Whereas the GOP fostered direct competition between members and made fundraising a pre-requisite for plum committee assignments, Pelosi sets targets and celebrates those who exceed them."

Encouraged by the intense pressure to raise money for the party, the growing entanglement between moneyed interests and lawmakers can be seen in other developments on the congressional landscape as well. Many leadership PACs now employ lobbyists as their treasurers (Berry and Wilcox 2009; Currinder 2009), and the GOP's K Street Project only further fortified the ties between moneyed interests, lobbyists, and GOP lawmakers (Hacker and Pierson 2005; Mann and Ornstein 2006).[2] The increasing use of LPACs also exacerbates the entanglement of members and moneyed interests by giving more members a second organization—in addition to their principal campaign committee—with which to solicit donors.[3] Other signs of an uncomfortably close relationship between lawmakers and moneyed interests include several fundraisers organized by lawmakers closely preceding key votes and markup sessions (Lipton and Lichtblau 2010) and a scandal in which clients of the lobbying group PMA "gained more than $200 million in federal earmarks from a roster of lawmakers who received hundreds of thousands of dollars in contributions from [PMA's principal lobbyist], his family and associates" (Eggen and Glod 2010). A story by *New York Times* reporters Charlie Savage and David Kirkpatrick about Representative Peter Visclosky (D-IN)—a lawmaker subpoenaed in the scandal—highlighted the link between Visclosky's fundraising and his desire to advance in party circles. "Although Mr. Visclosky rarely faces well-financed opposition in his overwhelmingly Democratic district," wrote Savage and Kirkpatrick (2009), "he has relied heavily on the lobbying firm and its clients to fill his campaign war chest, using much of the money to elevate his stature within the Democratic Party through donations to other campaigns."

Clearly, then, there is no shortage of stories suggesting that the new fundraising expectations parties have of members have tied lawmakers more closely to moneyed interests. But why, a skeptic might ask, should we care about the trends previously described, especially when countless studies by political scientists have demonstrated that interest group money has, at best, a limited and uneven effect on legislative outcomes?[4] To be sure, critics of the new party fundraising regime can offer isolated examples of its troubling implications for the integrity of congressional policy making, such as the Lewis case recounted earlier. But as social scientists, we ought to be wary of making generalizations from single cases.

The need to arrive at a more generalizable set of conclusions should serve as a challenge to future researchers. In our view, political scientists have failed to develop a model that assesses the influence of money on policy that even remotely captures the current political arrangements in Washington, D.C. Delineating the many flaws of the standard money-for-votes models typically used by scholars to estimate the influence of interest group money on legislative policy is obviously beyond the scope of this chapter. But we can say a few things as a way of guiding future researchers. First, such models were designed to capture money's influence when power in Congress was much more decentralized than it currently is. In a recent review essay on money and politics, Powell and Wilcox (2010) drive home the point. Studies evaluating the impact of money on policy, they write,

> assume the financial linkage is between the individual legislator and his or her contributors and the votes that the legislator casts. Increasingly, party leaders, committee chairs, and legislators who aspire to these positions have become fundraisers not just for themselves, but for the caucus. Any influence financial contributions have on leaders' and chairs' efforts to mobilize support for or against legislation in the party caucus will be missed in these models. In order to determine the influence of money on policy, we need to develop a measure that incorporates all of the various ways money may influence the content and passage of legislation. (643)

As an example of the challenges facing researchers attempting to trace the complicated flow of campaign dollars, Peters and Rosenthal (2010, 115) note that Speaker Pelosi would assist House Democrats in raising money (e.g., by appearing at fundraisers) so that members could, in turn, hand over to the party the funds they raised with Pelosi's help.

The standard money-for-votes models also fail to capture two other essential features of the current political arrangements in Washington. First, lawmakers have become increasingly aggressive in raising money from organized interests (Berry and Wilcox 2009; Mann and Ornstein 2006; Sorauf 1992). The Republican K Street Project is but one example of such efforts. Second, the models assume a national policy community populated mostly by pragmatic interest groups willing to work with either party. But as suggested by Sinclair's (2006) description of the increasingly polarized interest group community in Washington, such an assumption no longer holds.[5] Instead, groups have increasingly lined up with one of the two parties, either because of pressure from one of the parties or because only one party is willing to work with them. The standard models for estimating money's influence offer few clues as to how interested money would influence policy in such an environment.

In thinking about future research, then, scholars should focus on replacing outmoded models of moneyed influence with models that more accurately capture the essential features of the current political arrangements in Washington. At the very least, such models would need to offer a compelling story of how interested money—coaxed from donors by aggressive lawmakers who then turn around and redistribute portions of it to the party and its candidates—influences policy in a highly partisan and centralized Congress. The models could be fruitfully grounded in the theoretical perspective we offer, which characterizes congressional parties as political cartels seeking to monopolize not only legislative agenda-setting powers but campaign cash as well.

While more research is clearly needed, the preceding discussion suggests that the party fundraising trends we outline in this book may have troubling implications for the House's ability to function as a responsible lawmaking and representational body. The term *responsible* can obviously be defined in multiple ways, and any definition we choose reflects our biases about how we think representative government ought to work. Nevertheless, any normative evaluation requires a standard against which to assess the status quo, and toward that end, we find it fruitful to extend Representative David Price's definition of a responsible legislator to the House as a collective body. "A responsible legislator," writes Price (2004, 284), "takes the initiative in looking to poorly organized or non-traditional interests that the system might exclude and to broad, shared public interests and values that are inadequately mirrored in the 'pressure system.'" It seems unlikely that parties bent on monopolizing campaign funds will do a very good job of representing such interests and values.

Yet, compared to the later years of the period prior to the Bipartisan Campaign Reform Act, there may be a positive aspect to the trends we document. In terms of representing a broad array of interests, incumbent contributions are almost surely healthier for the parties than the six-figure sums of soft money the parties were raising prior to BCRA. After all, the money raised and redistributed by incumbents originates from a broader array of donors than do soft money contributions funneled to the parties by narrow interests. Incumbent contributions to the congressional campaign committees might thus be viewed as expanding and broadening a party's fundraising base by giving the party access (albeit indirect) to donors to whom it would otherwise have no connection (Heberlig et al. 2008). Of course, we are not claiming that donors who give to congressional incumbents are somehow representative of the overall population. Scholars have demonstrated this to be far from true (Francia et al. 2003). Moreover, the fact that lobbyists are likely responsible for bundling a nontrivial sum of the individual donations received by House incumbents makes it even less true.[6] Nevertheless, it is a safe bet that individual donors to House incumbents are, on average, more representative of the general public than are the narrow interests that, prior to BCRA, were funneling six-figure sums of soft money into national party coffers.

Furthermore, incumbent contributions have helped to strengthen party organizational capacity by allowing the party congressional campaign committees to mitigate the loss of soft money banned by BCRA and thereby remain an important presence in congressional campaigns (Corrado and Varney 2007; Dwyre et al. 2006). Indeed, the four Hill campaign committees made a combined $296.5 million in independent expenditures in the most competitive contests during the 2008 congressional elections,[7] and a healthy portion of the funds used to finance these expenditures were supplied directly by members of Congress.

Reforms and Their Challenges

Books such as ours often conclude with a menu of reforms. This is a difficult plan to follow in our case, because the trends we document in this book are motored by exogenous political factors that are largely unamenable to reform: namely, hyperpartisan polarization and, since 1994, a continuous struggle for majority control of the House. Likewise, the Supreme Court's skepticism of much campaign finance regulation, which has become especially pronounced in the Roberts court, suggests few opportunities for major restrictions on the flow of money in campaigns.

There are a few reforms, however, that may help curb some of the worst abuses associated with the new party fundraising expectations of incumbents. For example, the Federal Election Commission at one time proposed bringing a member's leadership PAC and principal campaign committee under a single set of contribution limits, which would limit members' ability to use LPACs to circumvent contribution limits governing their PCCs.[8] It may also make sense to place a reasonable cap on the sums members can transfer from their PCCs to the congressional campaign committees. Without such limits, incumbents are tremendously vulnerable to intense pressure from party leaders seeking to fill the party campaign committee's coffers. Additionally, one can imagine campaign money counting for less within congressional party circles if campaigns were less costly and if incumbents and nonincumbents alike had equal access to funds. In theory, then, reforms such as public funding that lowered the demand for private money in House campaigns might reduce the importance of party fundraising as a requirement for institutional advancement (which would heighten the relative importance of other qualifications).

In reality, however, public funding programs in the states have apparently not had this effect. Powell (2008) found that while legislators in states with public funding spent less time raising money for themselves, they spent more time raising money for the party caucus. Powell's findings speak to the problem with which we opened this section. Any reforms designed to curb the excesses of the party fundraising practices we document in this book would necessarily play out in the polarized and hyperpartisan political environment that has helped produce the current problems in the first place.

Money was important in elections long before competition for control of the House intensified in 1994. Party efforts to corner the fundraising market—by deputizing officeholders as financial supporters and extracting campaign funds from donors with business before the government—are by no means new. What *is* innovative is the pervasiveness of the congressional parties' efforts to control incumbent fundraising, the close linkages between institutional structures—particularly the advancement system—and fundraising on behalf of the party and its candidates, and the parties' success in generating substantial financial support from almost every member of their caucuses in a short period of time.

In an ideologically polarized environment, the battle for majority control has transformed the congressional parties. Political parties in Congress no longer act mainly as facilitators of legislative debate and executors of legislative procedures. Now more than ever, the congressional parties act in multiple and interdependent partisan capacities—setting the partisan agenda, building partisan floor coalitions, getting out the partisan message, undermining the opposition party's reputation, and funding the permanent and costly campaign for majority party control.

Notes

CHAPTER 1

1. In the five election cycles between 1992 and 2000, Peterson had donated only $5,000 to the DCCC and $22,375 to other Democratic candidates. During the same period, Peterson gave $82,600 to the Minnesota Democratic-Farmer-Labor Party. Thus, Peterson was willing to assume some electoral risk by giving to state party organizations, but he chose not to support the national congressional party or his fellow party candidates for Congress.

2. Though figure 1.1 begins in the 1990s, Bedlington and Malbin (2003) document that during the 1970s and 1980s, the sums of money redistributed by members of Congress remained under $5 million, roughly at the same level as in the early 1990s.

3. Congress raised the limit from $1,000 to $2,000 in the 2005 Appropriations Act (2 U.S.C. 432(e)(3)(B)). But the new amount was not indexed for inflation. See Metzler 2006.

4. http://www.opensecrets.org.

5. Since the industry data include soft money contributions, some of the trends surely reflect BCRA's soft money ban, which, starting in 2004, banned industries from giving soft money to the national parties. But this implies that House members' influence as donors has increased in the post-BCRA world.

6. *Colorado Republican Federal Campaign Committee v. Federal Election Commission*, 518 U.S. 604 (1996).

7. Federal Election Commission, press release, May 28, 2009, http://www.fec.gov/press/press2009/05282009Party/20090528Party.shtml.

8. Federal Election Commission, press release, May 28, 2009, http://www.fec.gov/press/press2009/05282009Party/20090528Party.shtml.

9. Federal Election Commission, press release, May 28, 2009, http://www.fec.gov/press/press2009/05282009Party/20090528Party.shtml; Center for Responsive Politics, "Democratic Congressional Campaign Committee," http://www.opensecrets.org/parties/indus.asp?Cmte=DCCC&cycle=2000; Center for Responsive Politics, "National Republican Campaign Committee," http://www.opensecrets.org/parties/indus.asp?Cmte=NRCC&cycle=2000.

CHAPTER 2

1. To be sure, there have been periods of strong parties in the House other than the current period (such as under the Reed Speakership [1889–91; 1895–99]), and it was not uncommon for U.S. Senators to head up personal statewide machines (Kolodny 1998, 21).

2. Joseph Schlesinger (1991, 186) notes that Johnson's 1940 push to raise money was "certainly an exceptional effort, if only because it was an era in which campaign expenditures were relatively small and probably less important in deciding elections than they became with the advent of television."

3. Through amendments, the 1974 measures changed nearly everything about the 1971 FECA, in effect amounting to an entirely new law.

4. In 2011, the limit was $88,400 for House nominees in states with only one representative and $44,200 for House nominees in all other states.

5. The limit was the greater amount, adjusted for inflation, of $20,000 or $0.02 per person for a state's voting-age population. In 2011, the limits range between $88,400 and $2,458,500 for Senate nominees.

6. Schiller (2000, chap. 6), for example, finds that same-state senators have different fundraising networks of PACs located within their state.

7. As we discuss later in this chapter, BCRA increased individual contributions to the national parties. See Dwyre and Kolodny (2006) for details.

8. Telephone interview by Larson, December 2, 1994. Since we do not have permission to publish this House member's identity, we refer to this member as Democratic Member of Congress A or Representative A (see the opening of chapter 3). Throughout the book, we treat all anonymous interviews in this manner.

9. The remaining 8 percent, $16,000, was contributed to the NRCC. Gingrich's contributions differed dramatically from those of his colleagues, who, on average, gave 47 percent to nonincumbent candidates, 22 percent to competitive incumbents, 10 percent to safe incumbents, and 21 percent to their party CCC in 1994.

10. http://www.fec.gov/data/LobbyistBundle.do?format=html (accessed April 10, 2010).

11. http://www.fec.gov/data/LobbyistBundle.do?format=html (accessed April 10, 2010).

12. Wright's interviews with PAC officials (1985, 403) showed that they are aware that incumbents may redistribute their contribution "to solidify or expand [the member's] influence within the House."

13. This section summarizes from a number of sources on the K Street Strategy: see especially Confessore 2003; Continetti 2006; Dubose and Reid 2004; Eilperin 2006.

14. The parties were remarkably evenly matched in soft money receipts in 2002 (and 2000) when all national party committees (Republican National Committee/Democratic National Committee, National Republican Senatorial Committee/Democratic Senatorial Campaign Committee, NRCC/DCCC) are summed: $250 million for the GOP versus $246 million for the Democrats.

15. Increases in spending by corporate-funded 527 and 501(c) groups suggest that some firms may be willing to take the risk. See Campaign Finance Institute, *Soft Money Political Spending by 501(c) Nonprofits Tripled in the 2008 Election*, February 25, 2009,

www.cfinst.org/Press/Preleases/09-02-25/Soft_Money_Political_Spending_by_Non
profits_Tripled_in_2008.aspx.

16. This includes the Democratic National Committee, the Republican National
Committee, and the House and Senate congressional campaign committees.

17. Federal Election Commission, press release, May 28, 2009, http://www.fec.gov/
pres/pres2009/05282009Party/20090528Party.shmtl.

18. Federal Election Commission, press release, March 7, 2007, http://www.fec.gov/
press/press2007/partyfinal2006/20070307party.shtml.

19. http://www.fec.gov/press/press2009/05282009Party/4_DSCCNRSCReceipts
08.pdf.

20. If corporations wanted to spend money in support or opposition to a federal
candidate, they could do so only through a separate segregated fund (i.e., a PAC) that
raised money in accordance with highly restrictive federal guidelines.

CHAPTER 3

1. This member ended up advancing to a high position in the House Democratic
leadership.

2. Although it would seem logical that someone would have developed a goal typology for parties similar to Fenno's list of individual goals (1973), Steven Smith (2007)
notes that studies of congressional parties traditionally have posited a single collective
goal and have failed to consider how parties and their leaders make trade-offs among
competing goals.

3. Based on interviews, Sinclair (2006, 88) develops similar criteria as necessary to
earn a nomination for a post within the Democratic caucus: being a "team player," casting "tough" votes, and raising money for the Democratic Congressional Campaign
Committee despite campaign debt.

CHAPTER 4

1. We focus on PCC contributions because LPAC giving to state and local parties is
very small: $146,310 and $39,848, respectively, in 2006.

2. Leadership PACs make very few contributions to CCCs; thus, we do not analyze
them separately. The fact that their contributions go almost entirely to other candidates—from whom the PAC sponsor can receive direct recognition—substantiates the
perception that the primary purpose of LPACs is to advance the sponsor's career ambitions.

3. We do not expect a relationship between a member's electoral security and leadership PAC contributions, since members cannot use LPAC funds for their own reelections.

4. The coefficients in table 4.2 are for expected conditional y—that is, the actual
expected sum redistributed by members with a given x (Long 1997, 209). Formally,
$\partial E(y|x)/\partial x_k = \Phi(z)\beta_k$, where Φ is the standard normal cumulative distribution function
and $z = xb/\sigma$. Since $\Phi(z)$ depends on the value of the xb's, the partial derivatives must be

calculated at specific values of the x's. For the dichotomous independent variables, the marginal effects represent discrete change in y when x changes from 0 to 1. For the continuous variables, the marginal effects are calculated at the mean of the independent variables.

5. We exclude the cash-on-hand variable for the LPAC regression since members cannot transfer extra money from their principal campaign account to their PAC.

6. This is an increase of one standard deviation in cash on hand, centered around its mean.

7. The member's decision to redistribute to federal, state, and local sources in the same election cycle would obviously suffer from simultaneity biases. Using federal contributions in the previous cycle allows us to control for the member's basic commitment to the practice of redistribution at the federal level and to measure whether that commitment is related to subsequent decisions to redistribute funds to state and local parties.

8. The absence of a relationship between party leadership responsibilities and contributions to state parties is not due to the inclusion of members total federal contributions in the previous cycle, which elected party leaders make generously. Holding an elected or extended leadership position is unrelated to state party contributions even when previous federal redistribution activity is excluded from the model. We will see in chapter 5 that elected and extended party leaders are significantly more likely to contribute to candidates from their states who are running for the House. But leaders' home-state generosity is limited to home-state candidates.

CHAPTER 5

1. Baker also notes that members can advance by giving contributions with their PCCs. So, although Baker focuses on LPACs, his critique presumably also applies to the process of redistribution generally.

2. Scholars studying LPACs (R. Baker 1989, 15–16; Sorauf 1988, 174–81) have offered a variety of reasons for why members form them. The reasons typically include paying for travel (which allows sponsors seeking higher office to build a national constituency), exploiting the higher contribution limits that govern LPACs (LPACs may give and accept larger donations than PCCs), building coalitions based on personal loyalty for use in leadership contests, and helping elect other party candidates.

3. Telephone interview by Larson, September 13, 1994.

4. Telephone interview by Larson, September 13, 1994.

5. Though Wilcox, Kanthak, and Currinder address similar questions to those we explore in this chapter, their papers suffer from methodological limitations. Wilcox only presents descriptive data. Currinder and Kanthak study only contributions from members' leadership political action committees. This limits their ability to compare the contribution strategies of different members of Congress, since mostly leaders form them (as the name implies), thereby preempting their ability to analyze the behavior of many rank-and-file members. Additionally, Currinder (559) excludes the "null" cases in which a contribution was not made, undercutting her ability to explain why members of Congress contribute to some candidates but not others.

6. Telephone interview by Larson, April 12, 1994.

7. Telephone interview by Larson, September 13, 1994.

8. We thank Gary Jacobson for generously allowing us to use his data on quality challengers.

9. Telephone interview by Larson, December 6, 1994.

10. Telephone interview by Larson, September 13, 1994.

11. The 2004 election cycle is a presidential election year, unlike 1990 and 1998, which are midterm elections. There is no theoretical reason to believe, however, that incumbents would shift their contribution patterns between congressional and midterm years. Indeed, Sorauf (1992, 129) stresses the increasing independence of the national party committees, which are mostly concerned with winning executive campaigns, and the congressional campaign committees, which for the most part focus exclusively on winning congressional majorities. Finally, aggregate amounts of incumbent contributions do not appear to vary between presidential and midterm cycles, as we show in chapter 4 (see also Bedlington and Malbin 2003).

12. We adjust for the clustering effects by the individual member because each incumbent member of Congress is entered multiple times—once for each incumbent and candidate pairing.

13. We collected data on all incumbent-to-candidate dyads. We did sample from the null cases and estimate the equations using sampled nulls and King and Zeng's (2001) estimation correction method in addition to estimating the equation with all the cases. The results are extremely similar statistically and substantively, though the substantive effects of independent variables are consistently larger when using King and Zeng's method, as expected. The differences do not effect the conclusions we draw from comparing the relative magnitude of effects of variables across members with different institutional positions within the House.

14. Because incumbents are the excluded category, members who contribute primarily to safe incumbents will have lower collective scores, even if the incumbent recipient does not match the contributor's home state, committee assignment, and ideological score as measured by the individualistic variables. Thus, party leaders who attempt to buy support from their caucus by spreading money widely among incumbents will have lower collective scores and thus lower party-orientation ratios than a member who contributes mostly to incumbent and nonincumbent candidates in competitive races.

15. Several other variables were tested in predicting DW-NOMINATE scores but were not included in the final model because they were not significantly related: African-American, blue-collar, foreign-born, or urban population percentages; numbers of government workers and of workers in manufacturing; median income; and number unemployed. Measures of all these variables were obtained from Adler 2003.

CHAPTER 6

1. Telephone interview by Heberlig, June 11, 2008.

2. See also Dennis and Whittington 2008. On the distinction between Democratic and Republican strategies for pressuring committee chairs to redistribute campaign funds, Barney Frank, Democratic chair of the Financial Services Committee, said, "They threaten. We shame" (quoted in Zeleny 2006).

3. The adjustment process boosts the value of contributions early in the 1990s, because their values were so low compared to contributions after party mobilization.

4. The figure for Democratic elected leaders was 35 percent.

5. As an example, elected party leaders often serve as ex officio members on all party committees, and nonelected leaders often serve in multiple capacities as well.

6. This occurs because the top elected party leaders do not generally hold committee positions and because Hibbing does not score their additional party positions.

7. For prestige committee memberships, this scoring system produces the somewhat counterintuitive result that the value of members' positions increases when their party loses majority status, because there are fewer seats available. Thus, we need to emphasize that we are measuring the value of the position as a selective incentive, not as a measure of power. In terms of absolute power, prestige committee assignments are certainly more valuable in the majority party than in the minority party. But as selective incentives that a party actually has to offer, prestige assignments are actually more valuable in the minority party than in the majority party, precisely because there are fewer prestige assignments in the minority than in the majority. The value of the position is relative to the positions one could get in one's own party. Additionally, the parties are really concerned about who gets the *new* positions, as those who already hold positions have property rights and are largely protected. If the minority party's steering committee only has a few positions to dole out on the Rules Committee or another prestige committee, it is going to be much more careful in its monitoring efforts, to ensure that it is placing the "right" people in power.

So, the criteria that we are arguing should be important for advancement (previous extended leadership positions, voting loyalty, and campaign contributions) should be most relevant when the party is in the minority. From the party's perspective, Representative X already has a very valuable position, and the caucus does not have an abundance of other positions to dole out as selective incentives to many members who want them. Thus, Representative X is unlikely to advance further unless he or she is spectacularly successful in demonstrating his or her commitment to the party's collective good (e.g., voting or campaign contributions). If the party reacts to losing prestige committee positions by increasing the number of extended leadership positions to provide service opportunities to more members, the value of those positions would drop, but they would be filled by members who are more "marginally qualified" than the members filling the rarer top positions.

8. We view the higher partisan selective incentive score of Rules Committee membership, compared to the other prestige committees, as entirely appropriate. The Rules Committee has substantial influence over the floor agenda, a critical power of the majority party. It is considered an agent of the party (Deering and Smith 1997; Cox and McCubbins 1993, 2005), and unlike in other committee assignments, its members are personally selected by the Speaker. While its members have some ability to pick up chits from their colleagues, this power is substantially limited by their overarching duty to the party. Thus, Rules Committee membership is of relatively limited value in providing direct policy or financial assistance to their constituencies in comparison to other committees. Members of the Appropriations and Ways and Means committees certainly have important influences over the party agenda on spending and revenues, but they also have substantial flexibility to serve their district interests.

9. We hasten to emphasize that we regard these numbers as approximations of the "real" value of positions within the party's arsenal of selective incentives. Inevitably, any

attempt to measure the value of positions will be approximations or averages within a particular political context.

10. We obtained these data from *Politics in America,* the *Congressional Directory,* and the *Congressional Staff Directory* for the relevant years.

11. There is both empirical and logical support for our decision to include the 104th Congress in the earlier, rather than the later, period. Appointments are made at the beginning of a Congress and are based on members' behaviors in the preceding session(s) of Congress. Given the numerous decisions that leaders of the new majority and new minority parties had to make at the beginning of the 104th Congress, old appointment procedures were likely to have been followed. By the 105th Congress, however, the parties began to understand the strategic implications of narrow margins of control and to use selective incentives to induce members to contribute. Empirically, transfer patterns in the 104th Congress look more like patterns found earlier in the decade than like those found later in the decade.

12. We control for the number of opportunities for advancement by including dummy variables for each session of Congress. Opportunities vary from one Congress to the next based on the number of positions opened by retirements, changes in committee ratios, and so on. We do not present the results for the session dummy variables, since they are not of theoretical interest. Additionally, we estimate the regression using a variety of different models, including a random effects tobit model. The results are quite robust across different models and qualitatively very similar to the results we present.

13. For the tobit model, expected y is given by the equation $Ey = \Phi(z)xb + \sigma\phi(z)$, where Φ is the standard normal cumulative distribution function, ϕ is the standard normal density, $z = xb/\sigma$, and σ is the estimated standard deviation of the residuals (Long 1997, 209). Since $\Phi(z)$ depends on the value of the xb's, the partial derivatives and expected values must be calculated at specific values of the x's. We compute the actual expected change in member position portfolios at various levels of redistribution. All control variables are held at their means.

14. The importance of proficiency on both dimensions may vary for specific institutional positions. Cann (2008) finds that the majority GOP selected chairs who both redistributed funds and voted based on party loyalty, with greater weight being placed on their voting. Given the importance of chairs to the passage of the party agenda, placing greater weight on their legislative loyalty is rational.

15. In other words, contributions made directly to other candidates potentially have the significant component of the exchange of selective goods if the recipients win office.

16. Members who already held elected positions were excluded from the analysis of new appointed positions, since any new appointed position they obtained would be a function of their elected position. Including the committee and subcommittee chairs in the appointed category does not affect the results.

17. This could reflect Ross Baker's (1989) observation that many incumbents are already committed to particular contestants in House leadership contests and that victorious nonincumbents may represent the best hope for ambitious members looking to gain support.

18. For comparative purposes, elected GOP leaders gave on average $134,000, or 10 percent of their total, to safe incumbents, while other members of the GOP gave them an average of $10,120, or 6 percent. So, the members of the Republican caucus consis-

tently gave more to safe incumbents, in both raw and percentage terms, but the Democrats weighted those contributions more heavily in determining who advanced.

19. Members who won special elections have the ability to work with the members of caucus and vote during their partial term; thus, we have included them in the model of returning members.

20. Consistent with our hypothesis that the redistribution of campaign funds is weighted more heavily in the minority party, redistribution is statistically significant for Democratic freshmen but not for GOP freshmen when the equation is estimated separately for each party.

21. Canon (1989) and Loomis (1984) observe, in passing, the importance of the Budget Committee for aspiring leaders.

22. Members of the Appropriations and Ways and Means committees who are assigned to the Budget Committee are excluded, because their initial appointment is not to the Budget Committee.

CHAPTER 7

1. Also, as Jacobson notes (1997, 27), "vote margins could increase without making incumbents significantly safer because electorates became more volatile and idiosyncratic across districts."

2. The scholarly verdict is mixed on the extent to which war chests can discourage quality challengers. For a good review of the literature, see Goodliffe 2007.

3. Isenstadt and Hohmann (2010) found that members spend between 10 and 15 hours per week raising money by phone or holding fundraising events.

4. In theory, members could probably safely finance their redistribution by spending more efficiently on their own reelection activities. Indeed, Fritz and Morris (1990) and Morris and Gamache (1994) show that House incumbent campaign organizations are anything but lean machines. But spending more efficiently would require risk-averse incumbents to set aside tried-and-tested strategies that have proven successful year after year.

5. By all accounts, House incumbents have become increasingly aggressive in their fundraising. As Mann and Ornstein (2006, 237) write, "the lawmakers themselves, in the zeal to raise ever-increasing bundles of campaign cash, regularly shake down lobbyists for money, using even more brazen threats to demand that lobbyists contribute personal and PAC funds to their fundraisers."

6. Access-oriented donors are donors who, in Malbin's conception (2003, 15), have money "pulled" from them by officeholders, in contrast to donors (usually with ideological or partisan goals) who "push" money into the system.

7. Following Cox and Magar (1999), we group corporate and trade PACs into the single category of business PACs.

8. For example, in the 2005–6 election cycle—a cycle with ample opportunities to elect Democratic nonincumbents—labor PACs gave 48 percent of their total contributions to safe Democratic incumbents, whereas only 5 percent of total labor PAC money went to safe Republican incumbents (Herrnson 2008, 151). A quick inspection of Federal Election Commission data demonstrates that labor's preference for giving to Democratic incumbents is not unusual. In the 1998, 2000, 2002, and 2004 election cycles, labor

PACs gave, respectively, 54 percent, 55 percent, 53 percent, and 56 percent of their total contributions to Democratic incumbents. By contrast, labor PACs gave an average of only 8 percent of their total contributions to Republican incumbents during these election cycles. Thus, labor PACs seem significantly less electorally oriented than nonconnected PACs, which gave an average of only 17 percent of their contributions to House Democratic incumbents and 25 percent to House Republican incumbents during these election cycles.

9. Gimpel, Lee, and Pearson-Merkowitz (2008) find that distant nonresident donors tend to give more to elected party leaders and majority party members, implying access motivations. Francia and others (2003) find that compared to donors driven by ideological concerns, "investor" donors are less likely to give to influence the outcome of a close race, more likely to be solicited by incumbents, more likely to be solicited by (and to give to) members on committees pertinent to their business or industry, more likely to be solicited by members of both parties, more likely to have spoken with a lawmaker or a congressional aide, and more likely to contact lawmakers for business purposes.

10. Defining a "large" contribution is obviously somewhat subjective. We define large individual donations as those of $750 or more in part out of convenience: the FEC data we used for this chapter disaggregates individual donations into four categories, with $750 plus being the largest. (The other three categories are $500–749, $200–499, and total.) But $750 is also very close to the amount ($500) used by Joe et al. (2008) to define large contributions in state legislative and gubernatorial elections, which typically cost less than U.S. House campaigns.

11. BCRA also substantially raised (and indexed to inflation) the limit on aggregate federal contributions (i.e., total contributions to candidates, parties, and PACs) that an individual could make. This allowed PACs to raise more money from individuals in the post-BCRA period than in the pre-BCRA period, which in turn gave PACs more dollars to contribute to incumbents when they came asking. Within the aggregate limit, there is a sublimit of $57,500 (indexed to inflation) on individual contributions to parties and PACs, no more than $37,500 (not indexed for inflation) of which may be given to organizations besides the national party committees.

12. A member had to run for reelection in at least two of the five election cycles because the model incorporates data from election cycle$_{t-1}$ and election cycle$_t$.

13. This is computed as the total dollars redistributed by an incumbent in election cycle$_{t-1}$ divided by the incumbent's total campaign spending in that cycle.

14. Following Cox and Magar (1999), we compute business PAC receipts as corporate PAC receipts plus trade PAC receipts. Besides being theoretically correct, this specification has the additional virtue of ensuring that there is not a reciprocal relationship between our dependent and independent variables of interest. After all, change in receipts in cycle$_t$ cannot cause crowding in cycle$_{t-1}$. We are not the first social scientists to estimate change in a dependent variable with static independent variables. For example, economists evaluating the determinants of economic growth cross-nationally often estimate models with static independent variables to account for change in growth (e.g., Mankiw, Romer, and Weil 1992). In the area of campaign finance, Milyo (1997) estimates change in campaign receipts with a mix of dynamic and static independent variables. See also Finkel 1995.

15. Incorporating fixed effects into the models allows us to control for difficult-to-

measure incumbent characteristics that are assumed to remain constant over time for each incumbent and that likely influence fundraising (Ansolabehere and Snyder 2000; Cox and Magar 1999; Goodliffe 2004; Romer and Snyder 1994). Examples of such factors include an incumbent's charisma, aggressiveness with donors, and taste for fundraising. If such variables are correlated with the dependent and independent variables included in the model, failing to control for them will result in biased coefficients for the included independent variables. Therefore, we follow the strategy of Ansolabehere and Snyder (2000) and Goodliffe (2004) and incorporate fixed effects into our regressions for each incumbent appearing in the data set. While the cost of a fixed effects approach is high in terms of degrees of freedom, the benefit is that it allows us to control for important omitted factors (Greene 1993, 466–69). An alternative strategy for controlling for such omitted variables would be to estimate a fully dynamic model. Such a model would control for factors that remain constant over time but that may impact campaign receipts cross-sectionally (Romer and Snyder 1994; Cox and Magar 1999). We experimented with an array of dynamic specifications, all of which produced results qualitatively consistent with the results we present.

16. It is unclear what effect institutional position will have on changes in labor PAC receipts.

17. Of the control variables, the most consistent and powerful predictor of change in receipts for all of the donor categories is the sum raised by a member from the relevant donor category in the prior election cycle. Indeed, the effect of prior receipts generally overpowers the effect of the other control variables, and the coefficient is negative and highly statistically significant in every regression. This demonstrates that the more campaign money a member raises from a specific donor category in a given election cycle, the less capacity the member has to increase his or her receipts from that donor category in the next election cycle.

18. By itself, the coefficient for the interactive term tells us only the *difference* in the effect of crowding on changes in business PAC receipts for Republicans (relative to Democrats); it does not tell us the *total effect* of crowding on changes in business PAC receipts for Republicans. To compute the latter, as well as the standard error for this coefficient, we must use the equations specified by Jaccard, Turrisi, and Wan (1990, 25–28). Abbreviating the equation to include only the variables of interest, consider the following model with an interactive term: $Y = a + b_1 X_1 + b_2 X_1 X_2 + e$, where Y = change in business PAC receipts, X_1 = crowding, and $X_1 X_2$ = crowding*party (X_2 is coded 0 for Democrats and 1 for Republicans). The effect of crowding on changes in business PAC receipts for Democrats (i.e., when $X_2 = 0$) is simply b_1. To determine the effect of crowding on changes in business PAC receipts for Republicans (i.e., when $X_2 = 1$), we must compute $b_1 + b_2(1)$ (Jaccard, Turrisi, and Wan 1990, 26). Similarly, to compute the standard error for this coefficient, we use the following equation: $[\text{var}(b_1) + X_2^2 \text{var}(b_2) + 2X_2 \text{cov}(b_1, b_2)]^{1/2}$ (Jaccard, Turrisi, and Wan 1990, 26, 27).

19. The median is 5.5 percent.

20. Also unexpected, the positive and statistically significant coefficient for crowding*LPAC in the nonconnected PAC regression shows that the impact of crowding on changes in nonconnected PAC receipts is actually greater for members with leadership PACs than for members without them. That the coefficient for crowding*LPAC is positive (if not statistically significant) in the other PAC regressions as well suggests that the

leadership PAC variable could be measuring a member's general fundraising prowess rather than the ability of leadership PACs to alleviate the tension between redistribution and reelection spending.

21. Again, this figure comes from summing the main effects crowding coefficient ($10,499) and the coefficient for the interactive term, crowding*BCRA ($3,714) (Jaccard, Turrisi, and Wan 1990).

22. The mean percentage of total campaign spending devoted to redistribution by House incumbents in the pre-BCRA period was 8 percent. By contrast, the mean in the post-BCRA period was 19 percent. The respective medians are 4 percent and 9 percent.

23. The increase in LPACs may also be partly due to the Federal Election Commission's relaxing of regulations pertaining to these committees. In particular, the FEC eliminated the legal possibility that it would ever rule a member's PAC and PCC to be affiliated committees (*Federal Register* 68 [2003]: 67016).

24. In the LPAC model, we do not include an interactive term for crowding*LPAC in cycle$_{t-1}$. This is because our analysis of LPAC formation includes only members who did not already have an LPAC.

25. We also estimated the model using duration analysis—a proportional hazard model with censored data—to evaluate the length of time until the member forms an LPAC. Duration analysis confirms that the greater the level of crowding that redistribution creates for reelection spending is, the more quickly the member will form an LPAC. Likewise, members involved in leadership contests form LPACs more rapidly.

CHAPTER 8

1. It is possible that members may have had their advancement blocked due to lack of fundraising or legislative loyalty, thus making this variable endogenous to the model. Excluding the interactive variable, however, does not affect the estimation of any of the other variables in the model; therefore, we retain it in our presentation.

2. They might also form and redistribute money from a state PAC, in which case the money would not be captured in our analysis. But giving money to state candidates from a state leadership PAC would allow the member to save his or her federal dollars for his or her own statewide campaign.

3. We exclude an analysis of career decisions in 1990 because we used lagged redistribution variables. Since we do not include redistribution data from the 1988 election cycle in our data set, we cannot examine behavior during the 1990 election cycle as we do in other chapters.

4. The relative differences between categories are extremely similar if we use the unadjusted campaign funds.

5. Making separate estimates for members seeking another office versus those seeking reelection and for members seeking retirement versus those seeking reelection produces results that are substantively and statistically very similar to those presented here.

6. A comment on the causal directions is warranted at this point. The fact that members redistribute less to federal sources does not "cause" them to run for another office in the same way that the disaffection hypothesis posits that low redistribution would push them to retire. Statewide candidates are not seeking higher office because of

their concern with party pressure to redistribute funds. Instead, they are saving their campaign funds, rather than contributing to other candidates or the party, because they are anticipating needing the funds for a statewide campaign.

7. We tested the relationship between redistribution and retirement in three additional ways. First, that retiring members redistribute significantly more than their colleagues in the election cycle preceding retirement ($cycle_{t-1}$) may be a result of minimal compliance with party expectations. They redistribute substantial sums, but it may not be as much as they could redistribute, given their status within the institution. Thus, we used a variation of the model of redistribution in chapter 4 to estimate members' projected giving. We then subtracted this estimate from their actual giving. "Disaffected" members, then, would be those who redistribute less than they could be expected to redistribute. We include this measure of redistribution into the same retirement model presented in the chapter and produce substantively the same results.

Our second variation was to test for nonlinearity, hypothesizing that members who had the capacity to redistribute but did not and members who did not have much capacity but did redistribute (thereby expending substantial efforts to do so) would be more likely to retire. We folded the redistribution measure—both the adjusted aggregate dollars and the actual measures minus the predicted measures—at their mean, so that extreme redistributors and nonredistributors would be at one pole and "average" redistributors would be at the other. These measures were unrelated to retirements when entered into the model.

Our third approach was to break down the analysis into three time periods: 1990–94, 1996–2000, and 2002–6. Members who are disaffected by the new expectations of redistribution should be more likely to retire in the middle period, as the party mobilization starts and expectations are put into effect. Party redistribution expectations are not severe in the early period (1990–94) and thus are unlikely to affect retirement decisions. By the later period (2002–6), expectations have been clear for a number of years, and members have had an opportunity to adjust their behavior. Thus, if there is evidence for the disaffection hypothesis, members who redistribute minimal amounts in election $cycle_{t-1}$ should be more likely to retire during the 1996–2000 period. Again, we find no supportive evidence. Redistribution is unrelated to retirement decisions in the 1990–94 period, as expected, since there was little to no pressure to engage in this activity. In both periods following 1994, the results are the same.

CHAPTER 9

1. According to the Center for Responsive Politics, the agribusiness dollars raised by Peterson's PCC went from $99,000 in 2004 to $388,000 in 2006. Additionally, when Peterson formed his LPAC in 2008, agribusiness was by far the largest contributor to it. See http://www.opensecrets.org/politicians/industries.php?cycle=Career&cid=N00004558 &type=P.

2. Mann and Ornstein (2006, 238) explain, "A core part of the K Street Project was to create a loop in which former lawmakers and staffers would be placed in lucrative lobbying posts that paid two to ten times what they earned on Capitol Hill, with the understanding that they would reciprocate by maxing out on contributions to the party and its candidates as well as to the leadership PACs of major lawmakers."

3. A 1997 editorial in *Roll Call* pointed out that "[Democratic leader Richard] Gephardt's leadership PAC, not surprisingly, gets most of its money from the same unions that deposited $1.5 million into his personal campaign fund. The same business PACs turn up on donor lists for GOP leadership PACs and campaign accounts."

4. For a review of this research, see Ansolabehere, de Figueiredo, and Snyder 2003; Baumgartner and Leech 1998; R. Smith 1995.

5. But see Cigler and Loomis 2007 for an alternative perspective.

6. New federal regulations mandating that incumbents report individual contributions over a certain threshold ($16,000 in 2009) that are bundled by lobbyists will give political scientists a better sense of the portion of a member's individual contributions that are bundled. See 11 CFR 104.22 for a detailed description of the new regulations.

7. Federal Election Commission, press release, May 28, 2009, http://www.fec.gov/press/press2009/05282009/20090528Party.shtml.

8. This proposal can be found in the Federal Election Commission's 1993 legislative recommendations. See http://www.fec.gov/info/LegislativeRecommendations1993.htm.

References

Abramowitz, Alan I. 1988. "Explaining Senate Election Outcomes." *American Political Science Review* 82:385–403.

Adler, E. Scott. 2003. "Congressional District Data File, 84th–94th Congress." http://soc sci.colorado.edu/~esadler/districtdatawebsite/CongressionalDistrictDatasetweb page.htm.

Adler, E. Scott, and John S. Lipinski. 1997. "Demand-Side Theory and Congressional Committee Composition: A Constituency Characteristics Approach." *American Journal of Political Science* 41:895–918.

Aldrich, John. 1995. *Why Parties? The Origin and Transformation of Political Parties in America.* Chicago: University of Chicago Press.

Aldrich, John H., and David W. Rohde. 1997–98. "The Transition to Republican Rule in the House: Implications for Theories of Congressional Politics." *Political Science Quarterly* 112:541–67.

Aldrich, John H., and David W. Rohde. 2000. "The Consequences of Party Organization in the House: The Role of Majority and Minority Parties in Conditional Party Government." In *Polarized Politics: Congress and the President in a Polarized Era,* ed. Jon Bond and Richard Fleisher. Washington, DC: CQ Press.

Aldrich, John H., and David W. Rohde. 2001. "The Logic of Conditional Party Government: Revisiting the Electoral Connection." In *Congress Reconsidered,* ed. Lawrence C. Dodd and Bruce I. Oppenheimer. 7th ed. Washington, DC: CQ Press.

Allen, Jonathan. 2010. "Nancy Pelosi Pals Gain Power in House." *Politico,* May 6. http://www.politico.com/news/stories/0510/36901.html.

Allen, Mike. 2000. "House GOP Goes Within for Money." *Washington Post,* June 14, A1.

Allen, Mike. 2005. "Hard Cash Is Main Course for GOP Fundraiser." *Washington Post,* June 14, A1.

Alston, Chuck. 1991. "Members with Cash-on-Hand Reach Out to Help Others." *CQ Weekly Report,* September 28, 2763–66.

American Political Science Association, Committee on Political Parties. 1950. *Toward a More Responsible Two-Party System.* New York: Rinehart.

Ansolabehere, Stephen, and Alan Gerber. 1994. "The Mismeasure of Campaign Spending: Evidence from the 1990 U.S. House Elections." *Journal of Politics* 56:1106–18.

Ansolabehere, Stephen, John M. de Figueiredo, and James M. Snyder, Jr. 2003. "Why Is There So Little Money in U.S. Politics?" *Journal of Economic Perspectives* 17:105–30.

Ansolabehere, Stephen, and James M. Snyder, Jr. 2000. "Campaign War Chests in Congressional Elections." *Business and Politics* 2:9–33.

Asher, Herbert, Eric S. Heberlig, Randall B. Ripley, and Karen C. Snyder. 2001. *American Labor Unions in the Electoral Arena.* Lanham, MD: Rowman and Littlefield.

Atkeson, Lonna Rae, and Randall W. Partin. 1995. "Economic and Referendum Voting: A Comparison of Gubernatorial and Senate Elections." *American Political Science Review* 89:99–107.

Austen-Smith, David. 1993. "Information and Influence: Lobbying for Agendas and Votes." *American Journal of Political Science* 37:799–833.

Austen-Smith, David. 1995. "Campaign Contributions and Access." *American Political Science Review* 89:566–81.

Babington, Charles. 2004. "Hastert Launches a Partisan Policy." *Washington Post,* November 27, A1.

Baker, Paula. 2002. "Campaigns and Potato Chips; Or Some Causes and Consequences of Political Spending." In *Money and Politics,* ed. Paula Baker. State College: Pennsylvania State University Press.

Baker, Ross K. 1989. *The New Fat Cats: Members of Congress as Political Benefactors.* New York: Priority.

Banfield, Edward, and James Q. Wilson. 1963. *City Politics.* New York: Vintage Books.

Baron, David P. 1989. "Service-Related Campaign Contributions and the Political Equilibrium." *Quarterly Journal of Economics* 104:45–72.

Barry, John M. 1989. *The Ambition and the Power.* New York: Viking.

Baumgartner, Frank R., and Beth L. Leech. 1998. *Basic Interests: The Importance of Groups in Politics and in Political Science.* Princeton: Princeton University Press.

Beck, Paul Allen. 1996. *Party Politics in America.* 8th ed. New York: Longman Press.

Bedlington, Anne H., and Michael J. Malbin. 2003. "The Party as Extended Network: Members of Congress Giving to Each Other and to Their Parties." In *Life after Reform: When the Bipartisan Campaign Reform Act Meets Politics,* ed. Michael J. Malbin. Boulder, CO: Rowman and Littlefield.

Bednar, Jenna, and Elisabeth Gerber. 2011. "Political Geography, Campaign Contributions, and Representation." Unpublished manuscript.

Benenson, Bob. 1986. "In the Struggle for Influence, Members' PACs Gain Ground." *CQ Weekly Report,* August 2, 1751–54.

Berry, Jeffrey, and Clyde Wilcox. 2009. *The Interest Group Society.* 5th ed. New York: Longman.

Bianco, William T. 1999. "Party Campaign Committees and the Distribution of Tally Program Funds." *Legislative Studies Quarterly* 24:451–69.

Bianco, William T., and Robert H. Bates. 1990. "Cooperation by Design: Leadership, Structure, and Collective Dilemmas." *American Political Science Review* 84:133–47.

Biersack, Robert, Paul S. Herrnson, and Clyde Wilcox. 1994. *Risky Business: PAC Decisionmaking in Congressional Elections.* New York: M. E. Sharpe.

Billings, Erin P. 2004. "Peterson, in Ag Bid, Pays Up." *Roll Call,* November 22. http://www.rollcall.com.

Billings, Erin P. 2005. "Democrats on Exclusives Face Review." *Roll Call,* January 24. http://www.rollcall.com.

Binder, Sarah. 2003. *Stalemate: The Causes and Consequences of Legislative Gridlock.* Washington, DC: Brookings Institution Press.

Birnbaum, Jeffrey H., and John Solomon. 2007. "Democrats Offer Up Chairmen for Donors." *Washington Post,* February 24. http://www.washingtonpost.com.

Birnbaum, Jeffrey H., and Jim VandeHei. 2005. "DeLay's Influence Transcends His Title." *Washington Post,* October 3, A1.

Black, Gordon S. 1972. "A Theory of Political Ambition: Career Choices and the Role of Structural Incentives." *American Political Science Review* 66:144–59.

Boatright, Robert G., Michael J. Malbin, Mark J. Rozell, and Clyde Wilcox. 2006. "Interest Groups and Advocacy Organizations after BCRA." In *The Election after Reform: Money, Politics, and the Bipartisan Campaign Reform Act,* ed. Michael J. Malbin. Boulder, CO: Rowman and Littlefield.

Bolton, Alexander. 2006. "Endangered Members Told: Pony Up." *Hill,* September 26.

Bolton, Alexander. 2008. "Stingy Senators Stiff GOP." *The Hill,* March 25. http://the hill.com/.

Box-Steffensmeier, Janet M. 1996. "A Dynamic Analysis of the Role of War Chests in Campaign Strategy." *American Journal of Political Science* 40:352–71.

Brace, Paul. 1984. "Progressive Ambition in the House: A Probabilistic Approach." *Journal of Politics* 46 (2): 556–69.

Brehm, John, and Scott Gates. 1996. *Working, Shirking, and Sabotage: Bureaucratic Response to a Democratic Public.* Ann Arbor: University of Michigan Press.

Bresnahan, John. 1998. "GOP Supporters Wonder Whether First Female Speaker Could Be a 'Dunn' Deal." *Roll Call,* March 30, 3, 56.

Bresnahan, John. 2000. "Hastert Backs Off Threats over Committee Slots." *Roll Call,* June 15, 3.

Brewer, Mark, and Jeffrey Stonecash. 2009. *Dynamics of American Political Parties.* New York: Cambridge University Press.

Brown, Clifford W., Jr., Lynda W. Powell, and Clyde Wilcox. 1995. *Serious Money: Fundraising and Contributing in Presidential Nomination Campaigns.* New York: Cambridge University Press.

Brown, Lynne P., and Robert L. Peabody. 1992. "Patterns of Succession in House Democratic Leadership: Foley, Gephardt, and Gray, 1989." In *New Perspectives on the House of Representatives,* ed. Robert L. Peabody and Nelson W. Polsby. 4th ed. Baltimore: Johns Hopkins University Press.

Buchler, Justin M. 2004. "Parties and Leadership PACs." PhD diss., University of California, Berkeley.

Burger, Timothy J. 1994. "Gingrich Hits Up Members for $3M to GOP." *Roll Call,* August 11, 1, 26.

Bzdek, Vincent. 2008. *Woman of the House: The Rise of Nancy Pelosi.* New York: Palgrave MacMillan.

Cain, Bruce E., John Ferejohn, and Morris P. Fiorina. 1987. *The Personal Vote: Constituency Service and Electoral Independence.* Cambridge, MA: Harvard University Press.

Canes-Wrone, Brandice, David W. Brady, and John E. Cogan. 2002. "Out of Step, Out of Office: Electoral Accountability and House Members' Voting." *American Political Science Review* 96:127–40.

Cann, Damon. 2008. *Sharing the Wealth: Member Contributions and the Exchange Theory of Party Influence in the U.S. House of Representatives.* Albany: State University of New York Press.

Canon, David T. 1989. "The Institutionalization of Leadership in the U.S. Congress." *Legislative Studies Quarterly* 14:415–43.

Canon, David T. 1990. *Actors, Athletes, and Astronauts: Political Amateurs in the United States Congress.* Chicago: University of Chicago Press.

Carney, Eliza Newlin. 2004. "In the Money." *National Journal,* July 10.

Caro, Robert. 1983. *The Path to Power.* New York: Vintage Books.

Carson, Jamie L., Gregory Koger, Matthew J. Lebo, and Everett Young. 2010. "The Electoral Costs of Party Loyalty in Congress." *American Journal of Political Science* 54:598–616.

Chappie, Damon. 1995. "DeLay's Leadership PAC Bagged Almost $200,000 in Corporate Soft Money in 1995." *Roll Call,* February 22, 3.

Cho, Wendy K. Tam, and James G. Gimpel. 2007. "Prospecting for (Campaign) Gold." *American Journal of Political Science* 51:255–68.

Chong, Dennis. 1991. *Collective Action and the Civil Rights Movement.* Chicago: University of Chicago Press.

Chwe, Michael Suk-Young. 1999. "Structure and Strategy in Collective Action." *American Journal of Sociology* 105:128–56.

Cigler, Allen J., and Burdett Loomis. 2007. "Organized Interests, Political Parties, and Representation: James Madison, Tom Delay, and the Soul of American Politics." In *Interest Group Politics,* ed. Allen J. Cigler and Burdett Loomis. 7th ed. Washington, DC: CQ Press.

Clausen, Aage R. 1973. *How Congressmen Decide.* New York: St. Martin's.

Clawson, Dan, Alan Neustadtl, and Mark Weller. 1998. *Dollars and Voters: How Business Campaign Contributions Subvert Democracy.* Philadelphia: Temple University Press.

Clucas, Richard A. 1992. "Legislative Leadership and Campaign Support in California." *Legislative Studies Quarterly* 17:265–83.

Clucas, Richard A. 1994. "The Effect of Campaign Contributions on the Power of the California Assembly Speaker." *Legislative Studies Quarterly* 19:417–28.

Cohen, Marty, David Karol, Hans Noel, and John Zaller. 2008. *The Party Decides: Presidential Nominations before and after Reform.* Chicago: University of Chicago Press.

Cohen, Richard E. 2010. "Pelosi the Campaign Boss." *National Journal,* May 8. http://www.nationaljournal.com/.

Collie, Melissa P. 1988. "Universalism and the Parties in the U.S. House of Representatives." *American Journal of Political Science* 32:865–83.

Confessore, Nicholas. 2003. "Welcome to the Machine: How the GOP Disciplined K Street and Made Bush Supreme." *Washington Monthly,* July/August, 30–37.

Connelly, William F., Jr., and John J. Pitney, Jr. 1994. *Congress' Permanent Minority? Republicans in the U.S. House.* Lanham, MD: Rowman and Littlefield.

Continetti, Matthew. 2006. *The K Street Gang: The Rise and Fall of the Republican Machine.* New York: Doubleday.

Cooper, Joseph, and David W. Brady. 1981. "Institutional Context and Leadership Style: The House from Cannon to Rayburn." *American Political Science Review* 75:411–25.

Cooper, Joseph, and William F. West. 1981. "Voluntary Retirements, Incumbency, and the Modern House." *Political Science Quarterly* 96 (2): 279–300.

Copeland, Gary W. 1989. "Choosing to Run: Why House Members Seek Election to the Senate." *Legislative Studies Quarterly* 14 (4): 549–65.

Corrado, Anthony. 1997. "Party Soft Money." In *Campaign Finance Reform: A Source-*

book, ed. Anthony Corrado, Thomas E. Mann, Daniel R. Ortiz, Trevor Potter, and Frank J. Sorauf. Washington, DC: Brookings Institution Press.

Corrado, Anthony. 2000. "Running Backwards: The Congressional Money Chase." In *The Permanent Campaign and Its Future,* ed. Norman J. Ornstein and Thomas E. Mann. Washington, DC: Brookings Institution.

Corrado, Anthony. 2005. "Money and Politics: A History of Federal Campaign Finance Law." In *New Campaign Finance Reform Sourcebook,* ed. Anthony Corrado, Thomas E. Mann, Daniel R. Ortiz, and Trevor Potter. Washington, DC: Brookings Institution Press.

Corrado, Anthony, and Katie Varney. 2007. "Party Money in the 2006 Elections: The Role of National Party Committees in Financing Congressional Campaigns." Washington, DC: Campaign Finance Institute.

Cotter, Cornelius P., James L. Gibson, John F. Bibby, and Robert J. Huckshorn. 1984. *Party Organizations in American Politics.* New York: Praeger.

Countdown to Majority Political Action Committee. 1994. "What Is Countdown to Majority: Why *You* Should Be Involved." Fall Newsletter, 2 (2): 1, 3.

Cox, Gary W., and Eric Magar. 1999. "How Much Is Majority Status in the U.S. Congress Worth?" *American Political Science Review* 93:299–309.

Cox, Gary W., and Mathew D. McCubbins. 1993. *Legislative Leviathan: Party Government in the House.* Berkeley and Los Angeles: University of California Press.

Cox, Gary W., and Mathew D. McCubbins. 2005. *Setting the Agenda: Responsible Party Government in the U.S. House of Representatives.* New York: Cambridge University Press.

Currinder, Marian. 2003. "Leadership PAC Contribution Strategies and House Member Ambitions." *Legislative Studies Quarterly* 28:551–77.

Currinder, Marian. 2009. *Money in the House: Campaign Funds and Congressional Party Politics.* Boulder, CO: Westview.

Damore, David F., and Thomas G. Hansford. 1999. "The Allocation of Party Controlled Resources in the House of Representatives, 1989–1996." *Political Research Quarterly* 52:371–85.

Deering, Christopher J., and Steven S. Smith. 1997. *Committees in Congress.* 3rd ed. Washington, DC: CQ Press.

Deering, Christopher J., and Paul J. Wahlbeck. 2006. "Determinants of House Committee Chair Selection." *American Politics Research* 34:1–20.

Dennis, Steven T., and Lauren W. Whittington. 2008. "Chairmen Sing Dues Blues." *Roll Call,* April 21. http://www.RollCall.com.

Dionne, E. J., Jr. 2005. "A GOP Plan to 'Fix' the Democrats." *Washington Post,* May 10, A21.

Dodd, Lawrence C. 1977. "Congress and the Quest for Power." In *Congress Reconsidered,* ed. Lawrence C. Dodd and Bruce I. Oppenheimer. Washington, DC: CQ Press.

Downs, Anthony. 1957. *An Economic Theory of Democracy.* New York: Harper.

Drew, Elizabeth. 1999. *The Corruption of American Politics.* New York: Overlook.

Dubose, Lou, and Jan Reid. 2004. *The Hammer: Tom DeLay, God, Money, and the Rise of the Republican Congress.* New York: PublicAffairs.

Dwyre, Diana. 1994. "Party Strategy and Political Reality: The Distribution of Congressional Campaign Committee Resources." In *The State of the Parties,* ed. Daniel M. Shea and John C. Green. Savage, MD: Rowman and Littlefield.

Dwyre, Diana. 1996. "Spinning Straw into Gold: Soft Money and U.S. House Elections." *Legislative Studies Quarterly* 21:409–24.

Dwyre, Diana, Eric Heberlig, Robin Kolodny, and Bruce Larson. 2006. "Committees and Candidates: National Party Finance after BCRA." In *The State of the Parties,* ed. John C. Green. 6th ed. Lanham, MD: Rowman and Littlefield.

Dwyre, Diana, and Robin Kolodny. 2006. "The Parties' Congressional Campaign Committees in 2004." In *The Election after Reform: Money, Politics, and the Bipartisan Campaign Reform Act,* ed. Michael J. Malbin. Lanham, MD: Rowman and Littlefield.

Edsall, Thomas B. 2006. *Building Red America: The New Conservative Coalition and the Drive for Permanent Power.* New York: Basic Books.

Eggen, Dan, and Maria Glod. 2010. "Ex-Lobbyist Paul Magliocchetti Charged with Campaign-Finance Fraud." *Washington Post,* August 6. http://www.washingtonpost.com.

Eilperin, Juliet. 2006. *Fight Club Politics: How Partisanship Is Poisoning the House of Representatives.* Lanham, MD: Rowman and Littlefield.

Eismeier, Theodore J., and Philip H. Pollock III. 1988. *Business, Money, and the Rise of Corporate PACs in American Elections.* New York: Quorum Books.

Epstein, Leon. 1986. *Political Parties in the American Mold.* Madison: University of Wisconsin Press.

Esterling, Kevin M. 2007. "Buying Expertise: Campaign Contributions and Attention to Policy Analysis in Congressional Committees." *American Political Science Review* 101:93–109.

Fellows, Matthew C., and Patrick J. Wolf. 2004. "Funding Mechanisms and Policy Instruments: How Business Campaign Contributions Influence Congressional Votes." *Political Research Quarterly* 57:315–24.

Fenno, Richard F., Jr. 1973. *Congressmen in Committees.* Boston: Little, Brown.

Fenno, Richard F., Jr. 1978. *Home Style: House Members in Their Districts.* Boston: Little, Brown.

Fenno, Richard F. 2007. *Congressional Travels: Places, Connections, and Authenticity.* New York: Longman.

Ferguson, Thomas. 1995. *Golden Rule: The Investment Theory of Party Competition and the Logic of Money-Driven Political Systems.* Chicago: University of Chicago Press.

Fineman, Howard. 2005. "The Disassembly of Tom DeLay: When a Majority Leader's State-of-the-Art Money and Power Machine Falters." *msnbc.com,* March 30. http://msnbc.msn.com/.

Finkel, Steven E. 1995. *Causal Analysis with Panel Data.* Sage University Paper Series on Quantitative Applications in the Social Sciences, no. 105. Newbury Park, CA: Sage.

Fiorina, Morris P. 1989. *Congress: Keystone of the Washington Establishment.* 2nd ed. New Haven: Yale University Press.

Fiorina, Morris P. 2006. "Parties as Problem Solvers?" In *Promoting the General Welfare: New Perspectives on Government Performance,* ed. Alan S. Gerber and Eric M. Patashnik. Washington, DC: Brookings Institution.

Fiorina, Morris P., with Samuel J. Abrams and Jeremy C. Pope. 2005. *Culture War? The Myth of a Polarized America.* New York: Longman.

Firestone, David. 2002. "To Retake House, Democrats Campaign on Buddy System." *New York Times,* October 31.

Foerstel, Karen. 2000. "Choosing Chairmen: Tradition's Role Fades." *CQ Weekly Report,* December 9, 2796–2801.

Foerstel, Karen. 2001. "Pelosi: A Tireless Fundraiser Sees Herself as a 'Fresh Face.'" *CQ Weekly Report*, October 6, 2324.

Francia, Peter L., John C. Green, Paul S. Herrnson, Lynda Powell, and Clyde Wilcox. 2003. *The Financiers of Congressional Elections: Investors, Ideologues, and Intimates*. New York: Columbia University Press.

Frantzich, Stephen. 1978. "Opting Out: Retirement from the House of Representatives, 1966–1974." *American Politics Quarterly* 6: 251–73.

Franz, Michael. 2008. *Choices and Changes: Interest Groups in the Electoral Process*. Philadelphia: Temple University Press.

Franz, Michael. 2011. "The *Citizens United* Election? Or Same As It Ever Was?" *Forum* 8 (4): Article 7.

Frisch, Scott A., and Sean Q. Kelly. 2006. *Committee Assignment Politics in the U.S. House of Representatives*. Norman: University of Oklahoma Press.

Fritz, Sara, and Dwight Morris. 1990. *Gold-Plated Politics: Running for Congress in the 1990s*. Washington, DC: CQ Press.

Froman, Lewis A., Jr., and Randall A. Ripley. 1965. "Conditions for Party Leadership: The Case of House Democrats." *American Political Science Review* 59:52–63.

Frymer, Paul. 1999. *Uneasy Alliances: Race and Party Competition in America*. Princeton: Princeton University Press.

Gais, Thomas. 1996. *Improper Influence: Campaign Finance Law, Political Interest Groups, and the Problem of Equality*. Ann Arbor: University of Michigan Press.

Garand, James C., and Kathleen M. Clayton. 1986. "Socialization to Partisanship in the U.S. House: The Speaker's Task Force." *Legislative Studies Quarterly* 11:409–28.

Gierzynski, Anthony. 2000. *Money Rules: Financing Elections in America*. Boulder, CO: Westview.

Gierzynski, Anthony. 1992. *Legislative Campaign Committees in the American States*. Lexington: University of Kentucky Press.

Gimpel, James G. 1996. *Legislating the Revolution: The Contract with America in Its First 100 Days*. Boston: Allyn and Bacon.

Gimpel, James G., Frances E. Lee, and Joshua Kaminski. 2006. "The Political Geography of Campaign Contributions in American Politics." *Journal of Politics* 68:626–39.

Gimpel, James, Frances E. Lee, and Shanna Pearson-Merkowitz. 2008. "The Check Is in the Mail: Indirect Funding Flows in Congressional Elections." *American Journal of Political Science* 52:373–94.

Godwin, R. Kenneth. 1988. *One Billion Dollars of Influence: The Direct Marketing of Politics*. Chatham, NJ: Chatham House.

Godwin, R. Kenneth, and Barry J. Seldon. 2002. "What Corporations Really Want from Government: The Public Provision of Private Goods." In *Interest Group Politics*, ed. Allan J. Cigler and Burdett A. Loomis. 5th ed. Washington, DC: CQ Press.

Goidel, Robert K., and Donald A. Gross. 1994. "A Systems Approach to Campaign Finance in U.S. House Elections." *American Politics Quarterly* 22:125–53.

Goodliffe, Jay. 2001. "The Effect of War Chests on Challenger Entry in U.S. House Elections." *American Journal of Political Science* 45:830–44.

Goodliffe, Jay. 2004. "War Chests as Precautionary Savings." *Political Behavior* 26:289–315.

Goodliffe, Jay. 2007. "Campaign War Chests and Challenger Quality in Senate Elections." *Legislative Studies Quarterly* 32 (1): 135–56.

Gordon, Sanford C., and Catherine Hafer. 2005. "Flexing Muscle: Corporate Political Expenditures as Signals to the Bureaucracy." *American Political Science Review* 99:245–61.

Gordon, Sanford C., Catherine Hafer, and Dimitri Landa. 2007. "Consumption or Investment? On Motivations for Political Giving." *Journal of Politics* 69:1057–72.

Grant, J. Tobin, and Thomas J. Rudolph. 2002. "To Give or Not to Give: Modeling Individuals' Contribution Decisions." *Political Behavior* 24:31–54.

Green, Donald Philip, and Jonathan S. Krasno. 1988. "Salvation for the Spendthrift Incumbent: Reestimating the Effect of Campaign Spending in House Elections." *American Journal of Political Science* 32:884–907.

Green, Donald Philip, and Jonathan S. Krasno. 1990. "Rebuttal to Jacobson's 'New Evidence for Old Arguments.'" *American Journal of Political Science* 34:363–72.

Green, Matthew N. 2008. "The 2006 Race for Democratic Majority Leader: Money, Policy, and Personal Loyalty." *PS: Political Science and Politics* 41:63–67.

Green, Matthew N., and Douglas B. Harris. 2007. "Goal Salience and the 2006 Race for House Majority Leader." *Political Research Quarterly* 60:618–30.

Greene, William H. 1993. *Econometric Analysis.* 2nd ed. Saddle River, NJ: Prentice Hall.

Greenstein, Fred I. 1987. *Personality and Politics.* Chicago: Markham.

Grenzke, Janet. 1988. "Comparing Contributions to U.S. House Members from Outside Their Districts." *Legislative Studies Quarterly* 13:83–103.

Grenzke, Janet. 1989. "PACs and the Congressional Supermarket: The Currency Is Complex." *American Journal of Political Science* 28:259–81.

Grier, Kevin B., and Michael C. Munger. 1991. "Committee Assignments, Constituent Preferences, and Campaign Contributions." *Economic Inquiry* 29:24–43.

Grier, Kevin B., and Michael C. Munger. 1993. "Comparing Interest Group Contributions to House and Senate Incumbents, 1980–1986." *Journal of Politics* 55:615–43.

Groseclose, Timothy, and Keith Krehbiel. 1994. "Golden Parachutes, Rubber Checks, and Strategic Retirements from the 102d House." *American Journal of Political Science* 38:75–99.

Groseclose, Timothy, and Charles Stewart III. 1998. "The Value of Committee Assignments in the House, 1947–91." *American Journal of Political Science* 42:453–74.

Hacker, Jacob S., and Paul Pierson. 2005. *Off Center: The Republican Revolution and the Erosion of American Democracy.* New Haven: Yale University Press.

Hall, Richard L. 1996. *Participation in Congress.* New Haven: Yale University Press.

Hall, Richard L., and Robert P. Van Houweling. 1995. "Avarice and Ambition in Congress: Representatives' Decisions to Run or Retire from the U.S. House." *American Political Science Review* 89:121–36.

Hall, Richard L., and Frank W. Wayman. 1990. "Buying Time: Moneyed Interests and the Mobilization of Bias in Congressional Committees." *American Political Science Review* 84:797–820.

Hamburger, Tom, and Peter Wallsten. 2006. *One Party Country: The Republican Plan for Dominance in the 21st Century.* New York: John Wiley and Sons.

Hardin, Russell. 1982. *Collective Action.* Baltimore: Resources for the Future.

Hasecke, Edward B., and Jason D. Mycoff. 2007. "Party Loyalty and Legislative Success: Are Loyal Majority Party Members More Successful in the U.S. House of Representatives?" *Political Research Quarterly* 60:607–17.

Heard, Alexander. 1960. *The Costs of Democracy.* Chapel Hill: University of North Carolina Press.

Heberlig, Eric S. 2003. "Congressional Parties, Fundraising, and Committee Ambition." *Political Research Quarterly* 56:151–62.

Heberlig, Eric S. 2005. "Getting to Know You and Getting Your Vote: Lobbyists' Uncertainty and the Contacting of Legislators." *Political Research Quarterly* 58:511–20.

Heberlig, Eric S., Marc J. Hetherington, and Bruce A. Larson. 2006. "The Price of Leadership: Campaign Money and the Polarization of Congressional Parties." *Journal of Politics* 68:992–1005.

Heberlig, Eric S., and Bruce A. Larson. 2005. "Redistributing Campaign Contributions by Members of Congress: The Spiraling Costs of the Permanent Campaign." *Legislative Studies Quarterly* 30:597–624.

Heberlig, Eric S., and Bruce A. Larson. 2007. "Party Fundraising, Descriptive Representation, and the Battle for Majority Control: Shifting Leadership Appointment Strategies in the U.S. House, 1990–2002." *Social Science Quarterly* 88:404–21.

Heberlig, Eric S., and Bruce A. Larson. 2010. "Congressional Parties and the Mobilization of Leadership PAC Contributions." *Party Politics* 16:451–75.

Heberlig, Eric S., Bruce A. Larson, Kristen Soltis, and Daniel A. Smith. 2008. "Look Who's Coming to Dinner: Direct versus Brokered Member Campaign Contributions to the NRCC." *American Politics Research* 36:433–50.

Herrick, Rebekah, and Michael K. Moore. 1993. "Political Ambition's Effect on Legislative Behavior: Schlesinger's Typology Reconsidered and Revised." *Journal of Politics* 55:765–76.

Herrnson, Paul. 1988. *Party Campaigning in the 1980s.* Cambridge, MA: Harvard University Press.

Herrnson, Paul S. 1994. "The Revitalization of National Party Organizations." In *The Parties Respond,* ed. L. Sandy Maisel. 2nd ed. Boulder, CO: Westview.

Herrnson, Paul S. 1997. "Money and Motives: Spending in House Elections." In *Congress Reconsidered,* ed. Lawrence C. Dodd and Bruce I. Oppenheimer. 6th ed. Washington, DC: CQ Press.

Herrnson, Paul S. 2000. *Congressional Elections: Campaigning at Home and in Washington.* 3rd ed. Washington, DC: CQ Press.

Herrnson, Paul S. 2004. *Congressional Elections: Campaigning at Home and in Washington.* 4th ed. Washington, DC: CQ Press.

Herrnson, Paul S. 2008. *Congressional Elections: Campaigning at Home and in Washington.* 5th ed. Washington, DC: CQ Press.

Herrnson, Paul S. 2009. "The Roles of Party Organizations, Party-Connected Committees, and Party Allies in Elections." *Journal of Politics* 71:1207–24.

Hershey, Marjorie. 2008. *Party Politics in America.* 13th ed. New York: Pearson Longman.

Hibbing, John R. 1982. *Choosing to Leave: Voluntary Retirements from the U.S. House of Representatives.* Washington, DC: University Press of America.

Hibbing, John R. 1986. "Ambition in the House: Behavioral Consequences of Higher Office Goals among U.S. Representatives." *American Journal of Political Science* 30:651–65.

Hibbing, John R. 1991. *Congressional Careers: Contours of Life in the U.S. House of Representatives.* Chapel Hill: University of North Carolina Press.

Hibbing, John R. 1993. "The Career Paths of Members of Congress." In *Ambition and Beyond,* ed. Shirley Williams and Edwards L. Lascher, Jr. Berkeley: Institute of Governmental Studies Press.

Hibbing, John R., and Elizabeth Theiss-Morse. 2002. *Stealth Democracy.* New York: Cambridge University Press.

Hirschfield, Julie. 2000. "Power Plays and Term Limits." *CQ Weekly Report,* November 11, 2656–70.

Hopkin, Jonathan. 2004. "The Problem with Party Finance: Theoretical Perspectives on the Funding of Political Parties." *Party Politics* 10:627–51.

Hunter, Kathleen. 2010. "Hispanic Lawmakers Eschew DCCC Dues." *CQ Political News,* October 3. http://www.cqpolitics.com/.

Isenstadt, Alex. 2010. "Nancy Pelosi to Democrats: Pay Up." *Politico,* September 10. http://www.politico.com/news/stories/0910/41995.html.

Isenstadt, Alex. 2011. "Key Committees Are Golden Ticket." *Politico,* January 19. http://www.politico.com/news/stories/0111/47770_Page2.html.

Isenstadt, Alex, and James Hohmann. 2010. "Freshmen: Massa Right about Money." *Politico,* March 11. http://www.politico.com/news/stories/0310/34244.html.

Jaccard, James, Robert Turrisi, and Choi K. Wan. 1990. *Interaction Effects in Multiple Regression.* Sage University Paper Series on Quantitative Applications in the Social Sciences, no. 72. Newbury Park, CA: Sage.

Jackson, Brooks. 1988. *Honest Graft: Big Money and the American Political Process.* Washington, DC: Farragut.

Jacobs, John. 1995. *A Rage for Justice: The Passion and Politics of Phillip Burton.* Berkeley and Los Angeles: University of California Press.

Jacobs, Lawrence R., and Robert Y. Shapiro. 2000. *Politicians Don't Pander: Political Manipulation and the Loss of Democratic Responsiveness.* Chicago: University of Chicago Press.

Jacobson, Gary. 1980. *Money in Congressional Elections.* New Haven: Yale University Press.

Jacobson, Gary C. 1985–86. "Party Organization and Distribution of Campaign Resources: Republicans and Democrats in 1982." *Political Science Quarterly* 100:603–25.

Jacobson, Gary C. 1987. "Running Scared: Elections and Congressional Politics in the 1980s." In *Congress: Structure and Policy,* ed. Mathew D. McCubbins and Terry Sullivan. New York: Cambridge University Press.

Jacobson, Gary C. 1990. "The Effects of Campaign Spending in House Elections: New Evidence for Old Arguments." *American Journal of Political Science* 34:334–62.

Jacobson, Gary C. 1997. *The Politics of Congressional Elections.* 4th ed. New York: Longman.

Jacobson, Gary. 2009. *The Politics of Congressional Elections.* 7th ed. New York: Pearson.

Jacobson, Gary C., and Samuel Kernell. 1983. *Strategy and Choice in Congressional Elections.* 2nd ed. New Haven: Yale University Press.

Joe, Westley, Michael J. Malbin, Peter William Brusoe, Jamie P. Pimlott, and Clyde Wilcox. 2008. "Who Are the Individual Donors to Gubernatorial and State Legislative Elections?" Paper presented at the annual meeting of the Midwest Political Science Association.

Jones, Bryan D., and Frank R. Baumgartner. 2005. *The Politics of Attention: How Government Prioritizes Problems.* Chicago: University of Chicago Press.

Kanthak, Kristin. 2007. "Crystal Elephants and Committee Chairs: Campaign Contributions and Leadership Races in the U.S. House of Representatives." *American Politics Research* 35:389–406.

Keim, Gerald, and Asghar Zardkoohi. 1988. "Looking for Leverage in PAC Markets: Corporate and Labor Contributions Considered." *Public Choice* 58:21–34.

Keller, Morton. 1977. *Affairs of State: Public Life in Late Nineteenth Century America.* Cambridge, MA: Belknap.

Kelley, Matt. 2006. "The Congressman and the Hedge Fund." *USA Today,* January 19, A1.

Kiewiet, Roderick D., and Mathew D. McCubbins. 1991. *The Logic of Delegation: Congressional Parties and the Appropriations Process.* Chicago: University of Chicago Press.

Kiewiet, Roderick D., and Langche Zeng. 1993. "An Analysis of Congressional Career Decisions, 1947–1986." *American Political Science Review* 87:928–41.

King, Gary, and Langche Zeng. 2001. "Logistic Regression in Rare Events Data." *Political Methodology* 12:137–63.

Kingdon, John W. 1989. *Congressmen's Voting Decisions.* 3rd ed. New York: Harper and Row.

Klein, Ezra. 2010. "More Money, More Problems: The Soul-Crushing Life of a Senator." *Newsweek,* November 8, 23.

Klinkner, Philip A. 1994. *The Losing Parties: Out-Party National Committees, 1956–1993.* New Haven: Yale University Press.

Kolodny, Robin. 1998. *Pursuing Majorities: Congressional Campaign Committees in American Politics.* Norman: University of Oklahoma Press.

Kolodny, Robin, and Diana Dwyre. 1998. "Party-Orchestrated Activities for Legislative Party Goals." *Party Politics* 4:275–95.

Koopman, Douglas L. 1996. *Hostile Takeover: The House Republican Party, 1980–1995.* Lanham, MD: Rowman and Littlefield.

Krasno, Jonathan S., and Conor M. Dowling. 2006. "How Well Do the Parties Compete in House Elections?" Paper presented at the annual meeting of the Midwest Political Science Association.

Krasno, Jonathan S., and Donald P. Green. 1988. "Preempting Quality Challengers in House Elections." *Journal of Politics* 50:920–36.

Krasno, Jonathan S., Donald Phillip Green, and Jonathan A. Cowden. 1994. "The Dynamics of Fundraising in House Elections." *Journal of Politics* 56:549–74.

Krasno, Jonathan S., and Frank J. Sorauf. 2003. "Why Soft Money Has Not Strengthened the Parties." In *Inside the Campaign Finance Battle: Court Testimony on the New Reforms,* ed. Anthony Corrado, Thomas E. Mann, and Trevor Potter. Washington, DC: Brookings Institution.

Krawzak, Paul M. 2004a. "Campaigns for Appropriations Chairman Approach Final Hours." Copley News Service, December 28. Accessed via www.newbank.com.

Krawzak, Paul M. 2004b. "Reversing Stance on Special Interests, Regula Raises Big Money." Copley News Service, September 12. Accessed via www.newbank.com.

Krehbiel, Keith. 1991. *Information and Legislative Organization.* Ann Arbor: University of Michigan Press.

Krehbiel, Keith. 1993. "Where's the Party?" *British Journal of Political Science* 23:235–66.

Krehbiel, Keith. 1998. *Pivotal Politics: A Theory of U.S. Lawmaking.* Chicago: University of Chicago Press.

Krehbiel, Keith. 2000. "Party Discipline and Measures of Partisanship." *American Journal of Political Science* 44:212–27.

Kroszner, Randall S., and Thomas Stratmann. 1998. "Interest-Group Competition and the Organization of Congress: Theory and Evidence from Financial Services' Political Action Committees." *American Economic Review* 88:1163–87.

Kucinich, Jackie. 2010a. "Cantor's Leadership PAC Is Tops in the House." *CQ Politics News,* June 6. http://www.cqpolitics.com/.

Kucinich, Jackie. 2010b. "NRCC Sends Crew to Collect Dues." *CQ Politics News,* April 20. http://www.cqpolitics.com/.

La Raja, Raymond. 2006. "State and Local Political Parties after BCRA." In *The Election after Reform: Money, Politics, and the Bipartisan Campaign Reform Act,* ed. Michael Malbin. Lanham, MD: Rowman and Littlefield.

La Raja, Raymond. 2008a. "From Bad to Worse: The Unraveling of the Campaign Finance System." *Forum* 6 (1): Article 2.

La Raja, Raymond. 2008b. *Small Change: Money, Political Parties, and Campaign Finance Reform.* Ann Arbor: University of Michigan Press.

Larson, Bruce A. 1998. "Ambition and Money in the U.S. House of Representatives: Analyzing Campaign Contributions from Incumbents' Leadership PACs and Reelection Committees." PhD diss., Department of Government and Foreign Affairs, University of Virginia.

Larson, Bruce A. 2004. "Incumbent Contributions to the Congressional Campaign Committees, 1989–90 through 1999–2000." *Political Research Quarterly* 57:155–61.

Lebo, Matthew J., Adam J. McGlynn, and Gregory Koger. 2007. "Strategic Party Government: Party Influence in Congress, 1789–2000." *American Journal of Political Science* 51:464–81.

Lee, Frances. 2009. *Beyond Ideology: Politics, Principles, and Partisanship in the U.S. Senate.* Chicago: University of Chicago Press.

Leech, Beth. 2010. "Lobbying and Influence." In *The Oxford Handbook of Political Parties and Interest Groups,* ed. L. Sandy Maisel and Jeffrey M. Berry. New York: Oxford University Press.

Lipton, Eric, and Eric Lichtblau. 2010. "Fund-Raising before House Vote Draws Scrutiny." *New York Times,* July 14. http://www.nytimes.com/.

Long, J. Scott. 1997. *Regression Models for Categorical and Limited Dependent Variables.* Thousand Oaks, CA: Sage.

Loomis, Burdett. 1984. "Congressional Careers and Party Leadership in the Contemporary House of Representatives." *American Journal of Political Science* 28:180–202.

Loomis, Burdett. 1988. *The New American Politician: Ambition, Entrepreneurship, and the Changing Face of Political Life.* New York: Basic Books.

Lowi, Theodore. 1964. "American Business, Public Policy, Case Studies, and Political Theory." *World Politics* 16:677–715.

Lowry, Robert C. 2005. "Political Money at the Source: Itemized Contributions in Federal Candidates, Parties, and PACs, 1993–2004." Paper presented at the annual meeting of the American Political Science Association.

Lowry, Robert C., Matthew Potoski, and Jeffrey Talbert. 2003. "Leadership PACs and Campaign Contributions in the U.S. House of Representatives." Paper presented at the annual meeting of the American Political Science Association.

Magleby, David B. 2000. *Outside Money: Soft Money and Issue Advocacy in the 1998 Congressional Elections*. Lanham, MD: Rowman and Littlefield.

Magleby, David B., ed. 2011. *Financing the 2008 Election*. Washington, DC: Brookings Institution.

Magleby, David B., J. Quin Monson, and Kelly Patterson, eds. 2007. *Electing Congress: New Rules for an Old Game*. Upper Saddle River, NJ: Pearson Prentice Hall.

Malbin, Michael. 2003. "Thinking About Reform." In *Life After Reform: When the Bipartisan Campaign Reform Act Meets Politics*, ed. Michael J. Malbin. Lanham, MD: Rowman and Littlefield.

Malbin, Michael J. 2008. "Rethinking the Campaign Finance Agenda." *Forum* 6 (1): Article 1.

Maltzman, Forrest. 1997. *Competing Principals: Committees, Parties, and the Organization of Congress*. Ann Arbor: University of Michigan Press.

Mankiw, Gregory, David Romer, and David N. Weil. 1992. "A Contribution to the Empirics of Economic Growth." *Quarterly Journal of Economics* 107:407–37.

Mann, Thomas E. 1978. *Unsafe at Any Margin: Interpreting Congressional Elections*. Washington, DC: American Enterprise Institute.

Mann, Thomas E., and Norman J. Ornstein. 2006. *The Broken Branch*. New York: Oxford University Press.

March, James G., and Johan P. Olsen. 1984. "The New Institutionalism: Organizational Factors in Political Life." *American Political Science Review* 78:734–49.

Masket, Seth. 2009. *No Middle Ground: How Informal Party Organizations Control Nominations and Polarize Legislatures*. Ann Arbor: University of Michigan Press.

Mayhew, David. 1974. *Congress: The Electoral Connection*. New Haven: Yale University Press.

McCarty, Nolan, and Lawrence Rothenberg. 2000. "Coalition Maintenance: Politicians, Parties, and Organized Groups." *American Politics Quarterly* 28:291–308.

McChesney, Fred S. 1997. *Money for Nothing: Politicians, Rent Extraction, and Political Extortion*. Cambridge, MA: Harvard University Press.

McGerr, Michael. 1986. *The Decline of Popular Politics: The American North, 1865–1928*. New York: Oxford University Press.

McGhee, Eric, and Raymond J. La Raja. 2006. "Changes in Party Contributions to Candidates for the U.S. House, 1980–2004." Paper presented at the annual meeting of the Southern Political Science Association.

Meinke, Scott R. 2008. "Who Whips? Party Government and the House Extended Whip Networks." *American Politics Research* 36:639–68.

Meinke, Scott R. 2010. "Adaptable Institutions: Growth and Change in the House." Paper presented at the annual meeting of the Midwest Political Science Association.

Metzler, Meredith. 2006. "Final Rules: Contribution Limits between Authorized Committees." *FEC Record* 32 (10): 5.

Miler, Kristina C. 2007. "The View from the Hill: Legislative Perceptions of the District." *Legislative Studies Quarterly* 32:597–628.

Miller, Tricia. 2010. "Safe Republican Candidates Earn Cred by Giving to GOP Contenders." *CQ Politics News*, October 30. http://www.cqpolitics.com/.

Milyo, Jeffrey. 1997. "Electoral and Financial Effects of Changes in Committee Power: The Gramm-Rudman-Hollings Budget Reform, the Tax Reform Act of 1986, and the Money Committees in the House." *Journal of Law and Economics* 40 (1): 93–111.

Moe, Terry M. 1980. *The Organization of Interests.* Chicago: University of Chicago Press.

Monroe, J. P. 2001. *The Political Party Matrix: The Persistence of Organization.* Albany: State University of New York Press.

Moore, Michael K., and John R. Hibbing. 1992. "Is Serving in Congress Fun Again? Voluntary Retirements from the House Since the 1970s." *American Journal of Political Science* 36 (3): 824–28.

Moore, Michael K., and John R. Hibbing. 1998. "Situational Dissatisfaction in Congress: Explaining Voluntary Departures." *Journal of Politics* 60 (4): 1088–1107.

Morehouse, Sarah M. 1998. *The Governor as Party Leader: Campaigning and Governing.* Ann Arbor: University of Michigan Press.

Morris, Dwight, and Murielle E. Gamache. 1994. *Gold-Plated Politics: The 1992 Congressional Races.* Washington, DC: CQ Press.

Moscardelli, Vincent G., Moshe Haspel, and Richard S. Wike. 1998. "Party Building through Campaign Finance Reform: Conditional Party Government in the 104th Congress." *Journal of Politics* 60:691–704.

Mosk, Matthew. 2007. "With Democrats Now in the Majority, Fundraising Shoe on the Other Foot for DCCC's Van Hollen." *Washington Post,* March 7, A15.

Munger, Michael C. 1988. "Allocation of Desirable Committee Assignments: Extended Queues versus Committee Expansion." *American Journal of Political Science* 32:317–44.

Murakami, Michael H. 2009. "Minority Status, Ideology, or Opportunity: Explaining the Greater Retirements of House Republicans." *Legislative Studies Quarterly* 34:219–44.

Mutch, Robert E. 2002. "The First Federal Campaign Finance Bills." In *Money and Politics,* ed. Paula Baker. State College: Pennsylvania State University Press.

Mutz, Diana C. 1995. "Effects of Horse-Race Coverage on Campaign Coffers: Strategic Contributing in Presidential Primaries." *Journal of Politics* 57:1015–42.

Nelson, Garrison. 1977. "Partisan Patterns of House Leadership Change, 1789–1977." *American Political Science Review* 71:918–39.

Newmyer, Tory. 2008. "Pelosi Bullish on the Future." *Roll Call,* July 28. http://www.roll call.com/.

Newmyer, Tory. 2010. "Democrats Shake Money Tree." *CQ Politics News,* June 29. http://www.cqpolitics.com/.

Novak, Viveca. 1988. "Mutual Funding." *Common Cause Magazine,* September/October, 34–39.

O'Connor, Patrick. 2008. "GOP Threatens Stingy Lawmakers." *Politico,* September 23. http://www.politico.com/news/stories/0908/13770.html.

O'Connor, Patrick. 2009. "Cantor Whips Votes, Counts Cash." *Politico,* January 27. http://www.politico.com/news/stories/0109/18004.html.

Olson, Mancur. 1965. *The Logic of Collective Action.* Cambridge, MA: Harvard University Press.

Oppenheimer, Bruce I. 2005. "Deep Red and Blue Congressional Districts: The Causes and Consequences of Declining Party Competitiveness." In *Congress Reconsidered,* ed. Lawrence C. Dodd and Bruce I. Oppenheimer. 8th ed. Washington, DC: CQ Press.

Ota, Alan K. 2006. "Boehner Promises 'New Vision.'" *CQ Weekly,* February 6, 334–38.

Overacker, Louise. 1932. *Money in Elections.* New York: Macmillan.

Parker, David C. W. 2008. *The Power of Money in Congressional Campaigns, 1880–2006.* Norman: University of Oklahoma Press.

Peabody, Robert L. 1976. *Leadership in Congress.* Boston: Little, Brown.

Pearson, Kathryn. 2001. "Congressional Leadership PACs: Who Benefits"? Paper presented at the annual meeting of the Midwest Political Science Association.

Peters, Ronald M., Jr. 1997. *The American Speakership.* 2nd ed. Baltimore: Johns Hopkins University Press.

Peters, Ronald M., Jr., and Cindy Simon Rosenthal. 2010. *Speaker Pelosi and the New American Politics.* New York: Oxford University Press.

Petrocik, John R. 1996. "Issue Ownership in Presidential Elections, with a 1980 Case Study." *American Journal of Political Science* 40:825–50.

Pianan, Eric. 2000. "House Party with a Twist; Rivals for Key Committee Post Pull Out the Stops." *Washington Post,* August 1, A1.

Pierson, Paul. 2000. "Increasing Returns, Path Dependence, and the Study of Politics." *American Political Science Review* 94:251–67.

Pitkin, Hannah. 1967. *The Concept of Political Representation.* Berkeley and Los Angeles: University of California Press.

Polsby, Nelson W. 1968. "The Institutionalization of the House of Representatives." *American Political Science Review* 62:144–68.

Potter, Trevor. 2005. "The Current State of Campaign Finance Law." In *The New Campaign Finance Sourcebook,* ed. Anthony Corrado, Thomas E. Mann, Daniel R. Ortiz, and Trevor Potter. Washington, DC: Brookings Institution Press.

Powell, Lynda. 2008. "The Time Legislators Spend Fundraising for Themselves and for Their Caucuses: Modeling Institutional, Personal, and Political Effects in State Legislatures." Paper presented at the annual meeting of the American Political Science Association, Boston, MA.

Powell, Lynda, and Clyde Wilcox. 2010. "Money and American Elections." In *The Oxford Handbook of American Elections and Political Behavior,* ed. Jan E. Leighley. New York: Oxford University Press.

Price, David E. 2000. *The Congressional Experience.* 2nd ed. Boulder, CO: Westview.

Price, David E. 2004. *The Congressional Experience.* 3rd ed. Boulder, CO: Westview.

Radcliffe, Peter M. 1998. "Now How Much Would You Pay? PAC Contributions, Timing, and Theories of Access." PhD diss., Ohio State University.

Ragsdale, Lyn, and Timothy E. Cook. 1987. "Representatives' Actions and Challengers' Reactions: Limits to Candidate Connections in the House." *American Journal of Political Science* 31:45–81.

Ranney, Austin. 1976. "Parties in State Politics." In *Politics in the American States: A Comparative Analysis,* ed. Herbert Jacobs and Kenneth Vines. 3rd ed. Boston: Little, Brown.

Ripley, Randall A., and Grace A. Franklin. 1991. *Congress, the Bureaucracy, and Public Policy.* 5th ed. Pacific Grove, CA: Brooks/Cole.

Rohde, David W. 1979. "Risk Bearing and Progressive Ambition: The Case of Members of the United States House of Representatives." *American Journal of Political Science* 23:1–26.

Rohde, David W. 1991. *Parties and Leaders in the Postreform Congress.* Chicago: University of Chicago Press.

Rohde, David W. 2010. "What a Difference 25 Years Makes: Changing Perspectives on Parties and Leaders in the U.S. House." In *The Oxford Handbook of American Politi-*

cal Parties and Interest Groups, ed. L. Sandy Maisel and Jeffrey M. Berry. New York: Oxford University Press.

Rohde, David W., and Kenneth A. Shepsle. 1973. "Democratic Committee Assignments in the House of Representatives: Strategic Aspects of a Social Choice Process." *American Political Science Review* 67:889–905.

Roll Call. 1994. "Vote-Buying PACs." August 8, 4.

Romer, Thomas, and James M. Snyder, Jr. 1994. "An Empirical Investigation of the Dynamics of PAC Contributions." *American Journal of Political Science* 38:745–69.

Rothenberg, Lawrence S., and Mitchell S. Sanders. 2000. "Severing the Electoral Connection: Shirking in the Contemporary Congress." *American Journal of Political Science* 44:310–19.

Rozell, Mark J., and Clyde Wilcox. 1999. *Interest Groups in American Campaigns: The New Face of Electioneering.* Washington, DC: CQ Press.

Rudolph, Thomas J. 1999. "Corporate and Labor PAC Contributions in House Elections: Measuring the Effect of Majority Party Status." *Journal of Politics* 61:195–206.

Sabato, Larry J. 1984. *PAC Power: Inside the World of Political Action Committees.* New York: Norton.

Sabato, Larry J. 1988. *The Party's Just Begun: Shaping Political Parties for America's Future.* Glenview, IL: Scott, Foresman.

Sabato, Larry J., and Bruce A. Larson. 2002. *The Party's Just Begun: Shaping Political Parties for America's Future.* 2nd ed. New York: Longman.

Sabato, Larry J., and Glenn R. Simpson. 1996. *Dirty Little Secrets: The Persistence of Corruption in American Politics.* New York: Times Books.

Salmore, Barbara, and Steven A. Salmore. 1989. *Candidates, Parties, and Campaigns: Electoral Politics in America.* Washington, DC: CQ Press.

Sandalow, Marc. 2008. *Madam Speaker: Nancy Pelosi's Life, Times, and Rise to Power.* New York: Modern Times.

Savage, Charlie, and David D. Kirkpatrick. 2009. "Subpoena to a Lawmaker Is Reported." *New York Times,* May 30. http://www.nytimes.com/.

Schattschneider, E. E. 1942. *Party Government.* New York: Rinehart.

Schattschneider, E. E. 1960. *The Semisovereign People.* New York: Holt, Rinehart, and Winston.

Schatz, Joseph J. 2004. "Claiming Appropriations Chair a Bit Trickier on House Side." *CQ Weekly Report,* May 15, 1128–29. http://library.cqpress.com/cqweekly/weeklyreport108-000001156034.

Schatz, Joseph J. 2005. "Lewis Wins Favor of GOP Leaders—and Coveted Appropriations Chair." *CQ Weekly,* January 10, 71–73. http://library.cqpress.com/cqweekly/weeklyreport109-000001480957.

Schickler, Eric. 2001. *Disjointed Pluralism: Institutional Innovation and the Development of the U.S. Congress.* Princeton: Princeton University Press.

Schiller, Wendy J. 2000. *Partners and Rivals: Representation in U.S. Senate Delegations.* Princeton: Princeton University Press.

Schlesinger, Joseph A. 1966. *Ambition and Politics: Political Careers in the United States.* Chicago: Rand McNally.

Schlesinger, Joseph A. 1985. "The New American Party System." *American Political Science Review* 79:1152–69.

Schlesinger, Joseph A. 1991. *Political Parties and the Winning of Office.* Ann Arbor: University of Michigan.

Schlozman, Kay Lehman, and John T. Tierney. 1986. *Organized Interests and American Democracy.* New York: Harper and Row.

Schumpeter, Joseph. 1942. *Capitalism, Socialism, and Democracy.* New York: Harper.

Schwartz, Mildred A. 1990. *The Party Network: The Robust Organization of Illinois Republicans.* Madison: University of Wisconsin Press.

Shea, Daniel M. 1995. *Transforming Democracy: Legislative Campaign Committees and Political Parties.* Albany: State University of New York Press.

Shepsle, Kenneth A. 1978. *The Giant Jigsaw Puzzle: Democratic Committee Assignments in the Modern House.* Chicago: University of Chicago Press.

Shepsle, Kenneth A., and Barry R. Weingast. 1987. "The Institutional Foundations of Committee Power." *American Political Science Review* 81:85–104.

Sherman, Jake. 2010. "Nancy Pelosi Power: $25 Million for Democrats." *Politico,* June 14. http://www.politico.com/news/stories/0610/38476.html.

Simon, Dennis M. 1991. "The President, Referendum Voting, and Subnational Elections in the United States." *American Political Science Review* 85:1177–92.

Simon, Dennis M., Charles W. Ostrom, and Robin F. Marra. 1991. "The President Referendum Voting, and Gubernatorial Elections in the United States." *American Political Science Review* 85 (4): 1177–92.

Sinclair, Barbara. 1982. *Congressional Realignment, 1925–1978.* Austin: University of Texas Press.

Sinclair, Barbara. 1983. *Majority Leadership in the U.S. House.* Baltimore: Johns Hopkins University Press.

Sinclair, Barbara. 1995. *Legislators, Leaders, and Lawmaking: The U.S. House of Representatives in the Postreform Era.* Baltimore: Johns Hopkins University Press.

Sinclair, Barbara. 2002. "Do Parties Matter?" In *Party, Process, and Political Change in Congress,* ed. David W. Brady and Mathew D. McCubbins. Stanford: Stanford University Press.

Sinclair, Barbara. 2006. *Party Wars: Polarization and the Politics of National Policymaking.* Norman: University of Oklahoma Press.

Smith, Richard A. 1995. "Interest Group Influence in the U.S. Congress." *Legislative Studies Quarterly* 20:89–139.

Smith, Steven S. 2000. "Positive Theories of Congressional Parties." *Legislative Studies Quarterly* 25:193–216.

Smith, Steven S. 2007. *Party Influence in Congress.* New York: Cambridge University Press.

Smith, Steven S., and Eric D. Lawrence. 1997. "Party Control of Committees in the Republican Congress." In *Congress Reconsidered,* ed. Lawrence C. Dodd and Bruce I. Oppenheimer. 6th ed. Washington, DC: CQ Press.

Smith, Steven S., and Bruce A. Ray. 1983. "The Impact of Congressional Reform: House Democratic Committee Assignments." *Congress and the Presidency* 10:219–40.

Snyder, James M., Jr. 1990. "Campaign Contributions as Investments: The U.S. House of Representatives, 1980–1986." *Journal of Political Economy* 98:1195–1227.

Sorauf, Frank J. 1988. *Money in American Elections.* Glenview, IL: Scott, Foresman.

Sorauf, Frank. 1992. *Inside Campaign Finance: Myths and Realities.* New Haven: Yale University Press.

Sorauf, Frank J. 2002. "Power, Money, and Responsibility in the Major American Parties." In *Responsible Partisanship? The Evolution of American Political Parties since 1950*, ed. John C. Green and Paul S. Herrnson. Lawrence: University of Kansas Press.

Squire, Peverill. 1989. "Competition and Uncontested Seats in U.S. House Elections." *Legislative Studies Quarterly* 14:281–95.

Steen, Jennifer A. 2006. *Self-Financed Candidates in Congressional Elections*. Ann Arbor: University of Michigan Press.

Stern, Marcus, and Jennifer LaFleur. 2009. "Leadership PACs: Let the Good Times Roll." *ProPublica*, September 26. http://www.propublica.org/feature/leadership-pacs-let-the-good-times-roll-925.

Strahan, Randall. 1992. "Reed and Rostenkowski: Congressional Leadership in Institutional Time." In *The Atomistic Congress: An Interpretation of Congressional Change*, ed. Allen D. Hertzke and Ronald M. Peters, Jr. Armonk, NY: Sharpe.

Strahan, Randall. 1998. "Thomas Brackett Reed and the Rise of Party Government." In *Masters of the House*, ed. Roger H. Davidson, Susan Webb Hammond, and Raymond W. Smock. Boulder, CO: Westview.

Summers, Mark Wahlgren. 2002. " 'To Make the Wheels Revolve We Must Have Grease': Barrel Politics in the Gilded Age." In *Money and Politics*, ed. Paula Baker. State College: Pennsylvania State University Press.

Taylor, Andrew J. 2003. "Conditional Party Government and Campaign Contributions: Insight from the Tobacco and Alcoholic Beverage Industries." *American Journal of Political Science* 47:293–304.

Taylor, Andrew. 2005. *Elephant's Edge*. Westport, CT: Praeger.

Thayer, George. 1973. *Who Shakes the Money Tree?* New York: Simon and Schuster.

Theriault, Sean M. 1998. "Moving Up or Moving Out: Career Ceilings and Congressional Retirement." *Legislative Studies Quarterly* 23:419–33.

Thompson, Joel A., and Gary F. Moncrief. 1998. "Exploring the 'Lost World' of Campaign Finance." In *Campaign Finance in State Legislative Elections*, ed. Joel A. Thompson and Gary F. Moncrief. Washington, DC: Congressional Quarterly Press.

Truman, David. 1959. *The Congressional Party*. New York: John Wiley & Sons.

VandeHei, Jim. 1999a. "Trying to Protect the Majority." *Roll Call*, March 25, 1, 22.

VandeHei, Jim. 1999b. "Would-be-Chairmen Hit the Money Trail." *Roll Call*, July 12, 1, 34.

VandeHei, Jim. 2006. "GOP Contest Guided by Lessons of Battles Past." *Washington Post*, January 13, A01.

Wallison, Peter L., and Joel M. Gora. 2009. *Better Parties, Better Government: A Realistic Program for Campaign Finance Reform*. Washington, DC: American Enterprise Institute.

Wawro, Gregory. 2000. *Legislative Entrepreneurship in the U.S. House of Representatives*. Ann Arbor: University of Michigan Press.

Wilcox, Clyde. 1989. "Share the Wealth: Contributions by Congressional Incumbents to the Campaigns of Other Candidates." *American Politics Quarterly* 17:386–408.

Wilcox, Clyde. 1990. "Member to Member Giving." In *Money, Elections, and Democracy: Reforming Congressional Campaign Finance*, ed. Margaret Latus Nugent and John R. Johannes. Boulder, CO: Westview.

Wright, John R. 1985. "PACs, Contributions, and Roll Calls: An Organizational Perspective." *American Political Science Review* 79:400–414.

Wright, John R. 2000. "Interest Groups, Congressional Reform, and Party Government in the United States." *Legislative Studies Quarterly* 25:217–35.

Zeleny, Jeff. 2006. "Of Party Dues and Deadbeats on Capitol Hill." *New York Times,* October 1.

Zeller, Shaun, and Michael Teitelbaum. 2007. "GOP Fundraising on the Quota System." *CQ Weekly,* January 12, 154. http://library.cqpress.com/.

Zelizer, Julian E. 2004. *On Capitol Hill: The Struggle to Reform Congress and Its Consequences, 1948–2000.* New York: Cambridge University Press.

Index

Note: Page numbers in italic indicate tables.